SUPER-
MEMORY
THE REVOLUTION

SUPER-
MEMORY
THE REVOLUTION

SHEILA OSTRANDER and **LYNN SCHROEDER**

Carroll & Graf Publishers, Inc.
New York

First Carroll & Graf edition 1991

Carroll & Graf Publishers, Inc.
260 Fifth Avenue
New York, NY 10001

Text designed by Terry McCabe

Library of Congress Cataloging-in-Publication Data

Ostrander, Sheila.
   Supermemory : the revolution / by Sheila Ostrander and Lynn
Schroeder. — 1st Carroll & Graf ed.
       p.   cm.
   Includes bibliographical references and index.
   ISBN 0-88184-691-0 : $21.95
   1. Mnemonics. 2. Success—Psychological aspects. I. Schroeder,
Lynn. II. Title.
BF385.087   1991
153.1′4—dc20   91-4501
                                                               CIP

Manufactured in the United States of America

DEDICATION

For all the dedicated new age pioneers
in fields from Superlearning to energy
medicine, music to NDE, whose leading-edge
discoveries inspired this chronicle of
memory breakthroughs

Special thanks to Christina Vandenboorn Gould, Donna
and Robin MacNeil and Trish Pfeiffer for their friendship
and help which surely made our way easier.

Contents

PART TWO

PART THREE

PART ONE

1.   The Memory Revolution

Stretching himself in the early sun of a Renaissance morning, Giulio Camillo surveyed the light-flecked halls, the fabulously furnished rooms of one of the most magnificent palaces in Venice. Satisfaction warmed him as he felt the quickening rustle and murmur of his vast household coming awake. Here he had gathered all the wisdom and wit he needed to walk as a counselor to kings, as a philosopher and dramatist of international repute. Here he returned always to sharpen his faculties.

The richly peopled palace Camillo surveyed was *invisible*. It was a memory palace, one of the invisible households, palaces, even towns that educated people of the day carefully constructed in their imaginations, constructs that let them remember almost everything, invisible palaces that generated a real creative energy.

They knew the secret. Memory isn't just something you're born with. Memory is something you can build, you can expand and keep lively for a lifetime. Today there are a multitude of new techniques to give you the know-how, 21st century techniques that even the master imaginer Camillo couldn't have envisioned. In the last two decades neuroscientists and musicians, educators, electronic specialists, athletes, plant biologists, and researchers of all kinds have ventured into the domain of memory to search down to the molecules of your genes and reach out to the "memory" of the cosmos. These explorers have returned with dramatic breakthroughs: new ways to improve memory, new ways to keep memory sharp into old age, and newly discovered powers of memory. They have even uncovered new ways of remembering the past that can change your future.

From one's career to social life, from school to job retraining, from sports to games, gambling to financial success, a superior memory is a great boon. It's something everyone needs. If researchers are right, the possibility of revitalizing your overall memory and tapping its resources may be closer and easier than you think. It may be as easy as pressing a button, swallowing a food capsule, or listening to unique patterns of high frequency music. Besides overall memory builders, there are fresh new memory systems—not memory peg methods—to help you recall the specific facts, figures, and languages. Even better, these 21st century memory methods are accelerated, stress free, euphoriant, global, and holistic. They can dynamize the entire personality into creative, expanded expression.

Do you know anyone suffering from memory slowdown or memory loss? The American Association of Retired Persons reports that 25% of seniors suffer some mental troubles. As we wrote this book, one of our personal research priorities was to find help for elderly relatives with alarming memory loss. We found that many common memory problems of the aged can be reversed; we found breakthroughs that can help seniors keep up in the information age.

"Are We A Nation of Nitwits?" groaned *USA Today* in yet one more feature on the dismal performance of U.S. students compared to those in other countries. 25% of our college seniors could not even remember when Columbus landed in America. Business foots an annual $25 billion re-teaching bill for this educational amnesia. Will forgetfulness bring us down as a nation? It doesn't have to. New cost efficient, effective ways to learn, retain, and recall are already in place in forward-looking businesses and schools—and among people who have decided that the only recourse is "do it yourself."

Transformative New Uses of Memory

New ways to stimulate memory have sparked an explosion of worldwide remembering, a different kind of remembering whose significance is as evolutionary as its impact is revolutionary. Does your memory exist before birth? Can it exist after death? What is your most ancient memory and how can evoking it help you today? Exploration of these questions has brought compelling discoveries about memory, so compelling that they have also brought better, more joyful ways for humans to arrive and depart the planet. Through these explorations the entire spectrum of memory itself—from birth to death—has suddenly expanded and with it has come a new image of who and what we are. This surge of remembrance "is a unique 20th-century phenomenon," says Dr. David Chamberlain, author of *Babies Remember Birth*. It's giving us hints too, about the 21st.

"Cosmic humans" are among us, not escapees from the Twilight Zone but people who have had unusual experiences at opposite ends of the memory spectrum. Some have arrived through "gravity-free" birth, the superbabies of Russia, New Zealand, and the United States. Others, the near-death experiencers, have undergone a "rebirth" thanks to medical technology. Members of both groups evidence expanded memory and capabilities. The near-death experiencers returned to report that their memories *did* work even though their vital functions were dormant. "It was like I knew everything," said one Virginian. "Everything I'd ever known from the beginning of my life . . . even little minute things." Not only did their memories work, some also returned able to recall things they didn't realize they knew, sophisticated scientific and philosophical information. Virtually every one of them claimed they had a profound new grasp of the uses of memory, here and hereafter. Memory is one thing you *can* take with you, they insist.

An old secret has begun to resurface too. Memory is far more than a storehouse of data. It's a primal, creative, cosmic power. From the Greek mystery schools of Pythagoras, through the teachings of St. Thomas Aquinas, to the memory magi of the Renaissance like Giulio Camillo, memory was known as a vehicle of self-transformation, something that could be used to create oneself anew. Can the hidden energies of memory reorder the future? This time the mystery school is open to everyone.

The Meaning of Supermemory

We wouldn't outlast the moment without memory. Memory is the substance we hang our lives on. It makes the notes that combine and recombine to weave the dissonance and harmonies of an individual life. Memory makes you a unique somebody. It is not surprising that Mnemosyne, child of heaven and earth, goddess of memory, has been around since the beginning. The surprise is how lively this ancient mother of us all is right now, as though she too were caught up in the feverish change cycling us into the 21st Century.

When we decided to explore supermemory, Mnemosyne didn't speak to us—she grabbed us by the neck and carted us off in unexpected directions. Suddenly we were seeing memory as a working partner of the immune system, memory alert in the womb, memory feeding into the mind subliminally to influence the way we act, think, feel. Solutions for problems seemingly far afield from memory began to appear—help for drug addiction, for one. We also began to get glimpses of the memory manipulators, people using the new breakthroughs for their own ends. For instance, rumors were abroad, diabolical rumors, about the use of memory as a weapon of war, about memory experiments that would curdle your brain cells. While we researched, news broke that the CIA would compensate nine amnesiac Canadians, people whose memories were erased when they became unwitting guinea pigs in cloak-and-dagger memory explorations.

As though on cue, the hottest new scientific theory of the decade ignited a firestorm of controversy. Not surprisingly, it's a theory of memory. "The past ain't gone, it ain't even past," says a Faulkner character. With his recent *Theory of Formative Causation,* Rupert Sheldrake puts it this way: "The past is pressed up against the present like a concertina." The past doesn't string out behind you like a film, it's all here now. All of nature, Sheldrake says, is suffused with memory. It's an ancient idea, a *world memory,* that one might attune to. The breakthrough is that Sheldrake's idea can be tested scientifically. So far, results are coming down on his side.

An extraordinary memory has always fascinated and earned its owner a place in the pages of history. Heinrich Heinekin won his few sentences early on. At a time when most of us are working up to "Mama," ten-*month*-old Heinrich could recall and recite long texts in both verse and prose. At fifteen months, he began learning history, as a two year old, Latin and French. By then he could write. Although he lived in Lubeck, Germany, Heinrich was fascinated by Denmark and could rattle off its geography and history. In 1725, the King of Denmark invited the four year old to visit. Courtiers perhaps suffered some pangs of inadequacy as little Heinrich answered questions in three languages, recited over 1400 passages from texts by famous Latin authors and recalled the entire genealogy of all the royal families of Europe. But after such an accelerated start, the tyke experienced burnout. He took only nurse's milk, his health declined, and the tiny whiz passed away age four years, four months.

Some people thought it served him right. Yet, if there is a constant to the brilliant achiever—the person who lights up his field—it's that almost every one has, at the least, an excellent memory. Some are legendary. French dramatist Jean Racine, for one, could recite entire plays verbatim after reading them once. Others, like Arturo Toscanini, have supermemory for music. One evening, just before a symphony concert, an alarmed bassoonist told conductor Toscanini that he'd broken the lowest key on his instrument and its note couldn't be played. In just a moment, Toscanini replied, "That note does not occur in the scores for the bassoon in any of tonight's symphonies."

Such effortless flashes of memory seem far afield to most of the people we've run into lately. "You're writing about memory?" they ask. "Hurry!" they chorus. Everyone seems to have complaints about memory. There seems to be a drift toward *sub* rather than super memory. As one wise child explained, "My memory is the thing I forget with." Even those who take measures to remember can have problems, as the mother of a Canadian diplomat discovered when she visited her son in Tokyo. His Japanese acquaintances exceeded even their usual lavish hospitality and entertained her royally. A farewell banquet was planned and the lady determined to say at least one important thing in Japanese—"arigato," thank you. To be sure to remember, she summoned a time-honored memory technique and associated arigato with alligator. That night the grateful woman gazed fondly at the assemblage of polite faces. "I just have one thing to say to all of you," she said with a warm smile, "Crocodile!"

Is there a memory pollutant on the loose? Is it spreading like a computer virus across the land making people's memories foggier than before? Or is it simply that in our accelerating age, everyday memory is being swamped with tidal waves of information and change, with proliferating things to do and seemingly less and less time to do them? Yes, is probably the answer to both questions. Psychologist Fritz Perls described normal consciousness as "chronic low-grade emergency." But a lot of help is coming over the hill.

Very real memory pollutants like stress, chemicals, and an electromagnetic world are being recognized and relieved. Can you eat to remember? It seems so. That power lunch can become a memory-power munch once you know the menu. One memory booster could even be considered a gift from the Garden of Eden. It's from the leaves of the Gingko tree, at 200 million years old a winner of the species longevity record. Other breakthrough substances have been discovered that quicken mental brilliance and creativity without addiction; a turn-on without a turnoff.

Help is also coming from some of the newest things around, machines that can stimulate and restore the human mind in ways never before known. Brain stimulators allow ordinary people to access heightened mental powers. One little-known sleeper of a machine might help people restore memory—and remember how to be young. Users claim it helps rejuvenate the body. Is there a high tech route to evolution? Some experts think so. In a decade, they claim, mind machines could bring the memory and mental agility once reserved for "geniuses." IQ-boosting machines will do for memory/mind what exercise machines do for the body.

With the press of a button, centuries-old prejudices about intelligence, what it is and who has it, could be swept away. "What we think of as intelligence is probably a pale shadow of the brain's actual powers and faculties," says Michael Hutchison, author of *Megabrain*. Robert Anton Wilson believes the new state-of-the-art HEAD (hedonic engineering and development) technology "will mark the most important turning point in the evolution of this planet."

Mnemosyne, goddess of memory, is also mother of the sciences and arts. Maybe that's why researchers have discovered that specific high-frequency sounds in music can nourish the memory. Frequencies have been mapped that can recharge the brain cortex, release new vitality, and strengthen your mind. In other quarters, researchers are using music to mask "beat frequencies," pulsations that raise imperceptible rhythms in the brain proven to heighten concentration, memory, and skill.

Memory Pegs and Supermemory

In the library of her New Jersey home, a schoolteacher quickly riffled through the pages of the latest issue of *LIFE*. Then her family checked her. Seemingly effortlessly, she correctly reeled off the contents of every single page, forward and backward. This "memory master," the mother of one of the authors, had plunged wholeheartedly into a memory course by Bruno Furst, a memory expert who wowed crowds much as Harry Lorrayne does today. "Page 19: Ford ad bottom right; article Eisenhower's cooking . . ." Soon the whole family got into the act. Memory pegs do work. Two or three of them may stick with you for a lifetime. But unless you practice with the discipline of a stage performer, the system fades in a month or two. The whole memory doesn't strengthen. You can still too easily leave your keys in the door or your card in the ATM, or lose your car in the parking lot. The new memory systems seem to nurture the whole memory.

Right now, can you learn two or even five times faster and remember what you learn? Can you begin to open up the global expanse of memory summoned by a Toscanini? Hundreds of thousands of people on five continents say you can and they can prove it. They are getting a boost at mastering almost any subject with accelerated learning. Superlearning is what we named our brand of this master method that lured us into the fields of memory over twenty years ago. *Lured* is the operative word. What attracted us so powerfully lay at the very heart of accelerated learning and sparked it to life. It's that old human desire for what scientists call *hypermnesia*—supermemory.

Two decades later, we were still wondering about supermemory. Is it "just" the ability to reel off facts with ease? That may be the lesser part. As we kept looking, our idea of memory kept ringing out further and further. It took a quantum leap when a friend, Dr. Raymond Abrezol, made an offhand remark. A tall, athletic-looking Swiss, Abrezol is an expert in creating both Olympic medalists and proficient self-healers.

"All disease is memory," the good doctor told us. When he said it, only a few years ago, it was a very odd remark. But it kept reverberating. Now mainstream science, hard science, is beginning to reveal how memory, like an invisible, essential enzyme, plays a dynamic role in making one sick or well. Researchers have tracked the ways in which our ever shifting memories affect even the secretions and substance of our cells. This brought up the flip side of memory: *forgetting*. If we don't want too much old baggage when we change centuries, we have to learn how to forget, how to notice and let go of limiting memory patterns bound away inside us. Memory masters of old made great conscious efforts to build memory palaces. Though we don't realize it, we are all building invisible memory structures and, in our unawareness, too often house ourselves in memory hovels and dungeons or sprawling worry factories. Now there are numerous, effective ways to help one remodel, to use memory *for* oneself, not against oneself.

Look at the world through the eyes of memory and you'll see new shades of meaning all around. You'll also begin to see that from physics to geopolitics and ecology, down to one's understanding of self, something basic is happening. A process of re-membering.

Re-Membering

Eventually it dawned on us why Mnemosyne seems to be stirring everywhere. The materialist mind that dominated the last 300 years saw the world as a giant machine and zealously took it apart, dismembered life to study life. It was a zeal that brought great gifts and, in the 20th century particularly, great ills. Years ago, William Blake sitting in the garden under the apple tree saw it coming—the fragmentation, the alienation, the disconnection from nature that would "weave old England's winding sheet." Today, scientist-philosopher Arthur Young, who has spent half a long life in a reexamination of evolution, sees something else coming: a dictate to regather and grow—or become "species extinct."

The idea of wholeness is on the rise in the collective mind, spreading its influence, not across the materialists' old impersonal globe but around Gaia the living earth. A new perspective is growing that emphasizes association, connection, interdependence, resonance—all, the dynamics of memory, all, the lifeblood of Mnemosyne. There's a move afoot to pick up fragments and knit them together. Like Humpty Dumptys resurrected, we are starting literally to re-member.

Scientists used to see you as a collection of parts. Now they speak of one process, "mindbody." Master teachers, who say education has taught only one sixth of the brain, now talk to the whole brain. Emotions are being welcomed back into intellectual pursuits. Your feelings, it's become apparent, play a vital role in your ability to remember and learn. To know ourselves whole, long-ignored states of consciousness are being retrieved. It turns out memory depends intimately on one's multiple states of mind. Across the board, disparate parts of human experience are coming home. Almost all have a connection to memory.

Like two mirrors flashing light back and forth, there is a dynamic feedback between memory and re-membering, they open each other up, bounce light into new corners. It becomes impossible to track one without the other.

"In Search of Time Lost"

As the 20th century dawned, the great French writer Marcel Proust launched his influential, massive exploration of memory. Seven intricate novels, well over a million words, flowed from him—all because of a cookie, all because of the echoing memories triggered by that famous lime-flavored taste of a madeleine dipped in tea. In *À la Recherche du Temps Perdu* (less aptly titled in English *Remembrance of Things Past*), Proust breathes life—flesh and blood—into philosopher Henri Bergson's theories of time. Time, near as our hearts beating away the measure of our lives, is yet elusive. Time can only be grasped by intuition and memory. Past and present have equal reality in memory, Proust realizes, as his long search culminates in *The Past Recaptured.* Memory lifts life beyond the withering tick of time.

Roaming in our memories, "recollecting in tranquility," is perhaps as close as many of us come to a sense of the eternal present, the eternal now. In this now, there seems to be a new resonance quickening the whole octave of human history. Beyond the personal, the fog that shrouds universal memory has started to lift. Spurred by the most relentless ancient memory of all, the ubiquitous cultural recollection of a lost paradise, scholars and archaeologists have uncovered intriguing new clues to help us remember who we are. Are we re-membering a brighter legacy? Is our picture of ourselves about to leap to a wider screen? Mayan scholar Dr. Jose Arguelles has a wide-angle view of history. He concludes that something is unfolding at this point in time, an impulse long ago predicted that will open evolutionary memory.

"We shall unlock ever deeper levels of memory," Arguelles says. "As primary patterns of resonance, memory shall come to be known as the radial pattern that unifies all levels of being and consciousness." This is cosmic memory or, in other words, a unifying field. It's a big concept, one the Renaissance memory magi also envisioned, one that becomes clearer as you venture through Mnemosyne's domain. Still, no matter how far any of us wants to journey, we have to start with our own quirky old memory.

Memory Lane as Superhighway

"Memory lane" has become a superhighway. The multitude of researchers who have gone down memory highway have opened it for the rest of us and made expanded memory readily accessible. "More has been learned about the workings of the brain in this recent period than in all history before," says George Adelman, editor of the *Encyclopedia of Neuroscience.* Life on the road to expanded memory can be exhilarating and rouse a sense of self-reliance and security. You have to take the steps, of course; it isn't magic. But the good news, something most people find hard to believe, is that you already have an extraordinary memory. It's standard equipment. The trick is knowing how to access your memory, how to treat it right and use it creatively. The 21st century memory breakthroughs in the following chapters will let you do just that.

2. The Master Memory Method

Hushed and peaceful as gently falling snow, the lovely, lingering melody of Vivaldi's *Winter* spread through the large hall. Four hundred Japanese students closed their eyes and settled into themselves—ready to learn electromagnetic theory.

In Ohio, the same sweet melody rose in a roomful of AT&T workers who breathed a sigh of relaxation and let go of worrying about how to remember the intricacies of new fail-safe equipment. In Toronto, a handful of freshly scrubbed boys didn't seem to be listening at all to Vivaldi's flowing melody. They lay flat on the floor, heads in a circle, breathing in the slow rhythm of sleep. But the prep schoolers were listening, this was one of their favorite classes.

Serene images, not the ones that usually come to mind when one thinks about how to keep up in the ongoing press to change, to learn and remember faster and faster. They are the images of a new approach. Instead of gearing you up to pace the treadmill faster, it gives you techniques to draw on innate ability, and to move from your own center in this accelerating age. The Japanese engineers, the AT&T technicians, and the Canadian preppies all learned faster with this approach. They learned faster because they remembered better.

Perhaps the most practical, all-around way to begin to empower memory lies with the developing methods of accelerated learning and Superlearning.® Just about anyone can use these master methods, six year olds to eighty-six year olds, the bright and the not so bright, students in class or individuals at home. They cost almost nothing and have a vast range of applications. They are master methods because their techniques can be used to enhance one's many "memorys"—the automatic memory built into sports and artistic performance, the memory that fuels problem solving, the memory involved in healing. They are master methods because as one focuses on a single subject, new facility begins to spread like light across the land to strengthen the whole mind and the whole memory. Some people say they bring a certain lightness of being. Executives, linguists, military people are using Superlearning to perform with more grace and punch. It's even easier for an eight year old.

Superlearning

The kids in Rosella Wallace's third grade class were making funny faces in the cafeteria line. Not only their faces looked funny, they were also scrunching up their whole bodies, tight as fists, then all of a sudden letting go with a shower of sighs. Rosella Wallace's class in Anchor Point, Alaska, had a mission, they were about to embark on something special that would lift them out of the spelling doldrums. "We're going to do Superlearning," she told them with her fingers crossed. This was her maiden voyage and so far, at least, the kids kind of liked the name. Blond-haired Rosella Wallace is a pleasant, respectable-looking woman with a glint in her blue eyes, the glint of an innovator, a rebel within the system who might overturn an applecart or two in her drive to find better ways to teach.

Before the lesson, Wallace asked her kids to get up, stretch, scrunch, and relax. Seated again, they closed their eyes; it was time to imagine they were someplace wonderful: they were outdoors on a glorious summer day, running free under a limitless blue sky. Sun beat on their bare arms as they noticed a fluffy white cloud drifting overhead. It was a magical cloud, a cloud to hitch a ride on and everyone did, each aboard a fluffy cloud floating along safe and secure so high in the sky. They were going to find that spelling would flow just as pleasantly, just as easily as riding on a cloud.

Back to earth, the children read along silently as Mrs. Wallace said and spelled each new word. She was talking in a rhythm. She would speak for four seconds, be silent for four seconds, speak for four seconds, be silent for four. The tone of her voice rose and fell in a repeating cycle too: normal . . . whispering and confidential . . . then commanding! When the lesson was over, Wallace told her kids to lean back and close their eyes as music began to play, not the kind they were used to, but Superlearning music, featuring the harpsichord and strings of the slow, classical Baroque masterpieces. "Don't try to concentrate," Wallace said. "Just let your mind flow between the music and the words." Then in the same rhythmic pacing, she read the lesson over again.

That's it—the core of the Superlearning system that allows people to learn two to five times faster *without* stress. You learn faster because you remember better. Instead of going over a new statistic or a Russian verb fifteen or twenty times, three or four repetitions can be enough to lodge it in memory. The method begins to draw out that vast natural memory everyone has in theory but until now few have realized in practice. This is education in the classical sense, a word which at root means "to draw out from" not, as one might think, "to stuff" as in sausage. Years of brain research, like that of the famous neurosurgeon Wilder Penfield, suggests that everything that has ever happened to you remains—somewhere. It isn't lost, "just" forgotten.

How can you retrieve what you perceive, when you want to? One secret lies in the way information comes to you. Another is the mindbody state you're in when trying to learn and remember. Accelerated systems move you into a "best state" for learning. To reinforce memory, you are fed data in a rhythmic pattern backed by slow baroque music in a specific beat. This special music can boost memory all by itself. Researchers at Iowa State played it during class and exams to find that memory improved by 26%. Lab tests in the USSR and Eastern Europe reveal that this baroque music induces highly beneficial, harmonizing changes in the body and brain. For those with an "open ear" there is another reason why the strings of the Superlearning music can evoke memory. The high-frequency sounds that energize the brain are also found in the harmonics of this special baroque music (see Chapter 10).

Besides music, a battery of other techniques weave through the seemingly simple accelerated systems, techniques that access the powerhouse intelligence of the subliminal mind, techniques to dissolve memory blocks and flood away stress. As detailed in coming chapters, you can use these many elements separately—from imagery to breathing patterns—to free up and strengthen your memory. You can also put them all together and enjoy a powerful, occasionally electrifying master method that's set many different kinds of people on the road to supermemory. Tests show they are remembering over the long haul.

Rosella Wallace is one of those born teachers most of us only meet in stories. She pioneered the development of Superlearning as a complete teaching method which involves a great deal more than memory embedding. Classroom support helps. Yet as far as the core part, empowering memory, goes, you can do it yourself. A great many people have, enabling themselves to remember rules for real estate exams, business caveats in foreign languages, or baseball stats for trivia triumphs.

"It's keeping my mind young," reports Ben Eizig, an eighty-seven-year-old San Francisco lawyer successfully Superlearning languages. Like a lot of olders, Eizig has discovered a kick with an antiaging effect. He's recaptured the joy of learning.

Pulitzer prizewinning journalist Charlayne Hunter-Gault jokes about asking an interview question and pausing—one, two, three, four—after she took up Superlearning Spanish on her own. "Once I mastered the exercises," she says, "I found they improved my interviewing, my writing, speechmaking, and just about everything else involving my memory."

At one of our lectures, a well-muscled man got up—a sanitation man it turned out, with a sense of the dramatic. "My coworkers thought I was nuts," he told the audience and us, "but I used Superlearning, baroque music and all, studying for the foreman's exam. . . . And I flunked!" Then he grinned. "It wasn't Superlearning's fault. I still remember everything I learned a year ago. It was just the wrong stuff."

When you pick the right stuff, the system apparently works whether you're trying to collect data on trash or the particulars of science. Brian Hamilton, an experienced social worker and therapist, decided to go back to school and take premed at Columbia. "I was getting Bs," Hamilton said when he dropped in at our office. "So I put my courses into the Superlearning format—and my grades turned to As." Definitely a member of the helping professions, Hamilton quickly began to teach the method to others. He trained teachers in an exceptional school, New Vista Academy in Brooklyn, a showcase school that daily proves advantaged and disadvantaged can both excel. Superlearning wasn't totally unknown at New Vista before Hamilton; the principal played Superlearning music over the PA. One day she forgot; a loud rapping sounded on her door. Would she please put the music on, students asked, they missed it.

What happened on the Alaskan frontier? "I saw a tremendous improvement in my class in the development of thought, concentration, and memory since starting Superlearning," Wallace reported. At year end, her kids scored in the 94 percentile on the standard spelling exam, highest in the school. When Wallace got the same good results with subject after subject, the Department of Education picked her program as one of only fifteen to explore in the National Curriculum Study. Wallace earned a Ph.D. with her innovations; a consultant now, she is working toward the realization of a magnet school that will use the new methods throughout. She also trains other teachers in this "better way," to help more kids, more 21st century citizens, learn *how* to learn—and love it.

Unexpected enjoyment pops up across the board with supermemory techniques. The Canadian Pacific Corporation ran experiments with executives, many of them disgruntled executives because they were required to learn French. They not only learned two to four times faster than before, but they liked it. Absenteeism nosedived, a real plus to trainers who found it dicey to admonish truant VPs. Liking what you have to learn gives one an edge, for the bottom line is that we remember what we *feel* like learning. But there's something else that makes Superlearning and accelerated learning particularly potent in business training. Rather than adding on more tension, the method automatically drains stress away, not just the stress of learning, but the stress of the job, of retraining, of life in general, the stress that dampens memory and that, in the long run, can even wear down areas of the brain all important to memory.

The stress-reducing effect showed in the Anchor Point kids. "It's my cloud that makes me love it," a young girl said in a taped interview. "I love riding on my fluffy cloud." "Do you think your teacher's crazy doing these things?" "Naah," one boy piped up. "She's not crazy. Before, I was getting Fs, now I get As." Kids felt good about themselves and behaved better, so much so that parents began to ask Wallace to teach them how to hitch a ride on a cloud too.

Bringing Memory out of Retirement

The memory of an eight year old is an open field compared to the labyrinthine memory of an adult. That's one reason we were intrigued to meet Commander Charles Croucher, a lean, tan man with a James Mason cut to his jaw, perfectly cast to have fought with the British Navy in World War II and to have served as dean of the Canadian Naval College. Language is a central love to Croucher and his wife, Hope, who both have degrees in linguistics. They retired and followed a dream to go to Spain, live in the sun, and pursue languages. So they did, until riding his bike Croucher was hit by a truck. In the hospital he was hit again by a stroke. He returned home to disaster. Suddenly much of Spanish, French, and German wouldn't come. Worse, nouns in English kept bordering out of reach. His general memory was weaker; doctors called chances for full recovery dim. "I could no longer function adequately as a translator and teacher," Croucher wrote the editor of *The Incorporated Linguist,* a British journal, "yet much worse was the thought of facing this enforced retirement deprived of the research and writing so long looked forward to. Not surprisingly, a state of depression set in."

Croucher's wife convinced him to visit Ray Alba, her brother in

New York, director of the Philosonic Society and a learning innovator on his own. Alba proposed what sounded like an odd experiment. They would teach Croucher Japanese, a language he had never studied; if it worked he'd know he still had enough memory to learn. In an interesting bit of psychology, Alba first gave the old-school Croucher the latest home-study course from the University of Tokyo. Every day Croucher would set to, learn a little, and forget a lot. It was hopeless. That's when Alba started Superlearning.

Before lessons, the Commander, buoyed by a waterbed, let his muscles relax and calmed his mind with an imaginary trip—wandering a fragrant garden in Spain, walking a salt-sprayed stretch of beach. Then, a graduate student from Tokyo read Japanese in four-second bits with cycling intonations. Breathing in a simple, rhythmic pattern, the Commander read along silently. Finished, he stretched out again as the strings of baroque music began to play in the special Superlearning tempo and key, and the lesson was repeated.

The doubting Croucher flowed through shock to elation. Tested at the end of seven days, he remembered 96% of what he'd learned. Teachers all, the group kept precise records. Hope Croucher Superlearned Japanese too, as a control. After fourteen sessions covering 150 Japanese phrases, the Commander retained 94% of what he'd studied, his wife 95%. They reported their "unqualified success" in *The Incorporated Linguist.*

"We were able to absorb a minimum of twenty to twenty-five simple Japanese phrases a day without stress. This means that studying half an hour every weekday, one could gain the basics of Japanese or any language in two months. . . . Unlike other methods that are known for quick learning and just as quick forgetting, tests proved a high level of retention for what we learned." Croucher adds, "The most immediate result for me was a renewed sense of hope and confidence that all was not lost."

Superlearning gets the credit for helping the Crouchers pick up basic Japanese in two months. But what about a disabled man suddenly able to learn and remember, who found the rest of his memory starting to work again too? Stroke victims sometimes just recover. On the other hand, teachers of the learning disabled tell us the method helps, the relaxation, the measured pace, and particularly the special music. Dr. Allyn Prichard, a pioneer of accelerated learning, faced what is usually called "a challenge," i.e., a dismal prospect. He was trying to rescue kids fallen way behind in reading, kids fast on the way to society's discard heap. Many of the young teenagers he confronted had learning disabilities, a couple were mildly retarded.

With Jean Taylor, his teaching collaborator at the Huntley Hill School in De Kalb County, Georgia, Prichard began accelerated learning with the reluctant readers. The startled kids picked up a year's work in twelve weeks. It wasn't a fluke. Under Taylor's direction such exceptional results continued a decade. Across the country, in the ghetto, on the prairies, the system has proved a natural for those who have to catch up, for those whom experience has taught, "I can't."

Before stretching Commander Croucher out on his waterbed, Ray Alba wanted to ask us some questions. Fortunately, we didn't connect until later —fortunately, because Alba probably would have heard, "A stroke . . . we're not sure . . ." But then, we'd spent a lot of years questioning accelerated learning. Right from the first, over twenty years ago, it sounded too good to be true.

The Communists and Supermemory

"Bulgarians are learning fifty times faster. They are approaching super memory!" trumpeted the *Sophia Evening News* in one of many reports on "Suggestology" that crammed our luggage as we trundled out of the train station into the Bulgarian capital. Sophia is a leafy, sleepy old city in a land filled with sunflowers and roses, a land where Ovid lived in exile, where it was said that Orpheus once roamed to enchant even the forest animals with his music.

What sort of enchantment was at work now, we wondered. In the communist world, tiny Bulgaria suddenly loomed as an educational tiger. The Soviets with their fierce interest in education had already scooped up Suggestology. "You can learn a language in a month," *Pravda* enthused. And again, "Workers attending night school find learning more refreshing than a nap." Was it all propaganda?

In Moscow, we'd met the man generating the excitement, Dr. Georgi Lozanov, founder of the state-supported Institute of Suggestology in Sophia and at the time Bulgaria's sole psychiatrist—a story in itself, another story. He was a man who could laugh wonderfully, with warm brown eyes and free-running, Einsteinian hair. He was very much of the school of thought that led Soviet scientists to tell us, endlessly it seemed, "The reserves of man, those are a country's greatest resource. We only use a fraction, maybe ten percent of our abilities." A hundred years ago, William James figured people use only five percent of their capability. "Only one percent," the Swiss Dr. Abrezol insisted recently.

Suggestology hit a responsive chord in the Soviets who had long delved into hypermnesia or supermemory. Probably the most gigantic memory ever probed scientifically belonged to the great Veniamin, "the man who remembers everything." A.A. Luria, the world-renowned Soviet academician, devoted decades to studying Veniamin and declared his memory "without limits." Apparently, Venianim really never did forget anything he experienced, down to the arrangement of plates and flowers on a table during an everyday tea twenty years before.

Lozanov knew Luria's voluminous work and he'd examined Indian and Bulgarian yogis who possessed total recall and photographic memory. But memory wasn't the goal when, with a long eclectic reach, he put together his new "ology." The doctor hoped to heal the sick. To do it, he reclaimed the old and gathered in the disciplines of the new. He drew from Raja yoga or mental yoga and Western hermetic tradition, melding them with the latest psycho-physical discoveries, especially the strongly invested Soviet research of suggestion.

"Almost miraculous!" was one assessment when we showed nuns at Rosary Hill College in upstate New York a Lozanov medical film, graphic evidence of the healing effect of Suggestology on the obviously wretched. Lozanov anticipated by thirty years today's burgeoning use of the mind's ability to heal the body, which sometimes brings the seeming miraculous. Suggestology relieved ills all right, but it often did something else. Patients seemed to strengthen all around, their intellectual powers and memory improved. Psychiatrist Lozanov, then treating a slew of overwrought university students, soon asked himself the right question.

"If we can have the painless birth of children why can't we have the painless birth of knowledge?" The accelerated learning and supermemory branch of Suggestology was born. Today it's not so strange that techniques that ease diabetes or cure heart arrhythmia can also boost memory. In ways Lozanov couldn't anticipate, it's becoming clear that from mind to molecule one's memory and health intersect and intertwine. Now researchers are spiraling around from the other side of the circle. They're using methods that spark memory and learning to prompt self-healing (see Chapters 16 and 17).

Unbelievable maybe, but Suggestology was intriguing and in 1970 we took just a few pages in our book *Psychic Discoveries Behind The Iron Curtain* to introduce the system to Westerners for the first time.

Apparently a lot of people were waiting. Waves of genius-seeking tourists, relief-seeking teachers rolled into Sophia. Tidal waves of mail rolled over us. Lozanov began to lecture in the West and was whirled around in Balkan intrigues until eventually his passport was lifted. "I was ruthlessly removed from the Institute of Suggestology, which I created twenty-five years ago, for insubordination to the totalitarian system," he wrote in the spring of 1990, when he was finally free to be on the move again. His brainchild had long since made it over the border, to be adopted and then adapted by a feisty group of Americans and Canadians who helped it grow in a new world.

Finally we were convinced that what worked in the authoritarian East also worked in Des Moines and Toronto. We got eclectic too, and in our book *Superlearning* put together a do-it-yourself program to help let everyone in on the discovery. The Superlearning system* draws on Lozanov's work and also from his sources—fortunately we were familiar with some of them or we might not have realized that something special was afoot in that tiny, faraway institute. We also drew from other mind-strengthening techniques particularly "Sophrology," the science of harmonious consciousness another new "ology" developed in Spain by another M.D., Alphonso Caycedo. It's a remarkable system too—three foreign universities have Chairs in Sophrology—yet it remains almost unknown here.

Does Superlearning sound like a fixed object? It isn't. All the accelerated systems are evolving. Yet from what we've seen over the last ten years, the part that enhances memory holds; it has been proved over and over again. (If you want to Superlearn a subject, see Appendix A for how-to instructions, or read the book.) Superlearning can jump start you on that road to supermemory. On the way, you might want to use it to pick up some foreign languages, because the journey has been joined all around the world.

* Superlearning is The Registered Trademark of Superlearning Inc., N.Y. NY.

3. "Learn Two to Five Times Faster"— A Global Turn-on

The colorful floral stamp on the letter read *Vanuatu,* a place we knew only from a TV special on "dirt diving." With a vine attached to an ankle, natives dove headfirst from the tops of palms trees to ground, not water. Vanuatu is a pinpoint in the Fiji chain. "Can you help me with Superlearning music?" the writer asked. How had he heard of it? What was he going to do with it?

Something more intriguing than a surprise is coming from accelerated learning. It's wrapped up with the urge to find more satisfying ways to live, to reach out and recover the parts of our lives and planet that have been ignored, repressed, steamrolled, wasted. We didn't realize it for a while, but it also involves a mystery that's beginning to emerge: the transformative energies of memory on a grand scale. One way to track this quickening is the hands-on response to accelerated systems. Do you sense that horse-and-buggy learning, fragmented learning, isn't going to cut it in the cosmic age? Then you're part of it. What is surprising is how global, how pervasive that sense is. It's as if someone were setting messages adrift in bottles.

Requests for data, and first-person accounts of successful Superlearning come from everywhere: from a Bantu teacher in South Africa, business schools in Singapore, the head of an Innuit settlement in Canada's Northwest Territory, dental groups in the Arab Emirates. Word comes from missionary nuns in a Philippine village, convicts doing hard time in Folsom penitentiary, the government of Finland, which incorporated Superlearning in its English training, the director of a large Mexico City drug clinic. . . .

"We are at a unique place at a unique time in the history of this planet," remarks Bruce Tickell Taylor, a leading proponent of the Society for Accelerative Learning and Teaching [*SALT*]. If we want a future, Taylor contends, we're going to have to work for it together. "One does not need to change human nature, but the unconscious beliefs resulting from childhood conditioning. Though such a task is considerable, it is not impossible. . . . The ability to change the unconscious through affirmation and inner imagery is a very important point that many of us in SALT are well aware of, though much of the population is as yet unaware of [it]. We are in a unique position to help." As the method boosts memory, Taylor sees it also bringing in powerful techniques to help re-member the global family.

Born to an international viewpoint in Korea after World War II, son of an American mining engineer and an English actress, Taylor settled down to three decades of teaching in the Windsor School District in California. He's another of the remarkable people we met through Superlearning. Taylor read the book, got up, and made something new happen.

Of four fifth-grade classes in his school, he took on the one with the poorest performance. In six months, his "slow" class had turned into superperformers. They were spelling at a level one year ahead of the best of the other classes. Working from kindergarten to teacher training, Taylor refined his techniques. "Do you have any memory tips?" we asked.

"Not the usual gimmicks, but I find it helps to think of a right angle triangle—a mini Superlearning device. The first angle is to do deep breathing, to pause and center yourself before learning something new. I used it to pick up ballroom dancing with good results.

"The next angle—do a relaxation routine and guided imagery. Then play the special music as you read material, preferably onto a tape.

"Finally, the right angle. Do the above but also listen to the voice and music tape just before sleep and on waking. That's what I did in a French class where the teacher *forbade* recorders. Using the right angle, I was constantly answering other people's questions and had to be silenced by the teacher!"

Taylor retired to work time and a half with his Accelerative Tutoring and Transformations Institute. At his own expense, he has placed taped lessons with teachers in eleven countries, hoping to wake up international academia. "Tithe a tenth of your time to help minorities," he exhorts SALT teachers.

Helping is the go word for the many who've taken up the method to prove in rather wonderful ways that one person still can make a difference. To relate what so many have accomplished and discovered around the world would be to write son (daughter?) of *Superlearning*. Instead, to show how convertible the system is, how many different kinds of memory it evokes, here are a very few highlights of what happened to people sparked by news of that obscure Bulgarian institute.

Acceleration Across the Board

"Je ne parle pas Français" is often the all-occasion sentence in Paris. We may have studied a language in school, but still draw big blanks confronted with a voluble cabbie overseas. That's what gave Bulgaria's Suggestology its initial cachet. You can pick up and remember languages quickly and easily. In one of the first experiments in the United States, at Iowa State University in Ames, Dr. Donald Schuster achieved a triple speed-up in learning Spanish. A psychologist with a nice mix of vision and practical gumption, Schuster became the pivotal person in the development of accelerated learning in America. He founded the field's professional society SALT, edits a quarterly journal, and with Charles Gritton, another tireless teacher, wrote a definitive text. Schuster has tested, teased, and tried the methods with subjects from A to Z. Not long ago, he zeroed in on a language more and more people have to grapple with: computer language.

If you were learning Pascal at Iowa, you'd attend three fifty-minute lectures each week and gain hands-on experience in the lab. Schuster's accelerated students got equal time in the lab but not in the classroom. He taught fifty minutes on Monday, twenty-five on Wednesday, and— happy surprise—not at all on Friday.

Final exams came. Schuster's students scored slightly higher than the three classes taught the usual way, but something else caused the excitement. Schuster's men and women learned Pascal as well, or actually a little better than their peers in *half the class time.* Better memory won the day. Besides proving that point, Schuster wanted to work with a class of over a 100, the ideal SALT group being twelve or thirteen. He followed the lead of Dr. Hideo Seki.

An inordinately good-humored enthusiasm for improving life, the universe, or whatever confronts him at the moment, makes Hideo Seki, now in his mid eighties, a great role model for anyone lucky enough to grow old. We know he is good-humored. As our host, Dr. Seki managed to trundle us and our mound of baggage twice as big as he on a never-say-uncle, fourteen-day lecture trip through Japan from top to bottom. Seki is a "retired" engineer and professor of computer sciences, and his colleagues, whom we met, are among the elder statesmen of Japanese science and academia. He easily grasped the potential of Superlearning and in the 80s developed it for the large classes typical of Japanese universities.

By mid decade, he was using his technique with a class of over 400 engineering students at the University of Tokai in a course that centered on a new edition of his own textbook, *Electricity and Magnetism.* For acceleration, Seki led students through three phases in his hourlong class. First he lectured in rhythmic pacing with intonations. As they listened, the young engineers breathed rhythmically in unison. The ins and outs of their breath followed a signal cleverly devised from the taped sounds of a running brook. Seki uses a brook sound because, he says, the frequency range is a basic, natural one that he also found in baroque music. Patterned breathing is a time-honored regulator of consciousness and memory. Centuries ago, yogis held their breath a minimum of seven seconds to focus or fix something in memory. More recently, the inventor of the floppy disk revealed that he too holds his breath, in a rather wild way, to catch his discoveries (see Chapter 9). American Superlearners try a simple maneuver: hold the breath while something is being said in the paced lessons, breathe in and out during the pauses.

Seki next gave a non-lecture. Students viewed special, colored diagrams and pictures. Meditative music played, not a word was spoken. The class wound up with the usual baroque music memory-reinforcing session. At the end of the semester, statistics showed "the number of students who got high grades increased remarkably, while the number with low grades decreased." Seki proved that the memory expansion methods can help large groups learn highly sophisticated material.

Far away on tiny St. Lawrence Island in the Bering Sea, teacher George Guthridge was making the most of a different kind of sophistication—you could call it street smarts except Guthridge's students look out on a tundra of snow and ice. "There's the Ben Franklin way of learning," Guthridge says. Kids explore using trial and error, then they're given specific facts. "It's a good thing for city kids." In the arctic, trial and error can swiftly lead to death. So Guthridge came up with "Daniel Boone learning, the natural way for bush children." A boy learning to hunt "starts out watching the father, memorizing what he does," Guthridge explains. "Next, he familiarizes himself with the tool. Then he conceptualizes. After some experience, that's when the son may start to be innovative."

Gutheridge uses the same approach with subjects like Middle Eastern History. First students memorize facts, names, dates, then come the lectures and creative projects building from memorized facts. Everyone used to learn that way. Today it's "reversed instruction" compared to usual teaching which begins with the general and leads finally to facts.

Teaching had reason to "reverse." Who gets fired up over a bunch of facts? Guthridge jumps over the boredom of such memorization by giving kids the facts rhythmically backed by baroque music as they relax in a dimly lit room. For his success with Superlearning "reverse instruction," Guthridge became the 1987 Alaska winner of the Department of Education's $25,000 Christa McAuliffe Fellowship.

As they stroll the trim lawns of one of Canada's most prestigious prep schools, boys at Upper Canada College in Toronto are about as far from bush children as you can get. They too have gotten a leg up from baroque music and rhythmic pacing. "Air conditioner: Carrier," says their teacher Lorne Cook in his measured, melodious voice. The ten boys lying on the carpet show no signs of recognition. "Mr. Carrier invented the air conditioner." For ten years, science teacher Cook has used Superlearning to teach a spectrum of science, to help bad test takers succeed, to help mathophobes relax, and swimmers stretch their limits on the school team. Over and over through the years, he's taught science tables to both Superlearners and control groups. Over and over, the results are the same. Tested later, the controls on the average score from 70 to 75%. Superlearners average 95% or better.

"There's such a huge gap between what we know about the brain and the way we teach," Cook says, and points out a common problem of Superlearning teachers. "There's a sort of conspiracy against success throughout our school systems. People get very suspicious if you use techniques that have the class average in the 90s."

If his colleagues weren't interested, Canada's largest paper *The Toronto Star* was, and interviewed nine-year-old Kristian Bruun. Previously math hadn't come easily to Kristian. "Superlearning helped me to learn better. My marks went up." On his own he'd taken to using the techniques to help him relax and remember every morning before tests. "I wasn't nervous. . . . Superlearning is really fun, and helped me get a lot accomplished."

But Kristian had another problem. According to his mother, violin recitals so unnerved him that he would drop his violin. Cook used Superlearning to help the boy relax, then run through and fix the entire performance in his imagination. "He played that piece like I'd never heard it played before," Mom reported. "He was outstanding." Cook is starting to train interested people beyond the schoolhouse walls.

Instead of kids from a specific culture, Dr. John Wade confronted a potential tower of Babel when he tried accelerated English learning in a project funded by the Australian Department of Immigration. In classes at Woden TAFE College, Wade looked out at students of varied age and education, from Japan, Argentina, Thailand, Czechoslovakia —ten different countries in all. He separated them into a control and accelerated group. Controls got textbooks and homework. The accelerateds just came to class.

After forty hours of learning, he tested their memory of idiomatic expressions; controls moved from a pre-class average of two to three. Accelerateds rose from three to eighteen. Could the immigrants retain their new English phrases? A test of long-term memory gave an average score of four for controls, ten for accelerateds. An outside teacher judged accelerateds were indeed speaking better, while results were unclear for the others.

"I like the music because it fixes the new words in your head better and helps concentration," one immigrant told Wade. "Successful," "comfortable," were the answers he got asking how they felt at the end of class. Students did have one caveat. It's a good thing we were all at the same level of proficiency, they said, or it wouldn't have worked. Yet prior to the class, their English had diverged so widely that Wade was advised that the group was "too disparate" and couldn't possibly work.

Memory on the Job

Rather than cultural differences, Matthew Rew dealt with physical differences. A young computer programmer blind since birth, Rew read *Superlearning* and realized that this mostly audio method might be an ideal way to strengthen memory so necessary to a blind student. He learned the techniques at the Lozanov Learning Center in Silver Spring, Maryland. Rew's computer work took a leap forward, enough so that his supervisors asked him to troubleshoot programming snafus. He relaxed, played baroque music, encouraged his unconscious, and found he could imagine and remember programs with ease. "I can mentally find bugs because I can see what's happening with the program." Quicker and better, he says, than anxiously running his fingers over a pile of Braille printouts.

With a grant from the U.S. Department of Health and Human Services, Lozanov Learning® set up a course with the American Technical Institute for Rew and a sighted consultant to teach blind programmers. The man behind Rew's success was Dr. Carl Schleicher, the only person with the know-how and patience to strike a deal with the Bulgarian government on the diplomatic level for the rights to Lozanov Learning.

Head of Mankind Research Unlimited, Schleicher jokes (we hope) that following up material in our books has ruined his life. It's true that he hasn't followed the track of his classmates at Annapolis or even a regular career in research and development. His research is on the far edges, particularly in what we used to call the Soviet bloc. Schleicher's unusual grasp of communist science, often quite different from Western science, allows him to spot promise that others miss. Until diplomatic agreements lapsed, he ran Lozanov Learning nationally for the public and helped bring the techniques into business schools here and in Germany.

Time is money, stress harms employees, change and retraining are the watchwords of the day—accelerated learning is a package that answers many needs. Don Schuster demonstrated how SALT can be used in industry when he taught a ten-hour course on the characteristics of paper to those involved in its purchase and use. Those Schuster taught with accelerative methods learned 80% more than people in the conventional class. Otto Altorfer, another long-time SALT member and a training specialist with Japan Airlines, has devoted years to testing the various elements of SALT in industry. Among the many benefits he found was accelerated *functioning* as well as learning.

Lately, baroque music has been playing in unusual spots like AT&T's National Product Training Center in Ohio. In spring 1990, C.L. Hallmark of the center added information from *Superlearning* and Superlearning tapes to his own expertise. He needed to teach workers, many of them older and being retrained, to handle complex control boards filled with light alarms. These are fail-safe systems for phone companies and "information must be ingrained in the workers' minds to allow prompt response to troubled conditions." Hallmark found Superlearning "well adapted" to this sort of training. His team thinks the system can find broad training applications in "this push-button world" right on up to teaching 747 cockpit controls. The AT&T trainers noted another plus, the by-product of stress reduction. "One of the people that it helped most," Hallmark says, "was a crusty old fellow I didn't think would even like the course. But he did."

After some years of searching, we've come to work with Karen Sands, educator, marketer, and former vice president of a major financial corporation, who used accelerated techniques to teach the fine points of highly sophisticated financial products. Training time contracted from weeks to three days. Sands is a disciple of Dr. W. Edwards Deming, credited as a major force in reviving Japanese industry after World War II with his philosophy of "continuous improvement" that leads to ever increasing quality in products and services. She is crafting her own unique combination of "continuous improvement" and Superlearning to help, as she says, "heal the wounded learner, create quality in wellness and to find ways to make the route to excellence accessible to people everywhere."

Re-membering Education

Your memory is your ability to: a) teach b) decide c) forget d) recall. By the end of the eighties, 70% of the nation's ten year olds couldn't remember what their memory was for, let alone how to use it better. That's just one more woeful statistic, the kind high-school teacher Albert Boothby of Sacramento loves to turn around. Boothby used Superlearning with kids who'd flunked history and failed to graduate. "We have such improved recall and understanding that our grades are A,B,C—or it's listen to the tapes and try again," he wrote us. Boothby fell prey to something that often happens to teachers who see for themselves the transforming power of accelerated learning. They don't burn out, they get fired up. Boothby too retired to work harder. A consultant for the Sacramento Unified School Districts, he tackled problem classes; one of the first included "some of the saddest cases, seniors with no motivation at all, from incredible poverty and abusive homes, kids who'd given up." Boothby promised them, "You can learn —and easily." To prove it, he quickly taught this class of unbelievers ten words in Portuguese. Observing teachers were surprised too. Their problem class was attentive, cooperative. "What I wanted the faculty to learn is that Superlearning is *fun* and allows everybody to learn." Boothby worked his "everybody can do it" magic even in classes for the gifted. "What brain power we unleashed!" he says.

Liberated teaching and liberating learning are growing. And yet, even in this accelerating age, accelerated learning has gained only a toehold. "What a help for Head Start, ghetto kids, third world countries, third world people coming here. . . ." We wrote that twenty years ago when we first introduced Suggestology. Now even more people have to catch up. More kids leave school with small memory of even the basics. We're still waiting for the trickle down.

Even when programs bloom, like Dr. Allyn Prichard and Jean Taylor's remarkable remedial reading course in Georgia, they can be cut off. Taylor helped failing readers for ten years until a new by-the-book administration canceled the class. Prichard, who's proved the system from grammar school to college with a batch of subjects, also served as Cherokee County's Democratic representative in the Georgia legislature. "People should remember that school boards are elected. They pay attention to mail," he says. "If you want change, you have to tell the boards, you have to support teachers working in new areas." Other SALT teachers have created successful courses of all sorts. The system isn't a panacea, but it's putting out strong signals that it's part of a solution.

Establishments resist novelty, it's an axiom. Change starts with individuals, especially those who, like nature, leave some open spaces for new growth. According to Don Schuster and his artist wife, Margaret, the good news is that something is happening inside post-industrial people that will bring an inevitable shift in how we learn. Many have studied the cycles of civilization, the rise from the physical building stage to the mental stage to the spiritual or artistic culmination. Unlike others, the Schusters sorted through three millennia to find the very different forms of learning that go with each stage.

Using data gleaned from everywhere—ancient Greece, aboriginal dream cultures, the curve of SAT scores—they created a model that reveals good reason why there is such dissonance in education. Our learning style doesn't fit the emerging character of the day. Our education, laid out, all dotted and crossed in a mental era, becomes increasingly out of sync as we evolve toward the artistic or spiritual phase of our culture.

No one wants to give up the great technological advances of the mental era, the Schusters agree. Yet as generations move into another way of seeing the world, they may not be competent in such fields. "Smarter jobs and dumber workers," as *The Wall Street Journal* says. "Our challenge," the Schusters warn, "may be to sugarcoat the mindstate educational system with spirit values and techniques." It's a challenge to re-member education by including such things as imagination, music, feeling, spontaneity, and an interest in the inner self including the subliminal self—the meat of accelerated learning, of the master memory methods. What's so handy is that these methods work for people at different cultural stages. They are ideal, too, for the newly literate in our immigrant cities who need to embed basics.

Coming from a different angle than the Schusters, Harvard's Dr. Robert Reich, in a report for the National Education Association, remarks, "People can't be trained as cogs anymore." Reich believes "the next economy will rely on a work force capable of fast learning," workers who have the ability to remember quickly and easily.

Those hyper headlines we saw years ago in Bulgaria and Moscow contained news after all. If you want to, you can turn into a "quick study." You can boost your memory, you can learn faster. This evolving master method is also bringing into more common use techniques that can strengthen other dimensions of memory—and techniques that can help you let go of the memories you need to forget.

4. Memory States and the Chocolate Factor

The rich, sweet smell of chocolate invaded the room, lapped around, and teased the taste buds of the Yalies bent over a test. The voluptuous smell hadn't escaped from the cafeteria, it was part of a memory experiment. If it worked, researcher Frank Schab would have a simple, surprisingly practical memory potion on his hands—one that might spur right reactions in an air emergency, or waft a grad student through a statistics final. Our senses are memory links. So are our emotions. To understand how chocolate, a surprise whiff of perfume, or a snatch of an old ballad can reach through time and vibrate alive forgotten smiles and long-ago faces, you need a sense of how a whole memory is formed. It has to do with inner ecology, our ever shifting inner weather, our multiple states of mind.

Altered states of consciousness aren't simply the pastures of mystic or tripper. They're everyday, all-the-time occurrences for everyone. "Altered from what?" is the mischievous question biofeedback pioneer Dr. Barbara Brown likes to ask. She has a point. Until recently, states of consciousness in the West came in a neat set of four: awake, asleep, coma, dead. Consciousness was talked of like a steady state, like a 60-watt bulb. Yet we all know our inner weather shifts constantly. Like light and shade in a photo, these shifts are imprinted on individual memories.

Do you remember things better when you're feeling good? Or when you're down? The question puts the cart before the horse. What counts is how you're feeling when you first experience something. How did you feel when you read that book, gossiped with your neighbor, listened to the lecture? Dr. Gordon Bower of Stanford University discovered that if you learn something when you're happy, you remember it best when you're again in a good mood. Those who feel sad during a new experience recall it best when they're feeling down. Memory and emotion seem to be as solidly bonded as atoms in a basic molecule. Even such a superficial act as putting on that happy face can influence recall.

At Clark University, psychologist James Laird had people read either Woody Allen's humor or muckraking editorials. Best recall of the funny bit came when people were told to smile. They remembered the angry piece most accurately when frowning. Apparently, if the face fits, wear it. The biggest holes in recall occurred when people smiled while trying to remember what the muckraker said, or frowned when trying to come up with Woody's jokes. Emotional state calls to emotional state in memory.

Feel melancholy while drifting through your memory and you'll pull back more sad recollections than usual. You'll also recall them more quickly than happy ones. Feel great and you're likely to tap into other good times. On down days, at least remember that your life hasn't been as unhappy as it seems, rather it's your mood striking alive only the weepy ghosts of other times. One's current state resonates with similar states in memory, just as surely as a G string on one guitar will resonate on its own when you pluck the G on a second guitar.

"Tears, idle tears," Tennyson wrote, "I know not whence they spring." The physical octaves of memory resonate too, hormones rush, muscles tense, or pleasure ripples through the body. On the extreme side, in the 60s this was the bugaboo of LSD flashback. Not a molecule of LSD glimmered in the brain, yet like a clang of cymbals a flash association would strike off a whole mindbody replay.

When we don't remember, we're more like the paper plate in the microwave, nothing happens to it because it resonates on a different frequency than the heating waves. If you're having trouble recalling something, try to recapture the state you were in when you first learned it. Try to feel your way back to it. If you rush into the kitchen and can't remember what you came for, go back to where you were, sit down, or otherwise take up the position you were in when the urge hit. Often the thought will strike alive again. In the same way, studying in the room an exam will be given in, or rehearsing in the place where you're going to give a presentation, can enhance memory.

The States of the Art

Like a seer scrying entrails, if you had the perception you could read a memory to know what was happening inside and outside a person when it was formed. Scientists call this "state dependent memory and learning." These states are like "different libraries into which a person places memory records," Bower says. "A given memory record can be retrieved only by returning into that library. . . ." Some libraries are easier to get back in than others.

There is the mild influence of everyday moods on memory, shading into the more pervasive influence of strong emotion and illness—or of getting tipsy, as forty-eight "martyrs" to science found out. They agreed to be plied with booze, then learn nonsense syllables. They managed. But when they were sober again, like the morning-after reveler who can't remember where the car is, they had trouble remembering what they'd learned. A little hair of the dog . . . as alcohol again flooded their brains so did the forgotten syllables. People on amphetamines and a variety of drugs have the same problem pulling memories over from one state to another. In a sense, they're not the "same" person, not in the same "place" they were when the memory formed. This may be an explanation for those who fall madly in love, then fall out of love and say, "I can't think for the life of me what I ever saw in her!" They'd have to be in the "love library" to see it.

Everyone's had this state-shifting problem bringing dreams across the borders of sleep. When we're half awake there they are, robust and alive. As we step into everyday consciousness, like friends left on the train platform they fade and are gone. Dreams often parade in outlandish costume. They're disguised, Freud decided, because we've repressed memories and can't face them straight on. Skewing images so they become bold, bizarre, farcical, and terrifying is a trick that memory experts have used since time immemorial to fix things in memory. Could it be that rather than playing hide-and-seek, some wild-haired dreams are trying to be remembered? If you want to hang onto a dream, try fastening onto its most outlandish feature.

Sometimes, one's everyday state of mind isn't conducive to memory. That state looks like a sieve or a great hunk of Swiss cheese riddled with an inordinate number of holes, according to mathematician Elizabeth Reudy. That's how her clients sketch their memories. Reudy immediately asks them to "forget something right now," so she can see their terrible memory state in action. Of course, they can't. Reudy, who can somehow look both studious and chic, is a Swiss now in New York. In the school system, teaching at the New School for Social Research and New York University or bolstering private clients, most of whom are mathephobes who face "impossible" graduate exams, she quickly found that people asked for help with more than numbers. "Help," they plead. "I have a terrible memory!"

Straight-faced, Reudy asks for a highly detailed description of a time when memory failed. After a while, as clients tell the stories of their terrible memories, recalling detail after detail, they start to look confused, or begin to laugh. Sometimes that's all you need, Reudy says, a little jolt to clear up a faulty self-image, to shake the self-fulfilling state of mind called "rotten memory." When real help is needed, Reudy has originated an unusual technique that strengthens the memory, not through the mind but by releasing the muscles and tensions of the body. (See page 82.)

Neuroscientist Dr. John Lilly has probably spent more time than anyone floating in the pregnant darkness of isolation tanks; he claims to have experienced hundreds of altered states. But too often he was like a zoologist whose rare specimens flew the coop on the voyage home. Back in "consensus reality," he couldn't recall his experiences. So Lilly came up with a memory "marker." When something interesting flutters center stage during an altered state, he purposely works himself into a strong emotion, the marker. Later, he hooks into that emotional excitement and can remember.

Once you know how state dependent memory works, like Lilly, you can do some leveraging. It isn't just Proust who was catapulted by his senses into the living world of memory. We all know the experience. Now, thanks to Frank Schab, science knows it too, from what might be called the fond-food-memory experiment. Schab gave various groups of Yale undergraduates a list of forty adjectives. "Write down the opposite of each." He didn't tell them that the next day they'd be tested for their memory of what they wrote. He said something stranger. "Try to imagine the smell of chocolate while you're working."

Schab treated one group to the real, rich-smelling aroma when they wrote and again when tested. Chocoholics will be reassured to know that this group remembered significantly better than those completely or partly deprived of the sensory fix. To work, the original memory had to have a chocolate smell and later a booster sniff was needed to bring it back.

If you're dieting, don't worry. Any distinctive smell can be a memory link, Schab points out, and suggests using different odors for different topics one learns in school. Why not at work? Mothballs for meeting notes, sausage for statistics . . . One caveat, you have to smell the real thing to resonate memory. Imagining didn't work, at least in Schab's experiments, though we suspect a practiced imaginer might just pull it off. Perhaps smells are so evocative because, unlike the sense of sight or sound, they shoot directly to the limbic area of the brain, switching station for memory and feeling. This lightning effect could be lifesaving in an emergency, Schab speculates. Why not use an odor when training pilots in emergency procedures, then automatically release the smell if an emergency strikes. It could "bring back a lot of information about how to do things, what to do next." All five senses imprint a memory. You can purposefully try any or all to cue back memory. Visualize former surroundings, listen to the same background sounds or music, sniff and sense yourself into that state where the memory lives. (For other Memory Shortcuts, see Appendix B.)

The Orange Juice Willies

Linked by association, all memories are separate to an extent. But sometimes the boundaries go up like the old Berlin wall, stifling association. State dependent memory becomes state *bound* memory. Recollection is bound away, partly or wholly inaccessible to everyday consciousness. These repressed memories can cast a long shadow and blanket away other memories, associations, and links that might lead to them. What binds memory? A savage beating, a three car smash-up, all the stuff of high drama or high soap. But so can everyday upsets. The state bound brings on the hidebound. Like electromagnetic patterns on tape, memory laid down below awareness plays on and affects behavior. Often this is the old baggage, the obsolete memories that limit life. A master at shaking them out was hypnotherapist Milton Erickson, increasingly recognized as a seminal genius of our times.

Erickson's uncanny ability to creatively engage his patients and cure their ills made it impossible for even the orthodox to ignore medical hypnosis. Erickson realized that people were often struck with a physical response, a body memory that kept playing over and over after the experience that caused it was long gone. A nagging backache, clenched teeth, unstable behavior, can be state bound memory and behavior that's living on its own. Bound away from recollection, the "tale" is wagging the dog. One case Erickson confronted will raise a sympathetic resonance in anyone who's ever thrown up after eating a certain food and could never look a steamed mussel or dollop of welsh rarebit in the eye again.

Could Erickson help, a young woman asked. Her aversion to orange juice was almost incapacitating. Orange juice had been her favorite, her coffee break, her champagne. Until one day, upset with a passing problem, she got intestinal twinges. Maybe it was the flu coming on. As a precaution she decided to chug some castor oil mixed with orange juice—only to later throw it all up for endless hours. On recovery, she'd done more than lose her thirst for orange juice. She couldn't even think of it; her family had to remove it from the refrigerator. In supermarkets, she had to avert her eyes from the pyramids of oranges or her stomach would begin ominous churning.

At an evening get-together, Erickson, who was legendary for the unconventional, asked the woman to be his subject for a demonstration of hypnotic age regression. He regressed her to a time two years before the awful orange juice incident. For twenty happy minutes, he let her live at that age and never mentioned oranges or sickness. Then the group decided to have some refreshments: orange juice. She joined in happily, after all, it was her favorite drink at that age. Remember nothing, Erickson said, and brought her awake. The rest of the evening, the young woman "kept rolling her tongue about her mouth and passing it gently over her lips as if she were trying to sense some elusive taste." Days later, she told Erickson she'd somehow spontaneously cured herself. She loved orange juice again.

Erickson took the woman to a time when her mind and body were set to experience orange juice as a treat. Then he let nature take its course, flooding away the adverse bound memory. If like Erickson you're clever enough to rouse it, deep down nature tends toward health. Dr. Ernest Rossi, Erickson's prime collaborator, points out that he didn't command away symptoms. He depended on the mind's innate ability to heal "without the intrusion of direct suggestion that could only be expressive of the therapist's limited view of how the cure 'should' take place." Erickson preferred an end-run around what he called "learned limitations" and what Rossi calls "state bound memory, learning, behavior."

The orange juice willies is a singular example of state bound memory that lingers and influences the body. It can get more exotic. Memories can be bound into states so discreet, so complex, that they begin to grow, and dance and jog on their own. Here you meet the three faces of Eve, or the ninety-two faces of Truddi Chase, all the alter egos of a multiple personality, each with its own expanding memory. Perhaps what is most bizarre is that here too memory retains its link with the physical. What does it mean that each bound set of memories, in other words each personality, has a different effect on the *one* body?

How often do you hear people speak of using hypnosis to program themselves or someone else? A highly uninformed idea, said Erickson, who defined trance as "creative reorganization." According to Rossi, the aim is not to manipulate, but to help a person access state bound memory so he can use it for problem solving and self-actualization. Creative reorganization—it has a better feel than thinking of your mind as a computer, which is rather analogous to thinking of your digestive tract as a garbage disposal. We aren't bolted like a machine into one square of spacetime. A memory isn't a dead byte. Memory is alive. Emotional memories fraternize. Remembering is a creative act; in today's jargon, every recall is a reframe. Which means that as memories are resummoned they are subtly changed, which can help you break out of the negatives. Every time you register a memory, you make a tiny but real change in living matter, your brain and body, and a change in your mind. This is what makes you unique. You may also be making a minute change in something a lot bigger than you are, in what Rupert Sheldrake calls "morphic forms."

Sheldrake has an audacious idea, to the average materialist mind a heretical idea. "A candidate for burning!" thundered *Nature,* the supposedly prestigious science journal, when it reviewed Sheldrake's theory. Another British journal, *New Scientist,* came down on the plus side, calling Sheldrake's work possible "scientific proof that science has got it all wrong." What wrong? How the world works. It isn't immutable law, splendidly isolate beyond time and space, that keeps the world running, Sheldrake says. It is memory, nature's memory in the here and now that keeps the world going and growing. Nature's memory exists as "morphic forms," patterns without energy that link to the world through resonance. You have your own unique morphic form. You also resonate to other, larger memory patterns in the world memory.

Cell geneticist and Fellow of the Royal Society in Britain, the Harvard-Cambridge educated Sheldrake contemplated an unanswered question in biology. What makes a birch tree a birch tree, a giraffe a giraffe, what makes a bit of fetal protoplasm, taken from a leg bud and placed where an arm should be, turn into an arm not a leg? Chemistry, DNA is a partial answer. Beyond that, scientists speak vaguely of organizing fields. Morphic forms shape us, according to Sheldrake. A memory pattern or morphic form rises with the first giraffe. Each succeeding giraffe resonates to the form and is shaped by it. At the same time, each individual giraffe feeds back its own minute bit of idiosyncrasy into the generic form, allowing change and growth. Nature's memory acts like the memory of habit. The hydrogen atom has resonated to its habitual form for so many eons that this pattern has become in effect immutable law. The rest of us have more leeway.

If you're a black woman from Santa Fe, you resonate most strongly to your own unique morphic form that's been building over your lifetime. You also resonate to morphic forms of American, black, female, and human to name just a few. Can you tune into specific morphic forms to enhance learning or multiply memory? Current tests are seeming to prove the idea (see Chapter 15). Certain people, like the Renaissance memory magi, may have always known how to tune into nature's memory. Sheldrake speaks of a morphic form for "French speaking." What about "healthy human body"? As will be noted in later chapters, the possibility that one resonates with nature's memory patterns could be liberating to both our philosophies and our abilities.

Theories of memory abound. They spring from experiments on chemical changes in the tails of slugs, they come from projections of holographic wave forms in the brain. Each fragment helps to bring the puzzle into focus. Of them all, two seem most pregnant with promise for our time. Only Sheldrake's universe-embracing theory seems large enough to begin to contain Memory with a capital M. The other concept, one that could help us become more universe-embracing ourselves, is state dependent memory.

Some researchers say we can think of memory itself as made up of infinite state dependent memories loosely connected by association and resonance. Understanding such a memory's hows and ways then becomes the route to knowing how to learn, function, and create better. It also brings a scientific underpinning to Dr. Abrezol's comment that "all disease is memory." Why do we lose so much of what we've experienced? How do we access what we know, but don't know any more? Why do we only use a smidgen of what is adjudged innate human ability? Perhaps we don't enjoy the exceptional functioning of the supermemory star, of the Olympic high jumper, the brilliant business strategist, even the miraculous self-healer, because *we don't know how to get into the state where these abilities live.* If we should get there by accident, we don't know how to recall those states again when needed. Understanding state dependent memory becomes a wide open way to pursue our possibilities.

How To Use the Joy of Learning

One of the simplest Superlearning techniques turned out to be one of the most effective for getting people into a state conducive to learning, remembering, and performing their best. It's the "joy of learning" exercise. The first time we mentioned it in a lecture, a few snorts erupted, then the whole audience roared with laughter. The joke was crosscultural. In Japan, the coupling of joy and learning sent soft ripples of giggles through auditoriums. Giggling, a ubiquitous Japanese response, seems to occur when something is funny or makes you nervous. This sounded like both. About the only people who didn't laugh were too young to talk much. If you want to see the joy of learning in the flesh, watch any old baby poking, sniffing, tumbling in the delight of discovery. All of us have experienced that rush, that high, when we discovered something, accomplished something. The idea is to resonate the memory of that mindbody state before you plunge into new challenges.

Conjure a memory of doing something really well, a time you felt terrific about yourself. Anything—giving a fine presentation at work, hitting a home run. The younger the better: when you got your driver's license, won a prize, first rode your bike—any moment of triumph. Relax by your favorite method. Then *be there.* Resonate that memory with every fiber of your body, every emotion, summoning all the awareness you can. See, hear, touch, taste, smell the scene.

Take your time. And slowly experience how your whole body felt, working up from your legs. Do you feel light, heavy? What's your breathing like? Are you smiling? On the outside, on the inside? Savor that glow of accomplishment. Give thanks for it. Press your left thumb and middle finger together as a marker. Realize you can press these fingers any time and circuit into this resonate memory of delight. Before sallying forth to learn and remember, before a speech or sports practice, take a moment and summon a mindbody memory of peak functioning, a success state.

Perhaps in the last decade of the 20th century, it's time to forget, to get rid of the hidebound, the state bound memories that no longer serve us. There's woe enough in our time, maybe the need is to resonate the joyful, to tune to, add our bit to that watershed of joy sustaining the life flow. It can help you remember and maybe re-member too.

5. Memories of the Subliminal Self

"It's okay to succeed." High-school underachievers discovered that this little subliminal suggestion can improve memory and strengthen learning. But that's hardly an iota of the story. An insider's view of how subliminal memories can be formed, how such memories can be changed, looks very much like necessary equipment not simply for self-improvement but for self-protection.

If you'd studied business law at Queens College in New York a few years ago, your eye might have caught an unusual catalog listing: Get an extra credit during a regular course. Just join "a study designed to see if subliminal messages can improve academic performance." If you'd been one of the sixty who opted in, you would have heard Dr. Kenneth Parker explain that subliminals involve information that bypasses conscious awareness but is picked up by the subconscious mind.

Parker planned to flash visual subliminals on a tachistoscope, a light device. Three times a week, you would look through the eyepiece of the tachistoscope. Suddenly, you'd see a quick, bright flash of light. Nothing more. Embedded in that light would be a single sentence. The four-millisecond flash would be too fast for you to perceive the sentence, but, according to the professor (a psychologist as well as a lawyer), your unconscious would get the message.

Parker divided the class into three groups. Each would get a different message, two that might enhance academic performance, one a control. What were the messages? "I remember everything easily"? "Study harder?" This was the one point the seemingly communicative Parker refused to discuss.

The first time students sat at the tachistoscope, Parker urged each to imagine an academic situation that made him tense—exams, answering in class, writing papers. Then each saw the flash. Once, then again. "Whenever you start to tense up in school," Parker advised, "remember the flash of light."

Subliminal effects increase with time, so Parker announced that two-thirds of the grade would be riding on the final. By then everyone had a full, forty-eight-flash dose of an unknown message. A month later, students were still wondering what the secret message was when they gathered to test their memory of what they'd learned. After that Parker revealed all.

As a group, those receiving the control subliminal scored in the low B range. If you'd gotten learning-enhancing suggestion number one, your group median was a high B. Those getting suggestion number two found that overall they'd been rewarded with a low A. Careful statistical analysis confirmed that the only thing that could account for the marked difference—about ten grade points—was subliminal suggestion. Subliminally strengthened memory lingered on. After four weeks, students who received the subliminal suggestions remembered more of what they'd studied than controls. (Experiments cited in this chapter are all well designed. For details see References.)

What are the "magic" messages that can so effortlessly improve one's ability to learn and remember? If you scored a high B, you might have been surprised to find that the message your unconscious took up was "The Prof and I are one." If you won an A, you might have been dumbfounded at what your unconscious took to heart: "Mommy and I are one."

It's hard to believe that the suggestion "Mommy and I are one" could, or even should, improve memory and learning, particularly in a law class. To grasp the potent, liberating effect of this seemingly childish suggestion, one has to follow a trail blazed by the late Dr. Lloyd Silverman of New York University, for over twenty years America's leading academic researcher of subliminals. Silverman's discovery of something that jogs memory was serendipitous. He was contemplating psychoanalysis. It seemed to help, yet its superstructure, psychoanalytic theory, remained just that—theory, because there were few ways to chart the subconscious objectively. Silverman had a flash of his own. If Freud rode dreams into the unconscious, perhaps he could blink subliminal suggestion into the hidden mind to light up its dynamics.

He knew he was on to something when he flashed psychoactivating subliminals to schizophrenics to stir up suspected areas of conflict. Symptoms boiled and became up to 70% worse. Conversely, when Silverman flashed different, wish-related subliminals, he could ease a patient's symptoms by almost as great a degree. What sort of magic was this that in a millisecond made schizophrenics, depressives, even stutterers a great deal worse, a great deal better?

Fired up, Silverman began contributing to a body of research that has accelerated mightily in recent years. It's a great, big body of research, but, like the twelve-foot purple elephant in the corner, most people are acting as if it isn't there. The elephant is unconscious processing. The question it trumpets is: Who's in charge? We like to think we're the captains of our souls, or at least that we choose to live as we do. Yet research reveals that a great deal of information enters our minds without our awareness. Like undercover agents, subliminal memories slip in, fraternize with other memories, and add their influence to the way we behave, feel, relate, believe. At the same time, subliminal processes are shaping our experience of the world.

Dr. John Ross, who studies sight, revealed how basic this shaping can be in clever experiments at the University of Western Australia. You go out in the street, look around, and see what's going on. Maybe. Ross discovered that you have a sort of visual memory bank in the unconscious. What you perceive enters your brain and is compared with this bank before it's sent up into consciousness as "what I'm seeing." This isn't a simple matching process, it works more the way an artist fills in a picture—include this, sometimes discard that. Ross calls it "a critical faculty capable of making decisions and of rejecting information, apparently on aesthetic grounds."

There's an old story, probably apocrapha, but one that makes Ross's point. As the story goes, when Henry Hudson first steered his tall ship *Half Moon* with all sails billowing into the Hudson River, something strange happened. Many of the native people could not see the ship. The medicine men could, some of the elders and children could, but many couldn't. What *really* doesn't fit a preconceived subliminal viewpoint doesn't make it into consciousness. Half awake, we actually are in a twilight zone. Who or what's "really" out there? As the innovative neurologist Oliver Sacks points out, "The world does not have a predetermined structure, our structuring of the world is our own—our brains create structures in the light of our experiences." But not all of these experiences happen in the light of awareness.

We often make up reasons for acting as we do and gloss over the fact that conscious "I" isn't exactly running the show because it's a frightening idea—at first. The subconscious through Freud's eyes was a dark, nasty realm repressed with reason. We're only now catching up with what some of his contemporaries saw. "A gold mine!" exclaimed classicist and consciousness researcher F. W. H. Myers, early on. He realized the subliminal mind connects us to transpersonal realms. "The spectrum of consciousness, if I may so call it, is in the subliminal self indefinitely extended at both ends." Mathematician Henri Poincare saw the genius of the hidden mind. "The subliminal self is in no way inferior to the conscious self; it is not purely automatic; it is capable of discernment; it has tact, delicacy, it knows how to choose, to divine."

Connecting with that talented subliminal self can improve memory. Learning to talk to the subliminal mind can help transform state bound, hidebound memories that live there and trip us up. It can help us forget what is no longer useful. Become aware of how the subliminal self pulls one's strings and you can begin to turn this powerhouse mind to advantage. Pinocchio did, after all, snap his strings and become a real boy.

The Mother of Subliminals

Could subliminals help everyone? Silverman decided to test the idea that a fantasy of merging, a symbiotic fantasy, can help people function more positively, or, to put it technically, can improve adaptive behavior. To spark such a fantasy, he came up with "Mommy and I are one." It proved an exceptional sentence. Mommy began to wind through research journals after she debuted in a weight-reduction class. Half the class received doses of the Mommy suggestion. The others were treated to a quick flash of the neutral subliminal, "People are walking." Whenever you feel tempted, dieters were told, think of the flash. Everyone underwent the usual course with dietary counseling and calorie restrictions. Even subliminally good mothering counts. People who got the Mommy message lost significantly more weight than controls. Even better, three months later the Mommy group had managed to keep off the lost pounds and continued to lose more effectively than the others.

The Mommy message has done a lot of subterranean housecleaning. It's helped alcoholics recover and smokers kick the habit. It's helped people dissolve phobias and others shake chronic anxiety. It's raised the math scores of high-school boys. Just how potent the subliminal can be in learning was revealed when Silverman and Dr. Rose Bryant-Tuckett tackled a difficult group at a Peekskill, New York school for emotionally disturbed teenagers. Could Mommy help their reading? Sixty-four boys and girls between ten and nineteen looked through the tachistoscope. Once again there was a control; once again no one knew what was hidden in the flashes.

The day of the standard California Achievement Reading Test dawned. The Mommy group got a good surprise. They really could read better, scores were significantly higher than controls. Maybe they weren't completely surprised, for things in general were looking up.

Inexplicably, their math grades had risen too. (Parker found a similar spillover with his law students.) Teachers noted that the group completed more homework than before and behaved better. Self-images improved. Obviously, something had changed, something helped these kids begin to rise above self-imposed limitation and blocks. The only something was the subliminal, Mommy, who apparently helped kids jettison a hodgepodge of problems.

News that a subliminal, particularly such an "undignified" one, could effect real change in people did two things in scientific circles. It raised a ruckus of opposition; it inspired others to go and do likewise. All manner of variations on a sentence were tried: Mommy is always with me; Mommy and I are two; Mommy and I are alike; Mother and I are one; Daddy and I are one. As far as your unconscious goes, Mommy is *it*. And she doesn't just help Americans. Dr. Sima Ariam tested subliminals in Tel Aviv to find that Mommy held sway there too. Mommy must be accompanied by *oneness*. Being alike, with, or the same as, doesn't move the unconscious.

Many psychologists still dismiss subliminals. Yet in August 1990, at the American Psychology Association convention, Dr. Joel Weinberger of Adelphi University reported a combined statistical analysis made of results concerning 2,562 people in seventy-two experiments with the Mommy subliminal. "There definitely is an effect," he concluded.

Why? Obviously it reaches to a very basic memory. Silverman spoke of symbiotic merging with "the good mother of infancy" that paradoxically allows one to become a self-reliant individual. If we mention Mommy in a lecture, two or three distressed-looking individuals bear down on us afterward. "But I didn't like my mother!" Just as baroque music, whether it's your style or not, enhances memory, liking appears irrelevant to the effect. It may be particularly helpful to those whose mother wasn't "good" or good for them.

Regular subliminals—"I remember easily"—can be converted into conscious suggestion, phrases you repeat to slowly bring the subliminal self around. Supposedly, Mommy loses power in the light of consciousness. She seems to be of a different order, like the elemental seed sounds that create basic Hindu mantras. There are a number of seed sounds. Has anyone found another basic subliminal? Eldon Taylor, who has long clinical experience with subliminals, reports that no matter what a client works on, he finds it necessary to include forgiveness subliminals: forgiving self, forgiving others, feeling forgiven. Forgiveness might be a seed subliminal. Or perhaps all-encompassing Mommy would clear that problem too.

Parker notes experiments which show that meditation enhances memory and learning. Perhaps, he suggests, this is because it triggers the symbiotic fantasy. That's one way to put it. Meditators agree that the practice can lift one to an indescribable sense of oneness, of connection to one's source. An insistence on re-membering, on reclaiming one's lost connection is at the heart of all major religions. Masters of old like Pythagoras and Plato believed this return to wholeness was a function of memory, of becoming aware of forgotten memories, subliminal memory. Would subliminals based on spiritual insights be helpful? Or would the unconscious still opt for Mommy? If so, there isn't cause for concern. Used on "relatively normal people," as Parker says, the Mommy subliminal doesn't seem to have any bad side effects at all.

What You Don't Know *Can* Hurt You or Help You

With all the ad pizzaz wrapping commercial subliminals, it's steadying to take a look at what controlled scientific studies reveal about subliminal memory. By the 80s, British pioneer Dr. Norman F. Dixon was able to gather well over 700 solid subliminal investigations in his book *Preconscious Processing,* and he came to an unavoidable conclusion. Only a relatively small amount of the information processing that goes on in one's mind and memory is conscious.

Subliminal information can channel to you through the sense of sight, hearing, smell, even touch in experiments involving subliminal electric shock. People didn't know they were buzzed, but it influenced them. Since the 30s, the Soviets have worked to develop the basic memory of conditioned reflexes subliminally. They can. Subliminal suggestions can influence your heartbeat, brain waves, threshold of perception. They can influence basic drives like hunger and thirst, and work best when tied to emotional drives. Your subliminal mind is a puzzle-solving whiz. Suggestions can be distorted—visuals embedded in other pictures, audios run at accelerated speeds. You still get the message.

Is it your conscious self that likes the white Cadillac, the deco sofa? You might wonder if you'd taken part in a psychology experiment at the University of Michigan. Unknown to you, geometric pictures are being flashed subliminally. You think the experiment simply involves looking at forms presented by Dr. Robert Zajone and telling him which you like best. Zajone is intrigued. Choosing freely, so you think, the forms you say you like are the ones embedded in the flash. We like what we're familiar with. This is familiarity, memory created without awareness. How often does it happen? Not through a secret flasher, but through suggestions flowing into memory from the environment?

Suggestions that one is unaware of can influence feelings about people and events. Subjects dosed subliminally with the words "happy" or "sad" described a neutral face in the expected direction. College men shown a simple picture of a man and a boy preceded by one of two subliminals, either "I am glad" or "I am ashamed," gave markedly different assessments of what that picture was all about.

Perhaps bigotry is called *blind* prejudice because it comes from subliminal memory, leaving us to make up reasons to fit our responses. In South Africa, Dr. T.F. Pettigrew and colleagues ran an experiment with echoing implications. They were doing dichoptic research, which means presenting different stimuli to each eye. The picture of a white face was sent to one eye, a black face to the other eye at the same time. English-speaking South Africans were able to fuse the images and see a face. Colored people also could see the face. But native Afrikaners couldn't fuse. They could not see a face. This is a compelling illustration of how unconscious structures, subliminal world views, influence our ability to perceive. We do not all live in the same world. To do so in South Africa or anywhere will take, it seems, more than outer sanctions.

Feelings are unpredictable; what about intellectual activity? Among others, Dr. Anthony Marcel of Cambridge University has shown that meaning doesn't have to enter the memory through consciousness. He flashed words on a screen too fast to be read, then unreasonably asked, "What are they?" A few students quit in disgust. The rest agreed to guess and came up right 90% of the time. Sometimes guesses were clearly connected by meaning. If the word was *blue*, people guessed another color like yellow. If we can read, Marcel concludes, "the meanings of words can somehow register without consciousness." Pondering such studies, he says, "I go along with philosophers who believe that consciousness is to some degree a social construct." Consciousness is learned to an extent which implies, Marcel observes, that people in radically different cultures might literally perceive and thus experience the world quite differently.

Surgical Memories

Most data we pick up subliminally isn't coming from a surreptitious scientist. It flows into memory hit or miss from the environment. It can hit hard when you're down, flat down on the operating table. In the 1950s, Dr. David Cheek, an obstetrician and Ericksonian hypnotist, discovered the unexpected. Though you are deeply anesthetized, your unconscious can keep right on picking up data—from the conversation of the surgical team. "What a mess!" or "She's a goner" would surely come over as an authoritative suggestion. What might be called surgical disinformation seems to come into play too. A doctor might call the guy who hit his car a "little bastard" or remark that another patient "can't heal well." The unconscious on the table can file the comment in memory, mistakenly labeled as referring to its body. Cheek's observations seemed too far-out at the time to rewrite operating-room chit chat. In the last few years others, particularly psychologists at the University of California at Davis, have gained confirming evidence.

There, Dr. Henry Bennett's team played taped suggestions to completely anesthetized people under the knife. The tape told them to tug on their ears during post-op interviews to signal that they had heard the message. When Bennett later interviewed them, 82 percent tugged their ears. None consciously recalled the tape or realized that they had pulled their ears. Another experiment involved people undergoing back surgery, who have a notoriously hard time urinating afterward and need a catheter. "You can relax your pelvic muscles and urinate easily," the repeating tape told anesthetized patients. Everyone who got the suggestion was able to urinate without a catheter.

One rather plump woman whom Bennett cites has the makings of a "conversational malpractice" suit. She was slow to recover after surgery, irritable, with intestinal problems. Suddenly, a week after her operation, the lady got mad. Her surgeon had insulted her, she insisted, and angrily told her nurse what the so-and-so had said. The nurse checked with a friend on the operating team. Sure enough, when the doctor approached his already anesthetized patient, he'd exclaimed, "My God, they've dragged another beached whale onto my operating table." After the memory blipped into consciousness, the woman's ills cleared and she was home in a day. This is an example of the Poetzel Effect discovered in the early 1900s, which holds that information subliminally seeded in memory tends to work its way into awareness, often in dreams, sometimes just appearing seemingly out of thin air.

Some people in surgery or coma or even in a catatonic state register what's being said. Why not make the most of it? Anesthesiologists at London's St. Thomas Hospital did. They suggested fast healing: no complications across the board. Writing for the team in the British medical journal *Lancet,* Dr. Calton Evans reported, "It is clear from our finding that these suggestions did get through in some way and improved recovery from surgery."

Extrasensory Subliminals

Anyone familiar with scientific psi research—the study of psychic phenomena—accumulating now for over 100 years, would be struck with a sense of familiarity looking into subliminals. Both elusive phenomena seem to circulate in the same shadowy areas of mind, a connection that Soviet scientists began to exploit shortly after their revolution. In an elegant Black Sea resort hotel, a young woman whirled across the dance floor in the arms of her partner. Suddenly, she stopped in mid step and fell into a trance. It wasn't Svengali who froze her in place but Dr. K.I. Platonov, who beamed a telepathic signal from an anteroom, a telepathic whammy he demonstrated at the 1924 All-Russian Congress of Psychoneurologists.

Platonov's feat led to heavily documented lab experiments stretching over sixty years in the USSR, which show that a telepathic signal can be registered by a subject's unconscious and affect his actions even though he is unaware of receiving a message. In the 1960s, American scientists at the New Jersey Institute of Technology, the nation's fourth largest engineering school, used impartial physiological monitoring machines to reveal that psi can be picked up subliminally and can influence a subject's body. That story is another book. But it's worth mentioning that there have been decades of rigorous lab work which reveal subliminal influence very different from the sort covered here.

In the 1930s, the electrical engineer B.B. Kazhinsky, a Soviet scientist so well known that he became a folk hero, began to explore both regular subliminal suggestion—messages embedded in movies—and subliminal psi. His findings led him to predict that one day subliminal telepathic suggestion would be used to enhance learning through a sort of memory implant. "Speech, pictures, books can be supplemented be a direct mental transference [by the teacher] of appropriate image concepts, sensations and feelings," he wrote. When we first met Georgi Lozanov, he was Bulgaria's leading parapsychologist and he too realized the subliminal telepathic element in teaching. He thought it was a way to implant positive suggestions to help open supermemory. Kazhinsky ran afoul of the Stalinists, and it wasn't until 1962 that the Ukrainian Academy of Science published his life opus, *Biological Radio Communication*. It was quickly translated for the U.S. Defense Documentation Center.

The "Flasher" in the Raincoat

Short of the KGB, the CIA, and no doubt every other cloak-and-dagger clique in the world, advertisers have explored subliminals more closely than anyone. Tracks of the hidden pursuaders are everywhere, some claim, probably in the magazine on the coffee table. Vance Packard broke the story years ago. Dr. Wilson Key followed with volumes of data in such books as *Subliminal Seduction* and *The Clam Plate Orgy*. The latter refers to old Howard Johnson placemats that feature a curling heap of fried clams—sneaky little buggers. When Key's students enlarged the picture, they saw a host of lascivious clams involved in orgiastic shenanigans. Unbelievable? Sure. That's why whistleblowers have trouble exposing attempts to manipulate your memory, to implant a memory tied to an emotional drive. Key tested over a thousand subjects, taught hundreds of students to detect subliminals in film and print ads; his dedicated graduate students worked like subterranean Nader's Raiders. *Library Journal* called Key "meticulously observant" and his work "essential for the public good." Still, his very vested adversaries have generally been able to pass him off as "the man who sees dirty pictures everywhere."

Dirty pictures because, compared to the scientist flashing his careful message, the adman comes on like the flasher in the raincoat. He works with sex and violence, Eros and Thanatos. Death heads to sell vodka, obscene words to push toys, it doesn't make sense and it's not supposed to. The message isn't aimed at the sensible mind, it hopes to attract the subliminal mind. Studies far beyond the subliminal show sex and violence raise quick red flags in the unconscious. The old reptile is ever vigilant to whiffs of danger and sex. Attention gained, advertisers hope your unconscious will remember the accompanying product and send up a little balloon of familiarity when you reach out to a store shelf. Manufactured memory, because we like what we're familiar with. What little public research exists indicates that subliminals might steer you to a brand, but won't prompt you to buy a product you don't like.

Let's hope not. In February 1990, Paul Tharp of the *New York Post* reported a new TV network soon to broadcast to large screens going up over the aisles of the nation's supermarkets. Soundless screens will "show 15 second computer visuals throughout the store to impart product information and subliminal suggestions to shoppers."

Can you find the concealed message on this Pepsi label? Discover how your subliminal memory can work *for* you to avoid mind and memory manipulation.

Be cool, be sexy, reach for a designer Pepsi. To celebrate the summer of 1990, Pepsi cranked out millions of cans of cola covered with bright zigzags and swirls—designer patterns, with perhaps more than one design in mind. If you stack one can atop another as is done on miles of supermarket shelves, and pause to look, you'll read SEX running vertically. *Time* (Sept. 3, 1990) ran a full color picture of the tempting cans and noted that Pepsi insists it was all an accident of computer design.

As Freud said, phallic or not, sometimes a good cigar is just a good cigar. Key and his students may sometimes "read in." But if you shift your eyes a bit and start to look, remembering that pictures can be distorted and words written backward without hampering communication, you may sight some ad subliminals yourself. They're like the hidden forms in children's puzzles gone wrong. Once you catch sight of a sex subliminal it's almost impossible *not* to see it—which can make your friends think you're weird.

The experience of a friend of ours made us open to Key's exposé. A textbook executive, she was summoned home from vacation. Disaster! A school in one of the largest systems in the country had sighted the old F word sprinkled through a history book. Embedded in the cross-hatching of borders and illustrations, one even uncurled in Lincoln's beard! Kids would have cracked up. The publisher, forced to recall the book nationwide, wasn't even smiling. The work of an illustrator, it was said, who'd lost his grip—on his embedding techniques?

Ironically, if a text publisher embeds subliminals to increase sales, he may unwittingly enhance memory. At East Texas State University, educational psychologist Dr. Bruce R. Ledford decided to project erotic and violent pictures on a large screen during class. Student innocence would be preserved, at least consciously. The slides shown by a rear projector at only one candlepower above the light in the room were imperceptible. Standing in front of the apparently blank screen Ledford lectured on subjects that had nothing to do with violence or sex. Exams came and clearly something had roused students' attention. Those treated to invisible, sexy slides remembered their lessons significantly better than students who really were looking at a blank screen behind the prof.

"If you were trying to bring down America through massive media subliminals, what would you use?" a filmmaker in search of a thriller asked Key. "Just what they're doing, sex and violence," Key answered. "No, seriously . . ." "Seriously!" Subliminal ad graffiti isn't the whole answer by a long shot to all the violence abroad. Yet, what does a steady dose of sexual violence injected in unconscious memory do to the interior climate? We know that mood shoots through memory and behavior.

"It is a strange and tricky game to mount the sweet enticing figure on a rotten ground." A caution from the best media mind of our century, Marshall McLuhan, an avid supporter of Key, who wonders, "Will the graffiti hidden under the lush appeal expedite sales or merely impede the maturity quotient of the buyers?"

Do Do-Good Subliminals Do Good?

Other subliminals, straight laced and upright, play to the public. "Thou shalt not steal." "Honesty is the best policy." Intertwined into the music swirling through stores, these messages are undetectible. Effects aren't.

At the beginning of the 80s, a New Orleans supermarket installed a subliminal system invented by Dr. Hal Becker, formerly on the faculty of Tulane Medical School. It was a dream investment. Pilferage dropped from about $50,000 every six months to "the astounding figure of less than $13,000," an all-time low. The manager reported an almost complete turnaround in cashier shortages from $125 a week to less than ten. Damaged merchandise, usually several truckloads a year, fell to a fraction of a truckload while at two other markets equipped with subliminals, personnel turnover dropped by half.

In Toronto, Canadian Tire, a chain of hardware stores, installed a subliminal device developed by Dr. Louis Romberg, founder of Audio Cybernetic Learning Systems in Burlington, Ontario. Employee theft dropped "considerably" while productivity climbed. Several Toronto real estate companies took up Romberg's motivating subliminals. Sales rose by 300%, one claimed. "That's because the unconscious is the biggest powerhouse we have," Romberg says. He experimented in a store stuck with a gross of puzzles. "Buy a Puzzle" played under music. Puzzles sold out. "Just a test," Romberg says, not something he'd normally do.

News of the transforming wonders of subliminals jumped out of the lab into the market. So easy, so effortless, such a quick fix, self-help subliminals held irresistible allure for customers and fast-buck operators alike. An electronic version of the Emperor's new clothes? After some shaking out, companies in the field today generally seem reputable. Do their products work? Do they really help people rewrite old memory scripts? There's been small scientific testing with ambiguous results and you can't track what people do on their own.

One man who's at least had a view from the working trenches is Dr. Eldon Taylor. If you'd tangled with the law in Salt Lake City, this tall, dark-haired man with a trim beard might have hooked you up to a lie detector. Or you might have felt yourself drifting into a different state of mind as he practiced his specialty, forensic hypnosis. A professional criminologist, wise to the working of the unconscious, Taylor became intrigued with the potential of subliminal suggestion to shift this powerhouse in a positive direction. He founded Progressive Awareness Research Inc., and ran the first jailhouse subliminal experiments in the country for the Utah State Prison System. Results were surprisingly good even with such tough problems as pedophilia, and led to a voluntary program. Taylor's firm is pursuing something else equally unlikely. If a doctor attests no counter indication, the firm, at no cost, takes on individuals needing nerve and bone regeneration. Could this really work? Warning that he has a very small sample, Taylor says data so far suggests that these subliminals are slightly better than 50% effective.

Taylor has collected hundreds of reports from people on the subliminal fast track who claim help with everything from bedwetting to maintaining an undefeated football season. "Subliminals are *not* a panacea," he warns. But Taylor thinks they'll soon be a "preferred method for effecting beneficial change," a way to finally escape what he calls "the condition/response that leads to victimhood," and what we would call resonating state bound memories.

Can You Hear Subliminals With Your Skin?

Have you ever thought of listening to a Bach fugue with your skin? Can you hear without ears? You can on a Neurophone.® Not every teenager is featured in *LIFE,* particularly in the days when it had the clout of network TV news, but the inventor of the Neurophone, Pat Flanagan was. Flanagan, a certified boy genius, has kept soaring above the secure gables of established ideas, developing science of the future. He's worked on very subtle ways to subliminally affect mental states, some not public, but the Neurophone is, and it may prove a particularly powerful way of delivering transformative subliminal suggestion to mindbody.

Practiced listeners can place one of the Neurophone's transducers on their stomachs, the other on their thighs, and with ears plugged hear tapes piped through the device. It's an odd sensation, we found. Hearing, scratchy as an old record at first, just happens in the head. At first too, there are "holes" in what you hear; it seems to take a while for the brain to kick in this unused channel.

Why would anyone even think of hearing with their skin? First you have to know that skin is embryonically the source of all sense organs. In the womb, the ear evolves out of the convolutions of the embryo's skin. Thinking of the deaf, it occurred to Flanagan that the skin, mother of sense organs, of the ear, might be capable of hearing. And so it is.

In the 60s at Tufts University, Flanagan, with hearing specialist Dr. Dwight Wayne Batteau, dug out the hows and whys of the Neurophone. Very simply, they found that the frequencies of our voices—whispering, shouting, singing—have little to do with the brain's ability to recognize intelligent speech. What does is the "time-rate-of-change nature of sound caused by time delays imposed by the mouth and nasal passages." This is the basic audio information our brains evolved to understand. The Neurophone capitalizes on this root function. It filters out the frequencies of incoming audio material, leaving just the time-rate-of-change information. "The electronic circuitry presents audio information to the skin in the manner that the skin was originally designed to receive and decode such information eons ago," Flanagan says.

Numerous devices let you hear through bone conduction. The Neurophone isn't one. Dr. Batteau, in definitive tests at Tufts, proved that the device does not work by bone conduction. Which means you have another sense channel, a sort of mother-root sense that can carry data to the brain. A small group of people interested in Flanagan's work played self-help tapes through this root sense. They report gains in memory, learning, and health.

Eldon Taylor compared the Neurophone to other ways of delivering therapeutic suggestion. He sent messages through the device, ones clients could hear. Then he turned the Neurophone down below the threshold level and sent subliminals that clients couldn't catch consciously. "In every instance in which we employed the Neurophone at subthreshold levels, the message was acted upon more consistently than when any type of audible communication, including hypnosis, was employed." More effective than hypnosis—a pretty significant statement from a man of Taylor's experience.

Flanagan cites reports from people who play resonant *om* tapes over the Neurophone. Considered by billions the creating sound of the universe, *om* supposedly balances living things. Flanagan's people said they indeed felt more centered than when *om*ing otherwise. More important, they noted an unexpected improvement in their health. There are tracers here to the data on mental healing in Chapter 16 and to Dr. Deepak Chopra's theory of cellular memory and health (Chapter 17).

The Neurophone works on what might be called a whole-body sense channel. Might it prove an optimal way to deliver therapeutic messages not just to the subliminal memory of the mind, but also to the memory of the cell?

Caveats and Manufactured Memory

"Never forget the SIN in sincere, the CON in confidence," McLuhan urged, eyeing subliminals. "As Zeus said to Narcissus, Watch Yourself." We found a few caveats when we finally made Superlearning subliminals. Superlearning was joined to the subliminal at birth; the most striking aspect of Dr. Lozanov's Suggestology was constant emphasis on the use of suggestion "on the double plane," i.e. always engage both conscious and subliminal mind. Checking the market, we found a few tapes with negative messages: "Smoking ruins my lungs," "Flabby fat is disgusting." Smokers often take up the weed again; dieters regain flab. Do you really want to seed ideas of disease or a disgusting self-image in yourself? Who knows, time doesn't exist in the deep mind, suggestions might even react retroactively. Well-crafted subliminals are phrased positively. If a company doesn't provide a printout of suggestions, claiming it diminishes their magic, go elsewhere. (Another option is to make your own subliminals, see page 96.)

And don't forget, as one woman did, that subliminals really aren't magic. "I don't understand it," she wailed over the phone. "I haven't lost any weight. Yet I play my subliminal faithfully after every big meal!"

Then there's "100,000 messages on a single tape." Wow! The idea appeals mightily to consumers and ad writers, yet so many messages on a tape produce a long high squeal. The unconscious can pick up the squeal, but as Eldon Taylor asks, "Is it meaningful?" The unconscious constantly picks up "noise" only to discard it. What creates limiting or liberating memories is that which is meaningful. Flanagan's discovery that the time element is basic to intelligible speech might be considered too. Parker's students received just forty-eight suggestions over six weeks, but they worked. Many users of a 100,000 message tapes claim great results. Maybe there is something to be proved, and certainly all commercial subliminals get a powerful push from the placebo effect which may be worth the price of the tape. There's also the way-out possibility that some squeals accidentally hit those high frequency sounds which have a positive effect on human capability (see Chapter 10).

Subliminals may liberate you from old patterns. Might they also implant patterns in memory you don't want? Dr. Dixon observed that it may be impossible to resist instructions which are not consciously experienced, though he was speaking about highly focused experiments not retail suggestions. Others maintain that subliminals can't prompt you to do things you wouldn't normally do. Is everyone in the supermarket normal? Or what might one "normally" do with a clever push?

Superlearning subliminals brought phone calls. "Now I never forget where I put my keys." "Boy, have I gotten creative!" Nice. Disconcerting were the many more calls like this: "My wife is too darn fat, she'd think it was just music. . . ." "I'd like to give my salespeople a kick. . . ." Happily, a key aspect to self-help subliminal success is the desire to change. More questionable were calls from two very different, very fundamental religious groups. Would we help them create subliminals to implant dogma in children? It could save the world! Whose world?

In May 1988, Francois Mitterand ran in a close election to lead France. A few days before voting, the French press exposed a new campaign tactic. Government-controlled TV was running "Vote for Mitterand" subliminals. Citizens took conscious note. Not that they objected. Mitterand won. And the first wave of self-help subliminals began to be snapped up in France.

There are obvious questions about the right to privacy, the right to make up your own mind for better or worse without the help of a subliminal Jiminy Cricket. In some instances at least, subliminals do seed their influence in mind and memory. Unchosen, that's manipulation. Chosen, subliminal suggestion seems to be one more way to lift above the law of averages, to rouse and reshape that living underworld of memory that makes us who we are, to have it work for us rather than against us.

6. How to Fine-Tune Memory With the Whole Brain

"A galaxy of stars, a vast galaxy continually twinkling on and off, with new stars lighting up. Think of your brain as a galaxy. See it filled with light," Sophrologist Raymond Abrezol urges clients. It's a galaxy beckoning us to explore. For "as long as the brain is a mystery, the universe, the reflection of the brain will also be a mystery," says neuroscientist S. Ramon y Cajal.

In the last two decades, people have engaged this mystery as never before. Fifteen neuroscientists have won the Nobel Prize in the last twenty-five years. The 1990s have to be the "Decade of the Brain." Congress made it official. With the rush of data, the mystery is taking a new shape. You will be closer to the truth, Nobelist Gerald Edelman remarks, if instead of thinking of your brain as a thing, you think of it as a process. This process also embraces news of other times that lives in the memory of the brains of the past still alive in us today. You will be closer to the truth too if instead of thinking of a process trapped in your head, you sense one filling the whole microcosm of your being, in two-way talk with everything from your genes to the afterimage of yesterday's joys and sorrows.

Breakthroughs in the brain/mind sciences have unlocked new ways to firm everyday memory; doors are opening to the creative ability of memory. High tech has brought unique concoctions of electromagnetic fields that act as "ambrosia" to the brain and others that get brainwaves "pumping iron." There is literally a re-membering, as we begin to reclaim the parts of the brain that have been cut off in polite circles.

Many of the breakthroughs support a premise basic to master memory systems: You are a multiplicity. You are a unique combination of right brain, left brain, emotional brain, conscious and subliminal mind, physical body and nonphysical spirit. These systems see you holistically and find that when you engage your whole self, you'll do better in any endeavor, from remembering a new book to drawing on memory to give a boffo performance, or solve a problem.

Left brain/right brain became an ad line in the 80s, so trendy it sounded as if Lizzie Bordon had given each of us a whack right down the middle of the head. Logical, committed to analytical a-b-c thinking, the figuring, writing, talking brain, that's the left brain. Its mate, the metaphorical right, is the imaging, musical, synthesizing, intuitive, and perhaps the healing brain. More or less right, but not close to exactly. The hemispheres aren't as compartmentalized as was first thought (a very left brain idea).

Nature is more freewheeling. Still, the general idea of two different *modes* of processing information holds. Added to it is the idea that there is a variety, a personal odor to the organization of any individual brain. Which isn't surprising in an organization of billions—billions of cells with the number of potential connections between them so large that they exceed the number of atoms in the known universe, billions of neurons so small that twenty thousand of them could, if not dance, at least network on the head of a pin. These galaxies of cells blink on and off, sending great waves through your brain, like a host of vast symphonies playing along simultaneously. The wider and deeper brain explorers follow this music of the "spheres," the more reason to exclaim with Shakespeare, "What a piece of work. . . ." And this piece of work doesn't want to just sit there.

Born To Be Challenged

"The brain is built to be challenged," asserts Dr. Jerre Levy of the University of Chicago, a specialist in teasing forth the secrets of the hemispheres. If you do simple tasks that only engage one hemisphere, attention span is low. Paying attention, as we all know, builds good memory. When there's enough going on to spark both hemispheres, attention snaps to. Complexity and challenge promote optimal functioning, Levy says. You attend to your experience, you remember it. That's why master memory methods bring in music, imagery, pleasure, hands-on sensation, novelty, and high expectations along with the intellect to mobilize many parts of the brain. To enhance memory, always try to engage both right and left brain. Boredom shuts down memory. Not just hemispheres, but the brain generally wakes up at novelty, at that which intrigues. Research puts a large question mark on the practice of watering down children's classics to already understood words, or simplifying college texts. There is nothing to demand attention, nothing to wake up the brain enough to remember much, as we cycle deeper and deeper into the intellectual drowzies.

Older people don't remember what they're learning as well as younger people. So it was believed. Finally, researchers thought to compare the old, not with college students actively hitting the books, but with young people who'd left school behind. Suddenly, there wasn't much difference. Use it or lose it applies to memory as much as muscle. Challenge and practice, much more than age, determine the strength of memory. Even Alzheimer's patients, it seems, respond to challenge. At the Memory Disorder Clinic of the University of California at Irvine, Dr. Curt Sandman asked victims' spouses to break up routine and take patients on a really different outing—out to the ball park, off to buy a new set of tires. Tested a week later, Alzheimer-afflicted people had no memory of routine days around that special event, but they could remember what they'd done on that different day. They even remembered what they wore.

New adventures, lifelong learning, are memory tonics. The emphasis is on lifelong—at least in rats. Scientists gave batches of baby rats extra attention in their first three weeks, handled and stimulated them. After that, they lived the life of their fellow rodents. When they hit old age, around eighty in our terms, the stimulated rats remembered how to run their mazes much better than others. Autopsies revealed hardly any of the usual age-related cell loss in the hippocampus, a mid-brain area vital to memory. Would this work for people? Certainly lifelong challenge keeps memory alert, association and actual neuronal connections growing. It might also help you get a lot more done. Levy thinks our brains may be designed to do two things at once even better than one.

Julius Caesar came, saw, and conquered perhaps because he was a whiz at time management. Pliny reports he could dictate four letters on important affairs at once. If nothing else required his simultaneous attention, Caesar could dictate seven at once. He could also listen simultaneously to four or five reports from his far-flung empire. At the University of Colorado, students tried working double time in an exploration of attention expansion. Can you read while writing competently on a different topic? Dr. Lyle Bourne's students could. They could also read while typing something else. Some could take dictation and read a book at the same time. They recalled the content of both. It sounds like a Ripley's feat, yet brain and memory are designed for challenge and perhaps the students' accomplishments only seem bizarre because, like fire walking, we simply never thought we could do it.

Jack Schwarz spent years proving to doctors at the Menninger

Foundation and Langley-Porter Neuropsychiatric Institute that the mind can control the body in ways they never thought possible. Expand attention, he often urges. Director of the Aletheia Psycho-Physical Foundation, Schwarz notes that as children we're told we can only do one thing at a time. The message sticks in the subconscious and we live by it "until we discover we can do many things at once. Instead of thinking of events as interruptions, we can think in terms of adding to our awareness, like peripheral vision."

Successful people have always been "whole brainers." To vault ahead, the highest profit making CEOs apparently combine facts with intuition, a supposed right brain talent. This showed in a massive study of intuition done at the New Jersey Institute of Technology that we reported in the book *Executive ESP*. With its mysterious connection to unconscious memory, as Kirk told Spock, "Intuition, no matter how illogical, is a command perogative."

Different strokes for different folks applies to communicating with your hemispheres. Speak the language of both, get both involved to anchor memory. The more numerous and varied your associations—conceptual, pictorial, emotional, sensual—the greater your chance of remembering; engaging both hemispheres leads to a helpful redundancy, a backup system for memory. Some people, however, might be interested in getting one hemisphere to remember and the other to forget. One savvy writer took note of the fact that hemispheres control opposite sides of the body, the right brain lifts your left hand, the left brain, your right hand. Whispering into someone's left ear sends the message to the right brain, the one that doesn't analyze. That's what happens when you're in the passenger seat of a car, talk goes mainly to the right brain. The writer swore that when his wife drove he found himself acquiescing more readily to her suggestions—"Let's buy a new car"—than when he was in the driver's seat and her ideas flowed mainly to his critical left brain.

The automotive approach to hemisphere manipulation isn't proved yet, but researchers do find they can fix suggestions in memory more readily if they speak through earphones to the right brain. At the same time, they talk through the other ear to the left brain and occupy it with busy work—repeating strings of numbers. It's too busy to analyze the suggestions. With this almost subliminal approach, ideas planted in the memory do take hold and begin to influence behavior. Outside the lab, such memory manipulation is the playing field of advertising and counterintelligence (See Chapter 20).

Ask Your Nose

Centuries ago, yogis observed that we move through the day breathing first through one nostril, then after about an hour and a half, through the other. They recognized this as a natural cycle. A whole discipline, Svar Yoga, grew around the idea that to live well some things were better done breathing through one nostril or the other. One prescription has a certain charm: when you wake, sense which side you're breathing through, kiss the palm of that hand, give thanks for the day, and step out of bed on that breath-favored foot.

In the last decade, the value of nostril breathing was another bit of old knowledge recycled into a scientific breakthrough at Dalhousie University, the Salk Institute of Biological Sciences, and the University of California at San Diego. Yes, they found we do switch breath with the average cycle lasting ninety minutes to two hours. But something else caught their eye. When you're breathing through your left nostril, your right brain is dominant, through the right, your left hemisphere dominates.

As the yogis long ago realized, some things are best done breathing through a particular nostril. Dalhousie researchers report that people's verbal and spatial ability "varied markedly" with the rise and fall of brain dominance. Verbal ability rose when the left brain was dominant. Spatial ability improved when the right cycled up. As one scientist put it, the nose then becomes an instrument to fine tune the brain, perhaps the whole body. In other words, to alter your state of mind, just press your nose!

To override current hemisphere dominance, close off one nostril and breath forcefully through the other. For instance, to wake up the left brain, press your finger against your left nostril, like Santa did just before he flew up the chimney. This is a pep up. Switching to a full cycle of dominance takes a little more, but not much. Press your fist under your armpit for a few minutes to activate the opposite side, or just lie down. Lying on your left side a few minutes will bring the right brain into dominance. Each brain has a personal odor, we said, and one recent test suggests that when some people close a nostril they activate the hemisphere on the *same* side. Discover what works for you. Dr. David Shannahoff-Khalsa of the Salk Institute points out that altering to the left brain could give an edge when doing language, math, or reasoning, to the right when creativity is needed. Or perhaps to defuse emotions.

People seek out actress/author Doe Lang to develop charismatic public speaking. Lang's is no easy job in this land where Gallup found that public speaking leads among "greatest fears," and where fully half of the timorous claim they fear giving a speech more than they fear death. Emotional jitters can bring on a speaker's greatest horror—a blank memory. Lang, a student of yoga, teaches clients to take twenty-six deep breaths through the left nostril to defuse such emotions. Image the air flowing up, across the corpus callosum (the bundle of nerves that connects the hemispheres), and into the right brain, "scooping it out as though there were nothing in it but limitless distance and pure, radiant energy." As you exhale, let all negative emotions flow away. One client of Lang's tried closing her right nostril when she phoned her difficult father. Finally, she said, she could talk without a fight—the debating left brain wasn't dominant.

Nostrils switch breathing, hemispheres switch dominance. Like so much else in nature, these are now recognized as cycles within cycles. They reflect a larger rhythm cycling through the whole self, body, and mind. We are designed to oscillate between action and rest, with emphasis switching back and forth between the sympathetic and parasympathetic nervous systems. We are set to focus out into the world, then inward into ourselves. It's a life rhythm, one we often override. Becoming aware of this basic rhythm can enhance memory, relaxation, and as Ernest Rossi finds, can help release negative memories to heal ourselves (See Chapter 16).

Sleeping To Remember

Half a century ago, America's best known psychic, Edgar Cayce, seemed aware of this basic body cycle. Internationally famous as The Sleeping Prophet, the entranced Cayce dictated a wealth of material much of which later proved accurate. In his *Readings,* he often instructed people not to study or ponder too long at one time. Superlearning also finds relatively short sessions fix memory best. Cayce's *Readings* advises too that immediately after learning one rest deeply or sleep to solidify memory. Recent research suggests that a catnap after study does enchance recall. Other experiments at Trent University in Petersborough, Ontario, have uncovered the profound, rather disastrous effect that tinkering with the sleep cycle itself can have on your memory. Do you sometimes burn the 2 A.M. oil cramming for a test or preparing a key business presentation? According to psychologist Carlyle Smith and his colleagues, your efforts can cut your ability to remember complex material by a full 30%.

After learning sessions, Smith kept volunteers awake, some until 4 A.M., others all night. The next day both groups remembered simple material like word association as well as the control groups. However, when the all-nighters confronted newly learned rules of logic, they found their retention weak and remembered 30% less than the controls did. So did the half-nighters, even though they'd slept late to get their full complement of z's. The sleep critical to memory is REM sleep, dream time. Students continuously wakened during REM periods found memory nosediving, those roused during nonREM sleep did not. Something curious cropped up in Smith's sleep lab, a "window of vulnerability" in the consolidation of memory. People deprived of sleep the night they learn or the night forty-eight hours later experienced the 30% drop; people kept awake twenty-four or seventy-two hours after learning remembered as well as controls. Apparently "a prolonged processing mechanism" is needed to fix complex data in memory, Smith says. Grandma was right when she admonished one to keep regular hours. Or if you must wing with the owls, for your memory's sake do it on alternate nights.

This sort of quirky finding isn't unusual in research. "The reality of the human brain, I've decided, is contentious, misleading, complex, and flirtatious," Dr. Levy says. "Nature hides and leaves false clues, and I seek. It wants a contest, a game." It's a game anyone can play. As Dr. Abrezol asks his clients on first introducing them to what's atop their necks, "What would you say to your brain?" You might want to have three replies ready.

Three Heads Are Better Than One

Your child steps off the curb. A car careens around the corner. Before you know it, you've leapt out, jerked your babe to safety, and are shouting choicest words at the disappearing speeder. It wasn't the hemispheric brain we're so proud of that saved you. It only told off the idiot after the fact. The mid brain, the maternal, nurturing brain had a hand, but at root you were saved yet again by the "old reptilian," the basic brain as old as Mnemosyne. We have a triune brain, really three different brains, and the oldest two are more intimate with memory than the "thinking cap" we've been discussing.

History is alive in our heads. Every brain recapitulates its evolution in the womb. Now that we're out of the womb, it's a good idea to recapitulate consciously, says Dr. Jean Houston. "In order to go forward you must recover the past." If you were in one of her famous workshops, you might find yourself lying on your belly, arms streamlined at your side, a fish rocking gently through a primordial sea. You'd act out, be, all the forms on the life wave up to human, then take an imaginative turn at the human to come. Many of the more than 10,000 people who've joined Houston's evolutionary play say the lasting reward is a new feeling of connection, spiritual and physical, a sense of being part of something that's growing and emerging. It's also the first time many have met their three brains, each different in personality, structure, and chemistry. The "triune brain," Dr. Paul MacLean dubbed it when first eloquently describing the three in his work as Chief of the Laboratory of Brain Evolution and Behavior at the National Institute of Mental Health.

You have a reptilian (primal) brain, an emotional (mammalian) brain, and a thinking (neomammalian) brain. The two older mentalities can't verbalize. "But to say that they lack the power of speech does not belittle their intelligence nor does it relegate them to the realm of the unconscious," MacLean makes clear.

Rising at the top of the spinal chord like a thick fist is the reptilian brain that's kept life crawling, flying, galloping since the beginning. The reptilian is the root brain of survival, involved with marking out and defending territory, with hunting, grooming, the mating dance, with social hierarchies and ritual. MacLean sees it as the basic chemistry beneath Nietzschean "will to power," beneath predatory urges and deception that can rise in our world as white-collar crime. This ancient of days has a very long, strong memory. It is the memory of ritual, of repetitive behavior. It is the memory of habit. This brain makes us feel secure in routine. It is a slow learner and does not like to change. It doesn't much like anything, for emotions blossomed with the next brain, which grew like a thick cap over the reptilian fist. Here are all the passions and feelings of life, the desire to love and nurture children, to be part of the gang.

Here too is the heart of memory, for the middle brain contains the hypothalamic-limbic system, the switching station of memory. Memory and emotion meet, mingle, and mate here. Ancient Taoists called this brain, which harbors the pituitary and pineal glands, the "golden room." Pain and pleasure light up in the golden room. So do playfulness and sex. Information from outside and inside, from the world and the body, flows through this golden room before going on to the thinking brain, before going into long term memory. State dependent memory knits together here.

The discovery of the importance of the emotional brain to memory and thinking is bringing changes. "At the very least, we will no longer be able to live with our separate distinctions of emotions and reason," says master teacher Dr. Elaine de Beauport. She says this with real feeling at educational conferences, enough feeling to make some in the audience squirm. It seems out of place and that's the point. "You're being emotional" is a putdown in and out of the classroom, a prejudice that trips up learning and memory and most of the other glories we aspire to. It's a left brain prejudice, apparent in "eggheads" like Adlai Stevenson, who remarked, "I find St. Paul appealing and Norman Vincent Peale appalling." Yet even the egghead's paper *The New York Times* recently headlined, "Research Affirms Power of Positive Thinking." Studies tracked people who instead of facing facts and being "reasonable" as left brainers often demand, flooded the facts away with feeling, upbeat feelings. The emotional optimists had more successful careers than the fact-facers. Over the long haul their health was markedly better too.

Dr. de Beauport, co-founder in 1969 of the highly regarded Mead School, now helps adults get in touch with the multiple intelligence of their three brains, particularly the limbic emotional brain. We remember what has significance to us, she reminds. We learn what we *feel* like learning. Is that where the old expression learn "by heart" comes from? If feelings are barred, part of us turns off too, and we grow up with overnight memory, cram memory. It will get you past tests, often brilliantly, but it won't give you an education. You miss out on the tranformative powers of memory. "Feelings take on very pragmatic significance when we realize that long term memory is based on feeling," de Beauport says. Some basic research suggests that memories are "labeled" by almost infinite shades of emotion to facilitate retrieval. Going further, explorations of state dependent memory show emotion is simply an inextricable part of a memory. The time is ripe to make the most of the feelings inherent in memory, time to give up insisting, like Dickens's pedant Gradgrind, on "the facts, nothing but the facts!"

Growing around the limbic mid brain, like a voluminous cap of many folds, is the much and rightly heralded neocortex—"the mother of invention and father of abstract thought," Paul MacLean calls it. There is a great big world beyond the nest of the golden room. The new brain developed to explore and adventure in it. This brain accesses memory and has ideas. It's a cool customer, devoid of emotion as a Vulcan. At least it was until the spectacular growth of the prefrontal lobes, the glory of the human brain. This front part of the top brain has at least some connections to the emotional brain, the golden room. Higher emotions are born: empathy, altruism. The prefrontal lobes—some call them a fourth brain in development—allow future planning. They can access past memory and present experience and project them ahead.

"The brain has acquired three drivers," MacLean notes, "all seated up front and all of different minds." And all with different memories. Like Houston's players, some people are breaking through to the three with mindbody techniques. Others use instruments like the Graham Potentializer, a curious revolving "bed" that helps harmonize the brains (see Chapter 19). This effort to look to the needs of all our drivers and get them communicating is one of the brightest bits of re-linking, re-membering going on. It has present survival value and future promise. Ignored, as de Beauport warns, "our emotional and reptilian brains continually sabotage us, undermine our choices . . . subvert us on the road to so many rational, intuitive, and artistic accomplishments." As we begin to remember the variety, experience, and depth of our brains, we may find our inner galaxy lighting up and stretching like the ever expanding universe that reflects it.

7. Tryin' Ain't Enough

"It's useless, it's useless, tryin' ain't enough . . ." runs a Kurt Weill refrain in *The Threepenny Opera*. If that's the kind of line your mind starts singing, maybe you should stop pushing away "negative" thoughts and listen. Sheer trying can do some funny things to memory. Princess Diana surely tried hard to get herself ready, to remember all the minutia of protocol for her "wedding of the century." All went swimmingly. Finally, the high point of the ceremony arrived, the hundreds crowding Westminster Abbey hushed as Diana turned toward Prince Charles. And plighted her troth to *"Phillip."*

A prominent New York decorator tried hard to remember dozens of details for a rush visit to a famous new client in San Francisco. Arriving at her client's mansion, she unzipped her bulging bag with the maid watching—and a mess of dirty sheets tumbled out. She'd forgotten which bag she put her clothes in, which her laundry.

The usually flawless interviewer, Robert MacNeil, carefully went over his notes for one of his first important interviews on CBC, Canada's national network. It was a big opportunity. On the air, MacNeil glowingly recounted the well-known man's achievements. Finally he paused, looked at his guest, and said, "I'm terribly sorry, sir, but I can't seem to remember your name."

Tension is static to memory. Dogged trying isn't the kind of concentration that builds memory. If a forgotten name is on the tip of your tongue, let it go. Soon it will saunter into your mind, as Emerson says, as carelessly as if it had never been invited. Can you relax your body at will? Can you calm your mind at will? We're exhorted to practice stress management, but we "just don't have time." One way to get more time is to master the art of mindbody relaxation. "The paradox is, you go faster by taking your foot *off* the accelerator," says relaxation expert Dr. Ken Dychtwald. Knowing how to relax can help you learn faster, consolidate memory quicker. It is intertwined with performing your best, from giving a speech to having a baby. It could save your life; it will surely give you a better life.

Stress can lower IQ, Dr. Bernard Brown of Georgetown University found when he studied more than 4,000 children. They were only seven years old, and there wasn't any single problem, but, on the average, a combination of changing, stressful factors tightened the kids up enough to rob them of fourteen big IQ points. Brown suggests chronic pressure diminishes one's ability to think.

A New York columnist recently said that no matter what topic she wrote about, the Big Apple is a place where somebody is always sure to object. "Except just once. I wrote the City Council had the IQ of a cucumber and nobody complained." Toronto's Addiction Research Center may have uncovered one reason bureaucrats' ability to think can hit the cucumber level. They tested municipal office workers for stress. And found it—at levels usually only recorded in *severely disturbed mental patients.* A call went out for Ely Bay, founder of Relaxation Response Ltd. and an early collaborator with Superlearning. As he had before with civil servants at all levels of Canadian government, Bay trained the frazzled bureaucrats in the art of relaxation. Test data and body parts eased back to normal.

Bay worked with Dr. Jane Bancroft, who, with degrees from the Sorbonne and Harvard, was perhaps the best credentialed academic to first pursue accelerated learning. She went early to Bulgaria and traveled many times to the Soviet Union and Eastern Europe, ferreting out important techniques omitted from official Bulgarian presentations. She's since gone around the world consulting and observing the varied growth of accelerated systems. Bancroft started Superlearning at the University of Toronto. At semester's end, students thanked her enthusiastically. "I've gotten over my insomnia," "my nervous headaches," "my allergy." Or, "I don't fight with my parents so much." "It really improved my relationship with my boyfriend." Bancroft was bemused. She wasn't teaching Psych 101, she was teaching college French.

They remembered French better than before, but students seemed more taken with what hit them where they live—techniques that drain stress away rather than adding it during learning. Bancroft confirmed what Moscow professors had told her. The system's built-in stress management can lead to surprising health benefits. That's why, after a long day's work, Soviets could go to night school and emerge feeling refreshed. In our culture now, Bancroft thinks that relaxation training may be a necessity for learning and remembering. Social turmoil, junk food, rock music, pollution, a hundred things take their toll on kids conditioned by TV to short attention spans. Compounding the insult, Bancroft says, "are crowded, noisy, ill-ventilated classrooms, chairs seemingly designed to promote bad posture, and learning methods appropriate to the Middle Ages." The rest of us live with the same swirl of pressure and them some. Which is probably why Superlearning do-it-yourselfers often tell us, "In the long run, perhaps the best thing I've learned with the system is how to get *myself* right." Good memory just seems to follow naturally.

Dynamic Relaxation: Secret of Mastery

Memory and learning are state dependent—the state one is in resembles a library you revisit to pick up memory. Being in the optimal state to learn and remember is central in all the accelerated systems. Body relaxed, mind calm and alert. Aldous Huxley called this "dynamic relaxation," the secret of the masters in everything from golf to prayer. "Don't strain and yet do your damndest," he advised. "Stop trying too hard and let the deep seated intelligence of your body and the subconscious mind do the work as it ought to be done."

To achieve dynamic relaxation, accelerated systems use exercises. Some like Prichard and Taylor start with physical routines—"I'm loose and limp, my arms feel like spaghetti." Vancouver radio commentator Pat Burns took a mental approach when he tried Superlearning to help a floundering student. Before the paced lesson, the teenager boarded an imaginary escalator that slowly carried him down through the spectrum of colors from red to violet, centering, calming his mind. As mindbody is one system, relaxation of either reflects in the other. Burns eventually reported, "I turned a failing student into a valedictorian."

Dr. Uschi Felix of Flinders University in South Australia interviewed over a hundred high schoolers learning language with the SALT methods. Did mind calming help memory?

"It's good . . . the words go quickly into my brain," said a tenth-grade girl studying German.

A classmate opined, "I think it does work with the work you have to remember, it helps you remember."

A ninth-grade boy thought mind calming okay because, "In the first term of German, I got a C, and in the second when we actually did the thing I got an A."

When we were on the PR circuit talking about Superlearning on the radio, a lady from Tampa called to discuss trying too hard. In high school she'd been considered slow, really slow, never college material. "But I always wanted to go." Finally, a community college took her on trial.

"It was my big chance. I decided not to do anything but study. I knew I could do it." She knew she could and worked and worked and finally, at the end of the semester—she got four Ds and an F. "Fortunately, just before, at a revival meeting, I'd been saved. When I saw those terrible marks, I thought about what the preacher said, *'Let go and let Jesus!'* So I did. I stopped struggling and turned it all over to Jesus. Since then everything's been fine. I got a degree in special ed and I've taught learning disabled kids for three years now."

As the fates determined, back in New York we immediately met someone else with an equally unusual approach. This young Japanese woman is among the very gifted, so much so that her old-guard family took the unusual step of sending her alone to study at the Julliard School of Music. She flew through undergraduate work and then her master's degree in an exceptionally short time with highest grades. "I know about Superlearning," she said. "I used that sort of technique to get through Julliard. I was a little fearful . . . about speaking English, New York, school. It was my mantra that helped me most." Unlike other people, she seemed to want to tell us her mantra. Who could resist a magic mantra to swing wide the door to super talent? So we asked.

"Well," exclaimed this petite, wondrously polite, exquisitely well-bred creature, "twice a day, for twenty minutes, I closed my eyes and said, "I don't give a damn! I don't give a damn! I don't give a damn!"

Both women proved a formula iterated by Tim Gallwey. "Performance equals potential minus self-interference." Tension tightens and diminishes performance whether in a physics class or on the ski slopes. Author of the "inner game" books, Gallwey says the single secret to mastering anything "is concentration, *relaxed* concentration." People sense this in sports. Concentration in full flower has been likened to the runner's high, to the euphoric flow of a perfect game. It's an altered state most people experience on occasion, times when you're so totally absorbed you're lifted out of yourself. Things begin to happen effortlessly. Mind and senses are sharpened, time fades, there is a current of joy, a fuller sense of life.

That's "a flow state" according to Dr. Mike Csikszentmihalyi of the University of Chicago, who a decade ago began studying peak performers, everyone from surgeons to rock climbers, composers to basketball players. Peak concentration seems to come when people are challenged a little bit. "Flow occurs in that delicate zone between boredom and anxiety," Csikszentmihalyi says. Flowing is the opposite of straining, even in brain patterns. Researchers who checked what happens in the brain when people concentrate often came up with conflicting results. Some found the cortex highly aroused. Others found a drop in activity. Which state enhances performance? Scientists at the National Institute of Mental Health may have the answer.

The desirable flow state of concentration shows a decrease in cortical activity. It is *forced* concentration, making yourself pay attention, that brings on bursts of activity in the brain "almost as if it is in the wrong gear for the work demanded," science writer Dr. Daniel Goleman says. He points out the resemblance between high-level concentration and meditation which also involves a feeling of relaxed alertness.

Oliver Sacks, the masterful doctor of *Awakenings,* discovered something else about harmonious concentration. Engaging his frozen patients in the arts—especially music—and in play, he could bring them alive for a while, concentrate them into selves. *"Concentration,"* he says, "acts as a 'cure,' albeit a temporary one, for Tourette's [and] . . . for Parkinsonism as well." Sacks tells of Jimmie, who suffered the extreme memory loss of Korsakoff's syndrome brought on by alcoholism. Jimmie was totally at sea—except at Mass, when he "would be enabled through its organic coherence and continuity . . . to recover, if transiently, his own continuity. He became, at this *un*pathological moment, 'a man in his wholeness wholly attending.' " The natural flow of concentration, it seems, can have mysterious powers, while strained concentration defeats itself and hampers memory. In turn, memory can generate strain that hampers us.

The Mating of Stress and Memory

Like most of his fellows, a Canadian medical student pushed to the breaking point. Bleary-eyed, aching with his own symptoms, unlike his colleagues Hans Selye began to wonder about stress as a medical problem. His aches set him on a career of classical research that defined stress in modern terms and more than anything established psychosomatic medicine as a real and reputable field. No matter what the stress, Selye discovered, the body reacts the same way. Change jobs, get flu, lose your spouse, face an important exam, breathe unacceptable air—the same alarm and repair system goes off. Selye called this the General Adaptation Syndrome, usually referred to by its apt acronym: GAS.

Your body strives, always, to maintain its inner equilibrium. You collide with stress. Hormones stream out like a SWAT team. Mobilized, the body shifts through three stages: alarm, resistance, exhaustion. Clenched muscles, churning stomach, insomnia, many of the re-actions sprung by alarm and resistance often remain when the stress has passed, Selye realized. The sirening is gone but the melody lingers on and the body keeps playing it like a needle stuck in a groove, wearing down and down. The body forgets to forget. It's easy to see how stress can bring on most over-the-counter ailments and factor in all ills from arthritis to cancer.

Dr. Paul MacLean speaks of the gut component in memory. A dog is conditioned to lift his leg as a buzzer sounds. When the experiment is over, the response is extinguished. Yet years later, at the sound of a buzzer, researchers can find a gut response, a racing heart. As one said, the dog forgets to lift his leg, but he remembers with his heart. This can generalize, the heart races at other noises. MacLean thinks the memories of two different brains are involved. The neocortex learns to lift the leg. But the conditioning buzzer also set off prolonged reactions in the limbic brain where memory and emotion cross, where there is close communication with the viscera. This is the memory that stays.

As a doctor, Hans Selye's prescription for the body's memory of stress was to cut across it with pills, shots, even surgery. He believed that shock treatment, popular in his day, worked not because it did anything specific but because it exploded general mindbody patterns. When the pieces settled, they might not fall back into the old pattern, into the rote memory of a symptom.

Selye didn't have the concept of state dependent memory and learn-ing, but it fits his observations. The hormones and chemicals that he found rush with stress are also involved with state dependent memory (see Chapter 16). If you don't have a scientific cast of mind, consider that there is a sort of poetry in the mating of stress and memory. Just as the harmonics of meaning and sound resonate above and below the conscious center of the great poem, current stress vibrates a universe of past stressful experiences. If your past reactions were maladaptive, unhealthy, they will reinforce the chord of present distress. Like the poet you can rewrite. Today many therapists, particularly Ericksonian ones, instead of seeing symptoms as something to excise see them as flags for creative action. Enter their universe, release or transform the state dependent memory, learning, behavior.

Mathematician Elizabeth Reudy releases a muscle spasm, stretches a back to help clients remember geometry. It all began with Vicky, a well-educated woman who to the European-reared Reudy's astonish-ment lacked even the rudiments of math. "Help me pass the graduate record exam." Teaching math to Vicky was tense. Reudy began consciously regulating her own breathing to stay calm and positive. She soon noticed that Vicky unconsciously began breathing in concert. This clue inspired Reudy to innovative teaching when they hit a bad plateau.

She tried one hour of Feldenkrais bodywork, followed by one hour of math. "That's when the surprises began," Reudy says, explaining that they focused bodywork on places Vicky felt weak, mainly her abdomen. As Reudy prodded, Vicky began reliving what made her feel weak until it was time for math.

"The changes were astounding," Reudy reports. Vicky's voice grew more authoritative, she became assertive about getting full explanations. "Geometry was suddenly much easier to her, she could take in the figures as a whole and understand the context. She worked faster, more accurately, in arithmetic." Finally in Reudy's doubly capable hands, Vicky passed her exam with high marks.

Unlike the mind, the body doesn't lie, Reudy points out, and it can be the shortcut we never think of to effective learning. She admits that memory problems can be small and localized, but insists that it helps to place them in the larger surround of self-image and body mobility. Get interested in the current state of your abilities, she advises. "It's much easier to change something we can accept than something we are trying to hide."

To effect that change, Reudy developed a bunch of mindbody techniques to help people remember the new and retrieve the old including them in her *Where Do I Put the Decimal Point?* A simple one may help when you just can't remember that name. Relax and start searching with any minute clue: sounds like . . . has two syllables . . . starts with . . . "Any close guess will be rewarded with a spontaneous deep breath," Reudy says, and notes that it's important to keep a sense of humor because first guesses may be way off yet contain clues. Rosella Wallace has also picked up on the body connection and sets memory dancing through the whole body with her "Memory Raps," handclapping, finger snapping, body bopping—"Nine, Eighteen, Twenty-seven, Thirty-six, Nines are magic, We know the Tricks . . ." published now in her *Active Learning: Rappin' and Rhymin.'* (For some Memory Shortcuts, see Appendix B.)

Your Own Safe House

We can't avoid stress and we'd be dull as amoebas if we could. We can, however, learn to ride stress in ways that create adaptive memories in the present, for the future. To help keep your balance you can say, "My right arm is heavy, heavy and warm." So begins Dr. Johannes Shultz's famous formula for relaxing body and mind at will—autogenics, literally "self birthing." Autogenics is widely prescribed by medical people and athletic coaches in Europe and the USSR. (If you're interested in an autogenics cycle the Soviets developed for cosmonauts and sports stars, see *Superlearning*.) Like all Sophrologists, in the interests of harmonious consciousness, Raymond Abrezol uses a form of modified autogenics. With it he and the Swiss Sophrology Association roused the attention of their thrifty countrymen. Over three years, they trained about 500 people in Sophrology and measured the effect with insurance claims. Medical expenses fell, depending on the town, 27% to 40%. (Somebody should tell Blue Cross.)

Progressive Relaxation is the other classic routine created by an M.D., Edmund Jacobson. That's the scrunching exercise Rosella Wallace's kids used. Beyond these two medical classics, relaxation techniques are ubiquitous, from yoga to Dr. Lester Fehmi's Open Focus to the Maharishi's Transcendental Meditation. In August 1988, *Fortune* reported to executives worried about health costs that people over forty who spent twenty minutes twice a day chanting TM mantras have 74% fewer doctors visits and 69% fewer hospital admissions than others. And *Newsweek* reports a study of nursing home residents. Some were asked to do TM, some other relaxation regimes, some nothing. The TMers showed the greatest gain in memory—and survival. Three years later, they were all still here, while 12.5% of the relaxers and 37.5% of the do-nothings had passed on.

Sort through the barrels of techniques and find one or two or even ten that suit you. And do them. Lisa Curtis lectures busy professionals in the United States and South America on how to turn stress into energy. She created a seven-minute cycle of very simple stress-breakers. For people in a hurry, even such a short exercise "can be a lifesaver," says broadcasting executive Nell Basset.

If seven minutes is too much, try an exercise that Yale psychologist Tyler Lorig claims is as relaxing as some used in therapy. Close your eyes and imagine your favorite dessert. See it, smell it, really taste it. That's all, though it's only fair to add that Soviet scientists found that people expert in autogenics could raise their blood sugar by just imagining . . . their favorite dessert.

Mindbody is one street with two-way traffic, so you might prefer to relax through mental means. Drifting on a cloud, feeling the host of golden daffodils brushing your legs, all manner of imaginary trips can relax and center. Set pieces work, but it may be more satisfying to create your own. Find a safe, nourishing place where you can let go, drop the load, be yourself and, if you wish, soak up the healing juices of nature.

For centuries, European esoterics taught initiates to construct imaginary safe houses: a forest lodge, a tower, even a small castle that often took months to construct, imaginary brick by brick. These are an apparent extension of the great invisible memory palaces that all educated people carried around in their imaginations for millennia (see Chapter 13). A footnote to history that links relaxation and memory. Not everyone will go in for castle construction, but the ability to escape to one's own special place for a few minutes is helping an increasing number get themselves and their memories together.

Relaxation exercise is a strategy and a good one. But overall it seems to be your basic attitude toward those slings and arrows of life that determines whether or not stress is a crippler. "Hold on lightly, let go tightly," an old Taoist saying advises. Because, we would guess, as a famous French actress of the last century explained, "Life may be desperate, but it is *not* serious!"

8.   How To Forget So You Remember Better

Many nights ago during the long cold war, a dorm full of young communists eagerly climbed into bed to do something peculiar to the Eastern bloc—successful sleep learning. Snoozing through "night school," students found they could grasp and remember material with much less wide-awake class time than usual. Then one night the psychiatrist in charge pulled the plug. Unknown to the kids, no lessons reeled through their sleep. Yet in class the accelerated effect held. It seemed the belief that they were getting an extra boost in learning gave them "permission" to use their innate ability to remember way beyond the norm. The experimenter, Georgi Lozanov, learned a lesson too. Sleep learning might not be necessary if one orchestrates suggestion artfully.

Suggestology, the science of suggestion, became Lozanov's name for his system of healing and memory expansion. Usually suggestion isn't so up front about itself. Usually we never notice how suggestion knits us into the fabric of society. From the moment we're born, perhaps before, we are immersed in suggestions, influencing everything about us, how we act, dress, eat, talk, how we feel about ourselves and others. More basic than good or bad, suggestion just is, with some suggestions affecting us positively, some negatively—unless we decide to stop living by the law of averages and take charge.

Lozanov was one of the first in our time to purposefully take out the randomness, to carefully organize *all* levels of suggestion, in the clinic to heal, in the classroom to trigger supermemory. The time had come; independently in Spain, Alphonso Caycedo, another medical doctor, was also crafting a surround of suggestion to heal and educate. A poem's "meaning," T.S. Eliot wrote, is like the steak the burglar throws the watchdog of the mind so the poem can do its work. Like artists, Caycedo and Lozanov shaped their message to engage, to enchant all shades of consciousness. They worked to avoid mixed messages, incompatible body language and wrong scenery, inappropriate voice tone and rhythm. Caycedo drew the name of his new "ology" from Greek. Athene herself was the Goddess of Sophrosyne, who harmonized all aspects of being through the fine art of persuasion. As

Sophrosyne, Athene was seen as greater than Apollo for she fused male and female, reason and emotion into a new harmony. To weave his cocoon of harmonious suggestion, Caycedo uses an art mentioned by Plato, "terpnos logos," a specific melodious, monotonous tone of voice, soothing and highly suggestive. It must be suggestive; Caycedo's sophrologists even reclaim the desperate street kids of Bogota who find life so tortuous that they lie in gutters to breathe car exhaust for the obliterating high.

As Caycedo knows, the shadowy influence of mixed messages often slides into memory from the background of life, from things that aren't subliminal but simply unattended to, suggestions that, like bits of radium, pulse an unfelt, pernicious influence. Pay attention and it's easy to see the different messages sent by a sterile, high tech hospital room and a home-furnished birthing room. Sickness and attendant alarm versus a warm family event. The signal power of things blinking on the periphery showed when Lozanov's team discovered that some part of us remembers even academic things on the periphery, like foreign languages.

Bulgarian students took tests on recall of foreign words. Teachers threw them a curve. They quizzed them on something no one had tried to memorize, the small-print foreign words in the instructions: "Will you please memorize this list?" Only 2.5% recalled the instruction words on the first test, though they did well with the vocabulary. Tests on following days traced the usual, well-known "curve of forgetting," a quick drop in recall for what they'd memorized, then a leveling out. But, and it's an important but, on succeeding days recall of the peripheral words began to grow. Until on the tenth day it was five times better than the first day.

This "curve of remembering" is a mirror image of the "curve of forgetting." The memory of what you experience with full awareness begins to partially sink away. At the same time, information you've picked up semiconsciously or subliminally begins to rise up into conscious memory. If you know that the mind remembers on different levels you can leverage the ability; as Lozanov urges you can work on the "double plane" and purposefully send messages to both levels of mind. Memory rising from the deeper level of mind is behind the snowballing effect in Superlearning. You learn more the third day than the first, the fourth week than the second. It's a sign that your whole mind is being engaged.

Memory Blocks

Suggestology noted three classical roadblocks on the way to supermemory and performance: the logical, emotional, and ethical blocks which often go unnoticed as they run automatically. Automatic memory is a good thing when it pockets the car keys from their usual spot or finds the light switch in the bedroom. But it has a flip side that can keep us running the same circles.

Some blocks or barriers are natural to the mind. If the mind did not have defenses against suggestion, the Brooklyn Bridge would have sold the first time. Artful suggestion has to dodge or satisfy natural mental barriers, so it can get on with its job of *desuggesting* the unnatural barriers we carry around. In other words, so we can employ the fine art of forgetting.

The logical block is the easiest to satisfy because it will listen to reason. You might grumble if a teacher asked you to learn two chapters overnight. If he said twelve, most people wouldn't even give it a shot. All by itself the structure of a textbook sends a powerful suggestion of how much it is possible to remember. We believe it, we never think about it.

If you want to expand memory and learning, by now it should be easy to convince your reasoning self that you can. Hundreds of thousands have succeeded with accelerated learning alone. If your reason is a doubting Thomas, go look up the reports. Or look into published results of new nutrition or mind machines. Or attend the seminars of people like learning maven Tony Buzon, who challenges anyone in his audience to prove she's really a stupid person. "If you can prove it, I'll take you around the world with me and we'll make millions!" Buzon says. Like many others, Buzon insists there aren't any stupid people in the old sense of the word, just people with "ticks or blocks" that dampen the innate capacity of the mind.

The defensive memory of the reasoning mind can dampen brawn as well as brain. A huge muscle of a man, Soviet weight lifter Vasily Alexayev could hoist 499.9 pounds. But not 500 pounds, of course, that was thought a barrier no human could pass. One day, Alexayev's trainers asked him to lift his personal best, 499.9. Then they weighed the bar and let him read the scale: 501.5 pounds. In the 1976 Olympics, Vasily Alexayev bent, strained, and lofted the gold medal weight —564 pounds! After Roger Bannister broke the impossible barrier of the four-minute mile, within a year fifty-two other men did too. Reason can be fixed in a suggestion that holds one back. Artful desuggestion can set it free. Remember, reason doesn't like to be unreasonable. No matter what you're trying to accomplish, to get your whole self behind you, make sure you think its possible.

Don't Be a Matter of Opinion

The fun begins with emotional blocks. Here's where the banana peel tricks of memory come from, sending one skidding. They build from suggestions like: "It's a good thing you're pretty, because you sure ain't smart." "No one in *our* family has ever been any good at math . . . sports . . . art." "Just mouth the words, you can't sing." Or worse, "Don't be too smart, nobody'll like you." "You're so clumsy . . . so stupid." "You have a mind like a sieve."

Everyone has their own batch of obsolete old humbugs humming along in the eternal now of the subconscious. Usually they are seeded when one is young with the full suggestive authority of parents or teachers, peers or society. They are such familiar old humbugs that we wave them with pride. "You wouldn't believe it, I have a mind like sieve!" "I couldn't learn math in a million years!" As we daily prove the power of self-suggestion, it might be worth pondering psychoanalyst Karen Horney's definition of masochism: "I can't-ism."

A simple shift of mind can start to reclaim all the parts you've cut off in yourself. This is an act of re-membering. Try making a list of everything you think you can't do, things you're no good at. After you're done, across the top write: *Opinions.* You've listed opinions about yourself, not facts. You don't have to be a matter of opinion. Awareness brings choice. Let's say one item is "can't learn languages." Maybe when you tried French you weren't really interested, maybe you feared being laughed at misspeaking in class, maybe you didn't like the teacher or she didn't like you, maybe your friends thought foreigners and languages were stupid. Or maybe like many of us you unknowingly suffered from a disease Lozanov uncovered. A serious health problem, he insisted, naming it "didactogenic syndrome," illness caused by poor teaching methods. There are dozens of maybes, if one of your impossibles involves performance, like dancing or public speaking, maybe you weren't physically or even emotionally ready.

Heraclitus let us know we can't step into the same river twice. Times change, techniques improve, you're not the same person you were when you were unsuccessful—unless you let old state dependent memory carry you back into a flush of ineptness. Some suggestions groove deeply and come to live as state bound memories. Often these form during the earliest, most basic experiences like a difficult birth, and become deep mindbody memories we carry through life (see Chapter 9). Could the alarming resonance from a hard birth underlie a fear of change? Or differently, might it lead us to use fear and anxiety as spurs to action?

Become aware of your self-opinions, those suggestive memories that start to resonate when you try to remember a speech or stick up for yourself at work. Then you can start to forget the outdated ones.

Sick Suggestions

There is another sort of ingrained memory we rarely question. "A winner never quits," your father used to say. "And a quitter never wins." Wise words, you've said them to your kids too when they needed a pep talk. You could use a pep talk yourself. The doctor reports your heart isn't doing too well.

Leo Rotan found that 80% of the men with heart problems he surveyed subscribed to proverbs like "A winner never quits" and "be you therefore perfect." A psychiatric social worker studying men with and without coronary troubles, Rotan says few of the fit had taken to heart such gung-ho proverbs. They preferred maxims like "little strokes fell mighty oaks," or "life is just a bowl of cherries." Watch what you plant in memory with full emotional agreement.

Anniversaries mean remembering. Even if consciousness forgets one, it seems the rest of the self may remember in ways that are disastrous. Elvis Presley and Mark Twain kept anniversaries by dying, others get sick, binge, or throw away money, according to clinical psychologist Barney Dlin. Elvis died on the anniversary of his very beloved mother's death. Twain, born as Halley's Comet streaked the sky in 1835, left when it returned in 1910.

In his patient records, Dlin noted that twenty-eight out of eighty-eight clients showed anniversary symptoms. Almost all were unaware of the connection. Anniversary reactions can be one shot or annual. A seventy-nine-year-old woman who suffered colitis and depressions for thirty-five years dreaded the end of February. Her ills always got worse, laying her low until mid-March. Finally, in therapy she made the connection: her only son had long ago been killed in Korea on March 12.

A forty-five-year-old doctor got a shock when he discovered his blood pressure had suddenly shot into the alarm range. It began to drop when an old friend reminded him that as a teenager he'd thought he wouldn't live past forty-five; he then remembered too that his favorite uncle had died at forty-five. Such anniversary reactions are more common than most therapists imagine, Dlin says. Often people mark the time of a parent's death or unconsciously develop anniversary symptoms when their own children reach the age they were when a parent departed. "A maladaptive reaction to stress" Dlin calls this. In our terms, its a stress-born state dependent memory yoked to time, that blooms sure as spring when the calendar swings around.

Then there is that barrage of suggestions all in a good cause that may paradoxically promote sickness. Consider a radio ad long heard in late night public service slots. Behind the words you hear a thumping heartbeat, known to enhance suggestion. "Do you have high blood pressure?" a pear-shaped, persuasive voice asks. "Millions of people do." Thump. "High blood pressure can kill you." Thump, thump. "Even if you haven't any symptoms, it can kill you." Thump, thump, thump. "At any time . . . Maybe *you* have high blood pressure. . . ." We'd lay odds that that ad raises blood pressure on the spot in many a listener alone in the night. "Millions of Americans are dying of . . . there is no cure . . . one out of four, one out of three . . . surely you or one of your loved ones will get . . . in the next thirty-six seconds someone will die of . . . everybody sooner or later . . . what you eat can kill you. . . ." A recent ad in *The New York Times* pictured a beautiful sunrise with a caption reading, "The greatest cause of cancer rose at 6:15 today." Is this really the best way to improve well-being?

Considering what's known about the real power of suggestion and its absorption by all levels of mind, one can question the "public service." Are we advertising sickness like soup? Are we creating a powerful mythos, seeding active memory of the inevitability and necessity of disease? Might not everyone profit if the good-hearted became more aware of suggestion and tried positive cautionaries?

You can flip the switch if a disease ad comes on. It can take a little more to release yourself from other suggested memories. Before exploring releases, there is one more block to mention, perhaps the strongest because it is the most subtle, the ethical block. This is the idea that somehow it isn't right to learn and remember too easily, to perform too artfully. Where does that come from?

Forgetting To Suffer

"The human mind is a natural resource," Lozanov said. "It is ethical to use resources in the most efficient way." Right. But as we traveled around and talked to many people, it began to dawn on us that the ethical/moral block might be the granddaddy of stumbling blocks. To take the easy part first, the very Soviet idea of mind and memory as resource: from biochemistry to Superlearning, the research mentioned in this book stands against struggle and sorrow as necessary or effective for learning and remembering. It points to ease, adventure, joy in learning. We came into this world designed for learning. Like outside ecology, recovering what we've cemented over inside is a necessity now. Hordes of the young are refusing to play the old amputation game and fit into the educational box anymore. The era of lifelong learning is here. The idea that after schooldays you don't have to learn anymore appears as silly as the idea that trees will stop putting out buds when they turn twenty—or forty or eighty. Learning is growing and growing is life. It's natural, and natural processes aren't designed to be pain-ridden. If you get a pain in your belly after supper, you think something's wrong. If learning is a pain, there's something wrong too. This is the turnoff that muffles memory.

With a little information it isn't hard for most people to drop the idea that they *ought* to flog themselves to learn and remember. That's not where the ethical block does most of its work. Anthropologist Ruth Benedict liked to speak of the cultural lens we all see through, invisible to us and focusing us. The ethical block is part of the curve of this lens. Most people don't think it affects them. Don't bank on it. You have to take a close look, for cultural suggestion builds into the tissue of our lives as noiselessly as the molecules of our dinners turn to flesh.

No pain, no gain reverberates way beyond the fitness center. If you're having too much fun, you must be doing something wrong. After all, life is hard, life is earnest, filled with 99 percent perspiration and one percent inspiration because nothing worth having comes easily. Which is good, suffering builds character. The righteousness of suffering, of being a victim, suffuses major strands of the Judeo-Christian tradition. There's a vague ground fog of feeling that we don't deserve to do well, as the old hymns sing, "We are but worms. . . ." And joy is suspect. You've probably known a church named "Our Lady of Perpetual Sorrow." Have you ever seen one named Our Lady of Perpetual Joy? Most Americans would think it was a bordello. There are all the cautionary tales about flying too high, tempting the gods, having your wishes come disastrously true, childhood stories that growl and roll over like sleeping dogs in the memory when things are going well—going too well, something bad is sure to happen! We called these vague prohibitions the granddaddy of stumbling blocks. A better name might be "Nobadaddy," the poet William Blake's life-squeezing patriarch Nobadaddy, personification of science, state, and church at their worst.

Remembering the Original Blessing

Often our "mind-forged manacles" as Blake calls them, were locked in place years ago at the suggestion of old religious dogmas. These are the most pernicious, says Dr. Joan Borysenko, for they cut you off from your source. Co-founder of the pioneering Mind/Body clinic at Boston's Beth Israel Hospital, Borysenko has identified a host of old memory patterns that shunt patients away from living life to the full. Yet she finds it is the moral and spiritual negatives that deaden most because they bar one from wholeness. Original sin or original blessing —which would you choose to generate healthy, joyous, creative life? Which would lead to repression, guilt, violence, pornography? If on close observation one finds some dogmatic manacles, he might flood them away by looking into the original blessing.

A new morning has broken, new voices within the broad spiritual traditions are calling us back to the still bubbling joy of creation. One of the most persuasive is the Dominican theologian Matthew Fox, who has lent his tough, artful scholarship to wiping clean again the bright face of the original blessing, the blessing of the beginning, of the creative Word that births creation. "And behold, it was very good." Fox calls this "Creation Theology" and shows it to be a much older spiritual stream than the usurping fall/redemption theology with its wicked load of unasked-for sin. The point is not to debate dogma. It's that looking through the life-giving eyes of the original blessing fits the business of forgetting and re-membering.

The move to reclaim the blessing is spirited by the same creative thrust that has brought the rise of the feminine, Fox says. It is part of a new energy directed toward healing ourselves and our earth, undeniable energy that has propelled the oppressed all around the world to claim their freedom, and is giving the global village a tingling sense of cosmic connection as we sprout into space. This is part of a widening embrace as we struggle to pick up forgotten pieces of ourselves.

One definition of spiritual is wholeness, which is what re-membering is about. For those involved in the grand task of re-membering, the original blessing holds great energy. It can lift strangling dogma from the past. It persuades toward freedom by reclaiming individual creativity. So does memory. The fanatic, the ideologue doesn't need much memory. He runs on automatic memory, like a knee jerk. A full memory, one that connects and synthesizes, that shifts the whole into an ever widening mirror of the universe, is the invisible modus operandi of the freedom bound.

So-called intellectuals often snipe at new agers running around saying, "I am a co-creator." Some are certainly sliding on the surface. But the idea has been around since the beginning. Does anyone call the great German religious Meister Eckhart trendy? "We are heirs of the fearful creative power of God," Eckhart wrote. He reminds us that creativity is an elemental power in us, and as Fox says, "Since we are images of God, our growing into this image, 'growing brighter and brighter into the image,' as Paul puts it, consists of us growing more and more brightly into birthers and creators . . . accepting the truth of ourselves as co-creators with God."

From either a spiritual or scientific stance, we do have an innate creativity. The times are calling us to unclog the pipeline, so we can begin to unclog the rest of the leftovers damming creation. It's time to forget the death-delivering patterns of memory, and time, it would seem, to remember who we are.

Is it a long leap from Lozanov's sleep learners to the original blessing? Maybe not so much as it seems. Lozanov's commitment was to help people remember themselves and what they might be. If you substitute the words Communist Party for religion, you have some of the things he wanted to say but couldn't. He was clearly aware that as people became educated to the ways that suggestion limits and shapes, they would begin to poke their heads above it and start to see through the bad old Nobadaddy of the communist state. It was part of his motivation.

"Briefest Therapy"

How do you get rid of the old dogs, the memories that can keep one running in place? For one thing you can teach them new tricks. Try dredging up a painful old memory, like being laughed at in class.

Relive the whole scene, but add high steppin' circus music or Dixieland jazz—and you have a different or reframed memory. "Briefest therapy" Richard Bandler calls this, a quick trick from Neurolinguistic Programming. Developed from Erickson's art, NLP is a system of healing change that Bandler helped create. Another briefest technique is to take an unpleasant memory and run through it per usual. Then roll it backward, quickly, a fast rewind. Run your movie again the usual way. It won't be the same. If you want quick methods of locating, befriending, and helping old memory patterns change to happier ways, you might enjoy NLP. The methods ride on the vast ability of the brain to learn quickly and point in new directions. Fast, but not a quick fix, NLP runs against the grain of the pervasive suggestion that change is a difficult, long-term affair. "If change work is hard," Bandler says, "or takes much practice, then you're going about it in the wrong way, and you need to change what you're doing."

Suggestive Jujitsu

One of the oldest ways to conquer blocks is to turn suggestion to one's advantage. Everyone knows about self-suggestion or self talk. We know about it, may give it a shot occasionally, but usually we overlook the self talk that really affects our lives, chattering endlessly at the bottom of the well as we go through the day. "I'll never have enough time." "I'll never remember . . ." "Dummy . . . stupid." Listen in. The vast preponderance of self chatter is negative. It's often said we'd never speak as impolitely to strangers as we do to our nearest and dearest. What's often not pointed out is that the near and dear who gets the most guff is our self. It's surprising how bracing it can be to take a break from this random chitty chat with some directed self-suggestion. Substitute it for the ongoing chatter as you take a shower, walk, sit in traffic, wake up, go to sleep. Make up a round of suggestions to talk or sing to yourself. Keep them short, pithy, positive, and in the present. "I remember my speech perfectly," not "I will remember my speech," a future tense that never arrives. The idea is to act "as if," as if you already are what you desire to be.

Have you ever tried this one? "I am very wealthy." "Naah, you're not," says a little voice inside you. Instead of giving up, use resistance to suggestions as one uses self-check health kits to detect hidden problems. Write down your suggestion, then listen to the little voice. For instance, "My memory is strong and powerful." "No it isn't." Why isn't it? "It would be too hard." Why? "Because I'd have to pay attention." What's wrong with paying attention? "I'd have to become involved." And? "I'm afraid to become really involved. I don't like what's going on." Tracing the thread backward can uncover root memories that need to be desuggested and forgotten before more conscious goals can be effectively suggested. Often these were once effective, even necessary patterns, now no longer appropriate. Though we know a lot of pop psychology, they can surprise. One woman who consciously wanted to quit smoking found that deep down she connected it with breathing, something she wanted to continue. Someone else we know discovered he originally started to smoke not to be part of the gang, but to distance himself from others.

Through whatever means, dredging up old negatives can take courage as they once again begin to thunder up and down emotional and physical octaves. It can help to remember that you're not jousting demons, that rather this is stored information, data bound away in mindbody, information that can be changed.

Whispering suggestions to someone as he drifts to sleep to implant better memory patterns is a hoary old technique practiced throughout antiquity from the healing temples of Greece to the high monasteries of Tibet. In this century, the most famous self-help writer of them all, Napoleon Hill, revived whispering to help a handicapped son. It did. About the same time, Edgar Cayce, in his *Readings,* began to speak of the effectiveness of "pre-sleep suggestion," an idea that continues in his Association for Research and Enlightenment. Most people wouldn't imagine that suggestion could help heal a critically sick, handicapped child, but A.R.E. member Cynthia Ouellette did. Lovingly, through countless nights, she made bedtime suggestions to her ailing daughter Jennifer. Results were so good that Ouellette used the technique with her other children. Bedwetting stopped, asthma attacks lessened, all-around self-image and health improved so much that Ouellette wrote *Miracle of Suggestion, The Story of Jennifer* to share the good news. (Full sensed imagining is another powerful way to shake away the old dogs of memory. See Chapters 12 and 13).

Homemade Mommy "Subliminals"

Dark-haired, with an outgoing bounce of athletic energy, Dr. Teri Mahaney is equally expert at teaching white water rafting and conducting brain booster seminars for CEOs. She's also another mother who first began a serious quest for transformative techniques to aid a child, her dyslexic daughter Jacki. Mahaney ranged through psychology, yoga, imagery, morphic forms, the Cayce *Readings,* to pick up a piece here, a piece there. Eventually, she came across Superlearning and the "Superlearning Subliminal Report." "Click," as she says, more pieces came together.

While an Associate Professor of Business at the University of Alaska, Mahaney created an intriguing, hybrid form of self-suggestion, called "Change Your Mind." CYM aims to accelerate change and help one drop old memory patterns in a hurry. Users, which include businesses, have unloaded a lot: the fear of success, PMS, or incapacitating test jitters. One previously thwarted client was finally able to pass the air controller's exam in the top percentile. "Subliminal," is how Mahaney tags her method. It's subliminal in the sense that you hear most of your do-it-yourself taped suggestions without conscious awareness, because you're asleep. Mahaney's "subliminals" follow a Superlearning format. First you tape a relaxation routine. Then custom-made suggestions are paced within eight-second frames, repeated three times, against a background of Superlearning music. Here too the rhythms seem to carry messages to deep levels of mind.

Mahaney made herself a tape to overcome a block: her academic training made it seem wrong to forge ahead when she didn't understand precisely how the technique worked. That barrier dissolved, she used experience, her own and that of hundreds of others, to develop her "empty the cup, fill the cup" approach. Everyone begins by emptying the cup of past memory patterns with a tape built on the Mommy subliminal.

The bare bones are: "Mommy and I are one. I now release and forgive Mommy for . . . I now release and forgive myself for . . . I now release and forgive myself for not . . . I transcend . . . (whatever needs to be forgiven)."

There may be many "forgive" phrases, check what floats to mind. From experience, Mahaney discovered that forgiving oneself both for doing and for not doing the same thing adds power. People go beyond mommy. They are one and forgiving with daddy, teachers, coaches, any suggestive authorities they can think of in their past. After listening to the emptying script for ten nights, clients tackle immediate change. Pick your subject and tape a few emptying phrases to be rid of past negatives. Then become one with the positive and tape suggestions for what you want to be, in the paced, repetitive, music-enhanced Superlearning format.

Mahaney's people claim fast, rather spectacular results. They may have an edge on users of commercial subliminals. Tapes require self-reflection and commitment to make. Suggestions can be specific and personal. The power of the specific showed when Mahaney and cohorts experimented with expanding the Mommy format, i.e., becoming one in a positive way with public speaking, success, memory. Or as one real mommy taped for her college daughter, Joan, "Calculus and I are one," "Western Civilization and I are one," including all five of her classes. As this was a genuine subliminal with words imperceptible behind music, Joan's roommate agreed to let it play in their room. Neither knew what the tape said. By midterm, Joan had As and high Bs in all her courses. The roommate also had As in Western Civilization and Calculus, the two classes they shared. She was getting Cs and Ds in her other subjects.

One client of Mahaney's came wide awake every night at a particular suggestion, an obvious need to trace the thread back to root resistance. Doing it yourself, you can fashion what's needed. If you're interested in Mahaney's system, details may be had from her company, Supertraining (see Resources).

"The Garbage Decade" is one name for the 90s. The landfills are looking like "deadfills" and recycling is the technology to invest in. Outside and inside. We can't afford the deadfill that sits in our memories much longer either. Suggestion is a recycling technology, a way to free up memory, to change. "Change is so very difficult!" Perhaps it's time to reverse that suggestion and say with Richard Bandler, "Change is easy." Teri Mahaney found that working with hundreds of people using thousands of suggestive scripts changed her mind too. "I now expect everybody to make it."

PART TWO

9. Your Most Ancient Memory

What's the earliest memory you have in your life? Some people think they can recall happy events—a second or third birthday party, a special parade. Some remember injuries, like tumbling out of the crib. Others recall traumatic events—losing parents, historic disasters, or wars. Some remember experiences shortly after birth.

A well-known French medical researcher says that we all have a particular ancient memory, one we all share, one that goes very far back, one that can be recalled today to enhance and enrich our lives. French scientist Dr. Alfred Tomatis has devoted a lifetime of research to exploring this ancient memory humans have and summoning it back to renew health, well-being, and creativity.

What is your most ancient memory? And why does it have the power to transform your life?

This earliest memory dates back to our time as "unborns." This most ancient memory is *the sound of our mother's voice carried to us through liquid,* through our fluid innerspace world as "unborns." Discovery of this most ancient memory and its surprising ability to spark life-altering changes has led to development of a whole new field of therapy, called Audio-Psycho-Phonology. Since its founding in France several decades ago, it has now spread worldwide and has been used by hundreds of thousands of people.

Dr. Tomatis (pronounced Toe-ma-*teece*) is a scientist whose curiosity and observations leap far beyond his medical specialty of eye, ear, nose, and throat. He was launched into what was to become a major breakthrough when, one day, he chanced to observe some ordinary birds' eggs. Songbirds' eggs, when taken immediately from the mother bird and matured and hatched by silent, nonsongbird foster mothers, produced birds that never sang throughout their lives. And no bird sang, he mused. There had to be a reason.

The key must lie in their prebirth life, he deduced. If the unhatched baby birds did not hear the repertoire of the mother bird's songs, they never learned them after hatching. Prebirth must be an extremely important time in the life of living beings, Tomatis reasoned. A lot of intense learning and remembering must go on that is essential to our functioning as adults. And the unborn's primary sense mode, he suddenly realized, was hearing—his own specialty.

If even a baby bird's entire life was shaped by "pre-hatch" hearing and remembering, how much more did a complex human benefit from prebirth hearing and memories. Did unborn human babies too need to hear a certain repertoire of sounds? And if they missed out, did this have a profound impact on a person's life, health, abilities, and well-being?

Moreover, what exactly *were* these sounds that bird and baby needed to hear? What were they like? How did they sound to our adult ears? *Why* were they so important?

Tomatis launched a cascade of experiments. How would a mother's voice sound to her unborn baby? Like a Jacques Cousteau of inner-space, he set up a kind of diving expedition. He would take microphones underwater to represent the unborn's listening post. He wrapped both a microphone and a speaker in rubber membranes and lowered them into a tank of water. Mike and speaker were each connected to different tape recorders. He played a tape of a mother's voice through the underwater speaker. The underwater mike picked up the sounds as they passed through the water and relayed them to a recorder. Tomatis felt a sense of excitement as his tape began to unveil the strange, all-important secret of exactly how a mother's voice sounds to her baby.

It was extraordinary! Mother's voice was a strange pattern of high-pitched squeaks and whistles, something like dolphin talk sounds. "It reminded me of a deep African night beside the river," he says. It was alive with unusually high-pitched sounds (about 8,000 hertz) as if coming through a thick jungle atmosphere.

Now he'd captured the secret sounds the unborn hears. What would happen if he played these strange sounds to a small child? Would the child remember them? Would they have any effect? He could hardly wait to try the newfound sounds on his young patients, many of whom had hearing and learning problems.

One of the first to hear the water-filtered voice sounds was a four-teen-year-old autistic boy. He'd cut himself off from communication with the world at age four. Tomatis made a recording of the boy's mother's voice filtered through deep water, and played it to the boy. He and the mother observed with anticipation.

At first, as the sounds filled the room, the boy seemed his usual noncommunicative self. Then suddenly he seemed to remember a strange, deep, ancient memory. He got up, ran to the wall, turned off the lights, ran to his mother, and curled up in her lap in a fetal position, sucking his thumb. Tomatis began to adjust the recording. He cut down the filtering until the voice sounded normal again. As the high-pitched squeaks became normal speech, Tomatis watched with fascination. The boy, who had not talked in ten years, suddenly began to babble like a ten-month-old child. It was a very dramatic moment for Tomatis, mother, and child—and the beginning of a new mode of healing for countless children and adults.

"This was a kind of 'sonic birth,' " Tomatis says. It was like making the passage again that we all make when we are born, from hearing through liquid, to hearing through air.

Playing the sounds of a mother's voice filtered through water calls back our most ancient memory: sounds heard through fluid. This in turn, he believes, "awakens a sense of our most archaic relationship with the mother"—of mother and child as one—a sense of wholeness, a kind of touching base with our oneness with the universe. Lloyd Silverman found the "Mommy and I Are One" subliminal enormously healing. Coming from a very different direction, Tomatis came to a similar realization. He thinks the healing power of his high-frequency sound rises from nudging people into a primary prebirth memory of wholeness.

Tomatis and colleagues developed a sophisticated electronic recording process to replicate our prebirth hearing process. The method has helped scores of learning-disabled, dyslexic, and autistic children—over 12,000 dyslexics alone have been cured at Tomatis centers in Europe, Africa, and Canada. The therapist records the mother's voice as she reads a story for her child. The voice is specially electronically filtered to heighten the powerful high frequencies. The child hears the tape played through a Tomatis invention, "The Electronic Ear." (See page 126.)

"These sessions are unforgettable," says one therapist. "You'd have to be there." When the child first hears these sounds, a kind of awakening and recalling goes on. "The child changes his relationship with the mother; becomes more affectionate and closer to her . . . she feels more loved and needed."

As treatment continues, playing on this basic memory, the child listens and understands better and can concentrate better. As the child's ear becomes trained, he can sort out the sound messages better, the universe becomes more comprehensible. Soon the child can learn in half an hour what previously took years to learn. Where it wasn't possible to use the mother's voice in the therapy, Tomatis found he could substitute something else—classical music, specially filtered to heighten the high frequencies and diminish the lower frequencies. Research shows the dynamic power of the technique is in the high frequencies. This was later to be the basis of another world famous healing method, Sound Therapy (See p. 123)

Tomatis' dramatic breakthrough regarding the importance of this early sound memory we all possess came long before research had established that the preborn could even hear. Since then, vast strides in monitoring unborn life show that the unborn baby's ear is functional from the fourth month of pregnancy and from that time on hears the mother's voice, heartbeat, and many other internal and external sounds.

In one of his most baffling cases, Tomatis was to find just how much our preborn hearing and remembering can shape our later lives. Four year-old Odile was autistic. She was brought to the Tomatis Center in Paris for his special treatment. Odile was totally mute and appeared not to hear. As the treatment with the special high-frequency tapes progressed, she gradually began to emerge from her long silence. Within a month, she was listening and speaking. Her Parisian family was delighted. They were also bewildered. After four years of silence, Odile now spoke—but to their astonishment, she spoke and understood *English* instead of French!

Where had Odile learned or even heard English? Her parents, brothers, and sisters naturally spoke French at home. Had Odile overheard her parents' occasional private remarks in English? But then why hadn't her brothers and sisters learned the same English words? Besides, Odile had appeared not to hear anything, no matter what language.

Dr. Tomatis, playing detective, tracked down Odile's mother's history until he discovered a clue to the mystery. Odile's mother had worked in a Paris import-export firm where only English was spoken all through her pregnancy. The unborn Odile heard *English* every day until her birth. The prebirth recall summoned by the high-frequency sounds had also brought memories of what she'd heard during that same period of time. Dr. Tomatis, also a Professor of Psycho-Linguistics in Paris, is convinced from his decades of research that even the rudiments of language may be developed when we are still unborn. He reveals more in his intriguing book, *The Ear and Language.*

Memories Before Birth

Not only are we affected by our most basic memory of high-frequency sound, but, scientists find, we can also be influenced throughout our lives by a host of things that sink into our unborn memory. Not surprisingly, many of these formative memories channel through our primary unborn sense, hearing.

"It may sound strange," says Boris Brott, conductor of the Hamilton Philharmonic Symphony in Ontario, "but music has been a part of me since before birth." As a young man, Brott was perplexed but delighted by an odd ability he had. He could play certain pieces of music sight unseen. "I'd be conducting a score for the first time," he says, "and suddenly the cello line would jump out at me; I'd know the flow of the piece even before I turned the page of the score." Instead of déjà vu, it was "déjà entendu." He mentioned the odd phenomenon to his mother one day, knowing that as a professional cellist she'd be interested in his affinity for the cello line in the score.

"Which symphonies were these?" she asked.

He told her the list. "I think I've solved the mystery," she said. "Those scores you knew sight unseen were the symphonies I played when I was pregnant with you!"

Dr. Thomas Verny, a pioneering Toronto psychiatrist, author, professor, and founder of Toronto's Center for Psychotherapy and Education, has devoted years to exploring the "new and truly exciting research" on the unborn in its natural habitat. A new generation of medical technology has unveiled the "secret life of the unborn," allowing Verny to uncover a dynamic picture of life before birth—"very different from the passive, mindless creature of the traditional pediatrics texts," he says.

A young mother in Oklahoma City peeked into her living room one day, drawn by the sound of her two-year-old daughter busily chanting a rhythmic pattern. Sitting on the floor, she intoned, "Breathe in, breathe out, breathe in, breathe out." She continued as though completing a set exercise.

"Maybe she's imitating something she saw on TV," thought the mother. Then it hit her. These were the words of the Lamaze exercises she had done herself! She had done them in Canada where she lived during her pregnancy. Her daughter was repeating precisely the *Canadian* version of Lamaze which differed from the U.S. version. She could not have seen it on American TV. The mother could think of only one explanation—her baby had listened in on her exercises and was now somehow remembering them.

Within the past decade, another new discipline has developed mainly in Europe—prenatal psychology. Psychiatrists, obstetricians, and clinical psychologists are pooling their rather amazing observations of the scope of prenatal memory and learning. In his psychiatric practice, Dr. Verny reports seeing hundreds of people who have been deeply scarred by negative prenatal events. He believes this new field can help an entire generation enter life free of corrosive mental and emotional memories.

Lifestyles of the Unborn

For the last thirty years, the unborn's life and memories have been widely charted. Dr. Dominick Purpura, of Albert Einstein Medical College and the National Institute of Health brain study section, and editor of *Brain Research Journal,* cites neurological studies proving the existence of the unborn's consciousness and memory. He pinpoints the start between twenty-eight and thirty-two weeks. At this point, the brain's neural circuits are as advanced as a newborn's, he says. A few weeks later, distinct brain waves are detectable showing waking and sleeping states, and REM sleep, indicating dreams. From twenty-four weeks on, the unborn listens continually—dominant sound, the mother's heartbeat. Dr. Verny believes the unconscious memory of the maternal heartbeat may explain why babies are comforted by a ticking clock.

Many audiologists like Dr. Michelle Clements of London have done extensive surveys of musical tastes of the unborn. If Vivaldi's music is played, even an agitated baby relaxes. Mozart is another favorite. Fetal heartrate slows and steadies and kicking declines. On the other hand, Beethoven and Brahms can start even a calm child kicking and moving.

The hard throbbing beat of heavy metal rock music is *not* on the unborns' hit parade apparently. Many kicked violently when they heard it. One of Dr. Clements' mothers-to-be was forced to leave a rock concert—the baby set off a storm of violent kicking. Dr. Albert Liley of National Woman's Hospital, Auckland, N.Z., discovered through physiological studies, that unborns twenty-five weeks or older will literally jump in rhythm to the beat of an orchestra drum. Worldwide, for the past fifteen years, new physiological monitoring technology has permitted an extensive exploration of prenatal reactions and preferences in different situations and cultures. These memories may later influence even career choices.

Verny believes preferences are established while in the womb that can have a great impact on later life. Many classical musicians, like Arthur Rubinstein, Boris Brott, and Yehudi Menuhin claim their interest in music was established *before* they were born. "In the womb," says Menuhin, "instead of hearing my mother's voice I heard music." Menuhin notes that musical interest and talents have often tended to run in families—for instance the Bachs and the Strausses. Of course, before the era of recorded music, a musical family was one of the few places an unborn might regularly hear classical music performed daily instrumentally, or by orchestras or choirs.

Not only sound memories influence our lives—motion memories too seem to be involved. The mother of Julie Krone, the record-setting, award-winning woman jockey, reports that Julie seemed to have learned to ride before birth, thanks to her own specialty continued during pregnancy of horse-riding competition dressage.

The explosion of new gadgetry made it possible to monitor, test, and explore the unborn's uncharted territory. Unborns were filmed, ultrasounded, EEG'ed, examined radiologically. Their living quarters were injected with cold water. (They didn't like it.) They were tested for conditioned response learning using loud noises and vibrations. (They passed). Amniocentesis needles were poked at them to determine sex and health; electrodes were screwed into their skulls for electronic fetal monitoring; they were even "fetoscoped"—illuminated with fiberoptics. (A preborn hand pushed it away!) They had bright lights shone directly on them, via mother's stomach. (They see light; it startles them; they look away from it.) A blinking light on the mother's stomach causes the preborn's heart to begin fluctuating dramatically. They've been jabbed, poked, pinched, and yelled at. (They quickly squirm away from the poking and kick furiously at yelling.) What sort of memories are being laid down by this high tech invasion?

There's extensive evidence too that the mother's thoughts and feelings can be picked up by the unborn. When the mother is upset, with major stresses like death of the father, accidents, war, stress chemicals flood through the placental wall to the unborn who also becomes frightened and anxious. Chronic stress had more impact than a passing scare. It seems we may acquire state dependent stress memories even before we plunge into the world, memories that have an even deeper, less conscious resonance than usual.

So things have come full circle. A century ago people used to say if you were afraid of horses it was because your mother had been scared by a horse before you were born. Folk wisdom realized the powerful effects of a mother's anxieties and fears, and women were warned to keep away from events like fires and funerals. Aware that events affected unborns, and that they remembered them, the Chinese had special prenatal clinics 1000 years ago to teach and shape them. Today, prebirth "schools" for unborns have sprung up again.

It appears our memories keep a record of all these events from before our births. More and more reports have poured in from hypnotists and psychiatrists about prebirth recalls. Psychiatrist Dr. Stan Grof, author of *Realm of the Human Unconscious,* reports on one man. Under medication he began to have a complete recall of his time as an unborn. He described his rate of growth—how big his head, legs, and arms were. How pleasant it was in the warm, amniotic fluid world. He could hear the comforting beat of his mother's heart and also his own heartbeats. Then he abruptly changed tone. "I hear muffled noises," he said. "I hear laughter. There are people out there yelling." Then he heard the brash blast of trumpets. The carnival celebrations were reaching a peak. Suddenly the man said, "I'm about to be born!"

Dr. Grof was intrigued by this vivid account. Was this a fantasy or an actual recall? he wondered. He phoned the patient's mother.

"Yes," she confirmed, "it was the excitement of going to the carnival that caused my son to be born ahead of schedule." She added details that matched her son's description. "But how did you find out about this?" she asked Dr. Grof. "I've never told anyone—not even my mother. She warned me not to go the carnival while pregnant because it could make the baby arrive!"

Dr. Verny is convinced that memory tracks begin to be laid down by the sixth to eighth month. "There is no question that the unborn child remembers or that he retains his memories," he says, pointing out that these "lost" memories remain alive in the unconscious, sometimes casting long shadows. For instance, there is the experience of an insecure young man who consulted San Francisco therapist Jack Downing. Under hypnosis he recalled a painful prebirth memory. When his mother told her husband she was pregnant, a tremendous battle began. "I've been saving to buy a Chrysler," said the father. There wasn't enough money for a child. The young man thought the recall strange because his parents didn't fight. Questioning them later, they confirmed having had the argument. They'd been so upset over it, they'd agreed never to argue in front of their son.

While the stresses and blows of life in the outside world can imprint the unborn with emotional or physical problems, there is a saving grace. The mother's attitude toward the baby can be a buffer. "Love is what matters most," Verny emphasizes. Love and nurturing weave a protective shield that decreases and neutralizes outside tensions.

Recovering Prebirth and Birth Memories

Dr. Stan Grof reports on thousands of clients who've used psychotropic drugs to recall prebirth and birth traumas and resolve them—problems such as physical and psychological rigidity, shallow breathing, anxiety, and other symptoms have yielded to the birth recall of impending suffocation caused by constriction of the umbilical cord or compression of the infant's body during birth.

Dr. Stephan Porges, organizer of a conference on fetal memory in Iceland, argues that "documenting the existence of long-term memory of the birth experience would change the way birth takes place." Currently, he says, newborns are considered to have no memory for procedures that give physical or psychological trauma, and they're done with no pain control (for example circumcision). He urges the medical profession to develop a more humane attitude to the newborn.

Dr. Frederick Leboyer, developer of the "Gentle Conventional Birth" has observed that it would be hard to think of a more frightening introduction to the world than the one obstetrics has devised for this generation of children. Birth has been moved from family experience to professional experience, and from female to male jurisdiction. Machine-age birth, with its overuse of chemicals, painful procedures, and traumatic separations, may be having an impact on society in terms of depersonalization, illnesses, violence, and child abuse, observes Dr. David Chamberlain, author of *Babies Remember Birth.*

On board ship one time, Dr. David Cheek, an obstetrician and hypnotist from Chico, California, met a fellow passenger suffering an acute headache. He'd had headaches for years. They always struck on the right side of the forehead above the eye. He agreed to hypnosis to ease the pain. Dr. Cheek regressed him right back to birth to track the cause. The headache sufferer recounted a violent birth. He felt his head crushed with severe pain—directly over his right eye on his forehead, and on the back of his neck. To Dr. Cheek, it sounded like a forceps delivery that had gone wrong. By chance, when disembarking, he bumped into his fellow passenger's mother. She confirmed the traumatic birth and the desperate, last-minute, high-forceps delivery. The patient had carried a lifelong, unconscious memory of his painful birth in the form of headaches in the injured areas.

Dr. Cheek tested four young men and women he'd delivered himself. He placed each one under hypnosis and asked each one to describe his/her birth. In particular, he asked each person to describe the position of his head and shoulders during birth over two decades before. He'd selected positioning as an accuracy test for birth memories, because he felt that there was no way subjects could know this.

After recording the birth descriptions, Dr. Cheek unlocked the delivery notes on subjects from his twenty-year-old files. Searching the obstetrical records, he discovered that each person had correctly described exactly how his/her head was turned, how the shoulders were angled, which arm was freed first and which delivery procedures had been used.

Cheek continued his hypnotic explorations of birth. He found that some patients who suffered from asthma and emphysema had been nearly suffocated during birth. He found that head pain is frequently associated with birth trauma. Hypnotic recall and resolution of the difficult birth was often enough to relieve migraine and chronic headaches.

Dr. Verny's files show that violent, traumatic, threatening births leave potent memories that may later require medical or psychotherapeutic treatment. He noted in particular that babies who have the umbilical cord accidentally wound around their necks at birth tend, as children and adults, to suffer from more throat-related problems such as swallowing difficulties, or speech impediments like stuttering. He also observed that many prematurely born people tended to feel rushed and harried throughout their lives. Birth-memory-recall symptoms can take many forms, even recurring dreams.

For years, Kathleen Burke of Toronto had taken her six-year-old son Ricky from doctor to doctor, trying to get help for his terrifying, recurring nightmares. Almost every night, just after getting him to sleep, she'd hear him thrashing around yelling and screaming. In a recurring scene reminiscent of *The Exorcist*, he'd spew out a stream of sophisticated curse words. "There's a bright light shining on me," he'd shout, then he'd pour out a sequence of words in a foreign language. Doctors could not diagnose her son's condition.

Finally, after consulting therapist Sandra Collier at Dr. Verny's center, clues began to fit together. Ricky had been born prematurely and almost dead after an extremely difficult labor. While struggling to save the infant's life, the exhausted doctors had cursed. A priest was called in and administered the last rites over the tiny form. Then, suddenly, Ricky had rallied. With a shock of recognition, Mrs. Burke pieced together the elements of Ricky's terrifying dreams. They were a replay of the memory of his frightening birth. The curse words were those the doctors had used. The light was the delivery room light. The strange foreign words were the Latin words of the last rites.

The late Dr. Nandor Fodor, the internationally known psychoanalyst, described many dreams and adult memory flashes linked with birth. One man, born on the Fourth of July during a bedlam of loud sounds that continued throughout his first twenty-four hours, developed an abnormal fear of firecrackers. Another, born near railroad tracks, had a lifelong hypersensitivity to train whistles.

Dr. Chamberlain documented hundreds of cases of birth/womb memory. He also researched in detail hypnotic birth recalls by ten mother/child pairs. He found mother/child reports matched, and contained many facts that were consistent and appropriate. Settings, characters, sequences dovetailed—one story from two points of view. Unbelievable as it sounds, daughters accurately described their mothers' hairstyles. One boy, whose mother reported he was placed in a plastic bassinet, complained about the "shiny plastic or glass walls around me. Things look blurry, distorted." Many grown children recalled being rejected at birth because they were not the "right sex."

Many adopted children have painful prebirth and birth memories of rejection. Another Chamberlain patient, David, reported in his birth recall, "There's no joy in this room. I feel like nobody's happy to see me. The whole room is very silent, like there is a death in the room . . . it's all businesslike." David was placed for adoption immediately at birth.

Adoptees placed later, report recalls of birth-time incidents. Cheryl Young stormed home from kindergarten one day in a rage against her parents. "I don't like my name! I'm mad at you for naming me Cheryl. Illeen! Illeen! I only like that name!" Her adopted mother felt a moment of shock. Illeen was the name Cheryl's natural mother had given her at birth, which she'd had for four months prior to adoption, and which she'd never been told.

Other adoptees, upon being reunited with their natural mothers, often discover they've had unconscious recalls of parent's and sibling's names and events. Lesley Brabyn of San Francisco, reunited with her natural mother in Ontario, discovered her natural brother's name was John Trevor. Lesley's husband's name is John and she'd named her son Trevor.

Birthdays Aren't Just Once a Year

It seems our "birth" day influences us unconsciously all year round throughout our lives. More than three decades of research now show that our prebirth and birth memories can have a lasting influence on us. Traumatic birth creates very powerful state dependent memories in the mindbody system, memories that many feel aid and abet disease. (see Chapter 4). So it's not surprising that researchers find life-threatening births appear to predispose a person to psychological damage, organic brain damage, psychosis, antisocial, or criminal behavior. Additional research in Nitra, Czechoslovakia, showed that traumatic births were more likely to happen when the earth's magnetic fields were turbulent as a result of solar flares and other factors (See chapter 20).

Dr. Sarnoff A. Mednick, researching twenty schizophrenics, discovered that 70% had suffered complications at birth or during prenatal life. Records of children without any evidence of schizophrenia showed only 15% had suffered complications during pregnancy or birth. Other researchers have made similar findings. Dr. Mednick then began to check out men who'd committed violent crimes. Out of sixteen criminals, fifteen had had extremely difficult births and the sixteenth had a mother with epilepsy.

Suicide by teenagers is now linked to difficulties during the birth process. Internationally known pediatric psychologist, Dr. Lee Salk, told a Toronto conference on childbirth that prenatal and birth memories play a key role in establishing mental health. The first few hours of life are crucial, he believes. Studying the medical records of Rhode Island residents under age twenty who committed suicide between 1975 and 1983, he and his colleagues at Cornell University found a high rate of birth complications.

Dr. Salk subsequently charted infant mortality rates and teenage suicide rates in fifty-five countries and found that where one was low, the other was high. Technology is saving babies who used to die, but the birth complications seem to predispose teenagers toward suicide. Swedish researchers corroborated Salk's findings and went further. They showed a frightening link between the *method* of suicide and the kind of trauma that happened at birth, says Salk. For example, teens who'd nearly strangled on the umbilical cord during birth chose death by hanging.

Birth memories may be so important that details of one's birth should probably be included in medical records. They could signal the need for early counseling to bring traumatic memories into consciousness and defuse them, to nip in the bud tendencies toward suicide and criminality. Beyond that, Salk insists we must do more in neonatal care. "I think it is irresponsible to bring children into the world if you cannot give them optimal conditions."

Birth practices may set the social character of an entire society, researchers reported at a 1982 Esalen conference. The way we greet our newborn members may have to do with the shaping of the overall character of a country and the health of individuals living there. "Childbirth is . . . the reproduction of the human race," says researcher Suzanne Arms. It's a personal, family, and social event, not just a biological or medical one. Immediate separation after birth deprives both mother and child of the chance for emotional bonding. James Prescott believes impersonal childbirth and lack of bonding may account for an alarming increase in infant homicides.

How To Recall Birth Memories

If memories of prebirth and birth play such a large role in shaping our lives, why do most of us recall so few of them? Dr. Verny believes laboratory animal research holds answers. When given the hormone oxytocin, animals develop amnesia and can't remember tasks they'd learned. During birth, the hormone oxytocin is produced in the mother's body and controls the rate of labor contractions. Oxytocin floods the mother's system as well as the child's. Our birth memories may be drained away by oxytocin during the birth process.

Why are traumatic births so powerfully seeded in memory? Another hormone may be responsible. ACTH has the opposite effect of oxytocin and aids memory retention. A flood of memory-enhancing ACTH in the mother's and infant's bodies, caused by the stress of a traumatic birth, might account for the powerful imprint and lingering influence of these memories.

Aside from hypnosis, birth recalls can often surface with psychotropic drugs. Most people in the birth memory research were born under the type of birth medication used twenty to forty years ago when medicated deliveries were standard. Psychotropic drugs may physiologically recreate the same state, thus triggering early memories.

"An awesome sign of memory," says Chamberlain, "is the reactivation of forceps bruises or a blue area on the throat where a person was being choked by the umbilical cord! That these marks come and go with the memory is a sure sign that memory has been preserved somewhere."

Soviet psychiatrist Dr. Vladimir Raikov, famous for "reincarnation hypnosis," found that with subjects in deep hypnotic regression, authentic reflexes of the perinatal period could be reproduced. Going still further back, many Chamberlain clients have remembered events concerning their conception—an apparent impossibility, yet later many details were validated. Ida described the when and where of her conception and her mother's drunken condition at the time. "Ida said she did not take up residence in her mother for three weeks and spent the interim floating in a comfortable place hard to describe and hard to leave. There were special swirls of light that felt good." It was so peaceful and felt so good, Ida later said it was the greatest religious experience she had ever had. Validation of these ultraearly memories has convinced Chamberlain that memory cannot reside in physical material and that memories coming from prebirth show a fully self-aware consciousness.

People under anaesthetic undergoing surgery have later reported full details of procedures and even doctors' comments and jokes about them. (See p. 57) Millions who have undergone near-death experiences have returned to describe in detail the efforts made by rescuers to revive them. They seemed to hover "out-of-body" above operating table, or car crash sight. (See p. 307) For people undergoing near-death or anaesthetic, says Chamberlain, ". . . memory is excellent, showing that memory and other cognitive functions lie in a protected sphere outside the body."

Says Verny, "Evidence for some sort of an extra-neurological memory system is growing." There are now thousands who have validated memories going back before the last trimester and these memories manifest through their dreams, actions, psychiatric symptoms, or other circumstances, he says. Research converging from a host of other fields also points to memory/consciousness being outside the physical body/brain.

The view of life related by people regressed to the moment of just-borns is an intriguing and mystical one, says Dr. Chamberlain. It's the view of aware, thoughtful minds of fully formed persons in little bodies knowing many things: knowing they cannot yet make their bodies work the way they'd like; knowing what they want and need, and who to trust; noting the strange behavior of doctors, the weaknesses of parents, the needs of siblings, and learning from everybody and everything.

Several new methods of birth memory recall have been developed aside from hypnosis and drugs. Dr. Grof created "holotropic" therapy which evokes early memories through a variety of sounds, music, movements, and breath control. *Rebirthing in the New Age* by Leonard Orr and Sondra Ray, explores a special breathing system coupled with positive affirmations that helps recall and resolve birth memory traumas. Leslie LeCron developed a finger signaling method for use with very light hypnosis. Arthur Janov's primal therapy is another method, and Dianetics offers its "auditor" system.

Dr. Verny highly recommends the Tomatis centers as the most innovative and effective nonverbal treatment (70% cure rate) for children who've undergone traumatic pregnancies or deliveries and appear to have psychological symptoms. At the Cagnes-sur-Mer clinic in France, each child undergoes several "rebirthing" or "reparenting" sessions in a tiny, egg-shaped room—a unique space designed to reproduce warm, reassuring, womblike feelings. The youngster is massaged with coconut oil and, while in the room, sits in a bath heated to the temperature of amniotic fluid. Ultraviolet light simulating the light an unborn sees when the mother is sunbathing, fills the room, and is color-adjusted according to the child's symptoms. (Blue if hyperactive; red if apathetic.) The recording of the water-filtered mother's voice—our most ancient memory—is piped in. Afterwards, the child is urged to play, paint, or sculpt in the playroom to relive and express old traumas.

Sixteen-month old Claude arrived at the clinic with his head in spasm so that it was pinned to his left shoulder. He could barely crawl and had very restricted movements. He constantly shrank back from his mother. Tracking prenatal events, therapists found that Claude as an eight-month preborn, had undergone amniocentesis. The needle nicked his neck on the left side. His prebirth memories caused him to develop the head spasm to protect his neck and to deeply distrust his mother. He was completely cured in six months.

Other researchers are trying to better prebirth memories by improving communications with the unborn. Rene Van de Carr, obstetrician and gynecologist, is president of a center in Hayward, California, with the tongue-in-cheek name, Prenatal "University." Twice a day, parents speak to the unborn while patting the unborn's habitat. More than 1000 unborns have been through the "school" and graduates are said to be more vigorous at birth—smile, sit, walk, and speak sooner, and bond well. Some believe prenatal stimulation technology will be the ultimate resource for the next millenium, revolutionizing how and when we learn.

Michelle O'Neil, RN, PhD. of the Institute for Noble Birthing in California, reports that she's been getting outstanding results with unborns through the use of Superlearning Music tapes prepared by the authors. Besides a comforting, slow 60 beats-a-minute tempo, Superlearning Music features a range of high-frequency sounds. Babies' hearing is open to these stimulating high-pitched tones. Dr. O'Neil uses the Superlearning Music for prebirth exercises and during the birth as well. She found the music shortened the first stage of labor by 20% for the mother and knocks out pain. It also made for a happier baby. Painful birth doesn't have to be part of the cultural context for either mother or baby, she thinks.

Remembering birth may be a unique feature of the 20th century, says Dr. Chamberlain, and these very real ". . . birth memories may provide a breakthrough to understanding," he says. Combined with other data they help give us a new picture of the difference between brain and mind, and open new dimensions of human consciousness. It's a chance to "look at one of life's most sensitive and awesome moments and catch a glimpse of who we really are."

Ideal Planetary Arrival Conditions

What would happen if we arranged for our arrival in this earth dimension to be the most beautiful, painless, most pleasant possible experience? According to people who've experienced it, both mother and child as well as the doctors who've arranged it, the answer is superbabies and superpeople, with amazing powers and abilities.

Over twenty years ago, Soviet Dr. Igor Charkovsky began to explore ways to make the birth process a pleasure for mother and infant. He was prompted by experience, the pain of seeing his own premature daughter badly injured at birth. Specialists held little hope for her. Charkovsky decided to try hydrotherapy; every day he lowered the frail baby into a tub of water. Soon she showed improved health and rapid growth. At three months she walked. At nine months she could talk. Eventually, Deirdre was restored to health. Today she is a fine athlete and top student.

Her recovery gave him an idea: gravity and water. What if you could have gravity working *for* mother and child during the birth process instead of against them? Labor would be shorter, easier, and less damaging. And water. What if the baby could emerge into life on earth in warm fluid, like the familiar prenatal fluid world. The transition from fluid to our air world could be made gradually and with far less stress, just like a deep diver surfaces carefully to avoid the bends.

He tried out the idea first with cats, rabbits, pigs, and chickens. The chickens popped out of their eggs underwater, and grew up able to swim just as well as ducklings. All the "water-born" animals were smarter and lived longer, healthier lives. Being in water at birth or in infancy had a profound effect on them. Many changed their basic behavior patterns. Cats, for instance, took to swimming and remained swimmers the rest of their lives. Charkovsky taught a pregnant pig to find food she liked underwater. Piglets born of that mermaid pig eagerly dove for tubes of milk deep in a water tank. The underwater piglets were healthier. They grew faster. Even briefly feeding underwater had a positive effect on their development. Charkovsky had beavers raise baby bunnies in water. The water rabbits became superrabbits, developing an unusually powerful build. (Helping with the dams, perhaps?) Like all his other water-born animals, *the rabbits lived twice their normal lifespan.* Weightlessness in water reduced oxygen requirements by 60% or more, freeing energy for growth, health, and development of potentials. If the method worked for humans, he realized, he might single-handedly be able to change the course of human evolution—a momentous undertaking.

Anti-Gravity Birth Memories

Next, Charkovsky developed an innovative submerged birth method for human babies. Experienced women swimmers and divers were first to try it. They reported that underwater birth was totally painless. In case histories several women stated they could give birth even while asleep in the water. The mother's feeling of confidence transferred to the newborn. This soothing, restful form of childbirth was ideal for the child, who also experienced little discomfort and swam out into the water like a gravity-free astronaut on his long life cord. The newborn is naturally amphibious, Charkovsky says, and swims a perfect, automatic breaststroke. The "water baby" went from her "weightless" fluid prebirth state into the weightlessness of the pool without stress or strain. Only after gradually surfacing would the cord be cut and the infant begin to breathe.

Charkovsky's water babies went right on swimming; thousands of newborns have been in the swimming pools in the USSR since their lives began. Some infants even learned to eat and sleep while floating safely in the pool. Charkovsky believes the greatest benefits come to the infants if they swim daily during the first three months of life.

The result of this euphoric, blissful, gravity-free birth method has been a generation of super babies, with ultrahappy birth memories. The children developed faster, with outstanding physical coordination. At three months they're at the level of a normal one year old, says Charkovsky. Many water babies can walk at four months, swim for miles when only six months. Mind and memory were vastly better. With higher IQs, water babies retain substantial advantages during their school careers. Freed of the handicap of machine-age birth trauma and its lifelong, corrosive memories, these children are also psychologically superior to average, say observers. They are happier, more sociable, even-tempered, and not aggressive.

Famous French diver, Jacques Maillol visited the pool where Charkovsky works. Maillol holds the world record for holding his breath and staying under water 100 meters deep, without a diving suit. He was bested at the pool by tiny tots who went on playing on the bottom of the pool long after the diver had to come up for air.

"Hydro-Obstetrics" is the medical name for Charkovsky's system. It could also be called "The Anti-Gravity Earth-Birth." A normal air birth suddenly subjects a baby to gravity forces similar to those that hit cosmonauts when the rocket blasts off. It's not surprising Charkovsky thought in terms of cosmonautics for birthing—his degrees are in engineering. He's also an athletics coach and has studied biology, psychology, and midwifery. He drew inspiration too from boyhood vacations with his zoologist parents near the Siberian-Mongolian border. There he met Siberian "healers" who'd preserved ancient knowledge and could direct their energies to healing and helping others.

Soviet medical records have tracked over 1000 boys and girls born by hydro-obstetrics. Most are supremely healthy, and retain a love of swimming underwater. Birth injuries are extremely rare. The floating position taken by the mother has a favorable emotional effect, as well as decreasing the pain.

Charkovsky also introduced a special hydrotherapy program for the handicapped and for children injured by standard birth procedures. They, like his daughter, have been restored to health. At least twenty-five Soviet cities now have pools like the one at Moscow's Institute of Physical Culture designed especially for the swimming babies. Infants graduate to aqualungs so they can swim underwater for twenty minutes at a time. Some 30,000 infants are in these water sprite programs.

Hydro-Obstetrics is now used worldwide, and Dr. Charkovsky has been named Honorary Professor at Columbia University, New York.

At the Natural Childbirth Institute in Culver City, California, results showed that immersion in experimental pools reduced labor from an average seventeen and a half hours to only five. Other experimental underwater births showed the child, once delivered, can remain under water still connected to the mother by the umbilical cord for up to twenty minutes, and it seems to ease the transition to the infant's new environment. The baby, gently guided to the surface to take its first breath, is often smiling instead of crying.

Charkovsky also explored the world of dolphins, long known for their high intelligence and friendliness toward humans. He had expectant mothers swim with dolphins in the Caspian and Black Seas. The unborns seemed to "receive" sound-signals sent to them by dolphins swimming nearby. High-frequency sounds, like those made by dolphins, have a vitalizing effect on the cortex of the human brain. When the water babies arrive, they too play with the dolphins. Soviets say they achieve an almost mystical camaraderie. Babies with dolphin playmates are more cheerful, emotionally stable, and have better mental capabilities than others, Soviets report.

Researchers who have followed these water babies through life believe they constitute a new stage in human evolution. Unlearning the genetic fear of water is the key to continued mental and physical development of the human race, Charkovsky asserts. Water is the cradle of life. "Human development has been at a standstill for many thousands of years; it has reached an impasse," he says in the book *Water Babies.* Gravity-free life in water offers new possibilities for developing human potential, he states.

Because the effect of gravity is greatly lessened, need for oxygen decreases. The body's energy is more efficiently utilized for learning, healing, development. Freed of the need to fight gravity, Charkovsky says, water babies develop the body and above all, the brain, mind, and memory. Water babies are totally mobile in water, instead of being flat out in a crib so they can investigate the environment, experience various stimuli, and acquire different kinds of knowledge at a formative age. Water babies *can create new brain functions* Charkovsky believes. Because of their evolutionary brain development, he insists, water babies will be able to solve problems and handle things impossible for us born and raised in the normal, handicapped way.

Adults too it seems can make some new and flashy brain connections underwater. One of the world's most famous inventors, Japanese billionaire Yoshiro NakaMats, who developed the floppy computer disc, digital watch, and 2,360 other patents was ahead of Charkovsky. For years, he's done all his inventing sitting at the bottom of his pool, holding his breath four or five minutes at a time. "The water pressure forces blood and oxygen into my brain, making it work at peak performance," he says.

Accelerated Evolution and Birth Memories

Can accelerated evolution be the by-product of positive memories of an empowering, nondamaging birth? Ultimate outcomes of Charkovsky's revolutionary birth methods are still not known. Will the water babies live *double* the normal human lifespan as the test animals did? Is "anti-gravity earth birth" the key to longevity? Will children of water babies inherit their superior abilities even if the other parent is not water born? Would memory research with water babies yield important information? Sophrologist Dr. Raymond Abrezol observed water babies born at the Hawaiian Pre-Natal Cultural Center in Molokai, directed by Daniel Fritz. Here he met thirteen adults and ten children from Argentina, Canada, France, the U.S., and Switzerland. Parents-to-be were undergoing special training and diet at the ranch and also swimming daily with dolphins, he told us. He and his wife joined the babies and dolphins. He photographed Molokai's first water baby, four-month-old Lanica, as she took her daily underwater dip in the Pacific. From the Soviets he learned that delivery in water protects the baby's brain from strain and possible damage inflicted by a sudden transition to the world of gravity. Because the physical instrument through which the mind expresses is not damaged by birth, water babies seem to come with deep memories of prebirth life, and possibly even past lives, Abrezol speculates. Some seem to tap into "Far Memory" skills, talents, knowledge. (See chapter 22) The water babies are further strengthened by happy memories of their earth arrival. Many are so outstanding, their gravity-free births and identities are being kept secret.

"It seems the Russians are creating a production line of geniuses," says Abrezol. Reflecting further, he suddenly realized that not only were they creating geniuses, but that "this method would transform the way these children think! In growing up they would become *positive* thinkers." Happy prebirth time followed by machine-age birth engraves a memory sequence of happiness followed by fear, anger, and hyperstress in us, he says. Throughout our lives a tiny interior sublimi-

nal voice in us constantly warns, "Happiness is followed by trouble—
and hyperstress." The result is an angry, fearful, stressed, sick society,
fearful of true joy. Change the birth memory and you change the
society. Sophrologists like Abrezol have spent decades teaching people
to overcome anger, fear, and negative memory programming, to let the
natural, in-born genius shine.

In *Sophrologie et Evolution—Demain L'Homme,* he observes that
our society is a sick one. "If children born in ideal conditions with an
ideal education become geniuses . . . will they perhaps be the basis of
a new society marking the debut of the predicted 'Golden Age'?" he
wonders. Will these new beings help us create a better world of love
and intelligence—one without drugs or functional illnesses?

The thrilled Soviet parents of these "super babies" believe these
"children of the ocean" may be the forerunners of tomorrow's "children of the cosmos," reports *Omni—The New Frontier,* the first U.S.
TV program to air documentaries of Charkovsky's water babies in
July, 1990. Birth and baby-training in weightlessness underwater may
be the key to speeding up the evolution of mankind, observes *Omni*
narrator, Peter Ustinov, and to creating a new breed of superhuman-
beings who will ultimately adapt to the weightlessness of life in space.
By returning to the sea, we move toward the stars. Closer to earth,
Omni asks, "Are the tanks of water also the cradles of tomorrow's
Olympic champions?"

Several years ago, dolphin expert Timothy Wyllie, author of *The
DETA Factor,* traveled to New Zealand to The Underwater Birth Conference at the Rainbow Dolphin Centre in Keri Keri. A group of
twenty water babies and parents meditated with 200 conferees at a
Maori holy place. Wyllie noted that the water babies were highly telepathic seemingly able to be in a full harmonious group contact. According to Charkovsky, the delicate head chakras (energy centers) that
govern higher sensibilities like telepathy and psychokinesis are not
damaged by water birth. Are the water babies our next stage, a highly
evolved seed group whose function is to midwife the rest of us into a
new age, a group of Galactic Scouts sent out ahead? "This is just the
tip of what we are going to be seeing over the next decade," says
Wyllie.

This evolution speed-up has passed virtually unnoticed in the West
for many years because reports often verge on the incredible. Normally conservative observers have returned babbling to us and friends
in tabloid headline-ese. Some reports are even a bit reminiscent of
a recent tabloid gem: "Baby Arrives Singing & Dancing: Nurses

Amazed." Every century there've been a few spontaneous occurrences of babies with supermemory who make it into the history books, like Heinrich Heineken who could talk at ten months. Charkovsky documentaries reveal dozens of water babies who talk and develop talents much earlier.

How many of these exceptional evolved beings are there? A decade ago we saw documentaries of the Soviet water babies brought out of Russia by American filmmaker Dmitri Devyatkin. Many are now adults. Aside from those birthed at centers in Australia, New Zealand, Hawaii, and California, thousands more have arrived through a "parents' underground." Western medical establishment hostility has driven water-birthing into secrecy. A quiet major planetary plan is being carried out, Wyllie believes.

The water babies' anti-gravity birth memories, new ways of recalling and reprogramming our own birth memories, near-death memories, past-life memories, and memories from other altered states —all these memory breakthroughs may help carry us into a new age of consciousness, says Dr. David Chamberlain. They may help us "discover . . . who *we* are. . . ." More and more birth memories are coming up, enabling increasing numbers of us to see that human consciousness is something that exists at all times—before, during, and after birth."

10. Gray Matter Music

A throng of fans gathered around the novelist guest of honor at a crowded, noisy, Montreal publisher's party. As the group enthusiastically discussed her latest book, the novelist drew back with growing horror and apprehension. With a feeling of desperation, she realized she could *not hear* anything that was being said to her. Embarrassed and upset, she abruptly fled the scene.

"I can't go to any more of these parties," she later told her daughter on the phone to Paris. "Over the background noise, I can't hear a word," she lamented. The cross-vibrations of sound were a jumble to her. Hearing aids at that time didn't filter out just one person's voice from the surrounding crush of noise or music.

Patricia Joudry, a well-known Canadian author, playwright, and broadcaster, was grappling with the frightening realization that she was truly losing her hearing. It was a problem for her professional life. Her quirky hearing was a special kind of pain on the personal level. Crackling grocery bags were spears. Traffic noise was an artillery barrage. Sometimes, panic gripped her. Could this be the prelude to total deafness? It ran in the family. Her own mother had become deaf and totally isolated from human society.

"I've just heard of something that might help," her daughter said sympathetically. "It's a discovery they've made here in Paris called Sound Therapy. Dr. Alfred Tomatis, a famous ear, nose, and throat specialist, developed it. He's highly regarded and a member of the French Academy of Sciences. A Montreal doctor I know will be setting up a Sound Therapy clinic and you can try it!"

Game for anything, Pat Joudry found herself in the Montreal Sound Therapist's office several months later. Following hearing tests pinpointing her hearing loss, she put on headphones, not on her ears but over the mastoid bone and the bone at her temple. She heard soothing, classical music, occasionally interrupted by soft hissing sounds. The specially prepared music emanated from a huge control center, a kind of recording studio filled with banks of machines that whirred and blinked. The prescription:—just listen three hours daily for the next six weeks to this electronically altered music.

Week after week she commuted sixty miles round trip to Montreal to the little music den in the Sound Therapy office. Was it helping? She noticed no improvement. It was hard to explain what was going on, and the treatment did cost several thousand dollars. The music she heard was mostly Mozart—violin concertos, symphonies, chamber music. The filtering made it sound strange and eerie sometimes. As the weeks passed, the sounds seemed higher pitched. The fourth week offered Gregorian chants. Occasionally she was to record phrases herself and listen to her own voice filtered back at very high pitch. She was also taught a special humming technique. By the fifth week she was experiencing major exhaustion and could barely drag herself around. The commute was devastating. The Sound Therapist said, "Good! It means the therapy's working! The middle ear is adjusting."

Then one day as Joudry drove home she began humming to herself. Suddenly she wasn't tired. She was brimming with new energy. She could stay up late at night, get up with just a few hours sleep, and feel totally refreshed. Insomnia vanished. Calm, pure energy seemed to spark through her whole body. Best of all, her mind and memory seemed to develop laserlike speed and clarity. Creativity soared. Writer's block was gone. A new novel bubbled up effortlessly. Now she felt as if she were in a perpetual state of exultation.

"I feel as though I've been plugged into the cosmos," she told the Sound Therapist.

Next came the hearing test. Could she hear the therapist while the music played through the headphones? She could. The audiometric tests confirmed it. The graphs traced out proof that her hearing was normal again.

She couldn't believe it until she conducted her own tests. She rushed into a department store. Could she hear the store clerk over the Muzak and babble of voices all around? She could! At the gas station with traffic noise all around—she could hear the attendant. At home with her family, her daughters could talk at the same time and she could hear each of them.

At her final music session, she begged the therapist, "Can't I continue this treatment at home? What if the effect wears off?"

"The equipment costs $20,000 and in addition you have to have the technical know-how to use it properly," he said.

But as the weeks passed, the radiant creative energy began to wane. Fatigue returned. Mental clarity retreated. Joudry's hearing remained cured, but dreaded writer's block struck.

However, whenever mind, memory, and energy needed a lift, she could simply make an appointment for a Sound Therapy session and inspiration flowed anew. Every music session yielded the wondrous mental boost: limitless vitality, serenity, joy, and a drugless high.

She became fascinated with her sound experience. What was Sound Therapy and what exactly had she been through? She felt absolutely compelled to live near places where Sound Therapy was available.

However, two years later, unexpected circumstances obliged her to give up her home near Montreal and move west to Saskatchewan. There she found herself under vaulting prairie skies on a remote farm. She was now thousands of miles away from the music that was ambrosia for her brain. She felt as if she'd been abruptly unplugged from the cosmos. Every day for two years she schemed new ways of getting back east to the soaring creativity and brilliant mental energy of Sound Therapy.

One day at dinner in her prairie farmhouse, a guest said, "Have you ever heard of St. Peter's Abbey in Muenster? They're using Sound Therapy with the students at St. Peter's College there."

She toppled over her chair. Muenster, Saskatchewan? The merest pinpoint on the map on the road to Saskatoon. Out of the thousands of miles of vast Canadian prairie she had somehow landed just forty-eight miles from "the kingdom."

The High Tech Monks of Muenster

Joudry was in Muenster the next morning at dawn. As Dorothy said to her dog when she landed in Oz, it was definitely an—"I don't think we're in Kansas anymore, Toto" kind of experience.

Shimmering under the prairie sun, St. Peter's looked like a monastery that might have landed on the prairies after a few orbits in outer space. Past stately gardens were rooms that looked like the command bridge of the spaceship Enterprise. They were crammed with decks of gleaming and glistening, whirring and blinking electronic equipment. The head of this evolutionary operation was a bearded monk, not in robes but in blue jeans and sneakers.

Father Lawrence De Mong of St. Peter's believed groups such as theirs should be at the cutting edge of new frontiers. That's why he'd installed many thousands of dollars worth of special sound studio and sound therapy electronic equipment and the new Electronic Ear. He had a vision of pioneering new heights in education, health, and personal transformation. Students had to put in several hours of listening each term. They just plugged in the headphones and went to sleep on the couches in the large bright listening room.

And something amazing was happening. Learning disabilities were vanishing. Students with long-term severe speech defects were 80% cured; cases of dyslexia, emotional disturbance, hyperactivity, hearing problems—all had yielded to the listening treatment. Students felt calm, relaxed, and stress-free. Concentrating was easy. And best of all, that radiant creative energy flowed steadily, improving mental performance in every sphere.

After she'd had dinner with the brothers, Father Lawrence handed Joudry a key. "Feel free to use the Sound Therapy center any time you wish, day or night." He quickly showed her where the special music tapes were kept and how to operate the equipment. "Music at 8,000 hertz gives the quickest recharge." He smiled, and sped off to prayers.

Joudry could hardly believe it. She had the key to the "kingdom"— and it was free! The large, bright "Buck Rogers" rooms filled with couches, headphones, electronic equipment, and mazes of wires soon became her second home. Within a week of listening to the special music, that dynamic mental clarity was back, the radiant, nonstop energy was back and so was the blossoming creativity.

Decoding Music That's Ambrosia for the Brain

The music program was the same one she'd experienced in Montreal. Now Joudry could unlock its secrets. Monitoring instruments showed that the low notes were filtered out of the classical music. The stereo favored right-ear dominance. Then these tapes were played through the Electronic Ear, Dr. Tomatis's invention, which bombards the inner ear with certain high frequency sounds that gradually allow the ear to hear a wider and higher range of frequencies. It made a slightly abrasive hissing noise mingled with the music. The sequence of selections made little difference; it just had to have high-frequency sounds in at least the 8,000 hertz and higher range. Those high sounds seemed to be ambrosia for the brain. After hearing the frequencies for 100 to 200 hours, the brain seemed to become harmonized and energized and sent out signals to reset the whole system.

One day as she arrived at 5 A.M. at the monastery, Father Lawrence spotted the Sony Walkman Joudry wore for her one-hour commute. A frequency response of 16,000 hertz—a portable tape player with a frequency response high enough to be used for the Sound Therapy music and the Electronic Ear effect! Within days they had metal cassettes of the music program and a revolution was born.

Until then, neither Father Lawrence nor the other monks had had time to spend several hours a day chained to headphones in the music listening center. Now with the Walkmans, they could have the phenomenal, healing, energizing benefits of this special mind music wherever they were. The student program could go mobile too. They could listen on Walkmans right in the college classrooms.

Joudry was ecstatic. Now she could take that precious music with her anywhere. It was like a stress shield to her no matter what happened, even when her aged Volvo broke down three times en route to the supermarket.

Couldn't others use this marvelous vitalizing sound? Who couldn't use a better mind and memory, more talents, more energy, more time, more serenity, more life? If the marvelous mind music could go mobile on Walkmans, it could reach thousands of people who had no access to Sound Therapy centers. But would people playing the special sound treatment on Walkmans get the same benefits that they got from the program at the regular therapy institutes?

She would have to create entirely new experimental music tapes and circulate them to the general public to find out. Joudry, a former technophobe who could barely change a fuse, soon found that she was a sophisticated sound engineer, devising a whole series of classical music cassettes featuring soaring high frequencies, filtered bass, fluctuating ear dominance, and special re-recording through the Electronic Ear. "The music did it," she says. It opened up a whole range of new potentials for her—and in particular, a new talent for technology.

Father Lawrence soon found that the Walkman with special music cured his insomnia. His energy bubbled over. He drove 2500 miles nonstop without sleep.

Soon the whole college was on Walkmans, including the monks, nuns, and janitors. At the Ursuline Convent in nearby Bruno, two elderly nuns suffering from Alzheimer's were put on the Walkman Sound Therapy. Six weeks later nurses reported the patients "greatly improved—more settled, less hyper, and enjoying the music."

High-frequency Sounds That Power Mind/Memory

Test subjects wrote in from everywhere. "After three days I was aware of an energy and mental clarity such as I had not experienced since before entering University, many years earlier," wrote Dr. Cliff

Bacchus from the Bahamas. An author and member of the American Academy of Physicians, he enthused, "My creative doors flew open . . . I now sleep better, think better, write better. . . ." He'd had zero dream recall before, suppressing the edges of nightmares. Now he had detailed, vivid dream recall and they were clear, happy dreams.

Linda Taylor-Anderson of Florida, author of *Carousing in the Kitchen*, found the sound recharged "my internal batteries that provide calm energy and a feeling of well-being."

Darrell Johnson, of Delisle, Saskatchewan, who suffered with Meniere's Syndrome (ringing in the ear, light-headedness, and dizziness) reported symptoms had cleared up after ten weeks. Fatigue and stress were gone. "It's like a new life."

John Westerhof's parents in Winnipeg reported, "Our son's showing terrific improvement in reading." His dyslexia had cleared up in two months of listening. He was off Ritalin prescribed for his learning disabilities. "It is like a miracle. . . ."

Parents of Carla Gaunt, a brain damaged, mentally handicapped Saskatoon teenager, told Joudry that Carla's speech and memory improved within three months—"great improvement in her ability to handle stress."

"Sound Therapy has transformed my life," wrote James Bragg of Kentucky. He'd gotten over a speech problem he'd had from childhood and also recovered from a hearing problem. He was over depression. "Energy is greatly increased; stamina and endurance greatly improved."

A Buffalo, New York, graduate student found not only enhanced learning abilities but recovery from fear of public speaking. "I call it Confidence Therapy."

Courtney Milne, a professional photographer with a grueling schedule, reported he now has "great inner calm" and never feels "harried or exhausted."

"Improved concentration," "ability to focus my mind," "improved memory and learning ability," "peace and tranquility," "boundless supply of energy," "easier, more efficient sleep," "sleep time shortened by two or three hours a night," "improved hearing," "recovery from hearing loss caused by aging," "recovery from disorders stemming from imbalance of inner ear fluid: nausea, dizziness, tinnitus," "recovery from stammering and speech defects," "help for dyslexia, hyperactivity, and behavioral problems," "cured snoring," "helped autism," "recovery from stress-related disorders from headaches to digestive problems. . . ."

Some people found the Sound Therapy helped them lose weight. The boundless energy and stress alleviation seemed to help weight problems to normalize.

Soon Joudry's test files were overflowing. *All* reported improvement —major or minor. It seemed the portable cassette system could definitely produce results for do-it-yourselfers. Though of course they were not exactly the *same* results that would be produced in a clinic with a Sound Therapist testing and monitoring, on the plus side, the effects did not wear off.

She had enough material for a book—*Sound Therapy for the Walkman*—an extremely lucid account, with an introduction by her friend, famed violinist Yehudi Menuhin. After the book was published in 1984 in Saskatchewan, Joudry was inundated with worldwide requests for the high-frequency music tapes. The Muenster monks worked tirelessly, hand-copying—not illuminated manuscripts as in other centuries—but "illuminating" music cassettes in "real time," and made them available for sale from St. Peter's Press. And something evolutionary began emanating from those distant Canadian prairies.

Mrs. Joe Bentley of Edmonton, Alberta, wrote that her daughter, a pianist, had suffered a severe bicycling accident, smashed her head on the pavement—two skull fractures, brain concussion, and coma. Diagnosis: she would never speak, walk, or have a memory. After five weeks listening to Joudry's tapes she could play the piano again and read music. Mrs. Bentley read Joudry's book aloud to her daughter. After six months of tape listening, she could read again, slowly. "The tapes have done so much for her. We thank you for all the help you have given our daughter."

Seventy-nine-year-old Marie Lyons of Newport Beach, California, was struggling with "inappropriate dopiness." After four months of steady listening, "foggy bottom has cleared. I am enjoying unaccustomed alertness and vivacity all my waking hours."

Elsie Edson of British Columbia found six weeks with the tapes calmed her frazzled nerves and cleared migraine headaches. "My thinking is clear and I have a strong sense of well-being."

Lorna Graham of New Brunswick who suffers from multiple sclerosis found the tapes helped stabilize her energy. "Nothing else has helped me the way the tapes have."

From Reba Adams, RN, of Dallas, Texas: Her eighty-two year-old mother, who'd suffered a massive coronary, had to live with her so she could care for her. After four months listening, the doctor said her mother was doing so well, she could now live alone again. "I give most of the credit to the Sound Therapy."

"It feels as if my mind has been put through a shower," wrote another. "Like having a new head"—"the sound clarifies my mind to a high sheen"—"sheer heaven"—"glowing feeling"—"tuned to the joy of life." The same reactions poured in from Canada, the U.S., and twenty-six countries.

Joudry told us, "First, improvement in memory, concentration, retention, and ease of learning is invariably reported by S.T. listeners. Parents report that they don't have to tell things to their offspring repeatedly anymore," she said, "and older people tell us that they too can retain information instead of it passing through their minds sieve-like. This is because Sound Therapy (among its other effects) unblocks neural pathways," says Joudry.

Various users speculate that Sound Therapy could give us an evolutionary boost because of this ability to deblock brain pathways. "It should be literally possible to leap from brilliant to genius through Sound Therapy," enthused Rollin Rose of Riverside, California.

Joudry recalled one man who was seriously dyslexic and had dropped out of school quite early. He found that after a few months of S.T. he was able to write and pass his high-school exams and graduate in his thirties. "The material made sense to him at last and stayed in his mind."

Musical memory too seemed stimulated. Maureen Imlach, a British Columbia music teacher wrote that after a few months of S.T., "I am thinking more clearly . . . I was amazed how quickly I re-learned repertoire not played for YEARS—the fingers and muscles seemed to know how to work without hours of labour. . . ." Months later without any practicing she could play well and *from memory* this same repertoire. "So that HAS to be Sound Therapy."

As research into Superlearning had shown, alert/relaxed states seem to help memory and mind function better. Joudry told us, "The *one main* effect that almost everyone reports from the therapy, regardless of the great variety of other conditions affected, *is stress relief.* They use almost the same words: "I am not stressed anymore. All the little things that used to make me uptight just seem to roll off me. I can shrug them off and not let them get to me. . . . So I feel that memory is being improved, and not always noticed."

Dr. Lois Plumb, a Toronto psychiatrist, uses the S.T. tapes herself and to aid patients with severe childhood traumas. The improved mental function helped suppressed memories to surface and the built-in stress shield aided patients in dealing with the painful recollections.

The tapes were soon used in prisons for behavioral problems and in schools for healing learning disabilities.

Joudry's determined commitment to make the Sound Therapy process more widely available took her on lengthy lecture and promotional tours. Soon there were thousands of "high-frequency freaks" and "trekkies" into new potentials of mind and memory. There was even a kind of "Mozart mania." That was too revolutionary for some of the old guard sound therapists. They brought lawsuits and demanded that Joudry's book be *banned*. Some bookstores even complied. The general public was not supposed to find out some of the amazing, little-known secrets behind vitalizing sound.

11.   The "Ear Force": The Overlooked Memory Power

It was deeply quiet at a remote Benedictine monastery in France. A young abbot had instituted new reforms. "Less chanting, more practical work," he ordered the monks. Soon he noticed they were growing sluggish. They slept longer hours but were still exhausted. A consulting physician put them on a conventional diet. But matters grew rapidly worse.

French ear specialist Dr. Alfred Tomatis was called in. Seventy of the ninety monks were sitting in their cells doing nothing, withdrawn like schizoid beings. He reintroduced their lengthy chanting schedule and the monastery rang with sound again. Soon, he said, they were sleeping less, working more, and feeling better.

"Some sounds are as good as two cups of coffee. Gregorian chants are a fantastic energy source. I work with them as background music and sleep only three or four hours each night," said Tomatis. Waking up and charging up the brain with taped sound to enhance memory and nourish the mind is one of the most promising breakthroughs around. To boost brainpower, Tomatis examined Gregorian chants and other music with an oscilloscope to see which sound frequencies emitted powerhouse energy and which sounds depleted energy.

Your ear is your primary organ of consciousness, says Dr. Tomatis. It is made not only for hearing, but is also intended to use sound to provide a charge of electrical potential to the brain. The cortex then distributes the resulting charge throughout your body. Tomatis has focused his research on the therapeutic effects of sound, the music of composers such as Mozart, and spiritual voice exercises such as chanting OM and Gregorian chants, which generate serenity and power.

Stress? Burnout? Fatigue? It could be your central gray nuclei. These cells in the cortex of the brain act like small electrical batteries, according to Tomatis. They generate the electricity for the brain to produce the electrical brainwaves you see in your EEG. Tomatis spent years researching how these "brain batteries" charged and discharged.

Inside the mysterious spirals of the snail-shaped cochlea of the inner ear there are 24,600 special sensory cells, the Corti cells. His discovery —the "brain batteries" were not charged by brain metabolism—they were recharged externally, by stimulating the Corti cells in this basal portion of the cochlea of the inner ear with sound. As he observed the process with monitoring equipment, he zeroed in on the precise frequencies. *High frequencies sped up the recharging process of the brain batteries.*

As sound was transformed into energy in the ear, he found that the cortex redistributed the energy throughout the body's entire nervous system, providing a beneficial dynamic flow to mind and body. Sound, transmitted along the auditory nerves, did two things: one nerve branch dynamized the brain cortex and the other branch, the vestibular nerve, determined posture and muscle tone throughout the body. It is this dual function of the auditory nerves that allows sound to recharge the mind and at the same time release stress and tone muscles. The ear, Tomatis observed, both sends and receives. As the ear transmutes sound into energy and sends it to the cortex, the cortex transmits feedback to the ear.

Can you just switch on your stereo and instantly recharge your brain cells? Not exactly, not unless you're already an inner ear athlete. The beneficial sounds can't help you if you can't hear them. To be able to hear high frequencies, most people have to have the inner ear "opened." To do this, Tomatis invented the Electronic Ear, a device that is like a "fitness center for the middle ear." Past your eardrum are aptly named structures, "hammer, anvil, and stirrup," operated by muscles that must tense and release and adjust the eardrum so you can hear properly. Tomatis found that varied high/low frequency sounds gave the middle ear a gymnastic workout so that it reopened its high-frequency hearing power.

He had a breakthrough! Once the middle ear had been tuned to high-frequency response, then the brain responded swiftly to the recharge. *Ear Force = Brain Force.* He saw the ear system in terms of electronics as an oscillator and resonator. Your vast, natural, cosmic vitality could be restored through the ear! And there is never any shortage of cosmic energy. Tomatis viewed the ear/brain link as a cybernetic system—the ear is meant to benefit the entire organism psychologically and physically.

8000 Hertz—Key To Mind Energy

But which particular high frequencies are the most potent for the brain? Seeking to decode the sounds that power the mind, Tomatis painstakingly worked through the spectrum of high-frequency sounds. His quest was an ancient one. The idea that specific tones can affect mind and body had been handed down from the earliest Semitic and Arabic sacred knowledge. Pythagoras drew on this knowledge to devise a modal music system which he said influenced both the gods and mankind—one mode banished depression, another grief, another passion. Pythagoras linked the frequency resonances to the planets, colors, and numbers.

After much experimenting, Tomatis discovered that the most powerful frequency for rapidly recharging the brain cortex was in the 8000 Hertz range, a note almost at the end of the violin's E string before going to overtones. Magnetic maps of the brain confirm that the brain resonates to certain sounds.

Brain Drain Sounds

Low-frequency sounds, on the other hand, he found, could act as brain drain sounds—poison for the brain. Low-frequency noise from traffic, airports, or construction sites not only could induce hearing loss but could actually drain the brain of energy. Sound pollution is yet another contributor to memory smog. Low pounding sounds of rock music are designed to force you into mechanical movement, Tomatis says, but can discharge your mental and physical energy. European studies show noxious environmental noise can cause high blood pressure and heart disease.

A recent breakthrough, magnetic brain-mapping (MEG) reveals that specific areas of the brain are tuned to specific tone frequencies. It seems our brains are like tuning forks. As Drs. Sam Williamson and Lloyd Kauffman of New York University beamed different tones at the brain, magnetic fields shifted, indicating that different frequencies do resonate different brain areas. Because low-frequency sounds discharge brain/body energy, when Tomatis linked his Electronic Ear with classical music, he found benefits increased when notes in the music under 2000 Hz. (about three octaves above middle C) were filtered out.

At the beginning of life, we all possess a wide-range keyboard of hearing—we hear sound waves pulsing from 16 cycles a second to 20,000. But both psychological and physical pressures can cause our hearing range to shrink. Noise pollution today has made hearing loss extremely widespread. Through Sound Therapy, combining filtered, high-frequency music with the Electronic Ear, Tomatis found a way to reopen hearing and nourish the brain and memory.

Dr. Tomatis' discoveries have been extensively tested over several decades. The Sorbonne University in Paris confirmed them too. His work is enshrined in science as "The Tomatis Effect." He was made a member of the French Academy of Medicine and the Academy of Science. He founded a whole new scientific discipline called Audio-Psycho-Phonology (APP), and the research fills volumes of scientific journals and books.

For over thirty years European therapists have used Tomatis' approach with great success to alleviate problems like deafness, epilepsy, hyperactivity, and autism. Stutterers found a cure too. Healthy people —singers, actors, public speakers, even language teachers have benefited greatly from his pioneering. Now, with the advance of electronics, perhaps everyone can tune in to boost brain vitality and a whole range of brain superpowers.

"We read with our ears," insists Tomatis. It seems, in particular, with our *right* ear! It was one of his most intriguing discoveries. He observed that the left ear has a longer, less efficient route to the language center in the brain. Could this lag time account for reading and speech problems? Working with thousands of dyslexics, Tomatis and colleagues opened their hearing to high frequencies and then fed more sound to the right ear than the left through earphones. 12,000 dyslexics in Europe and Africa were cured. What would happen if you read aloud and could only hear yourself through your left ear on earphones? A Belgian sound therapist, Dr. E. Spirig of Anvers, had people do just that. Normal volunteers soon became "magnificent dyslexics." Today, learning disabilities such as dyslexia are of epidemic proportions. And so are ear infections. Could reading, learning, and remembering be vastly improved with the Tomatis right-ear treatment?

Tests with actors showed that if they monitored themselves with the left ear while they spoke, they had difficulty with concentration, attention, fatigue—all things that affect memory. Conversely, singers who monitored themselves with the right ear through earphones as they sang, had more harmonics, better voice, and timbre, and felt a sense of well-being. People who speak well, act, or sing invariably have right ear dominance, reports Tomatis. His right ear training is now incorporated into the Sound Therapy program tapes and has proven a boon to those with a wide range of speech problems.

Stress, as we know, muffles memory. When the vestibular nerve (second branch of the auditory nerve) is stimulated with high-frequency sound, it tones and relaxes muscles throughout the entire body and is a powerful stress releaser, thus empowering memory. But effects can go far beyond even relaxation. Medical documents show spastic children and people with severe muscle problems have been greatly helped.

The Ear Force and Acupuncture

Why does the "ear force" have such a wide ranging effect on the body? In France, acupuncture was explored early and is widely practiced. Tomatis noted that acupuncture theory holds that the *entire body* is reflected holographically as points on the outer ear. (see diagram p. 173). Acupuncturists treat these ear points to stimulate and energize internal organs. Perhaps high frequency sounds conveyed through earphones over these points provide a sonic acupuncture treatment to the entire body. This may explain why symptoms as varied as phantom leg pain, high blood pressure, and tinnitus all yield to Sound Therapy. Acupuncturists maintain that chi (bioplasmic energy) circulates on meridians through the body. Apparently chi is highly sensitive to sound, and sound can travel these acupuncture pathways to reset and reorder de-energized conditions. This is the principle of another recent technological breakthrough—sonic acupuncture. Pioneered in Canada by Dr. Patrick Pillai of The Acupuncture Foundation of Sri Lanka and Niels Primdahl of Electro Medica of Toronto, Sonapuncture uses a sound wave generator, the Sonafon which emits mixed sound frequencies in the 10,000 hertz range. So far, tests show intrasonic acupuncture to be just as effective as needle acupuncture or electronic acupuncture.

The major acupuncture point for whole body anesthesia is #86 on the Heart/Lung meridian, on the shell of the ear. Electrically stimulating this point has now been proven to produce endorphins—the body's own natural pain/stress relievers and pleasure producers. Research in Hong Kong showed specific electrical frequencies enhance endorphin production. (See p. 326) There would seem to be endorphin-producing sound frequencies widespread throughout Sound Therapy classical music selections. These sound frequencies must stimulate this point on

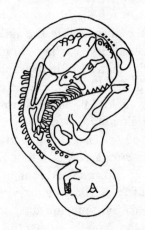

Our ears are an upside-down reflection of the entire body, says acupuncture theory and recent research. The diagram shows body treatment points on the ear. Addiction and withdrawal symptoms are treated on the lung meridian points on the lower ear shell.

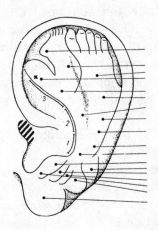

Stimulating these lower ear shell points with needles or certain electricity or sound frequencies has been shown to produce endorphines—the body's own natural pain/stress relievers and pleasure producers.

the ear through the earphones because virtually all Sound Therapy tape listeners report stress/pain relief and many report euphoria.

Yet another breakthrough makes visible the links between sound and chi energy. The Soviet discovery, Kirlian photography, an imaging process that uses electricity instead of light to photograph, reveals a brilliantly colored, light-filled field of energy around living things. Clearly visible in the energy fields of humans are the acupuncture points, showing as intensely glowing centers. Soviet biophysicists report that stimulation with sound, laser light, and colored lights all have a profound effect on the circulation of chi or bioplasmic energy. Photos show different kinds of music affect your biofield in a host of different ways. Before and after Kirlian pictures were taken of the finger of a person listening to baroque music, Bach's *Brandenburg* Concerto. After the music, the biofield of her finger changed to a fluted, more patterned light display.

Another surprising discovery was made recently about the "ear force." Italian physiologist Hugo Zucarelli revealed that our ears actually *emit sound*. Ear sound beams work like a kind of radar or reference beam. Through ear sound beams, we're able to tell which direction a sound is coming from. This is the basis of Zucarelli's 3-D sound recordings—Holophonics. Holophonics evokes synesthesia in many people—hear a match strike and you smell the sulphur; hear the crunch and taste the apple. This new sound discovery could greatly enhance full sense imaging to help memory and learning. Is this an easy electronic route to the sort of imaging done by Veniamin, the man who remembered everything? Would Sound Therapy be even more powerful if high-frequency sounds were recorded in holophonics?

"Giant Cricket" Music—Fiddler on the Grass

Tomatis discovered high-frequency sounds that can energize human beings and cure many afflictions. Another researcher has found high-frequency sounds so potent they could cure world hunger. That's what plant researcher, Dan Carlson of Blaine, Minnesota, believes he has discovered. For years, various observers had noticed that plants sometimes seemed to grow faster and larger when exposed to music, especially classical music. However, results were inconsistent. After many years of extensive research, Carlson isolated a *specific high-frequency in the 5000 hertz range*. Playing these high-frequency tones on an oscillating sound generator, he discovered that 5000 Hz makes plants

Effects of Music

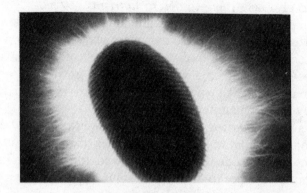

Different sound frequencies in music alter the body's chi energy circulation which recent research show is powerfully linked to memory. Before/after Kirlian photos of the biofiled of a finger of a person listening to baroque music show the biofield became more fluted and patterned after the music.

breathe better. If plants could breathe better through sonics, could the same sound also help them to *absorb nutrients* better?

Carlson decided to try growth stimulants on the test plants at the same time the high-frequency sounds were played. Results were spectacular. His sonics seemed to cause plants to absorb nutrients sprayed on their leaves with up to a whopping *700% greater efficiency than normal.* Sonics alone or spray alone produced modest effects. Together, they were dynamite!

Carlson's special *pulsed high-frequency sonics* of around 5000 Hz. produced on an oscillator, sounded a lot like a giant cricket chirping in a meadow. He imbedded the pulsed sound in Oriental, Indian, or classical music on tapes to develop a unique and listenable sound pattern—special dinner music for plants.

He played the special music tapes daily for half an hour and sprayed the plants with diluted plant nutrients (hormones and amino acids). The result? A phenomenal 99% growth increase for *any* plant. A 4½" purple passion plant treated to "giant cricket music" with dinner grew to *1400 feet* long in 2 ½ years. (Normal size—18". That plant grew right into the *Guinness Book of World Records.*)

There was lots of competition: a 15 foot tomato plant with 836 tomatoes; rose bushes with 75 blooms each; double yields on beans and potatoes; Jojoba seeds that expanded 40% bigger and germinated in 20 days instead of 1 to 5 months.

Since then, Carlson has demonstrated that various plant yields can increase two to tenfold with his sound/spray treatment. He took over an old plantation in Hawaii with elderly, spindly trees and soon had everblooming trees producing 25-fold harvests of delicious avocados and macadamia nuts. Thousands of users and many science labs have now confirmed his results. Carlson believes that sound/spray treatment could aid famine-stricken areas. The plants produced by the treatment are also more nutritious; they've absorbed nutrients better. He found that the sound could help replace chemical fertilizer. He grew trees so rapidly he believes the method could also help solve the greenhouse effect.

Like Tomatis, Carlson, working in the completely different fields of botany and agriculture, also discovered numerous ways in which high-frequency sounds can provide powerful benefits to living systems.

Does high-frequency sound work on both plants and humans in the same way? Could the Tomatis high-frequency sounds affect cell respiration in humans too? If you listened to high-frequency music at dinner would it also increase *your* absorption of nutrients? (As health food researchers are fond of saying, it's not what you eat, it's what you absorb.) Indian researchers studying Ayurvedic medicine chanted mantras over growing plants twice daily. Herbal medicines made from these plants were tested on a number of illnesses, particularly female problems. They proved more effective and potent than those extracted from mantra deprived plants. Pat Joudry noted that listening to high frequencies after eating prevented drowsiness after she ate big meals.

Instead of the wider ranging Sound Therapy music, would Carlson's pulsing 5000 hertz tones work for humans as well as plants? Could Carlson's "giant cricket" sounds help improve mind and memory also? Tomatis researchers found 8000 hertz seemed to give the fastest recharge to the brain cortex. However, high-frequency classical music would certainly contain 5000 hertz sounds too, and music is pulsed in structure.

Could these discoveries be applied in other areas? For instance, medical monitoring instruments that bleep out sounds by the hour beside patients—could these devices be pitched to higher, more helpful frequencies?

Longevity and Supersleep

It's often been noted that symphony orchestra conductors, who experience a daily diet of high-frequency sound from classical music, tend to lead very long, active lives. "Perhaps the greatest bounty of the Tomatis Effect is its gift of time," says *Sound Therapy* author Pat Joudry. Through Sound Therapy, you can accumulate a different kind of "retirement savings program," she says. You can accumulate the "fundamental currency of life energy" which flows through the sound/brain connection. Unless it is kept toned up, says Joudry, the brain merely deteriorates with the advance of years. Instead, with Sound Therapy, the ear can become the antenna for life force. As mentioned, stimulation keeps memory alive in the elderly, lack of it brings memory loss.

Joudry and her growing thousands of S.T. users often experience the phenomenon of "hypersomnia" or *Supersleep*. It's concentrated, compressed, doubly efficient sleep because the system has been energized and tranquilized through brain recharge. Supersleep is so restorative, that less of it is needed. Most S.T. users cut sleep by two to three hours a night. By Joudry's calculation you've lengthened your life by one sixth. If you are forty, with an eighty year life expectancy, it's a gift of an extra six super years. "More time means more life," says Joudry.

She found there was an incomparable feeling of richness about having abundant time, energy, and expanded mental faculties.

Sound Therapy—Insider Tips

We purchased the Joudry tapes and tested them over a period of many months. We found they really *do* give an extra energy boost. One of the authors observed that on days when she didn't listen to them, she felt a dip in energy. We did find the high-frequency hissing noise produced on the tapes by the Electronic Ear process was a bit irritating at first, but overcame it by listening with the volume low.

As for plants, one of us became a strolling player for her plants' dinner and performed the "giant cricket" tone on the violin (around the 2nd highest D on the E string) and misted the plants. A jade and rubber plant have both reached tree size.

Q. Could just listening to regular tapes of Mozart's high-frequency symphonies untreated by the Tomatis process give positive results too?

A. The full Sound Therapy music process includes: suppression of lower frequency bands below 2000 hertz; right ear stereo dominance; filtration through the Electronic Ear—yielding bursts of varied high/low-frequency sound alternating binaurally. Joudry has produced classical music tapes featuring both full and partial versions of the S.T. process and has still gotten good results. A British audiologist is conducting tests of Mozart's music without the processing. If you're playing regular music tapes, the tape recorder controls may allow you to turn up the treble and direct more sound to the right ear. If your ear is already opened to hearing high frequencies (a hearing test shows this), you'd probably be able to benefit from regular recordings. If you can't hear high frequencies, you'd need the full Electronic Ear treatment.

Q. Would listening to the tapes on speakers (car or stereo) work as well as headphones?

A. Apparently speakers give just modest effects. The headphones place the sound directly on the acupuncture points of the ear and also direct more sound to the right ear.

Q. Couldn't the powerful high-frequency tones be played on their own without the music?

A. That would probably be irritatingly impossible to listen to. Even the plants have their special tone imbedded in music. However, special music could be composed either highlighting or imbedding the most powerful tones. As Mnemosyne, the goddess of memory, was mother of all the arts, it's not surprising that the ancients encoded special secrets into the patterns of music—healing powers for mind and memory.

Ear specialist Dr. Jenkins-Lee of the Cleveland Hearing and Speech Center also believes the inner ear is like an electrical-chemical complex and, much like a car battery, can be recharged through the hearing apparatus. He broadcasts a low-frequency *radio* signal to the auditory nerves through a headset to stimulate and reactivate hearing and the whole system. Dr. William McGarey observes, "All the cells of the body are actually galvanic electrical units," and thus capable of being recharged.

Q. If high-frequency and baroque orchestral music of the past produced so many mind/body benefits, why weren't our ancestors all vitally healthy geniuses?

A. The number of people in past eras who ever got to hear full orchestras play these particular classical selections was very small, mainly aristocrats, church congregations, musicians, and physicians. In addition, they didn't have the complete methodology for therapeutic use of these orchestral sounds or the chance to listen to them for 100s of hours. However, ancient physicians of many cultures did use music to regulate heartbeat, cure melancholy, and regulate the body's "vapours" (probably electromagnetic fields). Contemporary recording technology has put music in the general public's hands for the first time in history. The Sony Walkman celebrated its tenth birthday in 1989. It's "revolutionized cultures around the world . . . For the first time . . . we now have the ability to program our lives to music," says New Age musician/author Steve Halpern. Joudry feels that it's been her contribution to make the previously restricted and little-known high-frequency Sound Therapy system available to the general public on cassettes for the Walkman.

Q. How long before improvements are felt?

A. Joudry suggests 100 to 200 hours of listening are needed. Three hours a day for about a month should begin to recharge the brain cells. You can listen on a Walkman at any time, while shopping, working around the house, or even while sleeping. Sound Therapists caution while you're trying to get recharged, cut down on the number of hours of heavy rock you listen to. If you listen to an equal number of hours of heavy rock featuring brain-drain low frequencies, the discharging low sounds will cancel out all the brain recharge the high frequencies provide. The high-frequency music cannot do harm and the longer you listen to it, the better, she says. At present, the tapes are not mass produced because high-speed tape duplicating machines suppress the high frequencies. The tapes are copied in real time on metal tape. Compact disc technology probably will remedy this situation. The Sony Walkman is recommended because it has the highest frequency response—up to 16,000 hertz which will even capture overtones. While Dr. Tomatis favors Mozart's music because it features very high frequencies, Joudry found baroque and many others with suitably high frequencies—Handel, Vivaldi, Boccherini, Rossini, Telemann, Haydn, Bach, and Tchaikovsky.

Boom boxes, boom cars, booming discos—a large percentage of the current generation is hooked on sound stimulation. It's a craving to stimulate the brain, Tomatis thinks. But in his opinion, they're going about it inefficiently. The more of this music they play, the more tired they'll eventually feel, and the louder they'll play the sound, says Dr. Tomatis. The recharging sounds of high frequencies are what's really needed, he says, to tone up body and mind and nourish memory.

We are all going to need to up our frequencies, says author-researcher Chris Griscom in her book *Ecstasy Is A New Frequency,* in order to survive and flourish in the new age. So perhaps it's up, up, and away with the "ear force."

Music That Makes You Smarter—Superlearning Music®

Superlearning Music is music to learn faster by. Really, it's supermemory music. Iowa State University tests found it upped learning by 24% and revealed even greater improvement in memory—26%. Scientific studies over the past thirty years show that people listening to this slow baroque music move into a state of *alert* relaxation, ideal for mental accomplishment. The music helps synchronize right and left hemispheres of your brain. It helps bring mind and body into powerful harmony. The slow, comforting tempo—about one beat per second—has been found to lower blood pressure and to entrain heartbeat, brainwaves, and other body rhythms into slower more efficient rhythms (see chart).

Superlearning Music-induced relaxation overcomes fatigue and increases physical and emotional well-being. It eases stress-related symptoms. Like mantra meditation, it is a mind/body link that helps open up inner awareness. Yet with this "Baroque Brain Booster" you don't have to do anything—the music does it for you effortlessly.

The ideal music, proven in accelerated learning experiments in lab and classroom in both Soviet Bloc and Western countries, the special music documented to enhance learning and memory, is music by 17th and 18th century composers such as Vivaldi, Telemann, and Bach. Just the slow, soothing, serene music is used—the largo (slow) movements from concertos, with a restful tempo of 60 beats a minute. Of course, this number is an average, and tempo can be from 55 to 65 beats a minute, and may fluctuate within a single selection. Music composed in this style by contemporary composers is also suitable as is music from other cultures such as the slow portions of Japanese Koto music.

Physiological Changes During Supermemory Sessions Compared to TM

	Supermemory Concert of Slow baroque Music (60 b.p.m.) During Intense Mental Activity (learning 100 foreign words)	Transcendental Meditation (Reciting a mantra)
Electroencephalogram (Alpha brain waves: 7–13 cycles per sec. Beta brain waves: over 13 cycles per sec. Theta brain waves: 4–7 cycles per sec.)	Alpha brain waves increase by an average of 6%. Beta brain waves decrease by an average of 6%. Theta waves unchanged.	Alpha brain waves increase. Some increase in Theta waves.
Pulse	Pulse slows by an average of 5 beats per minute.	Decreases significantly with a mean decrease of 5 beats per minute.
Blood Pressure	Blood pressure drops slightly (4 divisions of the mercury column on an average).	Tendency to decrease with intermediate fluctuations.
Body Motility	Sitting comfortably. Body relaxed.	Sitting comfortably. Body relaxed.
Awareness	Relaxed concentration	"Restful alertness"

Music therapist Janalea Hoffman, working at the University of Kansas, composed music with the 60 beats-per-minute tempo to enhance learning and also help people with heart arrhythmias, migraine headaches, and high blood pressure (lowered by 10 to 20 points). Her tests corroborated endless reports of increased health benefits coming to us from classrooms where the Superlearning Music was played.

High-frequency sounds apparently play a role in the effectiveness of Superlearning Music too. Almost from the first, researchers found that string music gave better results than music for other instruments. This is probably because music for violin, mandolin, harpsichord, or guitar contained the very high frequencies that Tomatis and other scientists found can help recharge the brain. Leading-edge brain researchers postulate that the neurons of the brain may resonate to the same harmonics that are found in this special music.

In Anchorage, Alaska, two innovative teachers at Mears Junior High, Anne Arruda and Tam Agosti-Gisler recorded all their French and Spanish study tapes with Superlearning background music. Students rated the tapes in a year-end survey. "On a scale of 1–10, the tapes were a 9," a student wrote. 85% found the music-backed tapes greatly increased comprehension and as one said, "helped me learn and REMEMBER. " Hyperactive students reported relaxed concentration and greater attention span. Other teachers called it a "miracle." Tape use jumped to 90%. As a result of these tests, Arruda and Gisler included Superlearning Music on their own full-length language programs based on the Total Physical Response method of language learning. Their courses are now widely marketed by the educational publisher Gessler.

Foremost North American Superlearning pioneer Dr. Jane Bancroft of the University of Toronto's Scarborough College, has a clutch of testimonials in her files from grateful students. At her suggestion, they switched from rock to Superlearning Music for studying. Concentration and memory improved enormously and marks soared.

Superlearning Music prepared by the authors is high-frequency music featuring compositions for string instruments in 4/4 time in ascending keys. People use it to relax—even in traffic jams—to balance the body, to achieve a best state for guided imagery and, of course, to enhance memory. Many programs are available backed by this special music.

Sophrology Musical Memory Booster

Dr. Raymond Abrezol, the Swiss Sophrologist, has taken a musical technique he developed to help people overcome pain and turned it into a memory booster. Aware of the body-balancing effect of baroque music, Abrezol created "Turning Sound"—baroque organ music with certain frequencies electronically altered, music that moves gently, rhythmically, back and forth from one brain hemisphere to the other. He added a breathing signal to further draw the listener into the rhythmic pattern, a harmonious pattern that seems to lift one into another state.

Abrezol gave tapes to his clients and other doctors. A popular form of pain control had been born! Throughout the 80s "Turning Sound" sold widely in Europe and has proven to be a great boon in natural childbirth. Investigating further, it occurred to Abrezol that "Turning Sound" created the ideal mind state for memorizing and learning.

He experimented and came up with instructions—place the material you want to memorize in front of you. Listen to the tape on earphones —let it carry you into that special altered state. Open your eyes and look at your material. Close your eyes again. Repeat this process in a paced, rhythmic way. According to Abrezol, "Turning Sound" is an all purpose memory technique and can be used to quicken learning of any material in any language. With practice, memorizing "becomes automatic," he says. Abrezol has now created "Turning Sound" memory-booster tapes using New Age music as well. Research continues at his center in Lausanne, Switzerland.

Boredom Beating Beats

If you're having trouble focusing attention, concentrating, and remembering, another new memory breakthrough has uncovered a whole galaxy of beats that beat boredom. In Tacoma, the sensuous strands of Kitaro's "Silk Road" swirled around sixth graders learning math. Vangelis's "China" played as third graders spelled, while Paul Horn's melodious sounds surrounded first graders embarked on creative writing. It wasn't just the music that was making teachers feel good about their kids' sudden spurt in ability. It was the special beats hidden in the music that imperceptibly tuned their students' brains and brought them into the "best" states for concentrating, remembering, or creating.

Robert Monroe, engineer, consciousness explorer, and founder of the Monroe Institute of Applied Science, devised the technique of using beat frequencies to propel the brain into specific rhythmic patterns. Your brain creates a beat frequency. For instance, if you don headphones, and a 300 hertz signal is sent to your left ear and 305 hertz sent to your right ear, your brain comes up with the difference. It resonates to five hertz. More felt than heard, this is not the same as experiencing this beat coming from outside the body, and it brings the whole brain into step in seconds. This is Hemi-Sync®, another effective way to use sound to enhance mind, memory, and abilities. You can use it to select from multiple brain states the one best suited to what you want to do—learn, image, or even weight lift.

In 1978, philosophy professor Dr. Devon Edrington brought Hemi-Sync into education to solve an equal opportunity problem, one we all fall prey to—wandering attention. Experimenting at Tacoma Community College, Edrington and colleagues fed specific beat frequencies via headphones to students pursuing a catalogful of subjects: ethics to drawing to Spanish. Would beat frequencies improve attention and concentration? Would the beat sound improve memory and performance? Psychology students who'd been shifted by Hemi-Sync into an optimal learning state scored significantly higher on a series of tests than those who tried to keep their attention focused by their own methods. There was only one chance in 10,000 improvement was accidental. Even the leery Dean of Instruction, after listening to a relaxation beat, urged Edrington to keep going. "I haven't felt so relaxed for many years."

"Wandering attention," says Edrington, "is the bane of education." By enhancing concentration and beating boredom, it looked as if Hemi-Sync could boost memory. Tacoma public school teachers soon wanted to get their classes in sync and concentrating too. Could the brain beats work for them? "The prospect of having thirty squirming six year olds tethered by headphone cords was terrifying," says Edrington.

First-grade teacher Jo Dee Owens absolutely insisted. What if they could broadcast beat rhythms masked by music over stereo speakers in the room? Edrington reluctantly rigged up the system. Earphones are better but still something happened. Soon parents, principal, and evaluators were beating a path to the room with the unhearable beats. The first graders were showing surprising concentration, independence, and cooperation. Kids completed work on the three Rs, and wrote stories while their teacher worked with others. "Then they read their stories," reported Tacoma Public School Systems Evaluator, Bruce Anaklev. "They gave one-minute talks and answered questions raised by classmates. FIRST GRADERS!"

To help teachers tune their kids into the helpful boredom-beating beats, Edrington came up with the Binaural Phaser, a kind of "beat-factory"—a synchronizer that lets you mix six different beat frequency patterns with music (see page 290). If kids whoop into class after a hot basketball game, a teacher might switch to a pattern that evokes slow, calming delta brainwaves for a few minutes. Then she turns to another beat frequency to help focus attention on history or biology and yet another for art or creative writing.

Adult minds can meander too. Master teacher Hans Heinzerling, at the University of Puget Sound, turned on Edrington's synchronizer in summer school classes full of public school teachers. It was vacation time and hot. Heinzerling was delighted by the group's sustained high-level attention, energy, and participation. "I would always choose to use the synchronizer," he says, "and would never work without it if I could avoid doing so." At Fort Lewis, Washington, the Army began using the beat frequencies in foreign language classes. Results were excellent, reported language instructors Yvonne Pawelek and Jeannette Larson. "A tremendous tool," they enthused, "in both classroom and language lab." Reports on the power of the beats that beat boredom and focus attention soon reached Army brass and education experts at national conferences. Many more teachers, trainers, sports coaches added the valuable beats to their repertoire.

Obviously conversant with the world's great thinkers, Dr. Edrington believes we need citizens who are not just trained but also educated, "people with expansive consciousness enabling them to appreciate other points of view, to tolerate paradoxes, to entertain ideals, to dream." Providing them with a simple way to overcome fragmented attention can help, he maintains.

Can beat frequencies become a crutch, an addiction? After a few months of exposure to the hidden rhythms, most people begin to have a "feeling" for focused attention and can shift into it on their own. It's an open question how many different states of being may be discovered and fine tuned with Hemi-Sync. As for concentration, it's a natural. Using rhythms to lead attention is as old as a mother rocking her baby or a preacher enthralling his congregation.

Different settings on the Binaural Phaser greatly assist attention focusing for different topics and different activities . . . one works well for guided imagery, another for studying, yet another for visual subjects like geometry. If you would like to add this breakthrough sound technique to your own repertoire, see Resources.

All across the board, new breakthroughs concerning our primary sense—hearing—are giving us powerful new ways to boost and access memory. New discoveries about music—from the powers of certain high frequencies to baroque beats, to beat frequencies help make the "ear force" a rapid route to evolutionary mind power. New sound technologies from the Walkman to holophonics are helping to open up the ancient mysterious connections between mind and music. There are enormous spin-off benefits too. "With the growth of sound awareness focused on health, we now have the opportunity to begin paying attention to sound as it affects our total health. In taking care of our own sound health, we may experience new vistas of self-discovery and aliveness that we never knew existed," says Steven Halpern. These new sound discoveries can vitalize and resonate our connections to the fields of memory, and give mind and body a "sonic bloom."

12. How To Imagine Better Memories

"What's the first thing you think of when I say *cup?*"

The room reflecting darkly in the mirror above the mantel, flame wrapped logs, dancing shadows in the fireplace, after-dinner coffee in gold-rimmed china on a black lacquered table . . . A scene one remembers, or fantasizes. Or maybe a picture in last month's *House and Garden.* It blinks on whole, all together, leading visual thinkers to make a quick maneuver on association tests. Saucer sounds reasonable, andirons might sound strange. It could well take a thousand words to describe the whole picture that is the real association. Imagery is the language of the right brain, the hemisphere that seems most intimately linked to the emotional limbic system so vital to memory; fortunately, the world is again becoming congenial to visual thinkers.

If you want to prove to yourself that a picture is worth those thousand words, look at a map. Perhaps because it carries so much information, so many associating parts, imagery is the stuff of memory. As the old line goes, no one says, "I'm sorry, I know your name, but I just can't remember your face." Countless experiments attest that visualization strengthens memory. To cite just one, Drs. Allan Paivo and Alain Desrochers at the University of Western Ontario coached students in both imagery and rote memory techniques. They weren't surprised that tests showed imagery boosted recall. They were surprised that students got *three times* better results with imagery than with repetition. If you can visualize something, you will remember it better. That's why concrete nouns are taught first in foreign languages. Dog, cat, table, they conjure instantly in the mind's eye. If you're having trouble remembering what you're reading, pause now and then, and make a movie of the last few pages. If that's easier said than done for you, try imagining yourself making a mental movie, seeing yourself rerunning it, remembering easily. Students of whole brain learning often journey right into the image. Slide down the lip of a lilly and feel your feet sticking to the pollen covering the stamen. . . . The birds and bees of plant life will stick in your mind. If you're interested in straight visualization techniques to remember anything or a hundred thousand things, check the extraordinary systems our ancestors built. Compared to them, our memory peg methods don't just pale, they blanch clear away (see Chapter 13). For Memory Shortcuts see Appendix B.

Streaming Images

As the century was dawning, Thomas Edison rolled back the roof of a small black building in West Orange, New Jersey. Workmen eased around the turntable on which the little building stood until the sun streamed directly through the opening in the roof. The camera clattered awake and the age of movies began. The outside finally caught up with the inside, for humans have been seeing movies in their minds for a long, long time.

Today people use their inner movies to help themselves accomplish all manner of things. These are the directed movies of the mind. Now people are solidifying memory with another kind of mental movie, a sort of inner cinema verité, an undirected stream of images that bears close resemblance to the stream of consciousness. Experts say this jostling stream rolls endlessly at the edge of consciousness, constant as breathing. People often notice it on the edge of sleep. If you close your eyes and pay attention, it's usually apparent anytime; a few are aware of it rolling all the time. This rich, innate stream of images might be tapped to help consolidate memory and understanding. Dr. Win Wenger is working on it.

The peripatetic Wenger, based in Gaithersburg, Maryland, is an education expert though he might better be called the Johnny Appleseed of brain/mind expansion. He uses his own priming techniques to churn up an abundance of fertile ideas that have been put to work by anyone with a brain, from problem solving executives to preschoolers. Wenger was another creative soul in the anchoring of accelerated learning in this country. He hasn't been content to sit within a set of supposed rules. The real debate point of accelerated learning, one that can get lost in nit-picking Wenger says, is its key element: does it effectively mobilize the "double plane," both conscious and unconscious mind. Results suggest that is its strength. "Since we perforce do address the unconscious in ourselves and others in *any* case," Wenger says, "why not find other techniques that also make use of this second plane of consciousness." Why not engage the stream of images?

Some will object, "I don't see images, never have." The brain devotes much more space to the visual sense than to other senses. Almost 80% of the brain's area has some visual involvement and most of this is subconscious activity. Which is one reason why many in the imagery field agree with Aristotle, that thinking is always accompanied by images, though in some people they may not pop through to awareness. Wenger has developed a battery of ways to connect with the streaming. "Pole-bridging" is one that works if you can catch at least a few images. With your eyes closed, describe the images that come, keep up a running commentary like a radio announcer describing a parade, if possible talk into a tape recorder. We've tried this and, as Wenger promises, with practice the imagery parade begins to flesh out, becoming rich, colorful, varied. The "bridging" links the right hemisphere with the verbal left and to Wenger's mind is an intelligence enhancer generally. Played back, taped descriptions can be surprisingly meaningful, particularly if you've posed a question. As Erickson said, "Your conscious mind is very intelligent and your unconscious mind is a hell of a lot smarter."

Wenger discovered this intelligence communicating through the imagery stream in a remarkable way during conflict-resolution seminars. Two bitterly opposed groups confronted him. He posed a few concealed questions aimed at combatants' unconscious. Warring parties closed their eyes and described their undirected imagery streaming. Wenger was surprised. Looking at the streaming of both groups, he says, "They unconsciously agreed unanimously on the best resolution of the conflict!" Getting this accepted consciously is another matter, he's quick to add.

Once people feel easy tuning into their own unique imagery stream, they summon it to integrate and fix memory. If you're having trouble grasping a lecture or a book, Wenger might say, "Even now, your mind's eye has prepared a picture for you to look at, which contains in some unexpected way the key understanding of this subject. Everything in this book revolves around this key understanding." Close your eyes immediately and see what the key is. Describe aloud or write or draw the key. Even novices who have no previous contact with a subject, Wenger says, very often "reported an immediate transformation from experience of difficulty and unintelligibility to transparent ease and richly meaningful intelligibility of the text or task." Streaming helps integrate talents and physical skills too.

Engaging the intelligence of the unconscious with streaming leads to long term memory retention and enhanced ability to recall just as Suggestology does, Wenger reports. The two techniques work synergistically. They boost memory in part because they work globally, integrating and associating, rather than the usual pigeonhole approach to learning. Streaming can be used to link different subjects, everything one takes in school or the data from various elements in a business, building an ever broader base of understanding, an ever stronger memory. That dozens of practical uses are being found for streaming isn't surprising. It's a matter of intelligence, drawing more of that vast, usually untapped resource into play.

If you enjoy revelations, pose the question, "What is it time to remember about myself?" Or, "What is it time to re-member about myself?" Then, catch the stream, remembering to describe what rolls. Try it now and then as you become more expert at streaming. People report surprises.

Memory in Your Fingers

Hooking someone's name to a funny image or imagining you're a satellite taking pictures of the earth's continents helps fix things in memory, factual memory. The directed movies of the mind that so many use often involve the memory you can feel in your fingers when you play the piano, in your whole body when you hop on a bike. An amnesiac may not remember her name, but she remembers how to drive a car. A man with a severe memory disorder can still play golf and improve with practice, though he can't remember that he played the last hole. Different than intellectual "semantic" memory, and from episodic, daily memory, skill or automatic memory seems closer to the bone and stays when others fade.

Some people have an inborn facility at body memory. Shirley Temple, for one, who seemed all-around competent at age three. She knew her way around a stage so well that she frightened adult co-stars like Adolphe Menjou, who called her an Ethel Barrymore at six and said, "If she were forty years old, she wouldn't have had time to learn all she knows about acting." One thing little Shirley realized on her own is that a movie set is a crisscrossing network of light beams. She picked up the varying patterns of heat as the unseen beams hit her body. "My knack involved sensing the difference between a patch of skin on my forehead and a cooler area on my cheek." Seemingly effortlessly, she remembered the patterns of heat and action during rehearsal. Unlike other actors, she always remembered where to be during takes, she could even "sense if my head was held in the right position."

Shirley also showed an almost flawless memory for her lines which she imbibed by a method a little reminiscent of Superlearning. While she relaxed in bed before sleeping, she went through three dramatic renditions of the next day's script with her mother. Then Shirley slept on it to be letter perfect the next day—not just with her own lines, but with everyone else's too! For those of us without Shirley's instinctive body memory and performance memory, imagery can help.

In our time, mental sports training first rose to Olympian heights in the USSR and Europe. Since the star-spangled gymnastics of Mary Lou Rettin and the godlike dives of Greg Louganis, both of whom worked out in their imagination, mental training has begun pumping in the United States. It wasn't altogether new. As they steamed across the summer Atlantic to the 1912 Olympics, members of the U.S. team pushed themselves in a lather of practice. All but one. While the others sweated, a coach noticed Jim Thorpe, the great track star, stretched out on a deck chair. "Why aren't you training," he demanded. "I am," Thorpe replied, and explained that he was imagining every inch of the track, every move, every breath of his run. More recently, American pentathlete Marilyn King ended up in bed with a back injury nine months before the 1980 Olympic trials. Rather than rue her fate, King spent her time viewing films of famous pentathletes, then visualized and experienced herself going through the event. In effect she was seeding memories of top-notch performance. King, now director of Beyond Sports, insists that her mental, not her physical, training won her a second in the trials.

Sophrologist Raymond Abrezol has 114 Olympic medals to his credit, not as Superman, but as a mental trainer who's coached clients to the top in sports as varied as skiing and skeet shooting, boxing and swimming. Mental movies roll at the center of this Sophrologist's coaching. They help to erase inept or faulty memories. They help inculcate skilled memories. If you're a tennis player, after practice Abrezol asks you to rerun your performance in your mind's eye, using all the techniques of a filmmaker: freeze frame, zoom, slowmo, wide lens overview. You correct any mistakes you made, if necessary backing up and running the film again and again until it's right. Bad maneuvers are not allowed to fix themselves in memory.

Beyond sports, you can try to edit out unproductive memories from any event while they're fresh. Rerun things the way you wanted them to be, which can be more liberating than it sounds. "Dog face!" You can hear "you look great" a thousand times, but the one "dog face" will stick with you. Negatives tend to stay more alive than positives in memory, they resonate like unfinished songs, music that hasn't resolved in a satisfying chord. If you immediately rerun and resolve unsatisfactory events in your imagination, it will help you forget.

SALT founder Don Schuster uses the mental movie loop after physical harm. If you sear your hand, for instance, as soon as possible run through the accident vividly, he advises. Schuster says this "psychological first aid" often brings faster healing, perhaps because expression allows the body to relax and bring healing blood flow to the injury, perhaps because it allows body memory to express and not fix in the cells.

In sports training, once you have a good take, Abrezol asks you to run through your performance again, but this time from the inside, to really be there, to bring all your senses into play, to look out through your own eyes, to feel, taste yourself connecting with the tennis ball. New-age coach Dyveke Spino goes further with full sensed imaging, and asks clients to imagine being a deer for speed, a panther to build power.

For competition like a track meet, Abrezol has you create a present memory of the future event. Day by day, for weeks ahead, you imagine every detail of the red-letter day. From digging into a power breakfast to the final hurrahs and the sweet smell of success, you try to experience events as though they were actually happening. You are building positive memories to draw on during that future day.

Abrezol carries this training into healing. Olympian Marilyn King has taken it into learning on the idea that as long as you can't imagine getting a good grade or mastering a difficult subject, you won't. "Once a kid grasps that potential is a state of mind, once a negative self-fulfilling prophecy begins to be replaced by a new script, a new film loop, watch out," King says. The natural tendency to rehearse in the mind is sometimes used to judge intelligence, probably because it connects to memory. Imaginative rehearsal is increasingly used for just about everything: to sell, have a baby, play the piano, propose marriage. It works, but why? If you can engage all your senses and imagine vividly, supposedly, your deep mind can't tell the difference between an imagined event and an actual one. You even produce micro muscle movements as you imagine performing. In effect, you are laying down mindbody memories. You are laying down memories of seeming past success which mobilizes to present and future success. There also seem to be more subtle mysteries involved, mysteries of the creative power of memory and imagination. Golf inspired one well-known Frenchman to pursue the mystery. He wasn't a champion, just a weekend duffer.

A well-placed sandtrap guarding a certain green had swallowed the man's ball more times than he could remember. As he headed down the fairway, his nemesis yawned like a moon crater in his mind. And his ball flew smack into the trap. Contemplating the "perfection" of his performance, Emile Coué came up with a famous law. "When the imagination and the will are in conflict, the imagination always wins."

A pharmacologist, one of the French fathers of the science of suggestion, in the 20s Coué inspired millions to chant, "Everyday, in every way, I'm getting better and better." But his study of imagination went way beyond a pop phrase. His law formulates an old esoteric idea: the will is what chooses, the imagination is what brings to fruition. It magnetizes, perhaps because it creates a desired mindbody state, a state dependent memory. Coué worked on the double plane and used imagery to rouse the subconscious and turn its energy to the chosen goal. Think of Coué's law next time you diet. Conscious willpower starts hanging by its fingertips if you let visions of chocolate mudpies dance in your head. "It must take a lot of willpower," people say to Marilyn King of her Olympic prowess. "While that may be true, I was never in touch with either willpower or discipline," she admits. It was desire, stoked by imagination, that got her early out of bed.

"I don't have any imagination. I can't do it." There are books full of techniques to prompt imagination. If visualization eludes you, perhaps touch is your dominant sense. Work from strength and cross over to other senses. Imagine running your hand down the rough bark of an oak or caressing the unearthly softness of a baby's cheek. Let the picture, the sounds grow from the touch.

The goal is full sensed imagining. Memory superstars like Veniamin, the man who remembered everything, bring extra-full senses to life. In Veniamin's case, senses were mixed in the phenomenon of synesthesia. Every number, every shape, every word and sound sent throngs of impressions stampeding through Veniamin's mind. "Letter *A* is white and long," he said. "*I* moves away from you. *O* comes from the chest, it's large and the sound goes downward. . . . I sense a taste for each too," he explained. "And numbers are not simple figures: *1* is sharp-pointed, independent of its graphic appearance, it's something hard and highly finished; *2* is flat, rectangular, whitish, sometimes grayish. . . ." One day as Veniamin and academician A. A. Luria walked past the gnarled stone walls of the Moscow Institute where their memory experiments took place, Veniamin said, "How could I ever have trouble finding your Institute? This wall has such a salty taste—it's so

wrinkled and it has a really strident sound. . . ." No wonder
Veniamin remembered. Full sensed imagining is something the rest of
us can learn to do, at least a little bit.

A recent discovery might give you a start-up boost. Hugo Zucarelli
found that our ears emit sounds that act similarly to the reference
beams that create holograms. Building on his discovery, Zucarelli invented something new and powerful: holophonics, 3D sound recording. If you listen to a holophonic recording, you're *really* there. The
first time you'll jump with surprise when you hear applause—you
didn't know someone was sitting behind you. For one reason or another, holophonics can evoke synesthesia. Listen to coffee perk and
sense the aroma and taste too. Holophonic guided imagery or straight
learning tapes could form powerful memories. Another way to exercise imagination is closer at hand.

Can you imagine the worst? We've never met anyone who couldn't.
Your spouse is late, he's probably been run over, his wallet dropped
out . . . the emergency room doesn't know who to call. . . . Or
you're not sure about the exam, you'll probably fail, lose your scholarship . . . have to leave school . . . become a bag lady. "Awfulizing," is what Dr. Joan Borysenko calls this. As Director of the Beth
Israel Mind/Body Clinic in Boston, she saw endless unhappy examples of where awfulizing can get you.

Next time you catch yourself rocking along on the awfulizing train,
yank the emergency stop. Take your train of thought back to the
beginning and run it through to a positive outcome. Your adrenals will
thank you. And without adding any extra time, it's an excellent way to
practice imagining. (For images that heal, see Chapter 16.) A general
discussion of imagery is beyond our scope, but guidance is easy to find.
On the scientific side, one exceptional investigator is Dr. Akhter
Ashan, founder of the International Imagery Association. On the per-
son-to-person level, Shakti Gawain is excellent. In part, they're both
engaged in creating future memories. So is Vera Fryling, M.D., one of
America's leading experts on autogenics, the classical relaxation routine which first brings the body to a warm and centered state, then
moves to creative imagery.

Creating Future Memories

Vera Fryling, a tall, stylish woman with a soft Deitrich-like German
accent, has flair in more ways than one. Most particularly, she has a
flair for surviving. During her teens in Nazi Berlin, on the run, with-

out papers, without food coupons, haunted by the Gestapo, she lived a sort of Anne Frank story with a happy ending. Except Fryling wasn't closeted, she was out and about in the harrowing life of the city, threatened by discovery on the streets and eventually by bombs tumbling from the sky. Imagery, she says, played a major part in pulling her through the knothole. Fryling proved the name of autogenics—"self birthing." This formalized system of relaxation and imagery became her specialty in private practice and on the faculty of the University of California Medical School at Berkeley. In recent years she has used it to help others survive and transcend life-threatening situations whether war, earthquake, torture, or incapacitating ills. Medicine, she believes, must attend not only to body and mind, but also to spirit.

Threats to survival force you to question the meaning of your life. Imagery provides a way of inquiry, adaptation, eventual transcendence. In the concentration camps, Fryling notes, often it wasn't the physically hearty who survived but those who could draw sustenance from a rich inner life. Victor Frankel, a triumph of a human being, survived the camps in part because he realized that "no matter how utterly desolate one's condition . . . man can preserve a vestige of spiritual freedom." He can insist on the one choice that's always left, the choice of one's thought. From memory, Frankel summoned his wife's face, "seeing it with uncanny acuteness. I heard her voice answering me. I saw her smile, her encouraging look, it was more luminous than the sun about to rise, and for the first time in my life, I saw the truth—love is the ultimate and highest goal to which man can aspire. . . ." Imagery allowed such radiance to unfold in the bleakest death camp. Frankel created future memories too. He imagined himself after the war at the University of Vienna, lecturing on Nazi psychology. He imagined in exquisite detail, down to seeing, feeling, hearing himself click on the lights in the hall. Frankel survived to catch up with his future memories. One day he clicked on the lights and lectured on Nazi psychology at the University of Vienna.

Fryling, only fifteen when her Jewish father fled Germany and most of her relatives were railroaded into death camps, didn't have as many past memories as Frankel. She clung instead, she says, to the German idealism of men like Schilling and Goethe; she made up her mind to become a psychiatrist to help heal the mental schisms underlying the horrors all about her. Not just naïve, but absurd at the time. Yet Fryling too began to imagine her goal in exquisite detail, laying down future memories. "Imagery helped me plot my survival strategy." It gave her the courage to eventually attend a private prep school under an assumed identity. It brought her through the death throes of Berlin, liberation by the Red Army, and finally out in the Berlin airlift to the University of Minnesota.

Soon after she gained her M.D., the years of stress caught up. Colleagues operating on Fryling for cancer only gave her a 50% chance of surviving five years. "Don't waste time and money studying psychiatry," they admonished. But Fryling had been imagining too long. She put her images to work on her health and again on her goal. Long since an internationally known psychiatrist with a busy practice, a few years ago, Fryling parked her car and ran into another survival threat, a mugger with a revolver. Shot again and again, it was touch and go for Fryling, but as you might imagine, she once more survived to pursue her very active life.

In the hospital, Fryling added music to her imagining. When sleep wouldn't come she used structured, slow baroque. Most of the time, she needed pieces like Beethoven's "Incidental Music for the Celebration of King Stefan," which energized emotional imagery of courage, strength, and transcendence. To heal, she also advises turning to memory and recollecting images of tranquility—a leafy landscape, a familiar, comforting voice, a reassuring touch. From these, "we can tap new sources of satisfaction to help us transcend the insults fate has dealt us."

Though it's usually not noticed, instructions on how to do full sensed imagining sound very similar—actually are identical to—descriptions of state dependent memories. They both have mood and temperature and engage the whole mindbody drama of an event. Imagining excitement or anxiety, for instance, can rouse and leave an imprint of the same hormonal activity as actual anxiety. As Lewis Carroll remarked, "It's a poor memory that only works backward." Frankel and Fryling in their intensity of imagination were creating state dependent memories of a future cast.

Memory can create without the restriction of time. As Milton Erickson and others have shown, it can even "change" the past. A client, for instance, might be regressed to early childhood and session after session experience the security and adventures of a warm family life— something in fact she did not have as a child. Eventually these newly buried memories can begin to pulse through time to the present and prompt the positive behavior and outlook that springs from a happy childhood.

Memory is such an intimate of time that St. Augustine's famous response when asked, "What is time?" might be extended to memory.

"I know what it is until you ask me!" Imagery rehearsal for skiing or sales talks is understandable, but the sort of imagining done by Frankel and Fryling blends off beyond the current view of our creative connection to the world. It fits with the perennial idea "act as if, and you shall become," as though the future, like liquid flowing into a mold, could be lured to flesh out imagined memories. Could strong imagining raise a morphic field, or hook into a generic one, organizing fields that grow stronger with the repeated imagining prescribed? Whatever your view, it's seems our memories have resources, usually untapped, that go far beyond "just the facts, ma'am."

13. The Magical Memory Tour

First stop, legendary Greece—and disaster. Rescuers and torchbearers swarm over a monolithic pile of rubble; a mansion has collapsed, the home of the mogul Scopas. A Who's Who of banquet guests, the beautiful, the rich, lie trapped in tons of marble. Only one has escaped, "the honey tongued" Simonides, the famous poet. His is a strange story.

"Scopas wanted me to compose a lyric in his own honor. I said I'd do it, *if* he paid me. Tonight, when I finished reciting, the self-centered old bleep said I'd only get half my pay. All because I added a few lines praising Castor and Pollux. 'Let the twin gods pay the rest,' he said. I was putting away as much of his feast as I could, when a servant whispered that two young men wanted me outside. I came out, but the street was empty. That's when it happened . . . like thunder it cracked and rumb . . ."

"Simonides, more tragedy!" a rescuer cuts in. The victims are so badly mangled not one is identifiable. How will the families know which corpse to bury, whom to honor? "Don't move those bodies!" Simonides shouts after a moment's thought. "I can see in my mind where each person was seated."

And that is why for the next two thousand years writers on the art of memory saluted Simonides of Ceos, discoverer of mnemotechnics. Like many legends, the story credits a master of an art with its invention. Simonides's memory was prodigious and lifelong. He won the Athens chorus prize in his old age. His story reveals the keystone of a memory system that later supported whole palaces, whole cities of memory: location and image, seat and person. Primacy of the visual in memory is doubly noted, for Simonides poetry was almost synonymous with stunning imagery.

In antiquity the legend commemorated another first, the first time a poet asked to be paid for his work. An act the gods apparently approve. No one doubted it was Castor and Pollux who called out Simonides to settle their debt.

Raiders of the Lost Art

There are a lot of tales about the boisterous Castor and Pollux, pages of stories about minor nymphs, water sprites, and tree spirits. That's what seemed so strange when we looked up the titan Mnemosyne. Memory herself. Mother of the arts. Mother of learning. There were no stories. Why was this mother of us all so strangely absent in historical account? Not absent it turns out, but like all mothering, invisible. As scholars begin to unearth the invisible art of memory, we are like Victorians with first reports of Egyptian tombs and shards of Schliemann's Troy—fragments that begin to summon the fragrance, the colors, the view of ancient eyes.

Invisible, yes, but Mnemosyne's art was more real and pervasive than any we know. The art of memory suffused our forebears. Educated people didn't just appreciate this art, every one of them practiced it. This is an art both hands-on practical and sublime. A leading, painstaking pioneer in reclaiming this lost art was Frances Yates, of the Warburgh Institute, University of London. Yates remarks that we can rightly call its practical side "mnemotechnics." The topless towers of Ilium are small town beside the memory palaces, citadels—even cities —that our ancestors built in their heads, invisible palaces which allowed them to perform everyday feats of memory that boggle the mind. Compared to them, we have no memory at all. We don't need one. We've created an artificial memory—books, tape recorders, cameras, TV, calculators, and computers that can raise the whole concordance of the Bible in a second. Equipped only with a wax tablet and a scroll or two, our ancestors had to remember *everything*. That they did, so gloriously, is a tribute to the human mind. Artificial memory meant something different to them: natural memory is what you're born with, artificial is the memory you train and develop. Mnemotechnics can still help us remember better. It might help us think better.

Mnemotechnics is the helping hand Mnemosyne gave humankind; her heart and soul, the essence of her art is something more creative, mysterious—and alluring enough to drive some of the best minds of Western civilization to Herculean efforts. The art of memory powered both Plato's and Aquinas's road to God, it helped form Dante's *Divine Comedy* and reveals to us the forgotten design of Shakespeare's Globe Theatre. The rules of mnemotechnics remained remarkably stable through the centuries. The art of memory, like any art, shifted with different cultures, shaping, being shaped by the tenor of the times. In our time, in our own way, we may still win gifts from this ancient art. It can help us, and not just to remember everyone's name at the party. It has power, it could help us stretch ourselves.

Imagine yourself on a different kind of magical mystery tour. To catch the flavor of classical mnemotechnics, make an image of each site we will visit, starting with the fall of the house of Scopas. Then, place the image carefully in your own house.

"House Beautiful"

Our next site is another house, the spacious home of an upper-class Roman family in the days of grandeur. Before the entrance, a student stands meditatively. Following the rules of mnemotechnics, to imprint the image on memory we will make the student bizarre, laughable. Easily done for that era by making our scholar a her—a her clutching the treatise *Ad Herennium.* She walks into her vestibule, looks in the corners, then slowly moves into the entrance hall, stopping a moment before the urn full of red flowers, then the candelabra, before turning into a large reception room. Pacing as though measuring distances, she circles the room, pausing at irregular intervals—by the divan, the window arch, the bust of Cicero in the corner. She looks at them reflectively, considering perhaps how to redecorate her house. But the interior design that so absorbs this student is of a different order. She's choosing her loci, the unforgettable places of her home where she will position memory images. The *Ad Herennium* advises that sites flow in a natural order, ample but differing spaces between, not too light, not in shadow.

When she's run out of places here, the scholar muses, she'll choose sites in her grandfather's house, the academy, perhaps her favorite temple . . . and giggles at the thought that she could ever study long enough to run out of buildings in Rome to store her knowledge.

Sites chosen, the student can now people them with memory images, invisible galleries that will let her remember anything and everything there is to know, limited only by her ability to generate potent images. She checks the rules in her *Ad Herennium.* Following nature, images are to combine those things that make us wonder: the beautiful, the ugly, the horrifying, obscene, comic. Make images lively, vivid, and moving. Weave into the picture famous and infamous people, goddesses, gods—Neptune, for instance, to signify maritime affairs. In starring roles, use family and friends, people you're familiar with. They can also exemplify traits. Dress them up dramatically—a bloody belt, tattered toga, or smear them with red paint. Use odd accessories like a large, lopsided crown. . . .

Borrowing perhaps the face of her mother, posing her as an open-mouthed goddess loaded with symbolic accessories, the student fashions the image she will put in the first place in the vestibule. If necessary, it will remain there for the rest of her life, reminding her of the first of the rules of Rhetoric, the real topic of the *Ad Herennium*. "In the first place . . ." we say, unknowingly commemorating the ancient art of mnemotechnics.

The *Ad Herennium* is sparse on examples of memory images. Not that they would ring many bells. What springs to mind at the sight of a seated man holding two tablets in his right hand, a cup in his left, with ram's testicles draped over his fourth finger? He's a detail of a complex picture a lawyer created to recall the case of a plutocrat poisoned for his money. The man is the defendant, the tablets call to mind the will, the cup the poison, the ram's testicles the "testes" or witnesses. But other recollections elude us. Why is the man seated, why ram's testicles, do they refer to Aries or other associations with rams? Why do the testicles grace the fourth finger, the "medicine" finger in Latin? If you know the whole answer, you're involved in a different facet of memory, one delved by Plato, far memory, the recollection of things picked up in past lives.

Even in its own time, there was strong reason for the *Ad Herennium* to spare examples. Do-it-yourself is the central belief in classical mnemotechnics. You must generate your own images and not use the pictures or associations of others, no matter how clever. The ability to birth living images is a skill, an art, one to be pursued as assiduously as a ballerina or sculptor pursues her craft. Skill in this inner generation is the secret of a powerful memory. It is the secret to winning knowledge and the real goal, wisdom. With wisdom comes self-transformation, Mnemosyne's gift.

The *Ad Herennium* was one more teacher's attempt to give advice on mnemotechnics. A master of images, perhaps, but the now nameless teacher could never have imagined that his simple how-to book would have a profound influence on the great minds to come, from Augustine to Aquinas, from Petrarch in the early Renaissance, to Bruno in the late, and still echo into the age of reason in the writings of Bacon and Leibniz. The *Ad Herennium* had greatness thrust upon it as the only complete set of mnemotechnic rules to survive the gutting of classical civilization. Other survivors said more fascinating things about memory, but omitted her rules—everyone knew them.

Aristotle Associates

The next strategically located image, if you've joined the expedition, involves a man in Greek robes, leaning over a wax tablet and making impression after impression with his signet ring. He shapes them into a picture: a train of elephants linked trunk to tail. Here is Aristotle, author of a lost book on mnemotechnics. Sense data falls upon and impresses memory the way signet rings impress wax, Aristotle said. This is the raw material to be worked on by memory and intellect. The key to both is imagery. The key to everything really, for Aristotle taught that you can not think without mental images—a famous dictum that goaded generations of students to roll up their eyes and try.

When you furnish your memory palace, Aristotle advised, concentrate on order and linkage. In a house you can start in any room and go to the back door or the front door. Similarly, if you've ordered your image-laden sites imaginatively, you can start at any site and move in either direction, effortlessly calling up more and more information. That's association, and Aristotle is credited with formulating its import in memory.

Building so you can move in any direction is behind a once popular memory feat that now seems a bizarre, not to mention impossible, way to show off one's intellect. Take the Roman Seneca, for instance. To wake up his students, Seneca would ask two hundred or more of them to each recite a line of poetry from any poem. When the last one finished, he would rattle off the whole of it perfectly from beginning to end. Before anyone could move, Seneca recited the whole again— *backward.* Such displays were the public relations of the day, when a master memory was highly esteemed and paid.

Half a world a way, fifteen hundred years later in 16th century China, it was still a good trick. Some intellectuals of Nanchang gathered for dinner. Though wearing the blue-trimmed purple robe of a Chinese literati, one husky guest was obviously something else again. He was the Jesuit Matteo Ricci, come to convert the Chinese. To gain their attention, Ricci planned to share the dazzling European art of building memory palaces. Ricci built his own memory house for Chinese characters, notoriously multiple and difficult to learn. At dinner, he asked his hosts to write on a sheet of paper a large number of different characters, in no order, with no relation to each other. After reading it once, Ricci recited the characters in perfect order. Then, "to increase their wonder," he wrote, "I began to recite them all by memory backward in the same manner, beginning with the very last until reaching the first. By which they all became utterly astounded as if beside themselves."

Aristotle drilled students in ordered memory for a different sort of conversion, to win debates. Linked images will rise into mind automatically in forceful progression when argument ensues. Since we've learned to consciously manipulate images to remember, we can extend this skill, Aristotle said. Deliberately choose images to think with, to explore and gain insights.

In Aristotle's scheme, imagination and memory inhabit the same part of the mind. The strength of their joint ability to grab hold of sense impressions is vital. Because, Aristotle believed, the *only* way we get knowledge is through sense data. Across the grove in academe, his teacher Plato thought otherwise.

Plato's Yoga of Memory

You might think about a man on a ladder, robes somewhat askew, balancing a plate on his head as he attempts a strange version of the Indian rope trick. His ladder leans on nothing and lacks rungs. Before he can move up a notch, he has to remember and see clearly in his mind's eye where that next rung should be. Slowly, rising upon his memory, he climbs toward the heavens.

Both Aristotle and Plato would agree with Pythagoras that "memory is a gift from God." Only Plato would have concurred with the elder philosopher's contention that this "highest of talents" allowed him to range across the boundaries of life and death and recall knowledge gained before this lifetime. Recall it and use it, in Pythagoras's case to help formulate his famous laws of harmony. Plato knew the value of a trained memory, his own was prodigious. But his interest, passion really, bypassed the "superficials" of mnemotechnics and dove straight to the essence of memory. Mother of all arts, he believed memory is the art that can lead us back to the realization of our own divinity, back to wholeness.

Memory certainly registers the bustling world of impressions. But these impressions are of things—chairs, sealing wax, kingly justice — that are copies, imperfect copies of the ideal reality that exists beyond our realm. "We come trailing clouds of glory," sings Wordsworth. We also come trailing memories of glory, Plato teaches. We have an innate memory, he said, of the realities beyond this world, of his famous ideal forms. The real art is to recover divine memory and fit sense impressions into this grander framework. That's how to climb back up the ladder that we descended at birth into this foursquare world. Plato's memory is a yoga, an art of enlightenment, of uniting with the divine source.

The Socratic method, perhaps the longest-lived teaching technique, is a way of jogging innate memory. At root, it is Plato's voice we hear when we say education means to draw out, not stuff into. Socrates drew from his students things they didn't know that they knew. Much came from calling back, recombining the myriad experiences of this life. But the hidden agenda of Socrates's method was to resonate and draw forth the innate divine memory. Plato pursued memory as the modus operandi of his theology, Aristotle as the key to his theory of knowledge. In the first century B.C., Cicero evoked Ethics from the invisible art.

Cicero and the Three Faces of Prudence

Romans listened when the brilliant Cicero spoke. His persuasive powers helped platonic philosophy blossom in Rome. Cicero too believed we are immortals with divine memory, but unlike Plato he was also a keen practitioner of mnemotechnics, a natural interest for this most famous teacher of Rhetoric. If an orator needed anything in the days before index cards and TV prompters, he needed a well-stocked and ready memory.

Cicero possessed some of the most elegant, far-flung invisible architecture of the day. He also trained in another classical memory system: a way to make a mental note, or notations, and remember words verbatim. It's a lost art, which may be just as well. The *Ad Herennium* considered it too hard to use and Cicero agreed that loci and images were enough. Some clue to these mysterious notations may come from the discovery that Cicero introduced a new way of writing to Rome, odd writing, sprung from the devil the church said, and condemned it in the Middle Ages as grievous heresy. Today we call it shorthand.

Cicero had also met Metrodorus of Scepsis. Counselor of kings, world famous in his day, Metrodorus too devised secret mental writing to jog memory. Cicero called him "almost divine." Later generations viewed his heavenly connection differently. Metrodorus raised his sights from architecture to the sky, to the zodiac. So rich in symbolism, so endlessly interpreted, this zodiac was a familiar place, its points recognizable in their individuality. Metrodorus used the 360 degrees of the Zodiac as sites for memory images. Placing images on a circle, he opened up new depth and overtones of association—think of the trines, the squares of astrology. Moving starward, he also cast the foundations for the mysterious magical memory patterns of the Renaissance.

Cicero made an equally lasting contribution. In *De Inventione,* he discusses prudence, the ability to know what is good, what is bad, and what is neither. An ability greatly to be desired, prudence is made of memory, intellect, and foresight. Memory is the mainstay, for it moves data from the past to the present and focuses it ahead. Not exactly a sizzling metaphor, but the idea stuck. Sixteen hundred years later, Titian could paint "Prudence," assured that viewers would catch the meaning. Titian portrays three male heads. One face looks straight at you. On either side is a head in profile; one looks backward, one looks forward. Memory, intellect, foresight.

Prudence seems just the ticket to build a successful society. As memory is its foundation, an upright citizen might think of memory exercise as a sort of ethical duty. Perhaps some Romans did. By medieval times, based on Cicero's reflections, memory development was indeed an ethical duty, a religious obligation in the service of born-again prudence, one of the four cardinal virtues of Christianity.

Remembering Hell

When the last embers of classical civilization guttered into darkness, learning went on a narrow retreat into monastic cells. The ancient art of memory sank into the darkness and transformed herself. The best picture of this metamorphosis can be seen toward the end of the period when Thomas Aquinas, with the care of the tapestry maker, worked the convoluted strains of medieval thought into an artful whole. Aquinas's memory was literally encyclopedic. As a boy he could remember verbatim what his teachers said. As a young man he impressed Pope Urban by putting together a compendium of writing by church fathers. He didn't copy it, he remembered it. We have no trace of the blueprint Thomas used to not only store his knowledge but to fit it together, into a structure that arched, spread, and soared toward heaven like the great Gothic cathedrals of his time. Like other medievals, he may have used the sanctified spaces of church and cathedral to store images, adding foreign sites, useful souvenirs he'd picked up on his travels.

From the perspective of imagination, Thomas was a saint in more ways than one. Images, along with everything else connected with the senses, the body, and the wicked natural world were in dangerous repute in the Middle Ages. St. Thomas threw his great authority behind imagery. It was a concession, he admitted, to the weakness of the flesh. Humans needed to use "corporeal similitudes" to fix their memories and discharge their ethical duty of keeping ever alive the memory of heaven, hell, and church teaching. *Ever* alive. As one religious recommended, when not working, young girls should be in their rooms vividly remembering the scenes of the Bible. Another, rearing the crucifixion in memory, said that with a "certain devout curiosity" one should imagine the sensation of putting one's finger in each of Christ's wounds, then thought to be over 5,000. Years later, St. Ignatius Loyola used the necessary mnemotechnics to deepen religious experience. His Jesuits were to practice full sensed imagining of the Bible, as daily devotionals and memory exercise became one.

St. Thomas did more than simply permit images. Cultivate the art of generating them, he advised. Traveling friars, like Thomas's Dominicans, became prolific imagers, spawning images to recall their sermons, images to fasten on the memories of listeners. They referred to these pictures in such glowing detail in their writing that later scholars were puzzled when they couldn't find the originals. But, of course, they were invisible. In the intellectual and emotional pressure cooker of medieval existence, one can wonder where this passionate inner embrace of images sometimes led. Novelists will tell you that characters take on a life of their own.

Think of "idolatry," dressed up to remember points in a sermon. Here comes a garish old harlot, blind, slobbering, with mutilated ears and stinking sores festering her body. Did she ever go careening off on her own through the neat memory rooms of a hapless preacher? Did a burnt-out friar ever slump into his barren cell, swing wide the door of his memory palace, and step into its fabulous halls forever?

Preachers carried the word to laymen: cultivate your own images. "What galleries of unusual and striking similitudes for new and unusual virtues and vices . . . may have remained forever invisible within the memories of pious and possibly artistically gifted persons!" Frances Yates writes. Sometimes, steaming and twisting, inner imagery did boil over into fantastic creations. Yates was the first person in modern times to recognize the almost all-pervasive influence of the invisible art of memory on the visible medieval arts.

The bizarre, deformed, beautiful, comic, obscene statuary of Gothic cathedrals, all the lurid, nightmarish, seemingly pathological paintings of hell, can be seen as the work of a distressed psyche—or they can be seen as the classical principles of the art of memory shaped by creative genius, a perspective that opens a vast, virgin field of study. To tempt a scholar or two, Yates writes that though it will come as a shock to them, Dante's *Divine Comedy* is a memory system, the apotheosis of the memory system. The ordered locations of images on the rings of hells, images of specific punishment for specific vices, tri-part prudence, all the other memory features we've mentioned, and many we haven't, are magnificently present working their art in Dante's sublime construction. Mnemosyne is the mother of the arts. Maybe it's time for our psychological era to trace her influence on her children.

With the great scholastics like Aquinas and extraordinary artists like Dante, the art of memory would seem to culminate in the service of the church. The rapid spread of printed books was just around the corner. But like the witch's cat, Mnemosyne had lives to come.

The Memory Theater in Venice

In the early 1500s, Giulio Camillo built a theater in Venice such as the world had never seen before or since (except for a replica he constructed in Paris for Frances I). Rumors ran through the French court and across Renaissance Italy that Camillo had whispered the real secret of his theater to the King alone. Frances never told. But there were many secrets to Camillo's Memory Theater and recently some have come to light. Camillo was another memory master or, in this case, magus, given the title "divine" by his contemporaries. The divine Camillo described his wooden masterpiece as a "constructed mind and soul," or a "windowed mind." He filled his theater with exquisite images—Apollo, the Three Gorgons, Pasipha and the Bull, Prometheus, and on and on in serried hosts, story images, proliferating before the viewer like the eclectic ferment of the Renaissance itself.

A warmer sun had risen. Rather than original sin, the original blessing galvanized Renaissance people. Man the microcosm reflected the macrocosm, his higher mind was part of divine mind. Plato, as neoplatonism, returned. The great hermetic philosophy of ancient Egypt given by the legendary Hermes Trismegistus was reclaimed and hungrily consumed. So were the shadowy wisdom secrets of the Cabala. Made truly in the image of God, the human was seen to be a co-creator in the universe. The purpose of the Memory Theater was to wake one to the memory of one's divine legacy.

As a theater, it reversed the usual viewer perspective. Camillo would stand his guest on the stage looking out on the fan-shaped rows, crowded not with spectators but memory images. He compared this to seeing the forest not the trees, to an overview, looking from cause through all the levels of effect. On the first level were the seven world-empowering ideas that sprang from the divine abyss symbolized as Cabalistic Sephiroths, archangels, and planets. The influence of each of the seven was seen moving up the auditorium through the crowded seven rings of existence, from super celestial to the material arts of man. Here memory images were connected, not arbitrarily, but *organically* to achieve unified, cosmic memory.

If nothing else, the viewer must have been stunned by the complex beauty of Camillo's design. But there was something else, Renaissance magic. Camillo first of all built it into the proportions of his theater. It reflected the geometries of the zodiac and earth, a kind of sacred architecture thought to create resonant space focusing cosmic energy. And Camillo's images were more than artful. He crafted them like the talismans fashioned by so many of his contemporaries. He was following the hermetic belief that certain patterns and proportions align with the universe and induce the flow of astral or "other" energies, energies that alter mind and matter. This was how, it was said, the ancient Egyptians made their statues come "alive." Today, in certain international circles, this is the science of Psychotronics.

This esoteric secret is also expressed in music like that of the baroque era, which we've come to see does have an effect on mind and body. Similarly, the Ciceroni, the latter-day followers of Cicero, incorporated esoteric patterns in their speeches to more powerfully impress their listeners. Cicero underlay many of Camillo's images—literally, in boxes crammed with pages of his writing, more ideas to be associated with this universe of image and place.

Strange as it sounds to us, Camillo's grand design fascinated his contemporaries. In the Memory Theater, many adventurous thinkers saw their most fertile ideas made, if not flesh, at least manifest. Projected outside, seen in organic connection, in divine proportion, they could be reinternalized to more powerfully work their transformative magic—to open cosmic memory. And with cosmic memory comes cosmic power, the goal of a magus.

Magic Memory Patterns

In 1482, the first printed book on the art of memory appeared. A slew followed. People no longer had to remember everything. Yet a long sunset glow lit the spacious halls and far-flung ramparts of the glorious invisible architecture. A century after memory saw print, the Jesuit Matteo Ricci was busy telling Chinese scholars about the noble Xi-mo-ni-de, a poet who went to a fateful banquet. Busy was the word for Ricci. While doing his best to win converts, usually a handful a year, he also taught the Chinese Euclid's geometry, Western chemistry, astronomy, optics, and clock making, wrote his most popular book, *Friendship,* quoting Western writers from antiquity to his own day, composed lyrics for Emperor Wan Li's eunuchs to sing, and created an annotated map of the world that hung in the emperor's palace. He did most of it from memory. His memory palaces were the best of the few possessions he carried around the treacherous cape of Good Hope into the very alien and, for foreigners, very dangerous Ming empire.

Ricci left no record of how many dry and secure sites he built in his invisible storehouses for his precious cargo. Perhaps they rivaled those of Francesco Panigarola who, a 1595 treatise reported, used 100,000 memory locations. By then, books on memory had proved perennial best sellers. Some of the most popular explained "how to develop a powerful memory for success," which sounds familiar. Other best sellers described how to boost memory with drugs, plasters, and special dietary regimes, one more lively current running through the ongoing art of memory (see Chapter 18 for the latest). Another old strain of the art also saw print: the magical memory patterns of the Renaissance. The hermetic glimpse of heaven that possibly prompted such designs may be alive in the deep space of your memory right now.

14.   The Seventh Seal of Memory

Like the alchemist pouring over brittle pages of arcane symbols, some would-be memory magi hunched for hours over magic squares and patterns. Repeating magic words over and over, Renaissance practitioners concentrated on a chosen design, impressing it into memory. Some contemporaries put this down as the lazy man's way to supermemory. The church saw magical designs as the devil's own, condemning them as blackest heresy. Later academics tossed the practice into the superstition bin. Yet concentrating on a specific pattern, repeating special sounds over and over, is reminiscent of the two great mind-tools of the East—the yantra and the mantra.

This little association turns into something enormously intriguing that floods out in all directions, raising other connections and a thousand questions. We can only touch on it. Yantras are geometric patterns for contemplation. The most famous, a sort of master yantra, is the Sri Yantra: a central dot framed by seemingly endless interlocking triangles within a rim of circles. For thousands of years, people have gazed upon the Sri Yantra, until they began to feel themselves drawn into it in a strange sort of motion that carried them to other states of consciousness. There, sometimes, came a vision of the structure of the universe. What is so intriguing is that the same basic apprehension dawned in the minds of Druid seers, Siberian shamans, Indian yogis, and Plato. Time and space are irrelevant to an archetype, a root structure of consciousness—or in other terms, to the jogging of innate memory, Plato's divine memory.

In his poetic book, *The Tao of Symbols,* James Powell tells the story of how this archetype revealed itself around the earth. What is it? A pole, a cosmic axis, tree, pillar. Atop is a light. Spokes, like the spokes of an umbrella, come down from the top. Ringing these spokes are seven circles of rainbow light like a seven-tiered umbrella. Each circle sounds a pure note. Finally, imagine these cosmic umbrellas nested within each other.

Of the many reports Powell retrieves, one is from the ancient Indian *Puranas.* There are seven heavens nested along the cosmic pillar topped by the pole star, the sages said, all revolving and bound to the star by fetters. Why was this vision so overwhelmingly desired even, we suspect, in Renaissance memory schools? Because the light at the top is true light, is Dharma, Cosmic law, the sublime harmony supporting all things. Once it truly lights up in a person, she knows divine harmony. Right action cannot help but flow from her. The ecstatic then is known as also the eminently practical. Ecstasy as highest practicality was understood by the magus.

Right now in the deep space of your memory—star aglow, rainbow lights shimmering, the cosmic axis is probably making its eternal rounds. In 1970, Dr. Jonathan Shear accidentally found a way to recall it while studying the master Indian teacher, Patanjali, author of the *Yoga Sutras,* textbook for the science of yoga. Patanjali's instructions are precise as chemical formulae; specific actions will bring specific effects repeatedly. Discussing siddas—subtle or supernormal powers—Patanjali said to meditate on the pole star to learn the motion of the stars. Not much of a supernormal ability, Shear thought. People have gazed at the pole star forever to chart the constellations. Curious, he had a group of experienced transcendental meditators follow Patanjali's instructions for the sidda. Everybody got a surprise. A number of meditators independently saw and, more tellingly, sketched the same vision. One notes it "appeared like an umbrella . . . ribs of cloudy white light, a circle of rainbow light at the bottom . . . all rotated counterclockwise. Another jotted, "Pole star has a wide shaft of blinding white light going through its center like a super highway. . . . an umbrella, rotates counterclockwise. . . ."

Shear went on an umbrella hunt through the world's story house and found his prize in Plato's *Republic:* the myth of Er. Er has what we call a near-death experience. He dies, goes to heaven, then returns to tell what he saw. As you might guess, Er saw a great shaft of light extending through the universe. Fixed stars crown the shaft. Rainbow belts of light come from the top, holding wheels, nested like bowls. A siren perches on each wheel singing a single, glorious note. Following the macro-microcosm idea, so dear to the Renaissance magus, Hindus find this pattern reflected in us as the subtle energy system of the body with its seven whirling chakras. Associated with each chakra are singular seed sounds. Shear believes the myth of Er confirms that the TMers sighted a genuine construct of consciousness, one of Plato's ideal forms, an archetype—or what?

Shear might find ongoing confirmation through the art of memory, all the ascending spheres within spheres of memory patterns, the rings of Dante, the seven arcing rows of the Memory Theater with a great light, the sun atop, leading the seven creating powers. (All endless sevens that reflect the mystery of the octave.) Did some Westerners use the magic memory patterns and incantations as yantra and mantra to glimpse cosmic memory, the harmonious relation of all things? Would it work today? We don't know. We have not hunted arcane schools of memory in other countries. Yates reports that when Appolonius of Tyana, master of the Pythagorean memory mysteries, visited India, a Brahmin recognized his devotion to memory, saying "That is the goddess we most adore." This is global terrain that needs multilingual and "multimind" explorers who delight in unexpected links. Giordano Bruno would have loved the challenge.

A Martyr to Memory

If we think of Giordano Bruno at all, it's to remember that the Inquisition burned him at the stake for supporting Copernicus's theory that the earth circles the sun. Superficially true, but more accurately he was burned for the overarching heresies of his extraordinary memory systems. Fire was the natural element of this ex-monk, burning with charismatic intensity as he blazed across Europe and England. Circe replaced prudence when Bruno left traditional Christianity behind in his Dominican monastery, to spread with what he called "furious love," the ideas of a universal hermetic religion wrapped in a memory system.

Bruno built monstrously complex memory systems. He created a book of seals, symbolic emblems often used in Renaissance systems. One example is the still common picture of a man with astrological symbols on appropriate body parts—Aries the Ram on the head, Taurus the Bull on the neck. Bruno strove to imbue his seals with emotional intensity and, of course, they were talismans designed to evoke astral and artistic energies. Seals were not just passive pictures. They were active; talismans to be contemplated, internalized, and set to work in one's deep consciousness. Renaissance people sought talismans of specific proportion and design, believing these could evoke specific cosmic energies. They hoped to strike alive in themselves this talent or that power. This might not seem quite so strange if we think of aligning with and evoking an archetype. Or aligning with or resonating with the morphic form of a desired ability. One seal that Bruno loved greatly was *Phidias the Sculptor.*

Frances Yates was a major biographer of Bruno, he led her to the art of memory. His use of the sculptor seal reminded her of Michelangelo's freeing his statues from the marble block. The sculptor, internalized, at work in Bruno's imagination, frees "forms from the inform chaos of memory. There is something to my mind profound in the Phidias Seal," Yates writes, "as though in this inner moulding of significant memory statues, this drawing out of tremendous forms by subtraction of the inessential, Giordano Bruno, the memory artist, were introducing us to the core of the creative act, the inner act which precedes the outer expression." Mnemosyne is the mother of the arts.

Images, or as he also called them "shadows" of things were particularly important to Bruno. He considered images closer to reality, shadows less opaque to the light than the material thing itself. The student was to work his way through the seals, internalizing their energies until the last seal of seals opened cosmic memory, the highest knowing.

In his great drive to organize the psyche so that it could realize its divine heritage, Bruno tried system after system and made a significant advance when he put memory images in motion on revolving wheels. A glance at just the central wheel gives an idea of the enormity of his system. The inner wheel held all the astrological and astronomical images—houses, decans, planets, one hundred fifty in all and all shifting, recombining as the wheels turned. As this wheel revolved *in memory,* one would know a great deal. Around it rode other wheels bearing one hundred fifty images each, symbolizing just about everything, moving in endless combinations. There is a resonance here to the *I Ching* which seems even more elegant in its economy than usual compared to the Western wheels.

So complicated were Bruno's systems that many believed them purposefully made to confuse and throw the uninitiated off the hermetic scent. Probably so, for the enemy had long teeth. When Bruno debated the Copernican theory at Oxford, he was necessarily under the protection of the French ambassador whose king shielded him in Europe. Bruno had extended reasons to defend Copernicus. Camillo exalted the sun in his Theater because to the memory magus it symbolized the One Light and its octave of influences. To the magus, the sun's rising prominence heralded the return of their Egyptian wisdom philosophy. The idea that we circle the sun was natural to Bruno's group. With Hermes Trismegistus, they believed the earth moved because the earth is alive, is Gaia. This was the culture broth that helped birth the heliocentric theory. It is only we, looking back, who separate supposed science from supposed magic.

Bruno created smoke screens, but heart and soul he believed in striving for a unified memory, the memory of a divine human which would restore our transcendental nature and give creative powers equal to those of the great beings of light, "the star daemons." His writings are vast, often brilliant, and occasionally strike a distinctly modern note. He was a holistic thinker. Unlike his peers, who put intellect, imagination, and emotions in separate boxes, Bruno taught that there was intercommunication among them. He railed against the fragmenting of knowledge. He didn't just use images as passive signposts. Renaissance magi practiced imagery to bring about changes in themselves and their world.

Throwing off memory systems as a dandelion throws seeds, Bruno went to the Germanic lands where there is reason to suppose he became a shadowy founder of the Rosicrucians. Lured back to Italy, Bruno was burned in 1600, an event perhaps not as traumatic to this fiery man as it seems to us. He had long before noted that martyrdom might be the price of seeding wisdom philosophy, a price that a magus who knew that life rings on might be willing to pay.

Like the Rosicrucians, around this period a great part of Freemasonry certainly evolved from the art of memory—the invisible architecture, the symbols or seals and pieces of hermetic philosophy stretching from Pharaonic Egypt through Moses and Solomon to Bruno. What influence might the old art have had on Washington, Franklin, and other founding fathers? All Masons, all aware of hermetic predictions for this new world.

The art of memory did have its influences on the Age of Reason. Baron Gottfried von Leibniz borrowed his famous "monad" from Bruno who had it from hermetics. The great German was the first to name the bright thread that runs through and knits together the world's great traditions—"philosophia perennis," the perennial philosophy. Leibniz wrote about both mnemotechnics and the inner art of memory. Like many a magus he sifted through myriad images, alphabets, and symbols, seeking those closest to reality. He was probably the first European mathematician to study the *I Ching*, sent to him by Jesuits in Beijing. Leibniz found his symbols of reality in numbers and created something new: infinitesimal calculus. He envisioned something greater.

Leibniz hoped to invent what he called "a good Cabala," a higher calculus answering questions of philosophy and religion. Once such answers were found he believed, like so many past memory masters, that harmony and right action would flow naturally through human society. In Leibniz and in the work of the emerging modern scientist, one driving current of the great memory systems finally found elegant expression, the drive for order, system, method in knowing. Other currents flowed on like a great subterranean river to feed artistic roots, most notably perhaps those in the orphic line: Blake, Wordsworth, Emerson, Rilke.

The Return of Mnemosyne

The hardy but rather pale ghost of mnemotechnics survives today in perennially popular memory peg systems and in late night "informational" TV shows where audiences are still being wowed by anyone who can remember a list. But something much more impelling is going on. Mnemosyne seems to be coming up out of the dark again; signs of a renaissance are all around. Her historic attributes are waxing. Imagery has made a vivid comeback. There are even echoes of magic seals as people concentrate on videos of golf pros and attempt to internalize them. Meditation considered requisite for the highest knowing by memory masters is on the rise.

With the physical half of the magi's questions answered, people are plunging again into the other half of Mnemosyne's art to experience the wide spectrum of memory. They are reclaiming prebirth memories, seeking memories of "other lives," and, like Plato's Er, bringing back belief-altering memories from near-death experiences. As the fog lifts, we are starting to reach toward memories of the universe itself. Like the memory magi, people are not just seeking but using "other" energies to empower consciousness in the push to become what Bruno called "star daemons" and we call "possible humans."

To open the 90s, two Nobel prizewinners and a dozen other best scientists met at the University of California in San Francisco to explore *Consciousness Within the Sciences.* Mind and matter are again seen as two sides of one reality and there is talk of co-creation. Holistic this and holistic that tell of an urge to unify. The mnemonic urge to associate and link has us sighting interrelationship, interdependence on all levels of the global village riding Gaia, the living earth.

We've touched on just a handful of the secrets that powered the old mystery memory schools as if one took five or six snapshots to convey a grand tour of Europe. Like Lord Carnarvon, when he swung wide the long-sealed door to King Tut's chamber to reveal a glittering unimagined world of the past, Frances Yates, the intrepid scholar, has opened the door to the treasure-laden invisible world of Mnemosyne. Memory explorers apply here.

Our era has created artificial memory that would boggle our ancestors, with 17,000,000 bytes on a personal computer instead of 100,000 locations. Our forebears carried their mnemotechnics inside themselves, cohabitating, live memory images. Ours is also outside, a sort of proliferating "global brain" we draw on/add to with the speed of light. The art of memory has a new playing field. What will be our vision of cosmic memory? With new adventure in the air, we may drink a cup of kindness yet for old Mnemosyne.

15. Multiplying Memory

"Pick a genius you want to be: Einstein, Edison . . ." two IBM trainers told students starting a Superlearning experiment. They hoped to leverage learning by using imagination as a springboard into other people's memories and talents. Academia is a little more modest. To boost memory, a high-school science student in Des Moines might choose to be Dr. John Baker, oceanologist in Maui, and begin to imagine how Dr. Baker would tackle a project. Special students at Moscow's acclaimed Maurice Torez Institute of Foreign Languages went further. Before the first Suggestology French class, these ranking party members chose Gallic identities and fleshed out full imaginary biographies. Then like method actors they did their best to be Mimi or Jacques. Even the embarrassment of making mistakes changed identities. Commissar Yuri didn't make the dumb mistake, Jacques did. These Soviets never did discover who each other were, a ploy more for security than pedagogy perhaps, but it spurred learning.

Imagining you are someone else is another recycled learning/memory strategy. It links to the old esoteric idea of imagining putting on someone else's head. It links to a Buddhist practice of crafting exceptionally detailed images of gurus that are internalized to live and work inside oneself. In the United States, Tim Gallwey in particular has popularized the maneuver for sports, when he asks people to imagine they are the tennis pro, the ski star.

Dissociating from your regular self is another way of circumventing blocks, as British professor Dr. Robert Hartley discovered. Struggling with grade-school kids who consistently performed poorly, he remembered an inspired tactic he hit upon in his own school days. He had drawn blank after blank trying to write a paper. Finally he thought of a famous radio commentator he much admired. How would he say it? Words began to flow.

Hartley presented his slow learners with a simple picture-matching test. "Think of someone you know who is very clever," he said. "Imagine you are that person. I want you to do the test just the way he or she would." Results were eye-opening, the grades of the poor learners rivaled those of the high achievers. They imagined they were clever and became clever. It was too much for some to swallow. "Wasn't me," one boy protested. "It was the clever one that did it!"

Some people seem to literally reach into other people's memories — telepathists. Many of them claim extrasensory impressions rise to mind just the way memory does, an idea confirmed by Dr. W.H.C. Tenhaef, director of the world's first government-supported psi lab at the University of Utrecht. "It appears that telepathic phenomena can be classified under the laws of memory known to us," Tenhaef declared after uncovering numerous similarities between the working of psi and memory.

Psi even follows the patterns of displacement and repression found in memory. Tenhaef handed one of his well-tested subjects a cap that belonged to a man suspected of murdering his unwed daughter's baby. The subject, a university student, grew agitated, flung the cap away, and vehemently insisted he could get no impression at all from it. Several days later, the student told Tenhaef he dreamed of a man smothering a baby with pillows. Did it have something to do with the hat? Tenhaef admitted that a baby had indeed been smothered with pillows. His student confessed that as a boy he had thrown bricks into his newly born sibling's cradle. "That must be why I repressed the information and couldn't consciously pick up anything," the student said. This is the Poetzel effect again: data that enters subliminal memory in time works into consciousness, often through dreams. Tenhaef's exploration of the curious connection between psi and memory moved into even more mysterious areas (see Chapter 21).

Sometimes aspiring to other people's memories seems to reach into that great broth of information we all live in, the collective unconscious and transpersonal memory. That there are techniques to help one open out into wider memory was proved to us over twenty years ago in Moscow when we learned about Dr. Vladimir Raikov.

Artificial Reincarnation

Sun streamed into the large studio as art students glanced from the model to their painting. Dr. Raikov tapped the shoulder of a girl intent on her work. "I want you to meet a visitor."

The girl introduced herself, "I am Raphael of Urbino." The visitor, a reporter, asked, "What year is it?"

"Why, it's 1505, of course."

The reporter held out his camera. Did she know what it was?

"No, and I don't know why you're bothering me with foolish questions. I've work to do," the girl retorted, and turned back to her easel.

The reporter spoke to other painters. One was Rembrandt, another Picasso. Director Raikov approached yet another busy Raphael. Using a hypnotic signal, he brought the young man back to normal consciousness. "Look at your painting!"

"That can't be mine. I can't draw more than stick figures!" said the young science student. He, like the others, had absolutely no memory of the hours spent as a great master, like the others he at first refused to believe he'd created his painting.

All the artists in Vladimir Raikov's studio were in the throes of what Soviet journalists called "artificial reincarnation." Supposedly psychiatrist Raikov found a new form of hypnosis, very deep but, unlike the usual somnambulism, also very active. People can learn and develop in this state. After some weeks as Rembrandt or Raphael, the talent, but supposedly not the reincarnated personality, begins to filter into consciousness. Some students even decided to switch to an art career. They aren't Rembrandts. But their efforts do look like good magazine illustrations. By living a few hours a day as someone else, they coalesced training that often takes years into a few months.

Raikov reincarnated music students as great virtuosos, engineers as inventors, alcoholics as teetotalers, and one woman as an obstreperous Queen Elizabeth I. There is an obvious flip side, particularly as Raikov was for a time attached to a psychiatric institute known for its political prescriptions. Why not reincarnate a dissident as a model citizen? After a burst of publicity, Raikov's work wasn't much heard of again until Glasnost. Apart from exploring prenatal memory, friends tell us he kept reincarnating, and recently conjured healers. Among others, he studied the famous Georgian healer, Djuna Davitashvilli, a great public success in the 80s who reportedly helped keep the long moribund Brezhnev walking, if not always talking. Can Raikov reincarnate other people as Djuna with the power to heal? So far it seems, the answer is "yes."

Certainly "permission" to use one's vast innate ability is evoked by Raikov's work. Beyond that question rise—how do you define the boundaries of oneself, how far may one reach? Did Raikov's students draw some of their talents from transpersonal memory? Or even from actual past lives, their own or others? Reincarnation therapy is popular today. Patients are regressed to supposed past lives and in one way or another find release from mental and physical problems. What would happen if therapists instructed clients to call in their chips and remember the knowledge and skills of their "former" selves?

C.G. Jung made us familiar with the collective unconscious, the realm of archetypal memory. Do talents, personified as legendary figures, roam this dimension? Can one draw on their energies? Jung delved patterns of mind rather than transfer of data. That has been the province of the esoterics and their Akashic record, an ever growing, impersonal record of everything that happens, a cosmic memory. Supposedly it was to these records that Edgar Cayce went in his sleep to bring back sometimes astonishingly precise bits of information. On what shelf, in what drugstore, on which street, in what town might a little-known patent medicine be found that would help a client's ills. That doctors have credited many of Cayce's prescriptions has overshadowed the arresting fact that he could so easily dip into an unseen information bank and bring back provable data.

Now we have channelers who speak of "light encoded data banks pulsing through dimensions." It's curious how the idea has persisted through history of an all-encompassing, pervasive world memory that one might tap (See Chapter 21). The Akashic record seems to resemble Sheldrake's morphic forms, nature's memory, a resemblance that no doubt helped ignite some furious antagonism. Critics ignored a major difference. Sheldrake's theory is testable. The germ of his idea came from scientific experiments in the first place, run in the 20s at Harvard by the eminent biologist, Dr. William McDougal.

Can you inherit learning, inherit memory? To find out McDougal taught swimming rats to get out of the drink through a lighted exit rather than a dark one. Children learned faster than parents. Others took up the experiment; generations of rodents learned faster and faster. But there was a big problem. Rats with no biological connection to previous learners also were learning faster. It wasn't genes, yet something seemed to be transferring memory. What was it? The build up of a morphic form, Sheldrake says. These composite patterns have no energy and are thus unhampered by time and space. If rats can resonate to a generic memory built by others and learn faster, why not people?

A leading Japanese poet supplied Sheldrake with three supposed nursery rhymes. Though similar in structure, one has been recited for generations, one the poet newly composed, and one was nonsense. Series of non-Japanese volunteers recited them aloud. Tested later, 62% remembered the traditional rhyme best—a highly significant number, only 33% would be expected by chance. This suggests learning got a boost from a strong morphic pattern built up by millions of people who knew the rhyme. In a like vein, people learned what they thought was Morse Code. Half was the real thing, half scrambled signals. Again, people remembered best what thousands had learned before them, which supports the idea of an ongoing, building field of information—nature's memory. Most, though not all, similar experiments suggest that one can tune into morphic fields, to outside memory. Morphic patterns shape the forms of giraffe's and crystal's, and they also reinforce the shape of behavior and knowledge, which has intriguing implications for the process of change. How might one try to tune to a desired morphic form?

Though nothing is definitive, there are hints. Whether crystal, embryo, or aspiring math major, a seed pattern or some bit of knowledge within is needed to begin resonance with a field without. In problem solving, one is told to saturate herself with data, then let go. That would give a seed and a further assist. As information is added, resonance should become more specific, more focused. Is this one reason why the advice to "act as if" seems to work? Does "acting as if" help one resonate to the shape of one's desire? In the Morse Code experiments, the apparent boost from morphic forms showed up in people who used feeling (in the sense of Jung's four functions) in an introverted way. In other words, they are accustomed to turning within to find knowledge, they don't see it as something apart from themselves, and are thus perhaps more sensitive to the subtle resonance of morphic forms.

Sheldrake's theory has just begun to reveal a little about the memory that pervades the cosmos. How far an individual's memory may extend, over what borders it may cross is still an open question. It's another frontier calling for adventurers. Adventure in the hair-raising sense describes the lives of a special group of people possessing many memories.

What the Twenty-four Memories of Billy Mean to You

Regan is a mean, strong man, the protector of the family. An expert in dangerous things, weapons and karate, he often lives up to his name, "rage again" in Serbo-Croat, a language he reads, writes, and speaks well. In heavy, Slavic tones, this committed Marxist describes himself as 210 pounds of muscle, with black hair and a long, drooping mustache. He's been seen to slug a heavy punching bag for twenty minutes when most men drop exhausted in five. Part of the secret is his ability to control his adrenalin flow at will. Regan's only physical defect is color blindness.

Though a year younger, the bespectacled Englishman Arthur doesn't care for anything so physical as exercise. When no immediate danger threatens, his rational hand steers the family, numbering two dozen. Deduction is his forte and some of the mysteries Arthur has figured out would not be elementary to Sherlock Holmes. Well versed in physics, chemistry, and medicine, he talks like an upper-class Brit, but he also reads and writes Arabic. Politically, Arthur is conservative to the core.

Labeled antisocial, Tommy can wiggle out of almost any situation, social or otherwise. Police turn red, hospital attendants gape when Tommy eases out of handcuffs and straightjackets with the aplomb of Houdini. His avid study of electronics gives him the know-how to repair the family's raft of equipment. In his spare time, Tommy plays the sax and paints colorful landscapes. Christine is another family member who likes to paint—and crayon. Butterflies and flowers are her favorite subjects, for she is only three, a perfect picture of a little girl with soft blond hair and big blue eyes.

Odd bedfellows even in the commune days, these four share the same house. They also share the same body, that of Billy Milligan. In a 1978 trial that drove Ohio headline writers wild, Billy Milligan became the first person judged not guilty of a major crime by reason of insanity, defined as Multiple Personality Disorder. A number of psychiatrists supported the diagnosis. More tellingly, so did the prosecutors and the judge. They had sat through eerie hours experiencing vying personalities seize control of Billy. If this was acting, it was of a different order, for no actor ever sent such a disturbing chill through them. They agreed that what they had under lock and key was a rare and pitiable creature.

Multiple Personality Disorder, MPD, a seemingly impossible phenomenon, has long fascinated people. Millions call it by another name: Jekyll and Hyde. In the 19th century, Robert Louis Stevenson wasn't alone in his absorption with the idea. Doctors, philosophers, and most particularly psychologists and parapsychologists pursued multiples. Here was a living lab in which to engage questions that fired some of the best minds of the day, men like Frederick W.H. Myers in England, Alfred Binet and Pierre Janet in France, William James in America. They wanted a scientific understanding of "dissociation," the splitting off of a group of thoughts or mental activities from mainstream consciousness. Dissociation is as old as trance and dreaming, as the altered states of artists and shamans. Understanding its dynamics, researchers thought, would lead to cures for a variety of ills. Many also believed it would lead, as James put it, "to superior dimensions of mind" not usually available, to an exploding realization of human potential. Dissociation is another way of talking about state dependent memory and learning. In a multiple, state bound memory isn't just a secret hidden away from consciousness. It's a secret named Arthur off to the library for books on hematology, or Regan heading to target practice.

Before early investigators found many answers, scientific fashions changed. Dissociation was out. Multiples became a back-shelf curio, until the 50s when Drs. Corbett Thigpen and Hervey Cleckley brought out *The Three Faces of Eve*. In the 70s, Dr. Cornelia Wilbur of the University of Kentucky Medical School revealed her pioneering work with the multiple Sybil. If you'd been at a conference led by Chicago's Rush-Presbyterian-St. Luke's Medical Center in the fall of 1984, you could have heard the beginning of an ongoing deluge of research, as doctors presented over a hundred reports at the First International Conference on Multiple Personality and Dissociative States. You also could have witnessed "Cassandra" try to convey what it's like to have dozens of alter egos sharing your body and brain.

As Robert Louis Stevenson realized, it's a horror story. That's why it seems worse than insensitive to find this disorder so exciting. But it is. In a strange, bizarrely dramatic way, MPD pulls together many of the most lively strands of contemporary thought. It's as though the underside of things got all dressed up in stripes and feathers, polka dots and rhinestones, and shouted, "Hey! Look!" to catch our attention. Of course there are ties to memory and brain research. There are also ties to new thinking about such disparate topics as hypnosis, near-death experiences, and evolution. There is resonance with explorations of subliminal memory, exceptional human talents, mindbody healing, and transpersonal concerns. All this from people who have almost always been horrifyingly abused as children, who are often trapped in jails and mental institutions.

Until the last decade there was little help for their horror stories. Imagine how you'd feel, suddenly surrounded by friends you'd never made, being congratulated for your prowess on the piano or in higher math, skills you have no knowledge of, or worse, waking up in L.A. when you live in Dallas, being labeled a liar, being fired, arrested for acts you can't remember. The holes in a multiple's memory truly are black holes. And always there is the stalking fear that someone is trying to take you over. As one victim said, "It's as if I'd put out a contract on myself."

Apart from all the fascinating implications for our ideas about memory, consciousness, and self, there is another reason MPD has grabbed scientific interest. Multiples are multiplying. MPD is still a rarity and, yes, there has been some faking, some misdiagnoses, but the truth is there are a great many more people with MPD than before. Jekyll/Hyde was a tidy dual personality. Clinicians report our multiples average eight to thirteen personalities. They've uncovered a few "super multiples" with over a hundred alter egos. Families have appeared with three generations of multiples, and at Odyssey House in New York, Dr. Arlene Levine treated identical twins each with six alters. Why is this happening at this moment in time, this arc in evolution?

Most multiples are smart enough to understand the implications of their problem. "I've never met a multiple with an IQ less than 110," says Cornelia Wilbur. Dr. David Caul, one of Milligan's doctors, notes that multiples are exceptionally perceptive. "They can smell a liar at a thousand paces in one ten-thousandth of a second." Exceptional functioning often shows up: photographic memory, extraordinary auditory and sense memory, paranormal abilities, artistic talents, and, as many clinicians attest, the ability to heal faster than the rest of us.

To escape overwhelming circumstances, the multiple turns inward and leaps into other states of mind. Once the leap is made, like a crystal from another planet, the glittering facets of personalities reflect in a distorted but nevertheless real way the mind's breadth and potential. Arthur sounds like a Victorian schoolmaster prodding his bodymates to make the most of themselves: study, practice, exercise, it will improve the family's chances.

What sort of memory does an alter ego have? One kind is the witness sort, like a court reporter's records. One of Cassandra's personalities, a bashful little girl named Stayce, rarely takes over the body, preferring to follow her original mandate. Years ago, she was "told" to "stay and see" what was going on when the young Cassandra was abused. She has.

"I taught the others all they know," claims Milligan's most extraordinary personality, called simply the Teacher. A seeming genius with a wry sense of humor, he has almost perfect recall. Teacher was a boon to Daniel Keyes, who interviewed his subject for two years before writing *The Minds of Billy Milligan*. Teacher remembered the highs, the lows, actually everything about the other personalities' experiences, and even gave an accurate account of a choking accident that sent Billy to the hospital at age one month.

Most multiples seem to have a Teacher somewhere, now usually called the "Inner Self Helper," a wise one with almost omniscient memory. It's as if one could finally talk to the sort of total memory we're all supposed to have but rarely connect with. Original personalities—the Billy in Milligan, whose surname has the ring of a Joycian pun—can't usually connect with this all-remembering personality. Nor without extensive treatment can they remember the knowledge, skills, or experiences of their alter egos. Usually originals are amnesiac and don't know they have bodymates. Which leads to strange introductions in therapy: "Billy, this is Tommy." Most personalities find the idea that there are other "someones" in their body hard to believe. Apart from the Teacher, of Milligan's personalities only Arthur and the child Christine realized what a queer situation they were in. Arthur deduced it. Try as he might, reason led him to the unreasonable conclusion that he was in a boardinghouse body. Arthur told Regan. Christine knew from the start. Perhaps her demonstrated ESP ability helped.

Alter egos often are able to share memories. Regan and Arthur became co-conscious and conferred in English. Regan was fluent in Serbo-Croat. Arthur knew Swahili as well as Arabic, but it didn't transfer. Billy knew only English. Bilingualism isn't rare in multiples. Personalities pick up languages just as they may become proficient in math, psychology, history. One multiple has a brilliant doctoral candidate among itself, while the benighted original has a rather mundane mentality.

The basic bond between emotion and memory came to light in an interesting way in multiples. A therapist listens to an alter tell about his vacation trip. Something doesn't ring true, the account doesn't have the emotional feel of a real memory, it sounds like someone recounting a story he'd been told—which in fact he had been by another personality who "took" the trip. Sometimes alters do remember factual things that happen to a bodymate, but are unable to recall emotional experiences or learned skills. This is state dependent memory writ big and bold. When you're in the Arthur state you know Arabic, in the Tommy state you don't.

Subliminal studies show that one can pick up information and fuse it into long term memory without being aware of the process. As striking as such subliminal feats are, they may be just a weak glimmering of the multichannels available to us. Cassandra, who fittingly studied brain sciences, has a modus operandi that would be the envy of any graduate student. "When I'm writing a paper on dichotic hearing, one of the others is composing the proposal for 'my' master's thesis. Someone else has prepared dinner and will later clean up the kitchen while I sleep. . . . I can no more prevent the others from working than I can prevent the change of the seasons. . . . We share the body so the time I am at the typewriter limits the others' use of the body. It does not prevent any one of them from using the brain to plan, design, or compose."

Compared to most of us, this is like switching from mono to twenty-eight-track recording and performing. What's hard to keep in mind about all this academic specializing, splitting of chores, and separate emotional responses, is that it's going on simultaneously in one brain. Apparently the multiple has found a way to activate that vast capacity of the brain the rest of us rarely access.

Most of us are aware that mind is somewhat fluid and has a certain plasticity. We can be of two minds, we can change our minds, we can imagine and daydream ourselves otherwise, we are different people in different relationships—boss, child, tennis opponent, lover. We know the stuff of mind is malleable. Just as surely we are quite certain that our body is pretty well fixed. Even to make it a little thinner or stronger or healthier takes quite a bit of doing. Unsticking our ideas about our bodies is perhaps where multiples can give us the most valuable insights.

Change Memories; Change Bodies

One, two, three—that's how long it takes multiples to switch personalities. In those same instants, they often switch handedness, righties turn into lefties, lefties into righties. This is an answer to the idea that multiples are "just acting." As any righty who ever tried left-handed scissors knows, handedness isn't something you flip off and on. Until now, it's been considered a fixed trait. So have such things as unique electrical and chemical patterns in our brains.

At the National Institute of Mental Health, Dr. Frank Putnam studied the brain wave patterns of three different personalities of each of ten multiples. "They seem to vary as much from one personality to another as from one normal person to another." Putnam thinks "multiples may, in fact, be one of those experiments of nature that will tell us a whole lot more about ourselves. . . ."

Dr. Robert DeVito of Loyola University studies blood flow in various regions of the brain in multiples. His findings suggest that alter egos show different patterns of biochemical balance. DeVito speculates that "the clinical switch from one to another may be the result of a biochemical switch process involving the complex phenomenon of memory." It seems that each personality settles in with its own biochemical "net" which repatterns the brain. *And the body.* This shift in body has profound implications for all of us.

You might not want to switch hands, but it would be handy to switch off hay fever or an allergy to orange juice or cats. Case histories are full of instances where only one personality has an allergy. Disease vanishes when another takes over the body. One alter may get poison ivy, the others can tramp unconcernedly through the woods—in the same body. An unknowing doctor might develop pathology himself treating a multiple. Fortunately, Illinois optometrist Dr. Kenneth Sheppard, knew "whom" he was treating. He recorded definite changes in eye pressure and corneal curvature as personalities changed. Astigmatisms came and went, farsightedness fluctuated. One nearsighted multiple required plural prescriptions. Her adults needed various strong lenses, but when she switched into a six-year-old alter, very weak ones gave her 20/20 vision.

Why do multiples heal faster than the rest of us? Many researchers note that they do. As yet no one knows quite why. Perhaps when a personality other than the one who sustained the injury switches in, it doesn't carry the cellular memory of the wound and so is able to repair more rapidly. A new "memory" or personality automatically brings a reprogramming of the biochemical and electrical patterns of the body. Or as Dr. Abrezol put it, "All disease is memory." A different sort of clue to rapid healing may come from Celeste, a flirtatious teenage blonde, another of Cassandra's personalities. Originally when Celeste controlled the body, she indulged in self-mutilation, a symptom of MPD. Maturing, she became interested in healing. Celeste practices mental healing through visualization and in the best tradition of modern imagery training, pores over texts to gain a clear picture of body organs and inner structures to aid her visualization.

Supposedly, Celeste can continue her healing imagery even when another controls the body. Could the rest of us learn through suggestion or otherwise to continue healing imagery on another channel while we went about our conscious business? This idea of another "personality" or state bound memory or autonomous construct of consciousness, whatever you want to call it, working away on its own, has a curious resonance to the practices of the memory magi. They attempted to internalize a talisman or a seal like Phidias the Sculptor. Drawing on senses and emotion, they strove to create an active image within themselves, one that took on a life of its own, rather like an author's characters, a poet's muse, a monk's saint. This imaginatively birthed construct of consciousness worked to an extent on its own to change, it was hoped, mind and body.

As a multiple's alter egos move in and out, they reorganize all sorts of physical systems. They change bodies as well as personalities. One unfortunate woman wound up with three menstrual periods per month, one for each self. Chicago psychiatrist Bennet Braun, another pioneer in the treatment of multiples, had a diabetic patient. Diabetes vanished when her alter ego took control. Epilepsy, dyslexia, and a number of serious diseases can be tied to different personalities. Some smoke, others can't stand the weed. Some shoot heroin, but their abstaining alters suffer no withdrawal. The message is straightforward. And shocking. *Change memories and the body changes.* Dr. Wilbur suspects multiples age more slowly than we do. What are we waiting for? By now it should be clear why almost anyone who looks into multiples can become seduced by the mystery, why therapists must remind themselves their primary object is to cure, not to play Dr. Jekyll in these living labs.

MPD is a pathology. Yet in a crazy way it's casting before us data to blow open our horizons. Why can't healthy people begin to access the extraordinary range of memory and talent that multiples have? Like a good novelist, perhaps evolution is sprouting multiples as a foreshadowing of humans to be. The American scientist-philosopher Arthur Young, in his monumental work on the arc of evolution, looked at what happened in other kingdoms, like the molecular and plant kingdoms, when they came to an all-important turning point in their evolution—a point he sees us at. A burst of expansion exploded in other kingdoms as they turned up the arc of evolution, a shift to complexity and multiplicity, to the bounty of growth. *Genius,* says Young, is the translation in human terms. That's where evolution is taking us, he believes, and notes that a few have already reached this stage where all-around competency and mastery are the watchwords.

Young conjures da Vinci in his studio amidst paints, portraits, blueprints. Friends arrive. Suddenly the master leaps high in the air, his feet kick, ringing the bells on the chandelier. You don't have to be a gymnast to paint. But as studies of the gifted show, the quality of competency often generalizes, there is a drive to live and excel in many areas: a Nobel chemist is a fine musicologist, a brilliant novelist is equally regarded as a lepidopterist, a mathematician as a mystery writer.

In a much milder way, this has been seen in accelerated learning since communist instructors first noted that when the mind wakes to itself in one area, the effect can become global, competency spreads and generalizes. An English major finally clicks in sports, language mavens do better in physics. Allergies suddenly disappear.

The techniques promoted today by accelerated systems could be seen to stand in a curious relationship to multiple personalities. They could be seen as healthy ways to access the talents that multiples leap to in terror. Suggestion is used to reach different mindbody states to activate different abilities. Suggestion and imagination shape new self-images, competent in specific fields. People call on visualization and imagination to create "future memories," to conjure the more masterful, more talented selves they want to become. Others imagine themselves as someone else, hoping to leave behind their old limited selves and take on the expert's abilities. Closely related is Stanislavski's school of acting.

As Soviet teachers were well aware, Stanislavski and Suggestology drew from many of the same roots, particularly Raja Yoga. Using their "soul imagination," actors strive to take on the mindbody memory of their characters. Once in a great while, one goes too far and gets lost like a multiple in another personality. Stanislavski wasn't trying to hatch multiples. In effect, Vladimir Raikov is, creating short-term multiples as his students spend working hours as Rembrandt or Liszt. Raikov's work seems to be on the borderline of healthy access to the multiple domain. Over the edge is the artificial creation of multiples pursued by the world's KGBs and CIAs (see page 292).

Dr. Jekyll said, "We haven't begun to discover what science can do to the body and mind of man." Thanks to the Jekylls and Hydes, we might amend that to: science is just beginning to discover what the mind can do to the body. Just as a deep pond takes on the colors, the eccentric shapes of clouds and birds wheeling over, so the bodies of multiples take on the reflections of the personages that come and go. Even flesh and blood isn't so fixed as we thought. A scary idea perhaps, but also a very liberating one. Fundamental change is possible. Time collapses, change happens, that's the striking part. It's as though one looped out of our dimensions one second and returned changed the next. What does it mean that a different state bound memory, i.e., personality, takes over and, on the instant, a body sickens or heals? Part of the answer may be coming from another new generation of scientists approaching the mindbody connection from a very different level, the microscopic domain of endorphins and genes.

PART THREE

16. All Disease Is Memory

"All disease is memory," said Dr. Abrezol as we chatted in his New York hotel before he gave a presentation on Sophrology to the Futurist Society. It was a remark in passing, on a snowy afternoon, as we looked out at the ghostlike trees of Central Park. It was a remark that kept resonating and rose to mind at odd moments like a Cheshire cat, something that held a wonderful secret that would grin a moment and fade.

All disease is memory. . . .

Your immune system does have the memory of an elephant and can recognize a virus it hasn't seen in twenty years. That's why vaccination works. Scientists find they can train an animal immune system just like Pavlov's dog and get a conditioned response. At the "bell," immunity strengthens or, depending on the experiment, weakens though no physical agent is present. That takes memory. Yet that appeared to be only a tiny part of what Abrezol meant. It seemed the place to start looking for the secret was in the hotly debated, little understood, often misunderstood area of mental healing, an ongoing story from the *National Enquirer* to the *Journal of the American Medical Association.*

Can your thoughts, moods, imagination have a direct influence on your health? Can they cause disease? More interestingly, can they cure disease? The idea that they can is rippling out from the robust growth of holistic medicine with its roots in folk medicine, Eastern medicine, spiritual healing. At the same time, modern studies abound showing that people can somehow use their minds to influence their heartbeat, lower blood pressure, increase infection-eating white blood cells and cancer fighting T cells. Children have summoned mind power to increase the oxygen in their tissues, adults to fire a single nerve, and the rare swami to grow a tumor on demand, then dissolve it again. Just a few years back, the notion that mind could so influence, order, and reorder the body would have been hooted at by almost everybody.

It still sounds rather incredible to anyone over ten. What makes even interested scientists queasy is that it's tough to understand just how a young cancer patient could visualize his immune cells as Ninja

Turtles massacring cancer cells and actually have his malignancy reduced. What's the pathway, the mechanism, where is the hard science? Finally, a leap of faith is being supplanted by a great leap ahead in understanding the body's communication systems, in discovering how the hypothalamic-limbic system, so involved with memory and emotion, translates the thoughts and images of the mind into information that courses through a web of communication networks: your nervous system, endocrine system, neuropeptide, and immune systems.

Dr. Candace Pert looks as if she'd be a lot of fun at a party. A dark-haired, outspoken woman whose smile seems as quick as her mind, Pert is one of the brightest stars in what may turn out to be the most extraordinary detective story of our era. She's involved in the discovery of the vast, interlocking, previously unknown communication network that is starting to reveal that your mind and your body are not two things, but one and the same. It's called mindbody and it is a single information system. Mindbody's image hasn't quite settled into everyday thinking, even in the professions. But the picture is rapidly gaining substance and circulation as more and more researchers puzzle the pieces together.

Connected to the Brain Bone

The yeasty field that Pert and others like her are pursuing draws from a bevy of disciplines and is so new that its name hasn't quite been decided. Some call it psychoimmunology or psychoneuroimmunology, or neuroendrocrinimmunology—and the list trips on. Things were getting so tongue-tied that *Brain/Mind Bulletin* ran a contest challenging one and all to come up with a handier name. Please! Marie Tait of New Zealand won with "emotio-immunology." At least for the serious-minded. Neither we nor Marilyn Ferguson, the *Bulletin*'s bright guiding light, can resist the two choices proposed by Cynthia Turich of Pittsburgh. Acronyms are the modern way, she says, and proposed HYFIHYB (said hiffy-hib) which means of course: How you feel is how you be. Or some might prefer THBCTTBB (said thib-ke-tibby): The health bone's connected to the brain bone.

The seeds of HYFIHYB are rooted in the early 70s when researchers, very much including Dr. Pert, then a graduate student at Northwestern, uncovered opiate receptors in the brain. A receptor molecule is usually imagined as a lock waiting for its key. The key might be the molecules of substances like codeine or valium that many of us ingest. The key finds its lock and opens up relief from pain or cool vistas of relaxation. Did nature, eons ago, really set up receptors for codeine in hope that one day we'd develop a thriving pharmaceutical industry? Obviously if there are locks, keys ought to be in the body too. Pert's team found some. Your body, it turns out, has long been running a more state-of-the-art pharmacy than any we patronize, manufacturing such things as opiates, tranquilizers, antibiotics, even, it seems, PCB, the notorious angel dust. Which must make Mother Nature smile. While we strained for drugs to get around her, the slowest among us was bubbling them up. Here again, it's as though we were set the task of making conscious what we already "know" in innate memory.

Our homegrown opiates are part of a larger group of chemical messengers, small proteins called neuropeptides. Once they knew what to look for, scientists quickly picked out an ever mounting number of them. With such a host of messengers, it became obvious that a whole lot of uncharted communication must be going on inside human beings.

Pert and her colleagues at the National Institute of Mental Health zeroed in on "hot spots" in the brain, places overflowing with opiates and receptors, the richest being that old familiar, the limbic system, central control for memory and emotion. At first, everyone thought they were chasing brain chemicals. Then their view of the communication network stretched mightily. These messengers are not only received but, more remarkably, they are also manufactured throughout the body, in organs like the kidneys, glands like the adrenals, even in the mobile immune system itself. The opiates of the immune system are in *two-way* communication. There's a conversation going on.

"It struck me immediately," Pert told writer Rob Wechsler, "if these sexy opiate peptides could do it, so could all the other neuropeptides I'd been mapping. I thought, 'Wow! What we're really talking about is how the mind affects the body!'"

Something else struck Pert, something pretty outrageous, she noted. She was looking at the biochemical basis of emotion. "When we document the key role that the emotions, expressed through neuropeptide molecules, play in affecting the body," Pert says, "it will become clear how emotions can be a key to the understanding of disease."

Emotions rise from the limbic system, from the golden room in the middle of your brain, so involved with memory. How they can link to disease showed when Pert and her colleague-husband Dr. Michael Ruff rounded up a batch of volunteers and said, "Solve these puzzles." Then they bombarded the group with racketing noise, making it almost impossible to concentrate. Subjects couldn't control the distraction. They felt helpless. Pert and Ruff examined subjects' blood factors, specifically the macrophage, a big broth of a cell that gobbles up disease and helps rebuild tissue. The macrophage isn't fazed by the nastiest virus. But apparently it does go into a bit of tailspin when its person feel helpless; it doesn't do its protective work as well.

Body conversation isn't a simple two-way fax. The world within us is a buzz of simultaneous conversation rivaling our global networks. Like individual correspondents, neurons can change messages as they flow, cells "overhear" their surrounding fellows, there is constant flux and change, and, unlike locks, receptor cells may change their shapes to pick up different messenger keys.

This partakes of the marvelous, as endocrinologist Dr. Deepak Chopra points out. "You think, 'I'm happy.' Instantly, a neuropeptide translates your emotion "into a bit of matter so perfectly attuned to your desire that literally every cell in your body learns of your happiness and joins in. The fact that you can inexplicably talk to 50 trillion cells in their own language is just as inexplicable as the moment when nature created the first photon out of empty space."

Mysterious and exciting, just beginning to flourish, Pert's field has attracted some of the most creative people of our time. We can only touch on it, mainly to reassure that the idea that mind, memory, and emotions can influence the body is not beyond the bounds of science. In fact, the hard science of this new discipline predicts such influence and demands it.

The Missing Memory Link

As the press quoted scientists of stature like Pert speaking of the possibilities of mental healing, Dr. Ernest Rossi noted a change in his patients. They kept asking for help with all manner of bodily ills. Rossi isn't an internist, he's a distinguished psychologist. A Freudian, then a Jungian, he eventually became the close collaborator of Milton Erickson, the canny hypnotherapist said to "cure the incurable." Rossi knew about strange little mental feats, for years noted and then set aside. Touch an eraser to a hypnotized person's arm, tell him it's a lit cigarette and watch a fat blister rise. Or, if you're a good hypnotist, don't touch him, just command him to raise blisters in the shape of your initials. Then there was the out-of-left-field healing so common with Erickson. A teenager with excruciating, embarrassing acne asked for help. Erickson commanded him to live in a place with no mirrors. The acne disappeared.

Rossi had file cabinets of statistics correlating mental attitudes with disease, yet as we too often forget, *correlation is not cause.* Something happens between mind and body. The time might be ripe to find out what, Rossi thought, and looked to see what hard scientists had put together. Not much, he found to his great irritation. Fascinating pieces of data were unearthed in a swath of specialties, but the synthesis was missing.

Irritated enough, Rossi took a whack at mapping the territory himself and made his way through mindbody experiments springing up like shoots after jungle rain. Beneath all the exotic details and data, he found common ground. He began to prod specialists with questions. Could your thoughts and emotions, working through the newly discovered networks, reach right down into the heart of a single cell? Could they actually influence your genes? Push an endocrinologist hard enough, Rossi reports, "and he or she will admit, 'Yes, it's true!' "

"Mind does ultimately modulate the creation and expression of the molecules of life!" Rossi declares.

It's a bold statement, the sort that's set scientific teeth on edge this last century. Yet Rossi unrolls a lucid map of the scientific discoveries that lead to mind at the summit. In *The Psychobiology of Mind-Body Healing* and other writing, he traces how information is transduced, or translated, from one communication network to another, all the way from mind to molecule. If he were to die right now, the prolific Rossi told colleague Jane Parsons-Fine, the few hard-won pages mapping how information moves through mindbody would be his greatest achievement.

How can we use the mindbody connection to heal ourselves? Rossi, the map-making healer, made a discovery of his own. He added one more piece. "It's the missing link," he says. State dependent memory, learning, behavior. That's what's missing, Rossi realized, in all previous theories of mindbody relationship.

Thoughts, emotions, experience, and the many messengers of the body's physical networks move together through the limbic "filter" of state dependent memory. Like the Fates, SDM knits them together, weaving the pattern of who we are, who we may become—the quick, or sometimes the dead, as state dependent memory resonates and sends information, chemicals, energy through the body, changing and figuring the substance of ourselves.

All disease is memory. . . . The remark was beginning to take shape. To look at healing through the eyes of SDM may be the next step up toward practical ways to get well and stay well. As far as feeling better goes, for years memory it seems has knit physical and mental into the most curious remedy we have.

For Half, Half, Half Relief

"I will please" is what the Latin '*placebo*' means. "Damn nuisance" is what doctors called it through the last half century, as they tried to get rid of the gremlin tilting their clockwork experiments. "The wonder is that scientists have invested so much effort in 'controlling' for it, and so little in identifying how it might be used to best advantage," remarks Dr. Jeanne Achterberg, Director of Research in Rehabilitation at the University of Texas. This nuisance or pleaser, depending on which side of the bed you're on, borders on being the mythical panacea. To list only a few, placebos are known to work with hypertension, diabetes, asthma, and radiation sickness, with multiple sclerosis, colds, cancer, and to mimic birth control pills. The placebo was telling us something, but it didn't fit our view of ourselves, so it was quarantined.

If a scientist announced he'd discovered a miracle cure that could help 85 million Americans suffering almost any malady, you'd think he'd been sniffing over his test tubes too long. Yet one out of three of us responds positively to sugar pills or other placebos—potions, shots, devices, even surgery if it has no curative properties. Dig deeper and placebos get curiouser and curiouser, as Dr. Fredrick Evans found at the University of Medicine and Dentistry of New Jersey. If you take what you think is an aspirin, but it's really a placebo, you'll get 55% of the relief you'd get from the genuine article. (Relief has been well verified in double-blind tests with the pain criteria used to test drugs.) If you pop a codeine placebo, you'll find 56% of the relief codeine brings. Given make-believe morphine, you'll experience 56% of the ease flowing from a real shot. Strange percentages are astir in more than painkillers. Lithium helps manage depression. So does a lithium placebo, being 62% as effective as the chemical. The constancy of the effect implies that there is a pervasive process at work, and may even imply, some think, that half of the effect of all medical procedure springs from this underlying healing process.

For half, half, half relief . . . try *nothing* in a capsule. Nothing must have interesting ingredients. "Just suggestion," were the magic words used to ward away placebos. Oddly, research shows placebos do not work through suggestion, at least not that associated with hypnosis. Imagination, mental makeup, a variety of factors kick off unconscious processing that seems to involve networks of state dependent memories, personal and cultural. Dr. Jeanne Achterberg is an expert in imagination's historic healing role. For centuries until science blanked it out, imagination was potent medicine; now it's making a comeback. Achterberg cites a study of people hospitalized with bleeding ulcers.

All received water injections. Half were told the medicine they'd gotten was very effective, a sure cure for their problems. The other half learned that their injections contained a new, experimental drug, which might or might not help them. 70% of the group that believed they'd gotten a sure cure showed "excellent improvement." A year later the sure cure was still working, improvement held. Of those who thought they'd gotten an unproven drug, 25 percent showed marked improvement. What sort of person saw "the cup half full" with the supposed experimental drug, and unconsciously kicked off the body's healing powers?

Which is something to think about the next time someone spreads the "false hope" alarm. Beware the purveyor, we're told, who sounds as dire as someone trying to trip a meltdown in the neighborhood utility. Maybe hope doesn't take an adjective. For mindbody, its presence is healthier than its absence.

An unhappy example of people who tie imagination to cultural norms surfaced recently. To test a cancer drug, half a group of patients was given real chemotherapy, the other, placebos, with no one knowing who got what. When results were revealed, doctors discovered that 30% of the people taking placebos had lost their hair, just what one might imagine with chemotherapy. M.D.s and witch doctors, both are power points that can energize a web of deep memory and belief. The witch doctor, however, usually knows when he's resonating the negative. Some call that a *nocebo,* the placebo's opposite, which elicits what one might christen "the worry response."

Relief, of course, isn't in the placebo, it's in our response. Faced with the outside authority of pills and personages, our minds—as long as we're unaware of it—docilely make us better, activating positive, healing forces, memories that echo perhaps to the roots of the species.

How can you tell whether you're that one out of three who can be helped with nothing in a capsule? Researchers portray the placebo responder as an open-minded, creative sort, someone who likes to embroider things with his imagination, who likes to search for patterns and synthesize. Open to change, the placebo person can damp down skepticism that springs from analytical thinking. This is a sensitive person, but not necessarily the shy and shrinking sort, as one of the authors knows from her grandfather, Carl Schroeder, who much to the hilarity of a large, boisterous family was a great placebo responder.

A hardy, bear of a man who loved to lead old-style political parades, he became known as "Carl, the actors friend," because he couldn't resist serving up free lunch in his restaurant to the struggling theatrical troupes that circuited through town. One night when a pounding head kept him tossing, he went into the darkened bathroom, groped in the medicine cabinet, found, and swallowed two anacin. His headache eased and he fell asleep. Come morning he discovered there was no anacin in the cabinet, but two of his collar buttons were missing. On another nighttime excursion, he rummaged around in the dark searching for his favorite liniment to ease his badly aching neck and shoulders. Where was the damn stuff? At last he found the jar and generously lathered neck, shoulders, chest. Back in bed, muscles relaxing at last, he fell into a peaceful sleep. Until his wife hollered. There in the dawn he lay, covered with great gobs of black shoe polish.

Automatic, cheap, with no side effects, the placebo is indeed a pleaser. "Proof," as Norman Cousins says, "that there is no real separation between mind and body."

Your Innard Image

It's also proof that the mind can radically affect the body. So are the extraordinary shifts from allergy to no allergy, from diabetes to no diabetes in multiple personalities, who when they change memory banks—becoming Arthur rather than Christine—"change" bodies. If mindbody can heal, why doesn't it? This is where Rossi's state dependent memory comes in, the old mindbody patterns that send information up and down the octaves influencing cells, organs, mind, patterns that shape us as surely as the memory named Arthur or the memory named Christine shapes their body. How does one change the memories that send unhealthy signals. There are choices. "Look back, find the seed patterns of your ills," we're often told. And sometimes, finding a forgotten "reason" brings a liberating and healing rush of energy. Yet there is a cautionary in the dynamics of state dependent memory when it comes to focusing on the past. Sad moods call to sad memories in the past; mindbody state resonates and reinforces mindbody state, which in illness may be carving the same grooves deeper. Rather than looking backward, many people prefer to seize the power of the present, the one opening all of us have to effect change in our lives. They use their creative forces to reframe or rewrite the script playing out inside their bodies at the moment. Then they summon full sensed imagining to create future memories of health, memory patterns that send healthy information through the mind and matter of the body.

Jeanne Achterberg is one health professional who wasn't surprised when she found experimental evidence that imagination can influence the body, for she's long delved into the curative ways of tribal shamans and the keepers of Greek healing temples. In her work at Parkland Memorial Hospital in Dallas, Achterberg draws on this old wisdom to successfully light the healing and pain-dissolving imagination of people in the throes of cancer and traumatic burns.

How do you image your body? Not the outside, but the inside. Our image of our innards, it seems, can speak of our lives as powerfully as our outer image. Achterberg and colleagues ask people in severe stages of cancer, "How do you see your immune system, your white blood cells?" "Describe or draw them." Then, "How do you imagine your cancer?" Achterberg's team pored over patients' pictures and scored them for fourteen aspects like size and vividness. They discovered something remarkable. They could predict with uncanny accuracy how the patient would do in the next two months. Reading imagery, they were 100% right about who would be dead or significantly deteriorated. The imagery told them with 93% accuracy who would be in remission two months hence. Called the Image CA, their method can also predict in arthritis, diabetes, pain.

What are the images of life, what are the images of death? That's the quick question Achterberg is loath to answer. Images are symbols, they tell a story about how one is enmeshed in life, about all the little memories that make you unique. They speak too of cultural memory. The Image CA was shaped from the inner pictures of educated whites. "Abominable" is what Achterberg calls her initial effort to read images served up by charity patients, mainly black or chicano. As you might expect, there was resistance to seeing "white" blood cells as the good guys. But what is the clue when a woman pictures her cancer as a lemon, "because it reminds me of my husband."

With strong caveats, positive images of the immune system include those that fight the good fight: Knights of the Round Table, cavalry charging over the hill (unless you're an Indian), top gun pilots. Then there are patients who say "My white blood cells are like clouds," or "like snowflakes." It's not a healing sign.

Achterberg's studies found it's the nonaccepting, fighting images that bode well—with one exception. In charity patients, imaging a symbiotic relationship with cancer can point to better health. Why, one wonders. Poor, with little power all their lives, have they learned to take more circuitous, accommodating routes to survival?

"Picture your cancer." These images tend to be more biological, less symbolic. Generally, omens aren't good for those who image cancer as ferocious, grasping, or crab- or insectlike. As other doctors also note, images of cancer as a weak critter, which it is, or textbook pictures point toward healing.

The idea isn't to force oneself to see the "correct" picture; what the Image CA is diagnosing is the life state one is in. If these patterns or state dependent memories are known, then perhaps they can be reframed. Achterberg's intensive study of shamans—the wise men and wise women who for so long served humanity as priest-healers—led her to appreciate their skill in dissolving sickness. Some shamanic medicine was dead wrong, she warns, notably that of those working on the physical plane, the lowest rung of the old healing hierarchy. Even here, however, the most dangerous drugs were reserved for shamans who used them to fly high into the altered state where healing power resided. Primitive medicine, yet Achterberg sees a parallel between this "and providing the *patient* with powerful dangerous chemicals. . . . The chemical crutches, in both instances, are only evolutionary steps in learning to use the forces of consciousness to heal."

How to Imagine Healthy Memories

If you want to activate healing imagination, practice twenty minutes twice a day, more in a crisis. Relax your body; calm your mind by going to a safe place in nature. Belief in a healing, transcendental connection in nature dates to the earliest medical systems like Ayurveda of ancient India. Mountains, meadows, beaches—if they stereotype, try summoning a masterful picture or a few favorite lines. "Feel the gladness of the May! . . . of splendor in the grass, of glory in the flower." Or, "watch the crisping ripple on the beach. . . ." Let the sights, smells, sounds, rise around you. Some wander the green pastures of a favorite psalm, resting a moment beside still waters. In this comfortable state, ask for and choose your healing images. Make sure they *feel* right.

Immune forces come sailing forth, all flags flying. Again, most choose the heroic, the invincible, from tigers burning bright to great white sharks or Kung Fu masters. Children can get caught up with play images—the insatiable PAC MAN gobbling disease. Some find success with a minimalist approach. Dr. Michael Samuels's patients see viruses as dots on a blackboard and erase them one by one. Attack, however, isn't the watchword for all problems.

A blue, soothing light, a drop of lubricating oil at a sore joint might be envisioned, or the touch of a healing hand, the palm of Christ. Feel out what works best for you. Dr. Vera Fryling, for instance, used slides to help a construction worker with a painful back injury evoke his imagination. After viewing dozens of photos, the man chose one of a cool, refreshing mountain stream. An anatomically correct picture of the back was superimposed on the slide to give him a soothing and healing image to summon at home.

A San Franciscan with AIDS, hospitalized by a threatening infection, used a more generative approach. The necessary treatment required a platelet count of at least 5000. "Yours is only half that," his doctor said. His death sentence? The man lifted the bedside phone and called Maggie Creighton, who with her late husband, James, pioneered the development of self-reliant cancer patients. Relax, she said, guiding him into his bones, into the marrow where blood cells grow. He began to see and sense blood cells "like grapes ripening on the vine," multiplying in a springtime of growth. Like grapes in a vineyard, he saw them differentiate into red and white cells and especially platelets. He imagined himself with abundant platelets, vital and renewed after the proposed treatment. Two days later his platelet count had doubled, he got his treatment, and left infection behind. Full sensed visualization is one of the powers awakened in cancer patients at the Creighton Health Institute, whose participants have a survival rate double the national norm.

Get information about your problem. There is a lot of cheering for infection-fighting white blood cells, yet if you have an autoimmune disease like rheumatoid arthritis or Epstein-Barr, the last thing you need is more of them. Today there are support groups, books, tapes, imagery societies, ongoing research; a warm world of help is available if you want to try the full complement of mental healing.

Eventually, as you learn to move easily in the healing imagination, Achterberg says, "physical sensations and word pictures disappear. . . . The imageless, wordless void is experienced as a state of unity, of divine harmony. The strife for physical health becomes irrelevant in the grand scheme, the magic remains, the spirit triumphs."

That's one answer to those who say mental healing is dangerous and burdens those who don't recover with self-blame and depression. Self-blame is a possible side effect, but is it worse than those of other methods? The critics seem to be looking from the old either/or level, the guilt level. In the best holistic therapy, the goal isn't so much cure as shedding the old baggage and finally really living the life one has. Guided from this perspective, no matter how things turn out, perhaps guilt need not apply.

In our battling times, a battle that could affect all of us is being joined in medicine; it's an ideological war which sometimes seems as full of enmity, half-truths, and a sense of divine right as the religious bloodletting of the 17th century. It's not so much a matter of one prescription or another, but a split in views on the nature of humans. The orthodox are entrenched on one side, the champions of myriad alternatives on the other. But middle ground has been won. Some physicians are adding the complementary arts of other medicine and mental healing to their practice, reviving the original sense of their title, *Doctor.* At root, it means, "to teach." Almost twenty years ago, we ran into a man who deserves the title. Carl Simonton was then a young cancer specialist in the warm grip of an idea: what is different about that small but real number of patients who experience spontaneous remission and live healthily ever after? (In 1989, Brendan O'Reagan, research director of the Institute of Noetic Sciences, announced a newly collected data base, culled from medical journals, of over 3,000 bona fide cases of spontaneous remission of profound disease.) Eventually Simonton, with psychologist Dr. Stephanie Simonton, worked out a nurturing, holistic protocol with heavy emphasis on visualization to help others become the kind of people who recover. The Simonton method has become a worldwide model.

The Simontons took a lot of potshots to open the way in this remembering of medicine. A number of exceptional doctors have followed, like Dr. Ahmed Elkadi, a cardiovascular surgeon and former professor at the University of Missouri Medical Center. "There are no incurable diseases," Elkadi says flatly. President of the Institute of Islamic Medicine for Education and Research, Elkadi brings a genuinely holistic approach to his international practice, combining allopathic medicine with herbal and European medicine, acupuncture, biofeedback. And he treats "negative memories, they have to be healed too for a return to health." Believing that only mainline scientific evidence will draw doctors to this wider approach, Elkadi tests his therapies with volunteers and in vitro and has gathered some eye-opening results. Like most holistic doctors, the occasionally Koran-quoting Elkadi also tries to bolster spirit as well as mind and body.

So does Bernie Siegal, M.D., a man beloved by his patients, if not by some of his colleagues who can't understand why this Yale surgeon says, "My hardest job is getting people to love themselves." Siegal works with people not "patients," a name he doesn't like. Think about it: patient, long suffering, submissive . . . Be the opposite, Siegal urges, be "heroic," grab hold of your unique gift of life. Being alive, he emphasizes, means some knocks, some frights that can freeze up a bit of life here, a chunk there. Work on them, Siegal says, don't be like Sadie, a woman reminiscent of the comic strip Momma Hobbs, who boasts, "Being sick is what I do best." When Siegal told Sadie he had a new shot that would "cure" her drastic ills, she somehow never had time to make it to his office and finally admitted that sickness was her way of getting on. "It's too late," she said, to learn to relate lovingly to herself and others. Sadie never discovered what so many who work at self-healing find: *every day is genesis.*

Even a vicarious experience of real love can spur the immune system, according to Dr. David McClelland. At Harvard, his students watched films of Mother Theresa as she ministered to the dying. Then McClelland checked students' saliva for a change in immune factors. Immunity increased. It didn't seem to matter whether the students were inspired, as about half were, or skeptical of what they'd seen of the good nun. "Perhaps she was contacting these consciously disapproving people in another part of their brains," McClelland says, "and that part was still responding to the strength of her loving care." Perhaps she touched off old state dependent memories of loving care almost everyone accumulates sometime in life. This is the reverse of what Hans Selye found, body memories of past stress and disease resonating in the present. It's also a bit of scientific data to back up another way of using memory to banish the shadows of disease.

How Sophrology Uses Memory To Heal

Say PER aloud, slowly. You'll sound like a tabby basking in a friendly lap. That's what Positive Emotional Reinforcement is about, using the healing glow of good memories to banish ills. In the hit musical *Cats*, Grisabella, with an assist from T. S. Eliot, sums it up when she sings her haunting "Memory." "Memory, turn your face to the moonlight / Let your memory lead you / Open up, enter in / If you find there the meaning of what happiness is / Then a new life will begin."*

* Text copyright © 1981 by Trevor Nunn/Set Copyrights Ltd. Reproduced by permission of Faber Music Ltd. London.

American are beginning to research the healing power of good memories; Sophrology has used memory therapeutically for three decades. One of the authors has her own good memories of attending an international Sophrology Conference in Lausanne, Switzerland and talking with Dr. Alphonso Caycedo, a stocky man in shaded glasses, a man who exudes strength—moral, physical, mental—and speaks softly. With Sophrology, Caycedo has introduced a new branch of medicine, or perhaps reclaimed and updated an ancient one, for like a medical Marco Polo he long ago embarked on a multiyear research expedition to India, Tibet, and the Orient to search ancient knowledge for techniques to heal modern ills. The Dalai Lama himself made it possible for Caycedo to study at Tibetan centers rarely opened to outsiders.

Sophrology, used for both physical and mental problems, means harmonious consciousness, and consciousness is seen as primary in this branch of medicine. According to Caycedo, doctors who don't take consciousness into account are working as veterinarians. Practiced by 20,000 professionals, mainly M.D.s in Europe and South America, Sophrology is a system of many parts. One is to move clients into a state of "dynamic relaxation." Another is to deliver therapeutic suggestions with *terpnos logos,* special incanting tones of voice which tests reveal also stimulate the thymus gland, an organ of the immune system that Caycedo says is highly involved with emotions. Sophisticated use of memory is also an integral part of Sophrology; there are techniques to banish negative memories, techniques to summon the healthy magic of good memories.

The first step of the negative-memory-erasing method, Caycedo explains, is to achieve the special relaxed state, using techniques drawn from autogenics and Zen, which he considers "perfected Raja Yoga." Then you begin "serial sophro-correction." This is accomplished in ten-minute visualization sessions once or twice a day. Let's say you have a bad memory of being thrown from a horse and severely injured. You approach the actual trauma gradually in your imagination. The first day, you might simply imagine getting into the car to go to the stable. Once you have the scene, immediately relax all the muscles in your face, shoulders, and body, and then, Caycedo instructs, imagine the scene as a happy, really upbeat one. In succeeding sessions, summon the memory ever closer, each time letting go, relaxing, and turning the scene into one of happiness and joy. You build to and through the actual trauma inserting happy memories, and little by little the corrosive memory loses its negative spin. Then, as Eliot said, a new life can begin.

A second Sophrology memory technique ignores the negative and makes the very most of the positive energy of good memories. "Divide your life into three sections and pick a positive recollection from each time span," Caycedo instructs. Then move each memory through five stages:

1. Evocation: evoke the positive memory from the past.
2. Fixation: concentrate on this positive sensation.
3. Association: associate colors, objects, and persons with this positive sensation.
4. Repetition: repeat the positive sensation so it is impressed on the mind.
5. Presentation: amplify this positive sensation in a written or oral form.

Caycedo and his many colleagues find that this technique can help dissolve not just mental hangups but physical ailments as well. Caycedo believes these warm, life-giving recollections raise a subtle energy in the body—"elan vital," he calls it—that floods through mindbody and washes away energy blockages caused by life's negatives. There are dozens of medical books on Sophrology and many more scientific reports, although hardly one, alas, in English. Alphonso Caycedo is another seminal thinker, perhaps the first person in our day to establish a fully elaborated working system, a branch of medicine, to treat body, mind, and spirit. In self-interest, perhaps it is time the English-speaking world discovered him. As noted elsewhere in this book, Sophrologists have moved out from the medical center to activate the inner alchemy of memory, to enhance learning and sports training.

Wondering Yourself Anew

Like rambling through a summer countryside, over a hill into a meadow, wondering is a pleasure of a more leisurely time. To heal, try a little wondering, Dr. Rossi recommends. As placebos show, the deep mind can often go about rebalancing health on its own. You don't always have to analyze, guide images, petition for relief. You can just wonder. The best wondering times are the rest periods of what Rossi calls ultradian cycles, those rhythmic shifts from one nostril to another, from one hemisphere to another, from outer to inner focus, that life rhythm we rarely make the most of (see Chapter 5).

Rossi stumbled on the rhythm in a Navy report. Inexplicably, even the sharpest radar operators tended to wander off a bit and daydream, about every ninety minutes. During this cycle, they were most likely to miss an immediate blip on their screens. An *Aha!* reaction hit Rossi. This natural rhythm must be behind his friend Erickson's ability to wield his healing magic through "the common everyday trance," a subtle inward shift in the patient that no one but Erickson seemed able to perceive. Finding confirmation in yoga and contemporary research, Rossi realized that riding these natural rhythms could leverage healing, self or otherwise. Rossi himself found that moving inward with the cycles to wonder brought him joy and sometimes deep creative and healing insights.

At some point during the rest cycle, which lasts about ninety minutes, find a comfortable place in your body. Connect with that comfort and let it spread. Forget suggestion, imagery, and everything else, simply enjoy the comfort. And wonder. Wonder lazily how your subconscious is going to deal with what's bothering you, knowing that mindbody's inclination is toward balance and health. Think of symptoms as helpful signals letting you know that some experience has become a state bound block to your birthright of health and growth.

Comforting yourself with short rest periods gives your subconscious a chance to use its extraordinary creative powers to reorganize and heal. Riding the ultradian rhythms, some people decide not to even wonder. These are the serious, or, really, joyful meditators who release themselves to the center of being.

In Solzhenitsyn's *Cancer Ward,* the ailing Kostoglotov chances upon something amazing in a medical tome on tumors. Struck, he reads it out verbatim to the other patients in the ward. " 'It happens rarely, but there are cases of self-induced healing.' "

"There was a stir throughout the ward. It was as though 'self-induced healing' had fluttered out of the great open book like a rainbow-colored butterfly for everyone to see, and they all held up their foreheads and cheeks for its healing touch as it flew past."

It's still amazing, but the butterflies are multiplying. And some of them seem to be rising from the fields of life cocooning every human body.

17. Healing Fields of Memory?

Literally anything cures somebody somewhere. We realized this finally after attending scores of alternative health conferences and roaming through the exotica of alternatives for years. If you keep looking and listening, you begin to realize something; there is a deeper reality at work. A something that at moments one almost, but not quite, catches sight of, like the sure sense that someone has just gone through the door. We sensed it in alternative therapy. Tracking the role of memory in sickness we came to the same place, to the same sense of something, as Wordsworth says, "A motion and a spirit, that impels all thinking things, all objects of all thought, and rolls through all things."

That motion, that spirit rolls through the Vedic texts, the accumulated wisdom of very ancient India. Veda means knowledge, and the four Vedas are designed to impart the knowledge of life, including the knowledge of reordering dis-ease and reclaiming the vitality of life. From their deep, cosmic perspective, the Vedas speak of the base perhaps of all healing. We rise into existence like waves, the Vedas teach, yet, realize it or not, we remain part of the all-embracing deep. That is perhaps another way of speaking about what the famous theoretical physicist David Bohm calls the "implicate order." Beyond space and time, it is the invisible, the realm of potential from which creation unfolds in the "explicate order." The work of quantum physicists like Bohm is finally beginning to shatter everyday materialist views and raise a panorama of reality much stranger, much less material, much more interdependent than thought before. And much more intelligent.

"Before this, science declared that we are physical machines that have somehow learned to think. Now it dawns that we are thoughts that have learned to create a physical machine." So says Deepak Chopra, M.D., who calls his intriguing medical approach "quantum healing." In physics, a quantum is an indivisible unit—a photon, an electron—any universal unit that can't be broken down into something smaller, something deeper. A quantum leap is a jump from one level of activity to another.

Chopra made the analogy to healing while contemplating Chitra, a patient whose advanced breast and lung cancer suddenly, miraculously, vanished. Like others with inexplicable cures, Chitra seemingly experienced a quantum leap in consciousness, a shift in awareness to a state where cancer didn't exist. It occurred to Chopra that the rare person who does this connects to a source level, the deepest level. The universe-creating quantum reality has a boundlessness to it and a different set of rules than the cause and effect we're used to. It is a world of potential, trembling on the threshold, flickering in and out of existence. Searching the human microcosm with quantum eyes, Chopra finds parallels, like the black holes of our memories where things are swallowed up forever. He explores quantum healing at the threshold, at that mysterious core where mind and matter meet. There one finds memory.

A doctor X-rays a tumor and finds the same one that was there a year ago. Yet materially speaking, it isn't the tumor he saw a year ago, for the stuff of our bodies turns over continuously. The cells of your stomach that "imbibe" your food are replaced every five minutes, your whole stomach lining every four days. You have brand new skin every month and even the skeleton holding you up right now isn't the one you had ninety days ago. This is why Chopra says memory is more permanent than matter. A graceful writer, in *Quantum Healing* he puts it this way: "As the atoms of carbon, oxygen, hydrogen, and nitrogen swirl through our DNA, like birds of passage that alight only to migrate on, the bit of matter changes, yet there is always a structure waiting for the next atoms." What is a cell? "A memory that has built some matter around itself, forming a specific pattern. Your body is just the place your memory calls home."

Once, explaining to an anorexic that she was driven by a skewed self-image, Chopra was brought up short when his patient murmured, "There really are ghosts. . . ." Chopra realized they were indeed talking about ghosts, the ghost of a memory stored in the body, very deep in the body. Another anorexic angrily told him that of course she knew what fueled her problem, but being conscious of it wasn't doing her much good. Awareness of the mechanism of problems is not always a healing answer to Chopra. Anorexia, addictions, cancer, heart problems—he sees them all as problems of distorted memory. Not memory as we usually think of it. He goes right down to the point where intelligence and memory transform into matter, to the infinitesimal mastermind of matter, to DNA living like the Wizard of Oz at the center of every cell. It is in cells and in DNA, the intelligent molecule with a prodigious memory, that Chopra looks to exorcise the ghost, the distorted memory of disease.

The only trouble is that medicine doesn't know how to commune with cells and DNA. At least ours doesn't, which is why, though well-known as a Western endocrinologist, Chopra also embraces an ancient science of his homeland—Indian Ayurvedic medicine. He reaches to the classical system laid out in the Vedas. Three basics at the heart of this ancient medicine have a curiously familiar ring. These are ancient ways to heal. What is startling is that they have an uncanny similarity to ways of influencing memory that we've discussed in this book. One is meditation to relax, to center the mind, to get in touch with deeper levels of self. Another is "primordial sound." Specific sounds are used as mantras to zero in on ills—a tumor or an arthritic knee. The idea is not to attack with sound but rather to overwhelm and, in effect, re-tune cellular patterns that have gone off key. As all matter vibrates, this is done by specific resonance. Finally, Chopra and his Ayurvedic colleagues train patients in the "bliss technique." Supposedly this classical maneuver lets one release into an ocean of pure awareness, of bliss. It is a quantum leap to another level of being. Sometimes the bliss is enough, Chopra reports, "to 'drown' a disease in awareness and cure it." This joy, this bliss, is perhaps what Achterberg points to when she says that in the healing imagination eventually there is only unity, only harmony. That the underlying joy is always there is something all spiritual traditions agree on. The trick is to wake up to it. "Once bliss is experienced," Chopra says, "the mindbody connection has been made."

Everyone isn't cured of everything at Chopra's clinic in Lancaster, Massachusetts. Yet his efforts to help people exorcise the persistent ghost, the distorted memory that plays beneath disease has evoked some remarkable and moving healings. He's helping to lift medical practice to a wider view, beyond sheer matter to the invisible fields where mind, memory, life, play on.

Back in the lab, biologist Dr. Glen Rein's basic research is revealing a quantum energy network that may underlie not just Chopra's work but also alternative therapies like acupuncture, psychic healing, and radionics. Candace Pert and colleagues laid bare an unsuspected bio-chemical communication network in the body. An even more dramatic breakthrough may be underway as Rein and others track an unrecognized energy flowing in mindbody. "Non-hertzian energy," Rein calls it, that rises in the realm of quantum potential, embedded in Bohm's implicate order. More subtle than electromagnetic energy, this newly monitored force might encompass what so many through history have pursued, the "other" energy. Prana, chi, mana,—it's been called a host of names and it prompted the internationally known Soviet physiologist, Dr. Leonid L. Vasiliev, to make a bold statement. The discovery of this energy, Vasiliev declared, "will be as important, if not more important than the discovery of atomic energy."

The well-credentialed Rein, who has researched at Harvard, headed labs at Mt. Sinai Hospital in New York and at Stanford University, now directs the Quantum Biology Research Lab in Palo Alto on a grant from the Fetzer Foundation. Using a special double-coiled device, he generates non-hertzian energy of specific character. Would it affect cells, like lymphocytes so vital to immunity? To say it did is an understatement. Non-hertzian energy increased activity "twentyfold, cells became 6,000 times more active," Rein reports. This boost apparently remains, unlike the mild stimulation of electromagnetic energy that soon fades. Rein infused water with non-hertzian energy and grew cultures in it. Again, cell activity leaped, showing that the energy can be carried by water.

This is red-letter basic research that could one day open a cornucopia of help for all of us. Rein and peers are spearheading what may finally be a scientific way of grasping and using that elusive, subtle energy long said to inform the body and weave many kinds of healing. "It is an energy," he says, "that links to consciousness." Rein's discoveries could also bring scientific underpinning to homeopathy, to those mystifyingly effective remedies that have been so diluted that not a molecule of substance remains, just its "memory" in vials of water.

The M.D. and the Subtle Bodies

Do you have a crick in your emotional body? Is your throat chakra sluggish? Shimmering subtle bodies and spinning chakras haven't attracted top medical minds in our time. Yet as holistic doctors struggled to push beyond sheer physicality, for the last three decades a singular pioneer, Dr. Shafica Karagulla, worked much further out on the frontier. A distinguished neuropsychiatrist and surgeon, she painstakingly accumulated data to define in our terms the subtle bodies of Eastern philosophy. Apart from the physical body, the idea goes, each of us also has an energy (etheric) body, an emotional (astral) body, a mental body, and four other bodies, all made of finer material and vibrating at higher frequencies than the physical, all interpenetrating the physical and each other, all of basic importance to health and memory. We also have seven chakras or energy centers, rising vertically from coccyx to crown, often pictured in Eastern art each with its own color, pattern, sound.

Subtle bodies, chakras—twenty years ago hardly a topic of common conversation. Today they're getting to be. More people than ever before report they see auras, while workshops to balance chakras or connect with the emotional body do brisk business. Swelling right along with the interest are confusion, claims, counterclaims, and from the outer circle, ridicule. That's why Karagulla's work is important: she built a foundation of data, information that points to something revolutionary—or better, evolutionary—about us.

Karagulla, who died in an accident in 1988, wasn't a floaty. She was two ways grounded. A Turk raised in Lebanon, she had that glittering eye of shrewdness which let her out-bargain just about any merchant in the casbah, a talent she occasionally managed to employ success-fully even in New York department stores. Her medical education was the best: the Royal College of Physicians, London, the Royal College of Surgeons, the University of Edinburgh for psychiatry. She became an expert on the sane and insane mind, in delusions and hallucina-tions, and went on to a three-year stint with the outstanding brain scientist of the day, Dr. Wilder Penfield. In Montreal, she assisted Penfield when he used his electric probe on the brains of epileptics, often lighting up whole mindbody memories of long-forgotten events. Penfield's work was part of the underpinning for the basic concept of accelerated learning, which holds that one already has a prodigious memory, that everything that has ever happened to you is there, some-where, that memory is never lost.

When she moved on to New York University, Karagulla's profes-sional life took an unexpected turn. Philosopher Viola Neal challenged her to look farther than the physical body. There is nothing supernatu-ral in the universe, Karagulla thought, just things we don't yet under-stand. So why not focus her scientific training on clairvoyants, seem-ingly intelligent people who claimed to perceive auras and subtle bodies, and relate them to medical matters. Mostly, she worked with underground psychics, people of reputation in other fields like business and medicine who perforce appeared under pseudonyms in the first 1967 publication of her findings in *Breakthrough to Creativity*.

"If evolution is a learning process, then why should not human beings begin to extend their perception?" Karagulla asked. It was a rhetorical question. She already believed that her data showed this is exactly what humans are doing. She developed a theory of *higher sense perception*—not ESP, but *HSP*—an emerging ability to tune into subtle realms, into the previously unperceived. The validation of quantum physics proved that we live in an infinitely more strange and subtle world than consensus reality ever thought. As a doctor, Karagulla determined to explore the finer realities of the human body. There weren't scientific detectors yet. But there was another kind of instrument, the finely developed clairvoyant with HSP.

In a massive twenty years of work, Karagulla carefully recorded what clairvoyants saw of subtle human energies, learning to filter out the individual bias of her "instrument" and build a picture of these energies in sickness and health. Her principal collaborator was Dora van Gelder Kunz, a highly educated, remarkable woman in her own right, longtime president of the Theosophical Society of America and born clairvoyant. Karagulla and Kunz studied outpatients at a New York endocrinological center. Kunz was never told what ailed a person or, as sometimes happened, that a principal gland had been removed. She simply related as accurately as possible what she saw of the colorful interplay of spinning chakras and subtle bodies.

Jack Schwarz is an accomplished sensitive with whom Karagulla did not work. But doctors at the Menninger Clinic did. Schwarz demonstrated that he too could accurately diagnose disease from the shifting energies around the body, even in patients he only saw on closed circuit TV. Now at his Aletheia Foundation, Schwarz teaches health professionals to do it too, and trains people in the art of self-regulation through exploration of human energy systems.

"The cause of the problem isn't in the physical body," Karagulla often heard from her clairvoyants. "It's in the emotional body." Sometimes, "It's in the mental body." Just as X-ray picks up problems in the body, they claimed to see abnormal patterns in the finer stuff of emotional and mental bodies that reflected in the flesh. Cure must ultimately come from these bodies, the clairvoyants said.

Dr. Rossi plunged into the body, following communication networks right down to the individual gene, and came up saying "mind modulates matter." Studying the fields around the body, Dr. Karagulla ended up saying the same thing, the whorls and kinks of mind and emotion link intimately with physical being. In broad outline, Karagulla's picture of the subtle bodies is probably easier to relate to than the intricacies of neuropeptides and receptor cells. It gives another perspective on mental healing. Does it make any difference which view you take? Probably not if you're trying to heal yourself.

In the long run it may make a difference if you exclude Karagulla's perspective. The dynamic, moving picture of the human being, which she built from countless bits of data, turns the usual idea of how we are made upside down. In her picture, the subtle bodies create the physical body and express through it. This has a better ring than the 20th-century idea of mind as by-product, an accident that befell busy little gray matter. To put it in Edgar Cayce's words, "Mind is the builder." Cayce's worldwide fame grew largely from his ability to scoop up successful cures from collective memory. Herbs, vertebrae adjustment—many of Cayce remedies don't sound strange today. One common prescription still does: he often recommended substances and improbable devices that he said worked on the body's subtle energies, energies that were as yet undiscovered by science (see Chapter 19).

Scientists in Moscow, Alma Ata, Novosibersk seemed to have secured the beachhead of that discovery. They too have pursued human force fields and subtle energies since the 60s. They are expert in Kirlian photography, photographing with electricity instead of light. With Kirlian, they first sighted a multicolor galaxy of light, flowing, flaring, glowing "a fire world" inside and around the human body. The bioplasma body, they named it. In the USSR an extensive scientific theory and a lot of heavy research, some of which is classified, has grown around the bioplasma body. It is of more subtle matter than the physical body. It is, Soviet biophysicists conclude, the matrix for the physical body. Disease patterns show up "ahead of time" in this bioplasma body before they can be detected in the physical body. It sounds familiar.

Where Does Memory Live?

What do subtle energies have to do with memory? Maybe a great deal. Their study fits with the re-membering urge, pulling into consciousness parts of ourselves we've been unaware of or perhaps have forgotten. Subtle energies, the Soviets point out, have been the basis of Chinese medicine for millennia. They are central to Indian philosophy and in the West to Theosophy, a concept Karagulla followed. The concept of subtle bodies may reveal a lot about our individual memory. Does memory reside solely within the physical confines of the body? (See Chapter 21) Clairvoyants often describe in colorful words how music mates and resonates with the aura and subtle fields of the body. Now scientists and new age musicians are exploring the effect of music on the known force fields surrounding the body. Soviet physicists, particularly at the University of Kazakhstan, are charting the very definite effects of music and sound on the bioplasma body. Is this resonance of music, bio-fields, and perhaps subtle bodies one of the means by which music can tune up or tune down memory?

Does personal memory resonate in these fields? Where does memory live in out-of-body experiences or in near-death experiences? If there is life after death, what vehicle carries memory? Two-thirds of the world believes in reincarnation. What retains the memory of the essential self, the string on which the individual beads of life are strung?

Back in the here and now, Dr. Karagulla concluded that it is the fields of the subtle mental body that connect us to larger memory, to the collective unconscious, transpersonal memory, genetic memory, the world memory that Cayce supposedly entered, traditionally called the Akashic records. What about the memory kinks that cause problems, physical or otherwise? Could some be transpersonal? Placebos suggest the activation of basic, perhaps even genetic and archetypal, memory. You can't scientifically prove or disprove most of the above right now. Yet more researchers around the world than most people realize are investigating subtle energies. Iconoclasts, perhaps, often behind closed doors, but well-trained scientists, some with quiet government funding. One place to find those who've gone public is the U.S. Psychotronic Association. In a different development, in 1990 a group of more mainstream scientists broke with tradition to form the International Society for the Study of Subtle Energies and Energy Medicine, based in Colorado.

We have a hunch that Karagulla's long effort is going to bear fruit in the healing arts. Not so much because it fits with an emerging worldview, or because of her fine, incisive mind, but because she was another of those genuinely joyful people, who delighted in life—making her, we suspect, one of the wise ones.

Memories of the Emotional Body

In the rarefied altitude of Santa Fe, Chris Griscom found "windows to the sky," acupuncture points that open access to subtle dimensions of energy, to the subtle bodies Karagulla's clairvoyants saw. A well-educated, attractive woman with long blond hair, Griscom's slightness belies a sturdiness that brought her through ten years service in the Peace Corps, from back-country villages in El Salvador to prison work and eventual directorship of the Corps in Bolivia. In the embrace of native cultures, she began to reexamine her own higher sense perception, a born talent tucked away during her mainstream upbringing. It flashed into practical use with acupuncture. Griscom observed shifts in subtle energies, particularly those of the emotional body. This is where memories live, she says. Memories are stored as energy patterns in the addictive, emotional body, old memories of hurt, fear, guilt, that keep waltzing us around the same dreary circles. Releasing these energy knots in the emotional body allows one's natural multidimensionality to express, Griscom says, and allows room for new emotional frequencies. Like what? Like the title of one of her books, *Ecstasy Is A New Frequency.*

Doctors, business people, artists, people of all sorts have journeyed to have their memory-laden emotional bodies toned up at Griscom's Light Institute in Gallesteo, New Mexico, an adobe village of four corners sporting a church built before the *Mayflower.* The land itself makes you unusually aware of light, Georgia O'Keeffe sort of light, a tonic on its own to the city folks who come from across the United States and Europe, especially from Germany where Griscom is well-known, thanks partly to a TV show involving her early client and supporter, Shirley MacLaine.

Memory imprints in Griscom's view are seen to come from this life or past lives. Like other past-life therapists, she doesn't squander time checking out "lives." She follows what works. Unlike the others, she emphasizes energy. At first through the golden needles of acupuncture, now increasingly through a type of acupressure and cranial manipulation, Griscom and her trainers try to free the fixed energy of negative memories in the emotional body. Releasing the energy of these memories supposedly mirrors in a shift in the physical body. That may be why some who journey to her institute claim such a deep sense of change.

"Are you talking about a real physical change?" one of us asked her. "If so, on what level?" "Yes," Griscom replied. "When memories are released, there is a real physical change. It's on the molecular level." Which is certainly reminiscent of Dr. Chopra's efforts to change memory on the cellular, molecular level. Coming from very different frameworks, the gist of Chopra's and Griscom's findings overlap. Chopra speaks of bliss, Griscom of ecstasy, Caycedo speaks of joy. Chopra thinks self-healing comes from connecting to "that level of which there is no deeper." Of her "windows to the sky" acupuncture, Griscom says, "These spiritually operative points permit the unmanifest to 'rain down,' to manifest. The formless spiritual body can consciously establish contact with the physical and emotional bodies. When it does, a powerful energy explosion is attained, so drastically accelerated in vibration that a frequency alteration results . . . this process alone is capable of changing the emotional body."

Griscom is an original to keep an eye on. She's a good news person using her gifts not only to help individuals but also the global family and earth itself. A multinational group of kids has landed in New Mexico to attend Nizhoni, Griscom's international school. Students don't just learn about classmates' cultures and Griscom's practical philosophy. They get the all-around education needed today that includes subjects like global economics. And Griscom is doing her part even more intimately to birth 21st-century citizens. She delivered her last child into the warm waters of the Caribbean—another water baby.

Griscom has traveled from Australia to the USSR, to discuss application of subtle energies to pollution. This would be making a shift in molecular memory on a different scale, transmuting pollution. It's a strange, probably nutsy idea to many, yet Soviet TV has already shown one of their psychics experimenting with pollution, and we ourselves have seen some interesting effects that so-called psychotronic energy, the "other" energy, has on polluted water. If there aren't subtle bodies and energies, there seems to be something very much like them. Chi, a vital force or energy is one of the oldest, most persistent concepts in human history. Maybe it's time to remember it and explore its possible dynamic interaction with self and memory. It's probably a good thing to have a down-to-earth mother of six, former Peace Corps leader on the trail.

Shout Hallelujah!

Once, down South, we chanced to turn on a radio evangelist. "Brothers and sisters, you can be healed," he declared, *"Put your hand on the radio . . . and shout HALLELUJAH!"* Ever since, we can lighten up by putting a hand on the radio. Perhaps some folks did get healed, but such performances make many people roll their eyes when you talk of psychic or religious healing. Yet there is long, documented human experience of such healing that keeps right on happening. Memory may link here too.

Etel de Loach is one of America's most accomplished healers. She's a healer who works only through doctor referrals, who has clients worldwide, who drew on her experience as a former teacher during a three-year stint at Johns Hopkins, informing medical people about healing. If you watched her work, hands swooping just above the patient's body, pausing, momentarily circling, then rippling on, you might be reminded of someone playing a musical instrument.

She has vastly improved and often healed a range of serious maladies. De Loach was studied with Kirlian photography. (Kirlian apparatus, now awarded dozens of world patents, is essentially medical equipment; in the 80s a leading Moscow medical journal reported that as a diagnostic tool in the USSR it was second in use only to X-ray.) Kirlian photos of de Loach's hands while healing revealed a bright increase of energy at the fingertips. Similar streamers and bursts of energy were photographed coming from the hands of Soviet healers. Is this the energy that heals? Not exactly, according to the current consensus. Researchers think what they are seeing is a transfer of information, a reminder, so to speak, of the innate pattern of health, a transfer that circumvents the conscious mind and sets off the body's self-repair mechanism. Could this data instruct the bioplasma body as some Soviets think? Or the subtle bodies? What about Rupert Sheldrake's morphic fields, the resonate memory spinning creation, more fundamental than subtle bodies. Could healing realign one with the morphic memory field of a healthy human body?

Sheldrake's theory of memory fields is in harmony with the idea that one can tune into or resonate with perfect health, with perfect being which is the expressed basis of some forms of spiritual healing. "There is but one life, that life is God, that life is perfect, that life is my life now." That is a truth for all of us, said Ernest Holmes, an exceptional American philosopher whose ideas are finally being explored by thinkers outside the Church of Religious Science that he founded in the 30's. Essentially Holmes is another re-memberer, who took the best of religion and perennial philosophy to create a practical, nondenominational set of principles or science that anyone can use. Science, because Holmes, like others in the New Thought movement from Christian Science to Unity, believed religion should work. It does work, according to a widening number of first person reports that claim healing of all sorts in *Science of Mind* magazine.

"Change your thinking and you will change your life," Holmes insisted, as he anticipated in well-reasoned texts much of what holistic medicine is starting to explore, a development that would have pleased him, for he believed in combining physical and mental therapy. Holmes also calls us to remember our true nature, our divine nature of wholeness, just as Plato taught that memory was the route to recovering lost divinity. The multidimensional world of spiritual healing is a book in itself. It's worth reiterating, though, that a new spiritual awareness is a common factor in most instances of successful mental healing. As Holmes so often said, "There is a power in the universe greater than you are and you can use it." Human experience attests that at least some spiritual healing moves past suggestion and placebo to connect with that power.

Is all disease memory? No, at least in the self-generated sense. Among other things, environmental factors—agent orange, asbestos, radiation—can incite disease. Though one could say they distort the memory of our cells. Is memory in the usual sense intimately intertwined with disease? Yes. Examining our afflictions through the patterns of memory, we can get fresh approaches to healing, including healing the social and global ills of our times. The basic memory pattern, the natural thrust of the life is toward health and growth. The multiple techniques we've discussed all attempt the same thing: to reach and release that healthy memory at the root of our lives.

"Think of your mind as a placebo that works," suggests Dr. Ellen J. Langer, Chair of Social Psychology at Harvard. Langer promotes "mindfulness" as a Western analog of meditation, and thinks it our most sure path to conscious orchestration of our health. Remember how you learned to ride your bike, she advises. You began wobbling along with a grown-up hand holding the seat. Eventually, without your realizing it, that hand let go, and you were breezing along without knowing you'd learned how. "We control our health, and the course of disease, without really knowing that we do," Langer says. "As on the bike, at some point we all discover that we are in control. Now may be the time for many of us to learn how to recognize and use the control we possess over illness through mindfulness." Mindfulness is another way of saying, be aware, remember yourself.

18.   Eat To Remember

You can make yourself vastly smarter, improve your memory, and increase your learning power, simply by eating natural, nontoxic food substances that are rich in elements now proven to increase intelligence. For instance, significant tests at the National Institute of Mental Health showed that a basic food substance found in egg yolks, fish, wheat, and soybeans, could make people up to 25% smarter. This substance, lecithin, breaks down into choline in the body, and choline has been proven internationally in scores of tests to bring about major improvements in memory and learning powers. Another "superfood" group for supermemory and enhanced brainpower includes whole wheat, soybeans, milk, and meats. These foods are all rich in glutamic acid, an amino acid that is a "high-octane superfuel" for the brain. You may have a "Cadillac" brain, but without quality fuel it just chugs along with poor performance ratings. Glutamic acid along with blood sugar (glucose) are the only compounds used for energy by the brain. Tests show that when people are given an added supply, IQ rises, even in the mentally deficient. High-energy brain fuel not only improves brain function and makes you more alert, it's also been found to fight fatigue and depression and stop cravings for sweets and alcohol.

Another super brainpower nutrient is found in cheese, milk, eggs, and meats. These foods all contain the amino acid phenylalanine. The brain manufactures an important substance, norepinephrine, from this amino acid; tests show that norepinephrine plays a major role in learning and memory as well as in relieving depression and stress. Dramatic new research has shown a form of phenylalanine may be one of the greatest breakthroughs in natural pain control discovered to date.

"Eat seafood—it's brainfood," Grandma used to say. This is turning out to be good advice, based on recent scientific studies. Fish, and especially sardines, herring, and anchovies contain a substance called DMAE (dimethyl-amino-ethanol). DMAE passes readily into the brain where it is converted to acetylcholine, which transmits electrical impulses in the brain and nervous system. Without adequate acetylcholine, you can display muddled thinking, confused memory, sluggish, slow reflexes, anxiety, and depression. DMAE also slows aging.

Fish, shellfish, and sardines, along with onions and brewer's yeast, all contain RNA (Ribonucleic acid), which is extremely important for intelligence. RNA improves memory, extends brain cell life, and prevents senility. RNA is essential to register information in the memory. It slows the aging process and helps extend your life span.

The "superfoods" menu includes chicken livers, cheese, bananas, avocado, yeast, meat, and fish. They contain tyrosine, which the brain converts into a substance that increases mental alertness, especially when you're under stress. In other exciting new studies, a natural substance called germanium, found in garlic, pearl barley, watercress, and ginseng, may turn out to be one of the most potent immune system builders ever found. Its ability to bring oxygen to the brain has made it a natural for brain-boosting. And the central essence of wheat, the wheat germ, has octacosanol, a natural substance so powerful it can not only aid mental retardation, but even repair brain damage.

Until about fifteen years ago, the idea that something you ate could make you smart or dull, enthusiastic or depressed, seemed absurd to scientists. Then a series of major breakthroughs occurred that opened up a whole new understanding of how the brain functioned. A growing number of researchers now report that our moods, our alertness, our sleep, our IQ, our ability to remember, even our perceptions of pain can be affected by what we eat. Their leading edge research has already brought safer ways of treating mind and emotions, new ways of rescuing people from a memory-less old age, new ways of boosting "memory metabolism." A torrent of biochemical research pouring in from labs around the world shows that with the right menu, the substances we munch daily can brighten our minds and memories—even those that have begun to flag.

One of the foremost brain explorers is Dr. Richard Wurtman, a physician and neuroendocrinologist at the Massachusetts Institute of Technology. Struggling to understand memory illnesses such as Alzheimer's, he focused his research on neurotransmitters, chemicals that the brain nerve cells (neurons) use to signal and communicate with one another at lightning speed. How did the brain increase its levels of neurotransmitters? How did they get formed and released? Fellow researchers had already noted that patients with severe memory loss such as Alzheimer's disease had an extremely low level of acetylcholine, an important neurotransmitter. The mystery of memory might be tied to neurotransmitters.

Studying groups of rats, Wurtman noted that tyrosine, a certain neurotransmitter in the blood, increased fivefold in the evening after dark. Even removing the pituitary gland from the brains didn't halt the unusual cycle. Why? he wondered. What released neurotransmitters in the brain so regularly after dark?

Finally, Dr. Hamish Munro, a distinguished nutritionist, supplied the key to the puzzle. Rats are nocturnal. They *eat* after dark. The secret was in the digestion cycle.

Brain explorer Wurtman was now stalking the trail of the nighttime neurotransmitters. The rats ate their evening meal of protein. Amino acids from the protein, including tyrosine, traveled from the intestine to the liver. The liver formed the aminos into enzymes which circulated in the blood and through the brain. In the brain they were converted into neurotransmitters. Tests showed that the amount of neurotransmitters in the blood was controlled directly by diet, and not by the brain as had been thought!

Wurtman tested human volunteers by having them fast. During a twenty-four-hour fast, blood levels of amino acids stayed constant. There were no ups and downs at all. Further research showed that the meal controlled the level of amino acids in the blood and the kind of meal dictated how much and how many neurotransmitters were made. Food influenced behavior and even disease!

There are over thirty neurotransmitters. When you think, move, or try to remember something, certain brain cells release neurotransmitters to signal other brain cells. Did food play a role in creating all of them? In addition, the brain is sheltered from various substances in the blood by the blood-brain barrier, a kind of sentry seal. Only brain fuel, blood sugar (glucose), and L-glutamine, travel easily through this barrier. How did these other food substances make it past the brain sentry?

Wurtman investigated serotonin, the neurotransmitter that makes you sleepy and eases pain. To make serotonin, the brain cells need an amino acid from protein called tryptophan. Wurtman gave his lab rats pure tryptophan and sure enough, they became sleepy. The level of serotonin in their brains soared.

Could drinking hot milk before going to bed make you sleepier? Milk contains tryptophan. Wurtman's studies showed that all the amino acids in the milk *compete* to reach the brain. Milk has lots of protein and lots of amino acids. Tryptophan is the scarcest one. In the race to the brain, the more plentiful and bigger amino acids get there first.

"It's like a traffic jam," says Wurtman's wife, Judith, of MIT's Nutrition Department. "Tryptophan is like an old Volkswagen that can't get through because all the other cars are bigger and faster."

How to get sleepy when you want to? Eat carbohydrates, say the Wurtmans. They found carbohydrates increase insulin in the body, which clears the blood of the other amino acids, making it easy for tryptophan to enter the brain. Eat protein to stay awake and alert. Eat starchy foods like cereals, whole wheat bread, a banana, or popcorn to fall asleep, they counsel.

Could some people be gaining weight because their brains are trying to ease depression, pain, and stress and bring on relaxation and sleep? The Wurtmans studied groups of overweight individuals prone to "carbohydrate binges." They found that carbohydrates started the insulin cycle, which pushed out the other neurotransmitters and allowed tryptophan and serotonin levels to rise. This in turn left obese patients feeling happy, less tense, and very relaxed. Treatment? The Wurtmans gave obese patients a drug to stimulate serotonin production in the brain. Result? Patients felt wonderful, stopped binge eating of carbohydrates, and lost weight.

Over the years, Dr. Wurtman's lab tracked the complex pathways, behavior, and interactions of these all important neurotransmitters. "The brain's ability to make certain neurotransmitters depends on the amount of various nutrients circulating in the blood," he says. The food breaks down into individual nutrients in the digestive tract. These nutrients in the bloodstream circulate to the brain where a few penetrate the brain's neurons affecting the production of neurotransmitters. "The brain is not above it all," says Dr. Wurtman. "It is intimately influenced by what we eat."

Choline and Lecithin: Memory Age-Proofers

"Our tests show that giving people choline increases their memory and learning ability . . . in other words, it makes them smarter," says Dr. Christian Gillin, government scientist and top official at the National Institute of Mental Health. Gillin ran the government's tests that showed that choline could make people a startling 25% smarter. Once you eat choline, a B vitamin, the brain manufactures acetylcholine from it. Acetylcholine is vital for the transmission of messages from one nerve cell to another and these "thought wave paths" are believed to be responsible for the memory process, according to government scientists. In scores of tests, choline has had a proven effect on memory, thinking ability, muscle control, and the nervous system in general. A substance rich in choline is lecithin.

"Lecithin accomplishes the same thing as choline," says Dr. Gillin. "It raises the body's choline level, and (thus) the amount of acetylcholine in the brain." In fact, says Gillin, government tests show lecithin "may be even more effective! We're very excited and encouraged by the results," he added, calling it a breakthrough in understanding the human mind.

Student volunteers in the government tests were required to memorize a list of words. After taking lecithin, students had a "significant" improvement in memory and learning powers, according to Dr. Natraj Sitaram, a NIMH Clinical Center research psychiatrist. "We're on the right track toward the development of a 'memory pill,' " he enthused. The choline in lecithin can act on your memory within ninety minutes and the effect lasts four to five hours. Dr. Sitaram suggests about 2 1/2 ounces (70 grams) of lecithin per day to power learning and memory.

Foods rich in lecithin include eggs (average size)—1.2 grams; 4 oz. salmon fillet—1.4 grams; lean beef—.8 grams. Lecithin supplements (made from soybeans) are widely available as granules, liquid, or capsules. A daily intake of 1 to 2½ ounces would be needed. If using granular lecithin, be sure the product is fresh and not rancid. Check product labels for the percentage of choline in the lecithin. The really useful form of choline, the power base of lecithin, is called phosphatidyl choline (PC). Researchers suggest that for the lecithin to operate successfully, you must have at least 30% PC—the higher the PC, the greater the success. Recently a concentrated form of PC has become available.

Dr. Allen Cott, a well-known New York City psychiatrist, prescribed lecithin containing 35 percent of the important PC to patients suffering poor memory and concentration. Results were excellent, he reports.

Dr. Wurtman, editor of the five volume series *Nutrition and the Brain,* believes that what is considered a "normal" level of lecithin in the diet may become insufficient as people age. "Choline or lecithin may even improve memory among otherwise normal young people with relatively poor memory functions," he says. Wurtman found that on an hour-to-hour basis, the amount of the neurotransmitter acetylcholine in the brain seems to depend on how much lecithin or choline-rich food you eat. If you have mental slump, or memory loss from stress or depression, lecithin can give you an immediate boost.

In one experiment, young people were given scopolamine, a substance which blocks acetylcholine. They immediately began to develop memory loss and learning problems as if they'd suddenly suffered premature aging. Researchers/authors Durk Pearson and Sandy Shaw report that conversely, people in their twenties, given a single 10-gram dose of choline, demonstrated greatly improved memory and learning abilities (they easily learned lists of unrelated words). A jolt of lecithin before exams or tests might greatly improve grades in school or college.

In the long run, can serious mental decline in old age be avoided by taking choline? At the University of Ohio, Dr. Ronald Mervis, director of Brain Aging and Neuronal Plasticity Research, calls his ongoing work with choline "very promising." He's found that levels of choline drop as we age and that levels were especially low in people with Alzheimer's. He gave lecithin to eleven Alzheimer's patients and seven of them experienced substantial improvement—50% to 200% in long term memory. Dr. Mervis believes lecithin can help diminish the effects of normal aging on the brain from midlife on. People who have a parent with Alzheimer's have a 40% greater chance of getting the disease themselves, he says. It would be especially prudent to begin taking a lecithin supplement as insurance, he says. "What looks exciting . . . is prevention," says Dr. Mervis.

Dr. F. Etienne of Montreal found that in using lecithin on Alzheimer's patients three out of seven could understand faster and had improved speech. When lecithin treatment stopped, learning ability dropped. All seven patients scored higher on learning tests when blood choline levels were high. In New York, at American Cyanamid, Dr. Raymond Bartus and his colleagues were able to get a "robust" memory improvement in aged rats by mixing the drug piracetam with the choline. Piracetam boosts the brain's metabolism, enabling it to benefit even more from the choline.

Age-proofing your memory with amazing lecithin sounds great, but the good news about lecithin involves *both* mind and body. Lecithin is found in every living cell, the highest concentration in the brain, heart, liver, and kidneys. Our brains show a dry composition of 30% lecithin. Acetylcholine helps maintain the brain synapses. In addition to being a brain tonic, lecithin works in the bloodstream to help prevent cholesterol and other fats from accumulating on the walls of your arteries and helps dissolve away dangerous deposits that may already be there. (A build-up of cholesterol can result in atherosclerosis and heart attack.) Lowering cholesterol helps mind-boosting oxygen reach the brain more easily. In the liver, lecithin metabolizes clogging fat and reduces the chance of liver degeneration. In the intestinal tract, lecithin helps the absorption of vitamins A and D and influences the utilization of other fat-soluble nutrients such as vitamins E and K.

Lecithin has been called "nature's nerve food" because it helps build the insulation around nerves called the myelin sheath. This insulator is like the covering on electric wires that insulates them from short circuits. Destruction of these nerve sheaths in the body can result in nervous system "short circuits" so you feel nervous and edgy, tired, depressed, or in pain. Lecithin has been used for years to treat nervous system illnesses and helps clear up slurred speech, shaking, and palsy-like reactions. It's even helped manic-depressives. Recently, Dr. Robert Becker of the Syracuse VA Hospital discovered that an electrical signal vital to healing is also carried in these nerve sheaths.

According to the U.S. Food and Drug Administration, lecithin is definitely not toxic or dangerous and has no side effects. Lecithin is found in the cells of all animals and plants. FDA spokesperson Marilyn Stephenson, a nutritionist, states that lecithin will not harm people. So it seems that for mind, memory, and body, a little lecithin can be a great boon.

Ginkgo, the Memory Miracle Tree

The Ginkgo tree has a long pedigree. It can trace its roots back to before the ice age. A species over 200 million years old, it was probably nibbled on by dinosaurs, and if there was an Atlantis, the Ginkgo's beautiful fan-shaped leaves probably graced its avenues too. This oldest living tree known to man is a hardy, vital tree, amazingly resistant to pollution, insects, disease, and stress. Originally found in Asia and the Orient, it's able to thrive in polluted European and North American cities—it can even "take Manhattan"! Gingko trees can survive from two to four thousand years. No wonder Ginkgo can help us with longevity.

Known in China as a sacred, medicinal tree, the recorded use of Ginkgo by the Chinese goes back at least 2,800 years. The Ginkgo's two-lobed fan-shaped leaf gives it its full botanical name, *Ginkgo biloba*. It is the extract from this lovely Ginkgo leaf that has been used in astounding, breakthrough medical research, which has shown that the Ginkgo can restore memory, reverse aging, and reverse the most harrowing mental deterioration.

"The quintessential brain food"—that's what European researchers have called Ginkgo leaf extract after many years of study. Others have called this multimillion-year-old memory tonic a "miracle." Here are some typical test results. Patients aged sixty to eighty years suffering with senile dementia were given 40 mg. of Ginkgo extract three times a day. In as little as eight weeks, memory and mental function were restored. There was "significant improvement" in all areas measured.

In a long-term study of 112 geriatric patients suffering from chronic cerebral vascular insufficiency, Dr. G. Vorberg reported in *Clinical Trials* in 1985 that Ginkgo extract "significantly reduced mental and physical signs of aging" in both subjective and objective tests. Long-term studies of the effects of Ginkgo on Alzheimer's patients are also underway at numerous medical centers in Europe and the United States.

In experiments designed to improve memory in healthy young women, researchers gave 600 mg. capsules of Ginkgo extract. Tests showed vastly improved memory. No side effects or toxicity have been found. In fact, researchers observed that it was a normalizing and balancing remedy. Healthy users report significantly improved reaction time, memory, awareness, and clarity of mind after taking Ginkgo.

California herbalist and naturopath Amanda McQuade of Sonoma County uses Ginkgo extensively in her practice, and has achieved outstanding results with patients. Just so her students at the California School of Herbal Studies could see for themselves, she asked the whole class to take Ginkgo. After three weeks students reported "overall increased ability to concentrate, an easier time recalling information learned in previous lessons, a general sense of well-being." Ginkgo led to A's on exams too.

European medical researchers have filled journals with reports of Ginkgo's amazing ability to improve general memory, restore short term memory loss, and aid mental efficiency and ability to concentrate. Ginkgo has relieved senility and age-related cerebral disorders including Alzheimer's. It can reduce stress and depression, ease vertigo and tinnitus. EEG studies of elderly patients showing signs of mental deterioration revealed that Gingko extract increased alpha rhythms and decreased theta rhythms, which helped bring patients out of an unfocused state of mind and back to the world around them.

Often, elderly people have failing eyesight and hearing along with memory loss, as if feeble senses were unable to even register events. Because of Gingko's ability to increase blood flow to the brain, it has helped restore long-standing hearing and eyesight loss brought on by poor blood circulation. It is helpful in vascular illnesses such as

Raynaud's disease, phlebitis, and diabetic conditions. It is beneficial too for hardening of the arteries and other circulatory disorders that can cause memory impairment. Ginkgo also aids the whole respiratory system. That's important because breathing problems are another known cause of memory slowdown. Better breathing means more oxygen reaches the brain. Asthma, allergies, even TB have yielded to Ginkgo.

Hundreds of European studies show that Ginkgo can help cerebral blood circulation and oxygen transport, intercellular energy production in the brain, brain reaction time, and nerve signal transmission. Its antioxidant, free-radical scavenging activity in brain cells helps reduce toxins from metabolism. All the components in Ginkgo extract appear to work together to help reverse mental and physical aging and increase mental performance.

The only potency of Ginkgo leaves shown to achieve remarkable results in European studies was the 50-to-1 concentration. (That means fifty pounds of leaves to form one pound of extract.) The leaf extract is then standardized to contain 24% active ingredients. Ginkgo has been widely used in Europe for years. Now Ginkgo extract has finally become available in U.S. health food stores. (Check the label for 24% activity.)

For anyone who wants to give mind and memory a "tune-up," to improve reaction time, awareness, and clarity, Ginkgo is ideal. This multimillion-year-old herb can be a great promoter of vitality and longevity. Chinese herbalists traditionally used Ginkgo to rebalance, rejuvenate, and invigorate the body.

For anyone already stricken with age-related symptoms—memory loss and mental disorders—*Ginkgo Biloba* extract from the tree that is a living legend can be a life preserver, a powerful nutritional ally for the restoration of mind and memory. According to European researchers, in cases of severe memory loss or senility, it takes at least four to eight weeks of at least 120 mg. of Ginkgo per day before any improvements show, and generally the minimum course of treatment should be three months.

L-Glutamine—Super-Premium Mind and Memory Fuel

Little Jane was nine and a half years old when she joined the research program. She babbled unintelligibly, could barely bounce a ball, had an IQ of 69. A few months after starting treatment, she developed an interest in reading, could jump rope and play ball, and suddenly loved arithmetic. The family noted a "remarkable improvement." Her IQ went up 18 points.

Peter was sixteen, but had a mental age of eight. His IQ was 50. He could not ride public transit alone. After treatment he began to read newspapers and took an interest in games. His IQ went up 16 points. He could go out on his own and could attend a regular school.

John was seventeen and had an IQ of 107. After six months of treatment, his IQ was up to 120.

These three children, along with 66 others, age five to seventeen, were in a treatment program run by Drs. Zimmerman, Bergemeister, and Putnam, at Columbia College of Physicians and Surgeons. Most were mentally retarded and some were epileptics. All were being treated with glutamic acid, an amino acid found in whole wheat and soybeans. Their IQs climbed 11 to 17 points. They showed remarkable improvement in alertness, drive, and ability to solve problems. Their mental growth (two-year advance) was twice as fast as untreated children. And the whole personality improved. The researchers believed glutamic acid could help boost the average person to brilliant and the brilliant to genius. When the glutamic acid was stopped, the test subjects began backsliding mentally.

These exciting results with intelligence-boosting glutamic acid took place about forty years ago. New nutritional breakthroughs show that if these researchers had given the children the "amide" form of glutamic acid, called L-glutamine, results would have been even more spectacular. Glutamic acid can't readily cross the blood-brain barrier. Glutamine can. Glutamine is unique. It's one of the few nutrients besides glucose that can travel easily through this barrier to be used as fuel by the brain cells. (Exceptions are alcohol and narcotics, which can also slip past the brain sentry.) But because of glutamine's rapid barrier-traveling abilities, it can even help counteract alcohol addiction.

Glutamine is a high-power energy source for the brain. Once inside the brain, it's converted back to glutamic acid. Taking even moderate amounts of L-glutamine causes a "marked elevation" of glutamic acid in the brain. That's how L-glutamine can give you such a "high" from fatigue or "brain fog." Because L-glutamine is a brain fuel, it's used to help people with hypoglycemia (low blood sugar) and it can even restore to consciousness patients in insulin coma. Low blood sugar, according to neurologist and aging specialist Dr. Vernon Mark, is one of the ten major causes of memory deterioration, one that's easily reversed with glutamine.

The second major function of glutamic acid is to control and buffer excess ammonia that forms throughout the entire body during biochemical processes, and prevent it from causing brain damage. According to Dr. Richard Passwater, "A shortage of L-glutamine in the diet, or glutamic acid in the brain results in brain damage due to excess ammonia." The result is a brain that can never get into "high gear."

Glutamic acid is also needed in the "citric acid cycle," the process by which the body extracts energy from food for body and brain. "Life's universal energy supply," is what *Life Extension* author Durk Pearson calls this obviously important cycle. This is yet another way glutamine reenergizes you while it empowers memory.

Dr. Lorene Rogers, at the University of Texas Clayton Foundation, was one of the first to test L-glutamine for its intelligence-giving properties. She gave L-glutamine to a group of mentally deficient children and then measured their IQ scores. Their IQs had soared. Famous nutrition pioneer Dr. Abram Hoffer of Canada reports exciting success using L-glutamine to aid mind and memory. He has also used glutamine to help overcome mental retardation, schizophrenia, and senility.

Glutamine has been used not only to improve learning, memory, and IQ, but also to speed the healing of stomach ulcers, to control craving for sweets and sugar, and to combat alcoholism. Alcohol, of course, is a known memory-damager. Dr. Roger Williams at the University of Texas researched glutamine's powers for years. He found that glutamine could protect the body from the toxic effects of alcohol. It also led to dramatic cures: one alcoholic stopped drinking when L-glutamine was administered daily without his knowledge. Even "alcoholic" rats responded to L-glutamine. It protected them from the poisonous effects of alcohol and stopped their "craving" for alcohol. Research appears to show that if you occasionally binge out on ice cream, candy, or alcohol, maybe your brain's fuel tank is running on low and needs glutamine.

"Sweet remembrance" turns out to be a genuine clue to improved memory power. Psychologist Carol Manning of the University of Virginia tested two groups of elderly individuals for memory and intelligence after giving them lemonade sweetened with either saccharin or glucose. The group receiving glucose had substantially higher scores for long-term verbal memory. Both glucose and glutamine, being brain fuels, can power up memory, but glutamine doesn't put on weight or include the health risks of eating large amounts of sugar.

If your memory and thinking could use a lift or if you sometimes feel you're in an "ammonia fog"—a *real* memory fog, or if you need more brain energy for better decisions in financial, personal, or career matters, L-glutamine, the premium quality brain fuel, may be ideal. Dr. Roger Williams recommends 1 to 4 grams a day. Dr. H. L. Newbold advises, "If you want to take it just for a potential lift, begin at one 200 mg. capsule three times a day for a week, increasing to two capsules three times a day the second week. If you are trying to control drinking or binging on sweets, 1,000 mg. three times a day." Nutrition expert Dr. Carlton Fredericks reports that 1 gram of glutamine daily will produce impressive improvements in the ability to learn, retain, and recall.

L-Phenylalanine Equals Neurotransmitters for Learning and Memory

The rats in the maze looked around baffled. They ran back and forth into dead ends. They could not seem to find their way out. The animals had been given a drug that blocked the amount of the neurotransmitter norepinephrine in their brains. Learning and memory were blocked. When scientists injected the rats with norepinephrine, their learning capacity returned.

Phenylalanine is an amino acid, which among other things is used by the brain to manufacture norepinephrine. And one of norepinephrine's main jobs is to help brain cells communicate with each other. Norepinephrine neurotransmitters are stored like baby kangaroos in very tiny pouches. These pouches are at the ends of the brain's nerve cells. When it's time to "transmit," the norepinephrine leaves the pouch, transmits its messages, and returns to the pouch, trying not to get shot down by enzymes.

If you take amphetamines or Ritalin, these drugs prevent norepinephrine from returning to the pouch. So there are more neurotransmitters out transmitting brain messages. Memory and learning improve because you can focus better. But once the norepinephrine supply in the pouches is used up, the amphetamines or other stimulant drugs stop working.

The more phenylalanine you eat (in beef, chicken, fish, eggs, soybeans), the more raw material you have to make norepinephrine. Phenylalanine supplements have been shown to improve attention span, improve learning and memory, and also relieve depression. The enzyme that shoots down norepinephrine increases in the body after you're over the age of forty-five. As people get older, more phenylalanine is needed to keep brain cell transmissions active.

Phenylalanine also is necessary for the production of thyroxine, the iodine-containing hormone of the thyroid gland. It also helps make the powerful hormone epinephrine, needed for constricting blood vessels.

In fact, L-phenylalanine is the raw material used by the body to produce a whole menu of extremely important compounds called "catecholamines," all essential for the transmission of nerve impulses. Once you've munched a little phenylalanine in your lunch, your adrenal medulla and nerve cells quickly produce L-tyrosine from it (important for alertness), then dopa and dopamine (important in Parkinson's disease), then norepinephrine and epinephrine.

All of these neurotransmitters help you feel "up," alert, and ambitious. Phenylalanine can greatly improve motivation and intellectual performance in test subjects, report Pearson and Shaw. For improved mental function, 500 mg. per day are suggested.

Because it is an extremely powerful antidepressive nutrient, L-phenylalanine has been widely used to treat people for depression and amphetamine abuse problems. One clinical study found that 80 percent of severely depressed subjects were entirely relieved of their depressions by taking 100 to 500 milligrams a day for two weeks. Good results were often obtained within two or three days. Neurologist Dr. Vernon Mark of Boston City Hospital observes that by far one of the most common causes of memory loss and intellectual deterioration, particularly among the aged, is depression. Slowed-down thinking and lack of concentration make it hard, sometimes impossible, to retrieve memories. Phenylalanine, like almost every substance mentioned in this section, is able to help ease depression, relieving one of the primary causes of memory loss.

Phenylalanine has also been successful as an appetite suppressant and diet aid. (A caution: Many diet sodas contain aspartame. This artificial sweetener is a peptide, made by combining phenylalanine with another amino acid, aspartic acid. [Two or more linked aminos equal a peptide.] In extremely large dosages, phenylalanine can increase blood pressure. If you consume a lot of diet soda and also take supplements of phenylalanine, check your blood pressure. In addition, some people report an allergic reaction to phenylalanine. It also should not be used by people with an inherited inability to metabolize phenylalanine.)

Miraculous Natural Pain Control Breakthrough

A dramatic major breakthrough—the nutritional control of chronic pain—has generated worldwide excitement in recent years. Tests on supremely grateful patients have resulted in reams of glowing reports from scientists, doctors, health professionals, and pain clinics. "Excellent relief from low back pain," "complete relief from whiplash," "excellent relief from osteoarthritis pain" . . . the list goes on and on. Relief from cramps, migraine, neuralgia, postoperative pain, fibrositis . . . All were patients who'd previously tried pain drugs and gotten no relief from them. Both pain and pain drugs, of course, can lower mind/memory abilities.

This natural food substance is totally nontoxic, has no side effects because it's not a drug, is not habit forming, is long lasting and safe. What is this amazing, miraculous substance? Phenylalanine, the now famous amino acid.

For pain, D-phenylalanine is used, the mirror image of L-phenylalanine. (L stands for "laevo" or left-handed, and "D" for "dextro," right-handed.) Some formulations, called DLPA, combine both D and L forms.

Research at both the University of Chicago Medical School and Johns Hopkins University School of Medicine showed DL-phenylalanine to be 85% to 90% effective for the control and reduction of chronic pain. Studies showed the analgesic effect of DLPA equals or exceeds that of morphine and other opiate derivatives. Morphine and other opiates frequently impair memory and mental functions, leaving people confused and disoriented. Nontoxic DL-phenylalanine could surely be an incredible boon to the approximately 50 million Americans suffering intractable pain from arthritis, back injuries, or osteoporosis. How does it work?

Endorphins to the Max

The brain produces its own powerful pain-relieving compounds called endorphins, similar to morphine. Pain signals during an injury tell the brain to release these pain-relieving chemicals. People have often reported crawling out of a severe car accident, unaware of their injuries, and feeling no pain until later.

Giving people endorphins directly to control pain requires injecting endorphins directly into the brain or spinal cord, a dangerous procedure. In addition, the body's enzyme systems constantly destroy endorphins.

In a major breakthrough, scientists found that DL-phenylalanine blocks the enzymes that destroy endorphins. Thus chronic pain could be controlled by the brain's own natural pain-relieving substances, and the endorphins lasted longer periods of time. In contrast to drugs, the actions of DLPA occur by completely natural means. DLPA relieves pain with absolutely no side effects—no "drugged" feeling, no memory fog, no clouded mind or fuzzy alertness as happens with many strong pain-relieving drugs. No addiction. Moreover, pain relief is selective: chronic pain is relieved, but you are not anesthetized, you can still sense a hot pot on the stove. Another big plus is that DLPA also eases the depression and misery that so often go along with debilitating chronic pain.

For pain relief, tablets of 375 mg. of DLPA, 6 a day, 2 before each meal, have been prescribed by researchers. DLPA worked even better when vitamins C and B6 were taken too. We have tried out DLPA for back pain and headaches and found it highly effective.

Endorphin Power v. Addictions

"An Intellectual Beverage," "A Brain Tonic!" These were the original marketing slogans for Coca-Cola in the 1890s. They referred to more than just the "taste of it." Coca-Cola's original formula contained cocaine (the federal government ordered it removed in the early 1900s).

Some people seeking a creative spark turn to drugs like cocaine for the rush of brilliance they feel it gives them. Cocaine, amphetamines, diet pills, and Ritalin release the neurotransmitter norepinephrine which boosts mental abilities, but the drugs soon deplete the supply, the brain stops making more, and there's a letdown or "crash" afterward.

It seems that natural substances phenylalanine and DL-phenylalanine can boost mental/creative abilities safely with no addiction. They can supply nourishment instead of a downer afterward. Phenylalanine works by causing the brain to increase both its production and its stores of the neurotransmitter norepinephrine. In addition, DL-phenylalanine relieves pain and depression and has a euphoriant quality because it prevents the destruction of endorphins and enkephalins, the brain's own natural morphine.

Recent studies have shown that people with drug and alcohol addictions are low in endorphins. Breakthrough research on new brain machines (see chapter 19) showed that they improved memory and mind by stimulating the brain to produce more endorphins. Would the mind machines be even more helpful combined with DLPA?

Both phenylalanine and DLPA have already proved a boon in helping some people get off addictive drugs, by providing the mental benefits with no side effects at low cost. One young Hollywood screenwriter, to beat fatigue and depression and to spur concentration, developed a heavy, very expensive cocaine habit. Tipped off by Durk Pearson that DL-phenylalanine could help, she tried 1,000 mg. a day of DLPA. "Results were very good," reports Pearson. She had high energy for mind and body, no letdown, and no depression. Plus she had confidence, and quality concentration.

Could phenylalanine and DLPA play a bigger role in the treatment of drug and alcohol addiction and in the treatment of "crack" babies?

It seems phenylalanine and DLPA can do a lot: make us bright and brave, empower mind and memory, ease depression and addictions, and control pain. Phenylalanine can help us de-stress for success. Phenylalanine is so important to brain functioning that it's been called the "learning and memory chemical."

L-Tyrosine for Mental Alertness, Stress Control, Optimism

Two troops of U.S. Army soldiers swung into action in a tough combat simulation test. Clad only in light uniforms, they suddenly felt as if they'd been swept upward to a mountain peak on a chilly spring day (15,500 ft. elevation; 60 degrees F.). Such instant elevation can produce hypoxia, a drop in brain oxygen. Under this sudden, extreme stress, they had to quickly record chart coordinates on maps, translate messages into code, and make complex decisions involving sophisticated equipment.

One group outperformed the other dramatically. They had a significant edge in alertness, mental agility, and rapid response. They were in a good mood, didn't feel anxious or tense, and felt they could think clearly and easily. They also suffered less from the physical stress of the test. These soldiers had L-tyrosine to thank for their mental agility and physical ease under stress.

In a report to NATO by the U.S. Army Research Institute of Environmental Medicine at Natick, Massachusetts, psychologist Louis Banderet maintains that L-tyrosine is superior to both stimulant drugs and tranquilizers. Drugs made the soldiers tense and jumpy. Tranquilizers made them dopey. Tyrosine can enhance mental and physical performance under stress, with no side effects.

L-tyrosine is another amino acid, one which the body can also make from the amino acid L-phenylalanine. It too produces the neurotransmitter norepinephrine. Like phenylalanine, it too can elevate mood and ease depression. Dr. Alan Gelenberg of Harvard Medical School's Psychiatry Department treated patients suffering long-standing depression, stubbornly resistant to drug therapy. After two weeks of tyrosine (100 mg. per day), "tremendous improvement" was noted. One patient, a young woman who cried frequently and took little interest in anything around her, improved visibly in two weeks. Then Gelenberg substituted placebos. All the depressive symptoms returned. When the tyrosine was restored, she improved again. Patients in Gelenberg's test were able to completely discontinue antidepressant drug therapy as long as they took tyrosine. Dr. Vernon Mark maintains that depression is one of the most widespread causes of memory decline. Both tyrosine and phenylalanine can boost memory by overcoming depression. The neurotransmitters they produce are "excitatory"—they keep you alert and ambitious and restore your *joie de vivre* while they enhance brain function. They also help to control appetite —an ideal way to diet, notes Durk Pearson, because there are no side effects.

So if you would like to turn stress into success, and perform mentally and physically at your best no matter what the circumstances, try a little tyrosine. Doctors suggest about 200 mg. a day. (Caution: An overdose can raise blood pressure.)

Vasopressin to Counteract "Brain Power Failure"

A young California nurse finally regained consciousness in the hospital after a severe car accident. She'd suffered serious head injuries. In addition, six months later she had amnesia—no memory of the months before and after the accident. At her doctor's office, she was given vasopressin, a pituitary hormone, in nasal spray form. Within a few minutes, she felt "a fog lifting in her mind." Her memory was back.

In England, Dr. Oliveros and associates reported in *Lancet* in 1978 that they'd been able to restore memory to amnesia victims by using vasopressin. Just 16 IU per day of vasopressin improved memory, concentration, attention, and fast reactions in a group of men in their 50s and 60s, according to Dr. Legros and coworkers. At the Jerusalem

Mental Health Center, Dr. Jacques Eisenberg and his colleagues tried vasopressin on a group of children with low IQs and severe learning disabilities. There was significant improvement in recall and learning. Many other scientific reports testify vasopressin is a potent memory booster.

Vasopressin is released by the posterior lobe of the pituitary gland in your brain. It has powerful effects on memory and learning. Old standby choline helps the pituitary release vasopressin when it's needed. Drugs such as alcohol and marijuana inhibit the brain's release of vasopressin, which is why, after quite a few drinks, some people don't remember where they parked the car. Cocaine releases vasopressin but soon depletes it. Vasopressin could be an aid to easing cocaine addicts from the drug.

In *Whole Earth Review,* an editor using the pseudonym R. Sirius calls vasopressin "an excellent tool for rapid learning and comprehension of complex systems of thought." He also calls it a "euphoric" memory-enhancing intelligence-increasing substance. It gave him a "charged up" feeling with clear ideation, but with no numbing, discomfort, or the hard edges of cocaine.

Mild vasopressin in the form of raw pituitary concentrate is available in health food stores. Suggested amount is about 25 mg. per day. (Full strength Vasopressin nasal spray is a prescription drug, Diapid.)

RNA-DNA: Memory/Mind Essentials

Learning and the production of new memories involve the creation of RNA (ribonucleic acid). RNA molecules act as messengers, receiving instructions from DNA (desoxyribonucleic acid) for correct protein synthesis. DNA and RNA exist in the nucleus of every cell. They carry our genetic code and direct the production of all body proteins. They are essential to brain development, to tissue repair and healing. Many nutrients are needed to make DNA/RNA. Without them growth and cell repair stop.

Startling experiments with rats and mice revealed the strange way in which past experiences of one generation could turn up in another. Rats and mice were "trained" by electric shocks not to go into the dark shelters of their cages, which they preferred. These "educated" rats and mice were then killed, and brain extract and RNA from their brains injected into "uneducated" rats and mice. These untrained animals automatically knew they must stay in the light without being taught by electric shocks. (Injections of brain tissue from "uneducated" animals had no effect.) Countless similar experiments indicate that RNA retains memories and is an important factor in learning from past experiences.

RNA and DNA are vital for the brain—there's more of it there than anywhere else in the body. A deficiency of nutrients needed for their production can cause brain damage and mental retardation. Experimental animals injected with an enzyme that destroys RNA were unable to learn. On the other hand, rats given RNA supplements learned readily and their life span was increased by 20%.

"Horrid Brown Age Spots" On The Brain

RNA is also an extremely important antioxidant (along with vitamins A, C, E, and selenium), and RNA protects the brain against damage caused by oxidation of fats. Those "horrid brown age spots" on face and hands, which ads deplore, come from the oxidation of fats. Lipofuscin is their official name. Tests reveal that they can also appear in your brain, where they interfere with its metabolism. These oxidized fats in the brain are carcinogenic, damage the immune system, cause mutations in the DNA blueprints for cells, and contribute to blood clots, deterioration, and aging. RNA protects the brain against these rancid fats.

Nutrition experts Dr. Earl Mindell and Dr. Kurt Donsbach both suggest 300 mg. a day of RNA to enhance brainpower and memory and to protect against oxidation and aging. (Caution: do not take if you have gout.)

Octacosanol to Counteract Brain/Nerve Damage

"Brain damage" is one of the most frightening diagnoses a person can hear about a loved one. Whether caused by accident or illness, the future prospects for the patient are usually bleak.

Here again a natural food substance found in wheat germ oil, alfalfa, grasses, and bamboo has been letting some people "refuse the verdict." Athletes have known about octacosanol for years, thanks to more than eighteen years of research by Dr. Thomas Cureton of the University of Illinois, who showed octacosanol could increase stamina and endurance, overcome fatigue, strengthen muscles, speed reaction time, and reduce oxygen debt.

For over thirty-four years, the late Dr. Carlton Fredericks, one of the great pioneers in the nutrition field, relentlessly tracked down the role of octacosanol in repairing neurological damage. His first case in the 50s was a little boy with cerebral palsy. He was a mentally retarded spastic in leg braces, his back muscles totally atrophied. Dr. Fredericks started the boy on wheat germ oil, which contains octacosanol. Within a month the leg braces had to be changed. He'd grown new muscles! He continued the therapy, and within months the octacosanol had powered up both his muscles and mental abilities — the family even reported "having trouble keeping up" with his newfound mental agility.

When Dr. Fredericks's own mother suffered a major stroke, she was left paralyzed on one side, with a drooping eye and mouth and serious speech difficulties. After just four months of octacosanol, vitamin E, and bioflavonoids, she was completely recovered. Amazed, her doctor tried octacosanol on twelve other stroke victims and had eleven successes.

More startling were Fredericks's coma cases. "Chronic vegetative state" was the neurologists' verdict for one young girl. She'd attempted suicide by breathing carbon monoxide from a car motor in a closed garage. She'd been in a coma for over four months. Doctors considered it a Karen Quinlan type case. The family removed the girl from the hospital, flew her to their hometown, engaged nurses, and had a local physician carry out Fredericks's protocol. Within three weeks, the girl came out of the coma.

Lori, a nineteen-year-old car accident victim, remained unconscious with three different types of brain damage. Surgery relieved pressure on the brain. But she remained unconscious month after month. Fredericks changed the intravenous feeding to fructose, minerals, octacosanol, and vitamin E. A short time later, Lori walked into Dr. Fredericks' home as a guest. She still had some muscle spasm and missing short term memories, but this was a vast improvement from a vegetative state.

Over thirty years of research on octacosanol are in Dr. Fredericks's files. Hundreds of cases of major brain damage diagnosed "hopeless," cases of the mentally retarded, brain damage with and without coma, epilepsy, multiple sclerosis, encephalitis, cerebral palsy, victims of cardiac arrest and oxygen deprivation, cases of brain poisoning from carbon monoxide and other toxic substances. The benefits of octacosanol range from slight to almost complete rehabilitation. In Fredericks's opinion, nutritional therapy should be tried for any case of retardation or learning disability, because we now know "the basis of thinking is in part biochemical."

In the opinion of Dr. Andrew Ivy, the famous physiologist, octacosanol is actually able to repair damaged brain cells. "Damaged nerves in the brain can be repaired," he insists.

Dr. Helmut Prahl, executive director for the Dynatron Research Foundation in Madison, Wisconsin, reports that in his clinical studies, "almost all diseases of the central nervous system, at least in some instances, are responding to octacosanol." It's being reported successful in reducing effects of multiple sclerosis, cerebral palsy, muscular dystrophy, and Parkinson's to name only a few.

Drugs and toxins are notorious memory/mind damagers. Today we seem to be inundated with pollution in air, water, foods. They bear toxic metals like mercury and lead, toxic by-products of air pollution, tobacco, alcohol, fats, preservatives such as formaldehyde. Researchers believe that octacosanol, along with the amino acid L-cysteine, can help protect us against this memory-numbing toxic invasion. Octacosanol is an "ergogenic," an energy-giver. But researchers don't fully understand the "how" and "why" of this energy delivery that's practically able to restore life. Many feel it increases the oxygen supply to the brain.

Little Jacqueline, a fifteen-month-old baby, was brought to Dr. Fredericks. Because of a botched delivery, she had never been conscious. Brain wave tests showed that her brain was wracked by continuous epileptic seizure waves. The baby received octacosanol and nutritional therapy, and as she neared her second birthday, her mother called Dr. Fredericks at the clinic and through joyful tears said, "She's opened her eyes and smiled at me. It's the first time!"

"Incurably autistic." That was the depressing diagnosis facing four-year-old Lee Ahmad of Toronto in 1983. Starting at eighteen months there had been tantrums, hyperactivity, bizarre behavior. At four it continued. He had no social interaction, no friends, no memory, a twenty-word vocabulary, and an IQ of 47. Authorities recommended warehousing him in an institution. His determined parents, Naseer and Monica Ahmad, heard about Dr. Fredericks's research. They gave Lee octacosanol, Di-methylglycine (DMG), and a complete vitamin/mineral program. Within a week Lee discarded diapers, rode a bike, and began to talk. To the amazement of his teachers, he never stopped. Memory and mental function steadily improved. Seizures stopped. By 1986, his IQ reached 104. Today he is a bright, well-functioning, athletic child. Naseer Ahmad, deeply impressed with the powers of octacosanol, wrote a book, *Not An Incurable Illness: The Story of Lee Ahmad,* and set up an organization to help other parents. "All kinds of amazing stories . . . about their children's improvement poured in," reports Ahmad.

For treatment of memory loss or nerve damage brought on by illness, accident, or toxins, Dr. Fredericks preferred octacosanol synthesized from wheat germ oil. Dr. Helmut Prahl suggests biomedical application dosage should be 10 to 100 times higher than for an athlete taking octacosanol for stamina. In Dr. Thomas Cureton's research, it took about four to six weeks of taking the supplement before effects were obtained.

Germanium Generates Mental Power

Breathing more and enjoying it less? The brain needs enormous amounts of oxygen, even more than the rest of the body. It's the single most necessary substance for living. We can't live for more than three minutes without it. So isn't it just great to know that the oxygen content of the air in many cities is down by as much as 50%. No wonder Tokyo's Takashimaya department store reported that one of their top-selling items in 1987 was gift-boxed sets of oxygen canisters!

Our cell metabolism works by using oxygen to burn food for energy. When there's little oxygen, it's like trying to burn damp wood: portions of it don't burn. Our cells accumulate unmetabolized waste products that clog them up and leave them a breeding ground for viruses and microbes.

In 1967, just when it was beginning to look as if we humans were about to sink under the worst levels in history of inner and outer pollution, and inner and outer toxic wastes, a landmark scientific breakthrough occurred. A brilliant Japanese chemist, Dr. Kazuhiko Asai, after a dedicated, seventeen-year quest, synthesized an organic form of germanium, a substance that is a miraculous oxygen bearer in the human body.

Oxygen, the single most important element for life, "may be the most powerful immune-stimulant of all," says Dr. Betty Kamen, in *Germanium, A New Approach to Immunity*. Germanium, acting as an oxygen catalyst and a detoxifier in the body, powers up the immune system to knock out the vast range of ills that accompany our contemporary oxygen-deficient lifestyles. In the twenty years since its discovery, germanium has been shown in scientific studies to help with cancer, arthritis, aplastic anemia, and glandular disorders, to name just a few. It's a powerful endorphin producer so it's also a potent pain reliever (4 grams of organic germanium have relieved cancer agony in fifteen minutes). Because it's an oxygen bearer, it's a powerhouse against viral diseases. (Viruses and bacteria thrive only on low oxygen.) Most importantly, because it's an oxygen bearer, it can power up your memory and mind.

As the acid raindrops are falling on your head along with several pounds of other airborne toxins, you can activate germanium as your own kind of "star-wars" system. Germanium "stars" as an interferon producer. It stars as a stimulator of T-cells, B-lymphocytes, and macrophages, and activates all the troops in the whole immune defense system. That's why it can muscle out allergies, food poisoning (salmonella), candida albicans, eczema, migraine, influenza, and a host of other illnesses. It's a proven life-span extender. Best of all, even in megadoses, germanium is nontoxic.

Germanium: Memory Defense System

The brain accounts for 2% of the body's weight, but uses 20% to 30% of the body's total oxygen consumption. Thinking and doing math boosts the brain's need for oxygen even higher. An illness such as hardening of the arteries, which decreases oxygen in cerebral nerve cells, can devastate memory and alertness. When oxygen supplies to cells and tissues are depleted, a disease called hypoxia occurs. Symptoms include senility, mental decline, memory loss, fatigue, acidosis, weakness, susceptibility to infection. Symptoms of aging resemble symptoms of hypoxia.

In extensive tests, organic germanium actually increased mental capacity. It relieved symptoms of mind-numbing hypoxia, mental decline, memory loss, and senility. Patients experienced improved mental abilities and felt the warm glow of increased circulation and well-being. Germanium's ability to promote endorphins alleviated depression.

Animal tests at Tohoku University in Japan showed that organic germanium increases the amount of oxygen transported by hemoglobin in the red blood cells. Germanium also decreases the viscosity of the blood, thus aiding its ease of circulation. In addition, Germanium has an oxygen-sparing effect, that is, it lowers the requirement for oxygen.

Dr. Asai, in his book, *Miracle Cure, Organic Germanium,* reports "dramatic" relief of mental disorders, including psychoses. He believes that "various types of mental disorders are caused by an oxygen deficiency due to a disorder in the blood circulation to the brain."

Many brain cells have been lost in the elderly senile and the remaining cells may get just enough oxygen to remain alive but not functionally effective. Dr. Edwin Boyle, Jr., research director of the Miami Heart Institute, reports that memory loss in the senile can be corrected by restoring oxygen to these oxygen-starved cells. He placed patients in closed chambers where they breathed pure oxygen at three times normal atmospheric pressure. He got good results, especially in arteriosclerosis cases. Patients regained ability to recall recent events and process new information. The improvement lasted six weeks to six months.

But, says Dr. Asai, oxygen you inhale must have its ions activated by enzymes to be effective. With germanium, the oxygen is ready to be absorbed immediately. Germanium is ready to renew brainpower right away.

A twenty-five-year old woman, unable to walk, talk, or write, was brought into one of Dr. Asai's clinics. She had ringing in her ears and trembling limbs. The specialists agreed that she had complete degeneration of the cerebellum area of her brain. Prognosis: incurable. At the clinic she was started on germanium. After one month she was able to speak again. Five months later, she could grip a pencil and write. Ten months later she could walk, and all her crippling symptoms had disappeared.

An autistic fifteen-year-old girl, diagnosed as schizophrenic, and distrustful of everyone, was brought to Dr. Mieko Okazawa's clinic. Germanium was started. After one month the girl brightened up and her personality became cheerful. Within a year, she was able to return to regular school classes.

"Mad as a hatter." The expression grew from real life: hatmakers worked with materials containing mercury that addled their minds. Today, mercury may be leaching out of dental fillings, and is certainly reaching us from food fertilizers and mercury-contaminated fish. Mind and memory are under attack by heavy-metal toxins. The germanium compound, says Dr. Asai, captures any heavy metal accumulated in the body and discharges it completely from the body about twenty hours after its intake. He has found that germanium will remove PCB poisoning as well. Japanese researchers report germanium has cured various mind/memory illnesses, toxin-caused or not.

Dr. Michael Rosenbaum of Mill Valley, California, reports outstanding results with germanium in increasing his patients' mental alertness and acuity. He adds, "I have been excited about the functions of germanium as an immune stimulant, (and) as a potential tool for the release of chronic fatigue syndrome."

A San Francisco scientist takes several capsules of germanium when he wants to work late on a project—it keeps his mind clear, he says. Brain-boosting germanium works through providing oxygen and clearing out toxins that clog up mind and memory function. But there's more.

Germanium: the Semiconductor and the Body Electric

That tape recorder or radio you're listening to or the TV you're watching all thrive on germanium too—the *nonorganic* kind. Metallic germanium is used for transistors because germanium is a semiconductor, which means that it accepts and transmits electrons.

The human body generates electricity (if it didn't, we couldn't measure brain waves and heart action). Organic germanium also functions in the body as a semiconductor, discharging excess electricity, stimulating the flow where needed, and generally balancing the body's electrical system.

Soviet scientist Dr. A.M. Sinyukin of Moscow State University discovered what he called "currents of injury"—wounds emitted a specific electrical pattern. Drs. Burr and Ravitz in the United States discovered that patterns of energy control the shaping of matter. (See Chapter 19) Dr. Robert Becker, showed that it's possible to regenerate tissue by applying electrical current. Nobel prizewinner Dr. Albert Szent-Gyorgi showed that the molecular structure of many parts of the cell support semiconduction.

Just like a mini acupuncture treatment, powdered germanium can be put on a Band-aid or bandage and placed on the skin externally to provide healing treatment. It can heal the pain of stiff necks, arthritis, tennis elbow, muscle strains, etc. It also increases blood circulation to the area involved. Germanium on a headband can relieve headaches and boost circulation to the brain.

Nutrition researcher Dr. Stephen Levine predicts that holistic energy medicine, such as that which germanium can provide, is the medicine of the future. "Like the electrical circuits in your home, your body is also electrical. Oxygen forms the positive terminal of your cellular battery. Energy from fresh natural foods provide the current. Trace minerals like selenium, zinc, iron, and manganese provide the wiring for the flow of electrical energy. Insulating material must coat and protect the energy transport machinery. For life, there must be a continuous flow of electricity, and adequate oxygen to draw the current."

Germanium appears to act on the body as a whole, rather than on any specific symptoms, says Dr. Asai, and because of its semiconductor nature may play a role in balancing chi energy too.

Germanium is found in such foods as garlic, watercress, pearl barley, and aloe, and in such herbs as ginseng and angelica, and a type of Reishi mushroom. Could the long-known curative powers of garlic and ginseng, wonders Dr. Asai, have to do with their high germanium levels?

Organic germanium in capsule, tablet, powder, and liquid form is now available in health food stores. Be sure the label says organic. For your mind/memory defense system, Dr. Betty Kamen recommends 30 mg. a day as a preventive measure. For minor problems, 50 to 100 mg. daily. For pain relief, or more serious problems, 1 to 1 1/2 grams.

Hyper-Oxygenation: Memory Insurance

An extremely effective way to bring oxygen to brain and body and an outstanding way to destroy memory-damaging toxins, viruses, and bacteria—that's what scientists, doctors, and patients are saying about hyper-oxygenation. A growing number of physicians and scientists in Europe and America have now turned to a form of supercharged oxygen as a potent defense against illness and as a brain booster. Over 4000 scientific papers testify to the effectiveness of this approach. Instead of attacking a virus with a drug that produces side effects, super-oxygen oxidizes the molecules in the shell of the virus. You can literally vaporize viruses with this space age virus zapper.

There are various hyper-oxygenation procedures. Some involve medical use of ozone, food-grade hydrogen peroxide, or oxygen electrolytes. German physicians in particular have pioneered ozone therapy for over thirty years. Medical use ozone is a nontoxic, supercharged form of oxygen. At the Bad Hersfeld Clinic, for instance, they draw a patient's blood, infuse it with ozone, and return it to the patient. Reports state virus-caused illnesses have been completely cleared up. Herpes, hepatitis, Epstein-Barr, cytomegalovirus, candida albicans —all have yielded to oxygen treatment.

Boost Your Memory Metabolism

"Perhaps the greatest potential benefit of the oxygen therapies is the reversal of the slight brain damage caused by long-term oxygen depletion, which can be observed in the 'average' human, and is sometimes not all that slight. The implications of constant gradual oxygen starvation in our cities somehow escape notice, despite the tiredness, depression, irritability, poor judgement, and health problems affecting so many citizens," says Waves Forest, writer and publisher of a health newsletter. Increasing the oxygen supply to the brain and nervous system, says Forest, an expert on oxygen therapies, will reverse these conditions.

Not only is the oxygen in the air down substantially, but even the oxygen in our water is low. Water has no aeration in building pipes. Even pet fish can't live in our tap water without an aerator. Besides that, contaminants are increasingly found in drinking water. Lead, a known memory-damager, was found in over 100,000 U.S. drinking fountains in the United States, particularly in schools. In Norway, an above average incidence of Alzheimer's disease was found in areas that receive the most acid rain and have the highest levels of aluminum in drinking water.

Medical researchers have come up with a new weapon against oxygen depletion and dangerous, toxic bacterial contaminants in water that can damage mind/memory. It's called "oxywater" and consists of adding a few drops of *food-grade* hydrogen peroxide (H_2O_2) to a glass of water or fruit juice, and drinking it once or twice a day. Even if it seems strange to you to drink drops of H_2O_2, you may have been doing so all along. H_2O_2 is the aseptic agent in drink box fruit juices. Today, oxywater is being tested and used more widely. (Caution: dosage of H_2O_2 must be very specific or it can become damaging.)

"The oxywater regimen improves alertness, reflexes, memory, and apparently intelligence," Forest reports. "Alzheimer's and Parkinson's are responding to it. [It] may offer the elderly a new weapon against senility and related disorders." On a somewhat philosophical note, he adds, "Oxywater may even cure stupidity."

According to Drs. Finney and Jay at Baylor University Medical Center in Dallas, hydrogen peroxide has also been able to help remove cholesterol from arteries, clearing the routes for memory-boosting oxygen to reach the brain.

Memory Pollution Solution

Are there "memory viruses" or bacteria on the loose, contaminating memory and browning out mind power? Many researchers think so. It was the famous Dr. Edward Rosenow of the prestigious Mayo Clinic who pioneered early work with hydrogen peroxide. In his sixty years of research at the Mayo Clinic, the late Dr. Rosenow discovered the cause of rheumatic fever, and in his day was considered America's most eminent bacteriologist.

In the 20s he came up with the idea that many problems of memory and mind—from schizophrenia to epilepsy, mental disabilities and learning problems to criminal behavior—could be due to microorganisms and their toxins in body membranes and blood. He cultured some of these streptococci and injected them into mice, pigs, and rabbits. The animals displayed many of the same symptoms found in mental patients. He tested more than 2500 patients at the Longview Hospital in Cleveland. Rosenow found evidence that all of them had damaging toxins from microorganisms. He also discovered a cure! Of all the substances he tested at that time, the only thing that could destroy all these microorganisms and toxins was hydrogen peroxide in a 1.5% solution. H_2O_2 appeared to work better than anything else because viruses and microbes are anaerobic, that is, they can only exist on low oxygen. As soon as high oxygen levels appear, they disappear. Dr. Otto Warburg, twice a Nobel Laureate, observed the same of cancer cells: malignant cancer cells are anaerobic and can't live in a high oxygen environment.

Chasing microorganisms with drugs has been a nonstop race. As the antibiotics grow stronger, the microbes mutate into ever more virulent forms (for example, so-called "hospital pneumonia"). This, Dr. Rosenow had also predicted. He'd performed scores of experiments showing that streptococci mutate by exposure to normal cosmic radiation and also by exposure to different environments and foods. For instance, in 1989, *The New England Journal of Medicine* reported that a "new" microbe, cryptosporidium, in drinking water in Georgia, had caused an outbreak of gastrointestinal disease. Chlorine won't kill it. Evidently, it's going to take hyper-oxygenation to get rid of it.

Recently, more and more doctors, scientists, and private individuals have tested oxygen therapies, and impressive streams of excellent results are beginning to pour in. In 1988, tests at the Bethesda Naval Hospital in Maryland, the VA Hospital in San Francisco, and by the

Medizone Company of New York showed that ozone effectively killed viruses without damaging those cells that had been infected. Dr. Charles Farr, a foremost expert on H202 infusion research, founded the International Bio-oxidative Medicine Foundation in Dallas, and publishes a newsletter. Farr calls H202 a flu cure par excellence, and has had an 80% success rate with viral illnesses.

Ozone therapy has been used now for over thirty years in European clinics. Some 3000 German physicians have announced positive results with viral and bacterial illnesses. In *Oxygen Therapies—A New Way of Approaching Disease,* Ed McCabe reports the latest developments on this hopeful modality that can boost memory and brainpower at the same time that it counteracts viruses.

Candida Epidemic, Memory, and Oxygen

Poor memory, zero concentration level, mental confusion, learning disabilities, depression—these are just a few of the symptoms that can arise from toxins given off by microorganisms. One in particular, a yeast infection called candida albicans, has reached epidemic levels in America and internationally, Dr. William Crook told us at a Canadian Health Food Conference in Toronto. Widespread use of antibiotics has allowed this normally benign inhabitant of the intestines to go berserk. Dr. Crook, author of *The Yeast Connection,* reveals that, just as Dr. Rosenow had suspected, a microorganism such as candida can cause severe physical, mental, and emotional problems. In his own medical practice, Dr. Crook has observed memory loss, serious learning problems, poor concentration, allergies, hyperactivity, tantrums, massive fatigue, muscle and joint pain, and a huge host of other problems all caused by candida. Standard treatment is the drug nystatin and diet.

Dr. Kurt Donsbach at his clinic in Mexico was becoming more and more frustrated by poor results with his candida patients. Finally, very, very cautiously, he decided to try hydrogen peroxide against candida. He reports excellent results. H202 can beat candida and its memory-numbing toxins, he believes. Patients exclaimed after oxygen therapy, "I'm thinking clearer!" "I can concentrate!" It seems that oxygen therapy may be a solution to "memory pollution." Donsbach's regimen requires twenty-one days of special H202 treatment. The elated Donsbach enthuses, "The recent explosion of interest in the internal use of hydrogen peroxide heralds one of the greatest advances in the treatment of the ailments of mankind in recent history."

Making Water More User Friendly

The ecological approach to memory, learning, and healing is beginning to catch on. New breakthroughs that can clean up outer toxic environments may bring the bonus of removing inner mental toxins as well. Cleaning up water supplies is one more way to restore brain-boosting oxygen and destroy mind-damaging toxins.

Supercharged oxygen—ozone—is now considered the preferred water purifier. It provides 5000 times more rapid disinfection and there are no toxic residues as with chlorine. It destroys all kinds of viruses and microbes, and it's cheaper. Los Angeles and twenty-nine other U.S. cities have ozonated water. In Europe, three thousand cities have ozonated water. Some spring water bottlers also use ozonation.

Izone International of Vancouver, which holds patents on several breakthrough ozone processes, reports that ozone can clean up virtually all toxic or hazardous wastes. Water pollution is at a crisis point, they say. "Unsafe tap water, polluted beaches, acid rain, mine effluent, fish kill, water courses so polluted they ignite spontaneously, PCB's . . ." The sickening list expands yearly: infectious hospital waste leaching into water supplies, oil spills, toxic industrial waste, strange new microbes in lakes and rivers. The good news is that ozone, the "supercharged" oxygen, has been found to vaporize bacteria like salmonella, viruses like hepatitis, and in certain cases AIDS, as well as parasites, fungi, and algae.

Could cleaning up our water and environment where food is grown give us an added bonus of increased memory and mind power? For instance, could ozonation or H202 help counteract the massive salmonella contamination of chickens and eggs in America? Some of the very foods needed for our brainpower potential have become contaminated. Aluminum, found in acid-rain contaminated water, has been implicated in Alzheimer's.

New Oxygen Therapies

The recent rush of research into the internal use of oxygen has brought additional benefits—safer forms of oxygen therapy. Many H202 researchers have sounded notes of caution. Using H202 in large dosages over a long period of time may result in release of the harmful hydroxyl radical, explains Dr. Farr of the Bio-oxidative Medicine Foundation. H202 should only be taken with antioxidant enzymes, he warns, or a free-radical scavenger such as gingko. Dr. Robert Bradford of the Bradford Research Institute also reports several negative side effects from long term H202 overuse.

Recently scientists have come up with several new forms of bioavailable oxygen. These are nontoxic catalyzed electrolytes of stabilized oxygen, a natural, safe alternative to hydrogen peroxide for internal use. It does not produce free radicals. According to researcher Dr. Bruce Berkowsky, this new form of oxygen supplement is stable and has the same electrical charge as atmospheric oxygen. You add a few drops to a glass of water three times daily. Oxygen electrolytes zap the harmful bacteria and viruses, but do not interfere with beneficial aerobic bacteria necessary for good health like lactobacillus acidophilus, the one that makes yogurt. The new forms of oxygen are beneficial, highly effective, and easy to use, say researchers.

"A lack of oxygen is why body organs grow old," says Sonya Star, author of *The Nutrition and Dietary Consultant.* Lack of oxygen "is the primary cause of strokes and degeneration of the brain." Can the new supercharged oxygen therapies offer us the route to rejuvenation of memory, mind, and body? Can we turn our water into a memory "fountain of youth" by adding a few oxygen electrolytes? More urgently, if germ terrorism should become a reality oxygen therapies could be an important defense. (See Resource.)

A B C s of Memory

All the breakthrough substances we've mentioned require the basic ABCs of vitamins and minerals in order to function. They work synergistically, as a team, to boost your brainpower and memory. Vitamins help the body absorb the memory-builders. There's plenty of evidence too that certain minerals and vitamins all by themselves can sharpen your mind and clear up memory burnout.

Three minerals, zinc, magnesium, and iron, are considered absolutely essential to good memory function. "The difference between a sharp mind and a fuzzy one could depend on the amount of zinc in your diet," asserts British physician Dr. Roy Hullin. Zinc is essential for the synthesis of memory substances RNA and DNA. Dr. Michael Weiner told *Prevention* that often symptoms in the elderly that look like senility are simply nutritional deficiencies. "To prevent senile changes in the nervous system, two minerals are absolutely critical—zinc and magnesium," he says.

Iron can also rebuild the anemic intellect. Children deficient in iron had short attention spans and trouble learning new material. When oxygen-boosting iron was given, learning improved. Dr. Don Tucker of the University of Oregon found adults too could improve alertness, memory, and even word fluency with an iron supplement. His research shows iron can help "turn the brain on." Dr. Earl Mindell believes that the easiest form of iron to assimilate is "hydrolyzed-protein chelated iron." It's organic and water soluble and doesn't neutralize Vitamin E. Dosage: about 320 mg. a day.

Minerals potassium and magnesium are both important for memory and thinking because they're involved with the whole nervous system. Calcium too has turned around faulty memories and slow learning. It helps release RNA. These three minerals are also electrolytes, charged particles found in the bloodstream within and around body cells. Brain function and ability to recall can decline without them.

If you've ever lost your car in a parking lot, or forgotten your keys in the door, you may need manganese, the mineral that helps overcome absent-mindedness. It's a memory-improver and nerve-nourisher, plus it helps produce thyroxin in the thyroid gland; 1 to 9 mg. a day are suggested.

Lack of vitamins and poor nutrition can definitely reduce your mental powers, report Drs. Goodwin, Goodwin, and Garry of the University of New Mexico School of Medicine. They tested 260 men and women over sixty years of age. Those who performed poorly on the memory and abstract-thinking tests had low intake and low blood levels of vitamin C, B_2, folic acid, and B_{12}. These vitamins are essential for production and use of all the memory substances.

Vitamin A helps delay senility and extends longevity. It's a good antioxidant. It helps prevent toxins from binding to the DNA in the cell. Take it in the nontoxic beta-carotene form.

The vitamin B complex is absolutely vital for the brain and good mental health. Memory loss, depression, confusion, lack of coordination, and mental illnesses can develop from B complex deficiencies. "Subclinical deficiencies can indeed lead to less-than-optimal mental performance," says Dr. James Goodwin, one of the University of New Mexico researchers. Neurosurgeon Dr. Vernon Mark goes so far as to warn that a diet lacking the B complex can produce "dementing brain disease."

Highlights of some of the brain-boosting Bs:

B_1 (thiamine): Anything that depletes B_1, such as alcohol, drugs, malnutrition, or stress can result in short term memory loss, poor concentration, and damaged intellectual functions.

B$_2$ (riboflavin): A deficiency can lead to depression.

B$_3$ (niacin): Essential for nervous system and brain function. It's been found to lower cholesterol, important in maintaining good circulation to the brain. Orthomolecular pioneer Dr. Abram Hoffer found niacin could help control schizophrenia. He has also successfully treated hyperactive children and poor learners with niacin. Close-to-home proof that his methods could reverse senility came when Hoffer's own mother developed memory failure and early senility at age sixty-seven. In addition to memory loss, she had degenerative ailments —nervousness, depression, joint pains, arthritis, poor vision, weakness, fatigue. He began a program of 3 grams of niacin, some B$_6$, C, B$_{12}$, E, A, D, and L-glutamine. Six weeks later, arthritis cleared, vision was normal, anxiety and depression were gone, memory returned. Twenty years later, at eighty-seven, she was writing her memoirs, proof that memory loss can be corrected. A deficiency of niacin can lead to nervousness, irritability, insomnia, confusion, anxiety, depression, and hallucinations.

B$_5$ (pantothenic acid or calcium pantothenate): Helps memory substance choline to work and counteracts stress which can cause embarrassing memory blank-outs.

B$_6$ (pyridoxine): Another essential for a healthy nervous system. It's vital in producing the 14 amino acids and the memory substance RNA. It's also needed for phenylalanine to produce neurotransmitters.

B$_{12}$ (Cyanocobalamin): B$_{12}$, folic acid, and biotin (all part of the B complex) help synthesize RNA and DNA. B$_{12}$ is a key nutrient for the health of the nervous system and brain cells. It improves concentration, memory, and balance. A deficiency can lead to trouble focusing and remembering, a stuporous depression, or even hallucinations. Dr. Vernon Mark warns that even low B$_{12}$ can bring on depression with memory problems, and a severe deficiency can bring on spinal cord degeneration and brain diseases.

B$_{15}$ (pangamic acid): An important oxygenator of living tissues. Soviet studies show it aids respiration of brain tissue and Soviets have used it for treating learning disabilities and mental retardation.

Vitamin C as ascorbic acid, or in the nonacidic ascorbate form, is needed to get neurotransmitters such as phenylalanine going, and it helps the body absorb oxygen-carrying iron. It's vital to building collagen, the connective substance in all cells of the entire body. It fights toxins, and is a powerful antioxidant and life-extender.

Adelle Davis, the doyenne of nutrition writers, reported that children with normal levels of vitamin C in the blood have higher IQs than youngsters with low blood vitamin C. When children low in vitamin C were given C, IQ rose an average 3.6 points. Dr. Linus Pauling recommends 1,000 mg. to 10,000 mg. per day.

Vitamin E is essential to the use of oxygen by your muscles and is also an important antioxidant and life-extender. According to Adelle Davis, when huge amounts of vitamin E were given to mentally retarded children, improvement occurred. Vitamin E helps supply oxygen to the body to provide stamina and endurance. Dr. Earl Mindell suggests 200 to 1,200 IU per day.

Reversing Memory Loss

As the authors can testify from personal experience, trying to cope with a relative displaying memory loss can sometimes be a panicky experience. There can be confusion over who's alive or dead in the family, inability to recognize friends, totally chaotic financial affairs, lost keys, documents, possessions, confusion about time sequence and locations, food preparation hazards. . . . In his book *Brain Power,* Dr. Mark lists ten reversible common causes of memory loss.

1. Depression. By far the most common cause of memory deterioration in Dr. Mark's forty years of experience. Loss of concentration and slowed thinking that come with clinical depression are readily treatable with medications or therapy (see phenylalanine and tyrosine). 2. Fluid imbalance. Too much or too little water in the body can disturb electrolytes such as magnesium, sodium, potassium, and calcium. Heat can dehydrate and slow mental functions, so keep fluid balance normal and/ or take mineral supplements. 3. Drug overdose. Various prescription drugs and combinations can sometimes lead to memory loss. Have medications checked out. For instance, international jet travelers report a whole new kind of global amnesia, with no recollection of the trip or business negotiated. Fortunately, it's temporary. Cause: some jet-lag medications. Pearson and Shaw suggest natural tyrosine instead. 4. Malnutrition. A diet lacking the vitamin B complex, especially B_1, niacin, and B_{12}, can produce memory impairment. 5. Low blood sugar. Blood sugar decrease can alter brain function and cause memory problems. Treatment is available (see L-glutamine). 6. Anemia and lung disease. Lack of oxygen in the brain can cause brain malfunction. Both anemia and lung disease are treatable (see germanium). 7. Head injury. Trauma to the head from an accident can damage memory circuits. This condition is also treatable. 8. Small stroke. There can be recovery of brain

function after a small stroke, says Dr. Mark (see octacosanol). 9. Poor blood circulation. This problem too is treatable. 10. Severe hypothyroidism. Affected person may appear vacant-minded, depressed, even demented. Therapy can reverse symptoms of this disorder too.

Dr. Linus Pauling, who won his first Nobel Prize in biochemistry, asserts that nutrition can readily boost memory/mind by correcting abnormalities in the chemical environment of the brain. On his list of nutrients for top-level mind and memory function are ascorbic acid, thiamine, niacin, B_6, B_{12}, folic acid, magnesium, glutamic acid, and tryptophan. Nutritional deficiencies in brain cells can affect alertness, memory, mental energy, and mood, says Dr. Roger Williams. Adding some of the brain-booster nutrients in this chapter can make any meal a "memory-power lunch or dinner." Dr. Brian Morgan, an eminent nutrition expert at Columbia University School of Medicine, maintains that "eating the right foods can make a tremendous difference in brain function, improve your memory, and boost your intelligence within weeks."

As in other spheres, discoveries in biochemistry, nutrition, and related fields are accelerating. In a forthcoming handbook, we'll cover some little-known memory breakthroughs, gathered from around the world, which can heighten a range of mental powers. Meanwhile, remember to eat, and eat to remember.

19. Mind/Memory Fitness Machines

An international jet taxied in from the runway at the John Wayne Airport on the West Coast. A man who looked "absolutely green and yellow" was carried off on a stretcher and hastily loaded into a waiting ambulance which sped off to an obscure clinic. A drug addict for years, he'd taken a particularly massive dose of heroin before leaving his home in London. At the California clinic, Scottish physician Dr. Meg Patterson attached a small device the size of a Sony Walkman to his head with electrodes. Within forty minutes the effects of the heroin had been counteracted, and within ten days of treatments with the device, the addict found he'd kicked his heroin/alcohol/cocaine habit completely—and without experiencing any withdrawal symptoms. He was rehabilitated, after having spent a fortune on treatments in various clinics worldwide. This man was Pete Townshend, rock superstar guitarist with The Who.

"It was incredible!" he says. "There was a sense of inner joy. . . ." Townshend had slipped into drugged oblivion following exhausting tours, a marital rift, and gross financial mismanagement that put him a million dollars in debt. Through the treatment "you learn something about your human potential," the powers you have to deal with whatever crises come your way, he says.

Meanwhile, the underground rumor mill ran overtime. What was this device? Who knew about it? Was the Pentagon involved? Was the Mafia involved? Who was trying to keep the devices from the public? Were big pharmaceutical companies, or even drug lords trying to suppress them? Were big investors involved? Were the Russians and Chinese involved? What exactly did the device do to the brain and mind? Was the FDA muddling around with it?

More news filtered out. The CIA was investigating researchers who said they'd found an electronic device that restored brain function in cases of Korsakoff's psychosis (loss of short term memory caused by alcohol). Rumor had it that these devices came from the Soviet Union. The Soviets were using them to treat generals and top brass whose vodka habits had cost them their memories. Researchers at a famous Washington hospital were using the devices to successfully treat American generals who had the habit of too much bourbon, scotch, or gin. According to some insiders, the CIA said, "Stop the research!" They grabbed the device and sped it to Garland, Texas to the Verro Instrument Company, one of the highest tech government-secret-agency suppliers in the world, builders of starlite scopes, infrared viewers, spy satellites, and other high-level spy devices.

More news leaked out. In cases of severe alcoholism, it generally takes eight years for short term memory to be restored—*eight years of total abstinence*. With the use of these devices, it was said, short term memory was being restored in *five days*.

The Verro vice president became so fascinated with the device he split off and set up his own company, Neuro-Systems Inc. They developed $50,000 devices and spent vast sums documenting the effects. The University of Wisconsin Medical School, the University of Louisiana Medical College, and the University of Texas tested the devices independently. The college studies showed loss of short term memory in chronic alcoholics reversed in three to five days after treatment with these devices. In some cases the test subjects had their original college records, and they compared the psychological and memory tests. Alcoholics of fifteen years had their short-term memory totally restored to original levels after five days of using the box forty minutes a day.

Were addiction centers interested? No, some said, because recidivism was their chief source of income. 75% of those treated backslid in six months and returned again.

"It's one of the most fascinating psycho-political stories that's emerged," Dr. Robert (Bob) Beck told us. He's a highly respected American engineer-physicist in the field of electromagnetics and he's been a longtime consultant to the U.S. Dept. of Defense, working on highly classified projects. Beck, a friend of Dr. Meg Patterson, soon found himself swept into the scenario. What was inside the box? What made it work? Why did it have a spectacular effect on memory? Where did the magic black box come from? 200 pounds of research material later, Beck was on his way to inventing his own neuro-electrical stimulator, the BT-5+ Brain Tuner. The story began back in China.

The China Connection

Dr. H. L. Wen, a Canadian-educated neurosurgeon, set out for China in the late 60s to study acupuncture for anesthesia. Chemical anesthetics during long brain operations can become a problem. Once proficient in electro-acupuncture, he set up practice in Hong Kong.

One of his first cases happened to be an opium addict scheduled for brain surgery. Dr. Wen "rehearsed" electro-acupuncture anesthesia with the patient several times prior to the operation.

A few days later the patient told him with amazement, "I don't have any withdrawal symptoms! And I don't even crave opium anymore."

Surprised and intrigued, Dr. Wen and his colleague, Dr. S.Y.C. Cheung, began experimenting. There was no shortage of addicts. Hong Kong is considered the drug capital of the world. Patients suffering severe withdrawal symptoms were treated three times a day for five days, for thirty minutes at a time. In most cases, within fifteen minutes withdrawal symptoms, cramps, nausea, coldness, and pain simply stopped. Within two days a normal appetite returned and the patient felt a growing sense of well-being. By 1973, Drs. Wen and Cheung had successfully treated 140 addicts ranging in age from seventeen to seventy-nine. Addiction duration ranged from three to fifty-eight years. Other research centers in Hong Kong independently got the same results. Wen's report was published in Volume 1 of *The American Journal of Acupuncture* (April–June '73).

Dr. Wen's treatment for addiction involved inserting needles into point #86 (Heart-Lung) on the inner ear shell and then running a current to the needles from an electrical stimulator machine. Soon he found the needles weren't necessary, that metal clips would do, and he also developed an electrical stimulator device providing higher frequencies, which he'd found more effective.

Some of Wen's addicts reported back that they'd tried a regular fix of heroin after the treatment and it didn't give them the usual effect. Some even got into fights believing their heroin was cut.

Dr. Margaret Patterson from Scotland, a surgeon at the Tung Wa Hospital in Hong Kong, became intrigued with Dr. Wen's results, which were steadily being confirmed by many local medical centers. She tested the method too, finding that if just a metal earring was clipped to the ear and an electrical current applied, people could relieve symptoms of withdrawal from tobacco and alcohol. It seemed to also work with stage fright. A friend of hers, a concert artist, told her he was suffering shattering stage fright. When he used the earring hookup prior to his performances, he felt completely relaxed and totally free of stage fright during his concert.

How Does Acupuncture Cure Addiction?

Why did the electro-acupuncture treatment work so effectively on drug addiction? Dr. Wen wondered. He began doing rat studies. One group of rats was made into heroin addicts. A matched batch was the control group. He studied sets of rats through all the varied stages of addiction and withdrawal, with and without acupuncture treatment.

Dr. Wen's idea was to track endorphins in the rats' brains because, he reasoned, the opiates as a class—opium, morphine, heroin—simply overload the body's production of normal endorphins. Endorphins (from *endogenous* and *morphine*—"built-in morphine") are painkillers the body manufactures and are many times more effective than morphine. When the body is given a massive dose of morphine, the part of the brain that manufactures neurotransmitters shuts down. When a person tries to kick drugs, the body is in agony because the neurotransmitters are depleted and the "little factories" in the brain don't start up production of the body's natural painkillers for some time.

Dr. Wen's heroin-addicted rats were abruptly cut off heroin. They were pretty miserable rats. It took three weeks before production of neurotransmitters started up in their brains again, bringing greatly needed pain relief.

Batch number two of heroin-addicted rats was luckier. They went cold turkey and then had electro-acupuncture stimulation through metal clips attached to their bodies. The rats were stimulated at 111 hertz. *Within forty minutes of applying the voltage, the brain's ability to produce its own neurotransmitters was rehabilitated. Within three to five days it reached normal.* Within forty minutes withdrawal pain was gone and within three to five days addiction withdrawal and symptoms were gone.

"The implications of this work are stunning," says Dr. Bob Beck, thinking of the millions of addicted people worldwide and the zillions of dollars involved, not to mention the drug trade and associated crime.

Meanwhile, Dr. Meg Patterson was still tracking down the mystery of how electrical stimulation halted addiction. Back in England, she began collaborating with biochemist Dr. Ifor Capel at the Marie Curie Cancer Memorial Foundation Research Department in Surrey. Using low-frequency electrical stimulation machines they made a dramatic discovery. Different neurotransmitters were triggered by different frequencies and wave forms. For instance, a 10-hertz signal boosts production and turnover rate of serotonin.

"Each brain center generates impulses at a specific frequency, based on the predominant neurotransmitters it secretes," says Dr. Capel. "In other words, the brain's internal communications system—its language, if you like—is based on frequency. . . ."

When electrical energy waves at 10 hertz are sent into the brain, cells in the lower brain stem that normally fire within that frequency range will respond. As a result, particular mood-altering chemicals associated with that region will be released. So, it seemed, electrical stimulation of the brain, at the proper frequency, wave form, and current, could quickly and sharply increase the levels of specific pain-relieving and pleasure-producing neurotransmitters in the brain. What was the frequency code for each different neurotransmitter? Dr. Patterson began experimenting with $50,000 devices developed by British instrument companies. It was one of these she brought to the United States and used on rock star Townshend.

Dr. Bob Beck, totally fascinated with the adventure of discovery, wanted to break the code of the brain's frequency language. Poring over worldwide research papers and conferring with Dr. Patterson, he learned that beta endorphins are stimulated with a pulse repetition rate of between 90 and 111 hertz, the catecholamines at around 4 hertz, the enkephalins at another frequency, and so on. Working with spectrum analyzers and other equipment he decided to develop a device that would broadcast all the frequencies at the same time instead of one by one. He focused on the three magic ranges: enkephalins, catecholamines, and beta-endorphins, the three most active known neurotransmitters. He set up the frequencies in bundles—the target plus some on either side of it. Instead of sounding the frequency for each neurotransmitter separately, he put 256 frequencies altogether like a rich, resonating chord of music played by a full orchestra.

Beck came up with the BT-5+ Brain Tuner, a device which produces over 256 frequencies, delivered simultaneously in each $1/1000$ second pulse. (The maximum output is less than $1/1000$ of an ampere and therefore safely below the limit for regulated devices.) The BT-5+ generates a sine wave of 10 hertz at millivolts. He believes it generates all the known most beneficial frequencies for the natural stimulation of the brain's neurotransmitters.

The BT-5+ has electrodes on a stethoscope-like headset that fits in the hollows behind the ears. Dr. Patterson and colleagues found these acupuncture points behind the earlobes are more effective and access additional acupuncture points on the "Triple Warmer" meridian. You wear the device only twenty minutes a day.

Beck is pleased at the below $500 price tag and public availability. "These overpriced devices available only on prescription are criminal. Anyway, that's my philosophy!" he says. The burly, wiry-haired Beck, a dedicated pioneer in this field, likes to kid that he's "crusader rabbit." The BT-5 + has been grandfathered through the patent process under the category of a TENS (Transcutaneous Electrical Nerve Stimulator) unit although it does much more than a TENS, which is used to control chronic pain.

One of the first people to test out the BT-5+ was a close friend of Beck's. She experienced a startling transformation in memory power. Following a spinal block operation during childbirth twenty-five years earlier, she'd been unable to recall phone numbers or addresses. After trying the device for one day, she was remembering telephone numbers without the phone book and recalling phone numbers she'd known twenty years earlier working in the aerospace industry.

"With the Brain Tuner," says Dr. Beck, "you'll find you can recall faces and places that you thought you had lost. They're just there. It does amazing things to the memory. It's also a specific for stress reduction. If you have any type of anxiety, depression, insomnia, if it's chronic, it takes about three weeks. If it's acute, it takes about one week."

Like its predecessors, the device in tests so far seems to overcome withdrawal symptoms of any kind of addiction. Double-blind studies were done at the University of Wisconsin, says Beck.

Can you get too much neurotransmitter stimulation? "Yes," says Beck. "There's a plateau. Forty minutes is the red line. If you go over forty-five minutes it won't do any damage, but it will undo the benefits."

One day Beck tripped in a parking lot and injured his hand. He applied the BT-5 + to his hand and immediately stopped the pain. Dr. Meg Patterson has also often used her black box device to ease pain. Like the original electro-acupuncture devices from which they sprang, the "tuners" are also excellent pain relievers like the TENS units widely used for pain control. Beck warns, however, that a TENS unit has a DC offset voltage built in deliberately and should never be used above the neck as a brain tuner.

The only troublesome side effect of the BT-5+? It stimulates lucid dreaming. Memories of dreams can be vivid and persistent. However, for those wishing to do lucid dreaming, it's ideal.

To date, users report BT-5+ reduces stress, increases energy levels, improves both short and long term memory, improves IQ, concentration, learning, and creativity, reduces anxiety and depression, and reduces sleep requirements. Recently published studies at the University of Wisconsin Medical College and University of Louisiana reveal the BT-5+ can also boost your IQ. Students were given sessions on the BT-5+ to reduce anxiety on final exams. The unexpected bonus was IQ gains of 20 to 30 points. BT-5+ stimulation appears to enhance neural efficiency, say researchers.

We and family and friends have tested the BT-5+ and recommend it. We all noticed stress relief and increased energy. (The headset tends to slip, we noted, and some didn't like the "pricking" sensation of the electrodes.) But for a fast, easy, highly effective route to new mind potentials, the BT-5+ is a definite plus!

The Graham Potentializer

You rush to your office early the day you're scheduled to negotiate an important contract. You want to get a head start on the day's work. But instead of rereading critical clauses, you lie down on a comfortable chaise lounge and appear to be snoozing with your head cushioned on a pillow. Very slowly, the chaise appears to be levitating. Then it gradually settles downward again. Actually, the chaise is slowly and gently traveling in counterclockwise revolutions about ten and a half times a minute. There's an enclosed motor under the chaise. Near your pillow there's a box that generates a pulsating electromagnetic field. As you revolve, you're moving through this weak electromagnetic field. You look calm and deeply relaxed. After twenty minutes or so, that stiff shoulder and backache have gone. Suddenly an idea pops up—a way to change a clause in the contract that will save years of aggravation. You get up from the chaise and stretch. You feel calm, but energized and focused. Your mind and memory feel clear and sharp as you head for your desk. That was no ordinary chaise lounge. That was the Graham Potentializer, an apparatus that's been proven over many years to sharpen mental efficiency, open up new mind potentials, and release stress.

"I call it a 'defogger,' " says Chinmayee Chakrabarty M.D. of Montefiore Hospital in the Bronx. She uses the Graham Potentializer in her private practice. "It focuses the mind," she says, "helps you to see yourself and your problem from a new perspective." She feels its greatest benefit is the improvement in clarity of thinking. "It seems to help integrate reason and emotion. It also produces a great increase in energy—you think and work more productively, because your mind has this new vitality and clarity."

Michael Hutchison, who tested the Potentializer and described it in his important book, *Megabrain,* found that "for several days after each use I felt refreshed and seemed to work better, think more effectively and felt surprisingly energetic and calm."

The Graham Potentializer has been spreading its mind/memory benefits for two decades and has reams of test data documenting its mind/memory-powering effects. Independent studies of the Graham device showed that it had spectacular capabilities for improving and accelerating learning. Tests showed a great leap in learning rate. Not only does it boost brain efficiency, but it also feels good.

"For some reason, this seems the most exhilarating of all the brain boosters around," says Robert Anton Wilson, author of *Illuminati.* Wilson, like Hutchison, has tested hordes of the new high tech mind fitness machines. "I have felt lingering effects two or three days after each usage."

We might have dismissed some of the claims for the Potentializer's abilities to open up evolutionary mind powers if we hadn't happened to stumble onto the early research going on right under our noses. The inventor, David Graham, is a Canadian electronics engineer in his late 40s. A native of northern British Columbia, he graduated from the University of Alberta and continued to study electromagnetic fields and human development at other universities in Canada. After an eight-year stint as a management consultant with the Canadian government, he launched his own business in the field of stress technology and relaxation research, and set up an office in Toronto where one of the authors resides part-time.

If his invention *really* was a brain-booster, the ultimate test would be to see if it could boost the mind power not only of the healthy, but of those most in need—the brain damaged and learning disabled. A large, ambitious research program got underway in the 70s involving over 1500 brain damaged and retarded children from the Toronto area. Over a period of months, these kids would only be treated by taking a ride on his rotating-couch invention, then called the "Electromechanical Therapeutic Apparatus." Dr. J.P. Ertl, a highly respected Canadian psychologist, well known for his pioneering investigations of the relationship between IQ and brain waves, developed a special EEG to measure "the most sensitive indicators of brain functioning." These objective tests would be carried out to see if the Graham apparatus really did boost brainpower, even in the impaired.

After the children had been treated for several months on the Graham ETA, Dr. Ertl completed brain tests on them. The average change in each subject was an enormous 25% improvement. Subjects showed increases in alpha waves and shifts in hemispheric dominance, so that right brain and left brain came into balance. Graham's machine definitely enhanced what Ertl calls the "Neuro-Efficiency Quotient"—a measure of how fast the brain takes in information. The machine "definitely does something beneficial to the brain waves," concludes Ertl. "The changes in EEG parameters were of great magnitude, consistent, highly significant statistically. . . . I am satisfied that the EEG changes observed were caused by the Electromechanical Therapeutic Apparatus."

The reams of statistics pouring out of Ertl's computer didn't begin to tell the behind-the-scenes story of exactly what it means to both child and family to boost the brainpower of the profoundly mentally disabled. There was five-year-old Bruce. He suffered from severe brain damage and was so hyperactive that he had to wear a helmet to protect his head. He never slept more than three hours a night and while his parents slept he became a house-destroying monster. They would awaken to find their home a shambles. After forty sessions on the Graham machine, he slept normally throughout the night. His mental functioning improved and he had better motor coordination. The family's entire home life was restored to normal.

Five-year-old Josh had a genetic blood condition. He never spoke until he was three and a half, had little coordination, and could not master basic self-care skills such as using the bathroom. He was considered unteachable in all other areas. After thirty-one sessions he experienced sudden, rapid speech development and coordination. His mental functioning took a big leap and finally he could look after his own basic functions. He became teachable by his parents and later by teachers.

Pat, who was twelve when she started treatments, had suffered severe brain damage at age three. She was spastic and autistic. She had speech coordination problems and spoke only incoherent, inappropriate, single words. She couldn't walk unaided. She slept twelve to fourteen hours a day and was totally withdrawn. After forty sessions she began talking in a meaningful and appropriate way. She had increased stamina, endurance, and energy. She could walk and handle utensils better. Excessive muscular tensions totally disappeared. She slept less and her attention span increased. She was classified as trainable for the first time in her twelve-year life by her school for the mentally retarded.

Stan was eight when he began treatment on the apparatus. Prior to treatments, his parents noted, he spoke only to doors and cats. He appeared happy but did not interact with other children and had never gone to school because he would not talk to people. After forty sessions over a twenty-week period, he slowly began to talk to his family. He began to interact with others, and, after he started kindergarten, teachers noticed increased attention span and improved class participation.

Nineteen-year-old Sterling was brain damaged at birth in both hemispheres. After thirty-five sessions, his mind and memory improved. He began to interact with others. Interestingly, the EEG tests showed *no* brain damage during the treatment and *slighter* reoccurrence of brain malfunction afterward.

A two-year-old child with Downs syndrome suddenly, in one month of treatments, developed all the fine motor responses of a normal two year old.

These are just a small handful of the cases we uncovered. They were genuine "awakenings," not just for the mind-damaged children, but for their entire families. We met one of the parents involved in the research program at a 1982 Canadian Health Food Association Conference at Toronto's Constellation Hotel. A single mother of a severely retarded son, she'd had to devote enormous amounts of her time to taking care of him. To bring him to Toronto for the treatments with Graham's apparatus, she'd had to commute fifty miles each way. "But it was worth it!" she said with a smile. After just a few sessions, he showed improvement. After five months of treatments, he was transformed. He could take care of his own personal needs, his schoolwork improved, and his interpersonal relationships improved. Though the sessions were over, he continued to improve. It was like a miracle in her life, she explained. Finally relieved of the burden of constant care he'd required, she'd had time for her own interpersonal relationships. She was engaged to remarry and was looking forward to a whole new life.

It appears that high tech mind-boosting treatment not only can transform the lives of the mind-disabled individuals involved, but the effects ripple out to the caregivers around them. A decade ago, the number of learning disabled in North America stood at 11 million.

Today it's higher. Could effective mind-boosters literally transform the lives of millions?

As research results kept pouring in, showing the amazing effects the device had even on the brain damaged and learning disabled, Graham fine-tuned his invention, and its name. Exactly how does this simple-looking couch increase intelligence, accelerate learning, and expand mental capacity?

The rhythmic circular motion is the key, Graham believes. It affects all the body fluids (we're 90% fluid) and the motion has a special effect on the inner ear. Motion causes electrical signals from the inner ear and the fluids of the semicircular canals to travel to the cerebellum, the back part of the brain that regulates balance and motor activity. The cerebellum has a network of connections with the limbic system (so involved with emotions, memory, pleasure, and pain) and with the "thinking cap," the neocortex. The motion, Graham believes, triggers increased neural activity in *all* parts of the brain, stimulating neurons and lighting up neural networks. Sort of a Nautilus fitness machine for the mind and for the triune brain—sparking connections among them, exercising all three segments at the same time.

"This neural activity is of an uncommon sort, not only stimulating many different parts of the brain, but causing the neurons to forge new connections. So what the rotation is really doing is altering and increasing the flow of neuroelectricity and neurochemicals to large areas of the brain. This . . . brings a dramatic increase in motor and learning capabilities. The 'exercise' has a brain-building effect, just as physical exercise has a bodybuilding effect," says Graham. "Movement is like a nutrient."

The rhythmic motion of ocean waves and human cerebral spinal fluid both average ten to twelve cycles per minute, and the Graham device operates at a rhythm of approximately ten and a half cycles per minute. The combining of this primal rhythm and motion helps produce the profoundly soothing, stress-relieving effect. At the same time, the weak electromagnetic field you move through interacts with and alters the body's own natural electric field. The action of Graham's apparatus is based on the burgeoning new field of bioelectric medicine. By externally changing the electrical activity, chemical changes are produced in brain and body. The Graham Potentializer produces a mild field of 125 hertz that Graham claims is highly beneficial. "In effect, an energy transfusion occurs," says Graham. "Your brain enjoys a highly effective exercising that improves its neural responses." The field balances and strengthens where needed. Graham has test evidence that under the right conditions brain cells can reproduce themselves just like the other cells of our bodies.

Clarence Cone, a pioneer in cell biology, while working for NASA at the Cell and Molecular Biology Laboratory of the VA Hospital in Hampton, Virginia, discovered that it *is* possible to stimulate neuron regeneration. Cone's patented system uses "direct electromagnetic changes across the cell surface" to regenerate brain nerve cells.

Graham's rotating couch in a weak electromagnetic field mimics the "earth experience." After all, as Graham points out, "as human beings, we experience such conditions all the time as we live on a rotating earth and move through its electromagnetic field." Current research is showing that when humans are cut off from the earth's natural fields, they start to have physical and behavioral abnormalities . . . fatigue, drowsiness, irritability. In addition to cutting ourselves off from our natural fields, we've added dangerous new ones—radiating computer screens, harmful fields from radio and TV towers, and electric power lines.

"Are there any negative side effects from using the Potentializer?" we asked Graham and his associates back in the 80s at his Toronto office. He loaded us down with reams of data. In over 1500 sessions with 500 people in Toronto and Ottawa over a four-year period, the reports show *"no* negative side effects reported or observed."

For over a decade we have scrutinized the Potentializer in action at various trade shows and conferences. Users generally emerge calm and deeply relaxed. Some told us it eased stress and relieved aches and pains.

In a controlled U.S. study involving reading, spelling, and math, both control and test subjects received twenty-one hours of tutoring from the same instructor. Test subjects had ten sessions on the revolving Graham Potentializer. Their math abilities in particular soared. They had a 2,100% increase in learning rate, Graham reports. Needless to say, Graham's own four children, who've been nurtured on these rotating devices, are extremely bright.

Can anyone benefit from the Graham Potentializer? "Definitely!" says Graham. He points to years of tests that show that his apparatus increases neuro efficiency. In addition, there are physical, neurological, and consciousness-raising benefits.

Famous Canadian geneticist Dr. David Suzuki, contemplating the current disastrous scenario humanity finds itself in, asks dismally, "Will limits of the human brain prove fatal?"

Megabrain author Michael Hutchison feels that human survival itself may well depend on the ability to increase human mental powers so that we can develop new strategies for overcoming our present crises. These proliferating new high tech routes to expanded brain power may be the answer, he thinks. "So mental enrichment, brain stimulation and the exploration of our mind's potentials are . . . part of a potentially beneficial, history-determining social process—one which can widen our knowledge and help determine the future of the race."

Graham Potentializers are available through a growing number of medical professionals throughout the United States and Canada. General uses include easing stress and pain, inducing relaxation, inducing positive emotions, increasing learning abilities, intelligence, and creativity, and improving motor functioning of the body. If the results continue, Graham feels the benefits to the individual and society "may be beyond imagination." In his opinion it could lead to an evolutionary breakthrough for humanity.

Memory Batteries and Rejuvenation

Fabulous techniques for rejuvenation of mind, memory, and body were said to be known by ancient secret priesthoods of Egypt and Tibet. Locked under glass in many museums of antiquities and fine arts around the world you can find remnants of what some people believe are these extraordinary ancient healing and rejuvenating devices. They might be labeled "ritual devices" or even "vril" sticks. Egyptian paintings and sculptures too sometimes reveal priests holding strange rods of carbon and lodestone, or vril sticks—metal tubes made of "electrinium," a secret mixture of gold, silver, and quartz. With the "vitic force" or increased vitality and nerve energy invoked by these devices, it was said you could heal any illness. You could almost double your life span. You could enjoy brilliant mind and memory powers into a vigorous old age. These ancient priests were said to have uncovered the secret of total mastery of life force and could use it to restore and rebalance any condition. Is there a kernal of truth to these legends?

What may prove to be the story of the recovery of at least some of this lost healing technology, a technology that could be a boon to all, began many decades ago in Kentucky. Edgar Cayce, in his *Readings* for distant patients, began to describe the plans, construction, and uses of unusual and seeming nonsensical devices. Asserting that he could access the Akashic record and read off the data stored in humanity's universal memory record, Cayce carefully dictated precise instructions for building bioenergy generators. Of the ancients' carbon rods, gold and silver were among the basic components. The design was updated. Place two five-inch bars of carbon steel in a sixteen-ounce tin can or copper container, Cayce dictated. Separate them by two one-eighth-inch-thick sections of glass. Surround them completely by bars of carbon on all four sides. Put the assembly into crushed hardwood charcoal inside the metal container. Run copper wire leads from each of the carbon steel bars. Pass one wire through a jar containing a solution of gold or silver.

When completed, the strange device looked like a lantern battery. The two wires from the battery were to be attached to the user's ankle and wrist. Place the device in a pot of ice, Cayce instructed. The cold helped instigate bioenergy circulation that would carry the vibrational force of carbon and gold to the patient. The generator would then activate a powerful balancing force that could heal and restore vitality to every cell in the body, Cayce explained. It will "revivify the elemental forces that create energies in the body itself," claimed Cayce. It is "beneficial to all human force of life—good for anyone!" he urged. "It can keep the body in almost *perfect* accord for many, many, many, many, MANY days!" The silver and gold conveyed in vibrational form to the body through the generator, *"may almost lengthen life to its double,"* insisted Cayce. For those with memory loss, senility, or brain damage, the device was paramount. It can produce "almost a new brain," he said.

Had Cayce really uncovered the secrets of the ancients—mastery over vital force? Was the legendary "fountain of youth" a fountain of "vibrations"? Detectors to chart any subtle energy or vibrational force generated by the device did not exist at the time. Acupuncture and chi energy were unknown in the West back then, much less scanners to monitor chi circulation. Double-blind testing and lab analysis of chemical changes induced in the body by the battery were to come decades later. Whatever the thing did, there were absolutely startling results with patients.

In March 1938, twenty-nine-year-old Florence Evans of Toddesville, Kentucky was literally "turning to stone" with incurable scleroderma. Treated with the battery, nutrition, and massage, she was fully recovered by the following May. She went on to an outstanding career as an organist. Sidney Kalugin of Jackson Heights, New York, a 1968 scleroderma patient, was called a "walking miracle" after treatment

The Edgar Cayce bio-battery, a neglected but primary element in Cayce's holistic health system. Sixty years of use and recent scientific research suggest it *does* perform as Cayce said. Can it really restore memory and rejuvenate mind and body?

with the bio-battery. By 1972 he was fully cured and enjoying an active lifestyle again.

Tony Castello, an intelligent, skinny six year old, was carried to see Edgar Cayce in April 1930. He couldn't walk and his attempts at talking were jerkings and writhings. He had cerebral palsy. After treatments with the battery, osteopathy, and nutrition, within eight months at the Cayce center he showed marked improvement which steadily continued at home.

In 1969, Birmingham, Alabama, physician Dr. John Peniel developed incurable rheumatoid arthritis, rarely leaving his bed. In 1972, after using the Cayce appliance for three months, he was up and about again.

Suzy Paxton, a twenty year old diagnosed as having neurasthenia, had also suffered from hyperactivity and mental/motor incoordination for fifteen years. After eight weeks of treatment with the battery in 1930, she was cured. She married the next year, led a fulfilling life, and by 1969 had seven grandchildren.

At the Association for Research and Enlightenment (A.R.E.) in Virginia Beach, there are meticulous records of decades of achievements with the bioenergy devices and volumes of testimonials on file. The case histories show the devices have helped alleviate virtually every known ailment. They have restored memory, cured senility, overcome drug abuse, stress, hypertension, deafness, and weight problems. They have helped heal all manner of serious illness from cancer to arthritis to cerebral palsy. In the 70s, we personally witnessed a woman with a terminal illness slowly overcome it with the use of the device over many months.

The large A.R.E. library houses some 15,000 pages of *Readings* Cayce gave while in trance. Out of the 2,100 readings dealing with health, a whopping 25% told patients to use these bioenergy devices. Altogether, a total of 1,150 readings discuss the bioenergy devices.

"Cayce stressed these devices more adamantly than anything else," says Phil Thomas, a health researcher from Ithaca, New York. "From my examination of the readings, I feel confident in saying that the Cayce devices are crucial to his treatment of illness," emphasizes Thomas.

The Cayce readings repeatedly extolled the all-around benefits of these rejuvenators: "Found to aid the body in EVERY direction"; "Necessary for anyone that uses the brain a great deal"; "This we find would be well that everyone use such an appliance, for the system would be improved in every condition that relates to the body being kept in attunement"; "The vibrations from same are well for every human individual."

Alleviating Memory Loss

Cayce prescribed the bioenergy devices in particular for cases involving memory loss. Whether the condition was amnesia, senility, mental deterioration (later called Alzheimer's), insanity, or brain lesions and tumors, the devices could help, he insisted. Brain malfunctions that may have started very early—mongolism, retardation, brain incoordination, cerebral palsy—could also be alleviated.

"Memory is never lost!" Cayce asserted. Only our ability to access memory could be lost. Peering inside memory-loss victims with a clairvoyant eye, he said it was like seeing a "fouled-up telephone switchboard." In Cayce's view, memories are stored safely outside the physical body. Restoring vital energy with bioenergy batteries can help us reestablish our communication system with our memories, he believed.

If a patient suffered memory loss due to brain deterioration, or whether senility was caused by old age or brain disease, the bio-batteries used along with osteopathy for a full course of treatments could virtually produce a new brain, he explained. We are constantly repairing and replacing the cells in our bodies. By using the bioenergy battery, the replacement cells are attuned back to their correct pattern. It was a mechanized way of doing what Deepak Chopra accomplishes with sound and mantra. (See page 213). Even dimmed senses of hearing and seeing and taste in the aged could be restored, he claimed. The bio-battery could give stability and strength to the system, and bring proper coordination and proper resuscitation. It could rebalance, equalize, purify.

The Rejuvenation Solution

The different solutions for the jar that connects to the bio-battery are all-important. As the ancients had known, gold and silver are extremely beneficial to the body. They may turn out to be the quintessential rejuvenators. Recently, gold injections have benefited arthritis patients, but the treatment has to be monitored carefully because there's danger of toxicity. We aren't built to absorb or eat metal. Gold conveyed to the body through the bio-battery, however, is completely safe. The body absorbs the vibrations of gold and silver, said Cayce. The metals don't have to pass through the physical organs of assimilation. Cayce specified that solutions of gold chloride and silver nitrate are the best. Gold chloride is exceptional in Cayce's view. "Gold chloride can rejuvenate any organ of the system." Gold chloride and silver nitrate could be alternated. *"Given properly, silver and gold may almost lengthen life to its double,"* said Cayce. Did the legendary fountain of youth consist of vibrations from gold and silver? Did the ancients know how to tap the vibrations from the gold and silver vril sticks? Do acupuncture's gold and silver needles convey vibratory force?

Cayce dictated plans for a second type of bioenergy battery called the "Wet Cell Appliance," or "B Battery," a single-cell battery. Two poles (nickel and copper) are suspended in a jar containing a liquid solution of distilled water, copper sulfate, powdered zinc, and sulfuric acid. This battery generates a small electrical charge. Wires run from the battery poles to the user's body. Like the other battery, a solution jar can be used with it. The Wet-Cell battery too was prescribed for conditions from senility to brain tumors, mental retardation to insanity.

A Battery That Generates Good Luck?

Surprisingly, Cayce claimed that these bio-batteries could bring you "good luck"! The bio-batteries help you get centered and tuned-in to inner guidance which can help you with any situation, he observed. The days when you use the bio-battery "will be found to be, if it may be so termed, the 'lucky' days, or the periods when there is a closer association with Creative Forces about the body."

Cayce frequently emphasized that the vibrations from the bio-battery enable people to communicate more easily with the unconscious mind. This makes it easier to speed healing with positive affirmations or to achieve a desired goal by visualization. After using the device, answers to problems, creative solutions, fortunate decisions might come in dreams, he said.

With so much going for them, you might have thought that Cayce's bio-batteries would have become widely used. With many people worldwide suffering mental and physical illnesses, many battling toxicity of every sort, many who could use repair and regeneration, you might have thought that leading-edge researchers would be investigating rejuvenation through bio-batteries. But, unfortunately, like the beautiful gold and silver Egyptian vril sticks in the Boston Museum of Fine Arts, the precious bio-batteries too were set aside like museum pieces. Countless books were published outlining the Cayce remedies, but few mentioned his rejuvenating, health-restoring bioenergy devices. Like the vril sticks, few understood how and why they worked.

In addition, the devices were inappropriately named. Because of the vibratory forces involved, Cayce had dubbed them "Radial-Active Appliances" or "Radio-Active Appliances" or "Impedance Devices." (Of course they have nothing to do with "radioactivity" in its currently understood meaning.) This moniker brought regulatory authorities sniffing. According to the science of the time, the devices did nothing.

Authorities attributed cures to the placebo effect. For years, the devices languished in an underground and only insiders got to benefit from their powers. They became "like a gift left unclaimed on the doorstep," says Harvey Grady of the A.R.E. Researcher Phil Thomas lamented, "It's as if the very backbone of Cayce's holistic health philosophy had remained dormant."

Regenerating the Regenerators

Finally, in the 80s as worldwide discoveries in bio-magnetics, bio-electricity, acupuncture, subtle energies, and vibrational medicine opened up totally new horizons for healing and rejuvenation, the Cayce bio-batteries began to be looked at in a new way. The long-sought secrets of the bio-batteries at last began to be unveiled.

The Fetzer Energy Medicine Research Institute launched rigorous, scientific, double-blind studies of the Cayce device in 1987. The Cayce devices used in the tests were a high-quality version developed and trademarked "Radiac" by Bruce D. Baar of Downington, Pennsylvania. To rule out the placebo effect, the institute had dummy devices built to match the Cayce devices. Neither volunteer users nor medical staff knew which was which. Elaborate before/after biochemical analyses were done by independent labs.

Conclusion? Tests showed the genuine Cayce device had a measurable effect on the human neuro-endocrine system. Blood levels of the neurotransmitter dopamine increased. This neurotransmitter (see p. 237) helps you cope with stress and aids relaxation, blood circulation, and improves fine motor control.

Harvey Grady, director of Research Programs at the A.R.E. Clinic in Phoenix, Arizona, reports that, "The study offers a promising suggestion . . . the Cayce Device actually performs as the Cayce readings suggest." Grady, a longtime user of the device himself, says its benefits improve with time. Like an unclaimed inheritance, he says, "the device could become a resource for health maintenance as a body energy balancer and stress reducer. . . ." Writer Toni De Marco, who tested the device during a month of harried business travel, says it not only eased stress but also gave her a surge of energy. Aerospace engineer James Beal, after trying the device, calls it "a harmony generator."

Bruce Baar, who has researched Cayce devices for twenty-nine years, told us that he has personally witnessed individuals with prenatal problems such as monogolism achieve a recovery, using the battery plus special solutions. In cases of such life-long problems, the course of treatment is slow and took seven years.

The effectiveness of Cayce bio-batteries is also being investigated by Phil Thomas of the U.S. Psychotronic Association. At their 1988 international conference, he reported he'd constructed and given bio-batteries to two quadraplegics. Could they help nerve regeneration? A twenty-seven-year-old man, who'd suffered brain damage shortly after birth, made slow, steady progress with the device. After eight months, his mother reported, "He's much brighter now than before. Memory and concentration are both improving. He can speak sentences now instead of fragments. He can focus on objects and ideas which previously would have gone undetected. He has some improved motor function in his left hand." A thirty-five-year-old man from D.C. felt sensations returning to the center of his body after eight months on the device. A forty-year-old Virginia Beach woman who'd had severe rheumatoid arthritis for eight years, was up, walking, and off medication after six months' use of the bio-battery. Swelling and pain were gone, she stated.

Tom Johnson of Virginia Beach's Heritage Store, a Cayce remedy center, told us he has seen a great many people who credit their recoveries to the Cayce devices. He believes the solutions in the jar used with the bio-battery "transmit elements from these solutions into the body's system vibratorially. This apparently stimulates the body into producing its own needed elements." Aside from gold and silver, solutions for specific problems include tincture of iron, spirits of camphor, or Atomidine (iodine).

Exactly how does the device work? According to Cayce, when the bio-battery is placed in ice or cold water, the carbon steel becomes electrolized. A discharge is set in motion by the difference in temperature. It travels from the body to the carbon steel and back again. The metal then produces a form of electronic vibration, which becomes a form of vibratory motion for the cells of the body. Each atom, element, and organ of the human body has its own unique electronic vibration. When a cell or organ becomes deficient in its ability to reproduce and maintain the necessary equilibrium for sustaining its physical existence, it lacks this vibratory energy. These deficiencies could come in many ways, Cayce said, through injuries, disease, poor elimination of toxins, etc. An abnormal condition in the human body is caused by a lack of equilibrium, he said, which in turn is caused by the lack of an element to produce a vibration in a certain part of the body.

The wires from the battery are alternated in their locations. The first day, the positive lead goes to the right wrist, negative to left ankle. Next day, + to left wrist, − right ankle. Third day, + left ankle, − right wrist; fourth day, + right ankle, − left wrist; and repeat. Acupuncture theory postulates a chi energy exchange at the hands and feet, exactly where Cayce said to place the electrodes from the device. Perhaps the bio-battery balances chi energy, or even generates it. Acupuncture rebalances chi energy when there's too much in one location and not enough in another. The Wet-Cell Battery, which does actually generate electricity, may function like electronic acupuncture.

Stanford University physicist Dr. William Tiller theorizes that the Cayce devices balance the energy flow in the body through the acupuncture meridians. The devices, he says, may set up a gentle oscillating energy flow through the meridians, causing electric current to flow out of some acupuncture points and into others. The currents are less than one millionth of an ampere, he says. Dr. William McGarey, co-director of the A.R.E. Clinic, a longtime user of acupuncture in his practice, agrees with Tiller.

Decades before the discovery of "The Body Electric" (see p. 283), Cayce anticipated it and designed a device that could facilitate using the body's electrical system to help heal itself. "Just as a battery may be charged or discharged, so may the human body be recharged by the production of coordination by the Appliance," said Cayce. "Vibrations are controlled through the activity of the Appliance . . . [T]his takes energies in portions of the body, builds up and discharges body electrical energies that revivify portions of the body where there is a lack of energies stored." He clarified that the Appliance is not electrical itself, but runs on the body's electrical forces and redistributes and equalizes them. He also emphasized that the device was totally safe. The bioenergy battery should be kept in use for the body "as long as it lives, for it would be good for it all the time."

"When the body is tired, depleted or when there are disturbances in any portion of the system, this should be used again to bring the desired effects in allowing the body to rest, in bringing about better digestive forces, better circulatory forces and—most of all—a better coordination in the cerebro-spinal and sympathetic system," he instructed.

New breakthroughs seem to back up Cayce. In 1983, the distinguished Swedish radiologist Dr. Bjorn Nordenstrom of Stockholm's Karolinska Institute, published a revolutionary book, *Biologically Closed Electric Circuits: Clinical, Experimental, and Theoretical Evi-*

dence for an Additional Circulatory System. He reveals decades of research into his "astounding" theory, that biologically closed electric circuits exist in the body and play a key role in health and healing. The circuits, he found, could be switched on by injuries, infections, tumors, or normal activities of the body's organs. Voltages build and fluctuate. Currents course through arteries, veins, and capillary walls to balance the activities of internal organs. The currents, he says, are the foundation of healing and are critical to the well-being of the body. He too developed a biological battery. Dr. Nordenstrom has documented scores of cures with his battery to back up his claims. Today, worldwide, the science of electro-medicine is making a surging comeback.

Some years ago, we were taping a TV show in Washington, D.C. with the late Hugh Lynn Cayce, Edgar Cayce's eldest son. During a break, he undid his tie and loosened his collar. "Look", he said, pointing to a metal rectangle on a chain around his neck. "It's a small piece of carbon steel," he said. "I wear it to ward off colds and keep up my energy level during these hectic PR tours!"

We found details in reading #1842: "If the entity will wear about its person, or in its pocket, a metal that is carbon steel—it will prevent, it will ionize the body—by its very vibrations—to resist cold, congestion . . ." and throat problems. There's also a mini-appliance you can take with you anywhere for any emergency. Attach a one-inch-square piece of carbon steel to a length of copper wire. "Charge up" the carbon steel in a basin of ice water, and then run the copper wire in a circle around your waist.

Over the years, we have occasionally tried out the full-size bio-battery. It really does relieve stress and fatigue! It gives a restful, centered mental focus. Cryopac icepacks were helpful in providing the large amount of ice needed. As the years keep passing, we're beginning to be inspired to try the gold solution to rejuvenate.

Cayce's devices, with sixty years of use behind them, are prime candidates for testing with the new subtle energy technologies: Motoyama acupuncture meridian detectors, thermo-luminescence devices, MEG and SQUID scans, Kirlian photography, and others.

"Is it possible that a concept as profound and potentially far-reaching as this has been left idle all these years?" asks researcher Phil Thomas. "Is it plausible that the very backbone to the Cayce holistic philosophy could remain dormant, while his legacy is known to millions? Is this the missing shred of information which could reduce the pain and suffering of those with virtually every known ailment?"

As for these bio-batteries that can "almost produce a new brain,"

Cayce made predictions. "There will come those days when many will understand and interpret properly." Perhaps these *are* "those days."

Mind/Memory High Tech

"We have new technology for enhancing consciousness, rapidly, safely, right now, with no side effects," says Dr. Bob Beck. It seems the technological supermemory revolution is here.

The evolutionary impact of devices like those developed by Beck, Patterson, Wen, Graham, and others has just begun. Neuroscientist Dr. Aryeh Routtenberg of Northwestern University observes that catecholamine-enhancing drugs facilitate learning, and the centers and pathways of brain reward are also the centers and pathways of *memory* consolidation. Routtenberg was one of the first to discover that electrical stimulation triggered the release of large amounts of the catecholamine neurotransmitters (including dopamine and norepinephrine). These have an effect on the brain similar to cocaine, which also works by stimulating the catecholamines in the same areas. Routtenberg's discovery helps show why Beck's BT-5+ improves memory and learning. When something is learned, he concludes, the learner is rewarded and the activity of the reward centers and pathways facilitates the formation of memory.

Superlearning rats—that's what Dr. James Olds got as early as 1954 when he too stumbled on the idea of stimulating the brain with electricity. He implanted electrodes in the pleasure centers of the rats' brains and they could electro-stimulate themselves by pressing a pedal. The rats kept pressing those pedals. They learned mazes with astounding speed and accuracy and passed rat intelligence and memory tests with high marks. Twenty years later, the mystery was being solved—electro-stimulation triggered endorphins which enhance learning and memory. Says Routtenberg, "The improved learning may be due to the fact that the animals self-regulate the amount of stimulation, thereby self-reinforcing their behavior."

The discovery of devices that can easily stimulate your brain's learning and memory pathways has startling implications. Says Michael Hutchison, author of *Megabrain,* it means that at a touch of a button, you can enhance your ability to think, to absorb new information, to combine ideas in new ways, to consolidate facts into memory, or to recall or remember information already stored away in your brain. Users would hook up to a brain-boosting tuner or electro-acupuncture device, then study afterward while endorphin and peptide levels are high.

"I think that one day mind machines may be seen as the brain-training counterpart to the sleek Nautilus and Universal machines, and ergometers and rowing devices and cross-country ski contraptions," says Hutchison. "It's not hard to imagine serious brain athletes getting their gray matter in shape by pumping peptides and neutrotransmitters."

How much could you improve your memory? How much faster could you learn? These are the questions of the 1990s. Dr. Donald Kubitz of San Francisco, one of the first American doctors to study Dr. Wen's work, believed electro-acupuncture could not only help treat addicts, but could greatly aid autistic children as well.

Could certain groups use these devices to make themselves into a powerful elite? On the other hand, could the addiction-releasing powers of these devices help break the power of the drug lords who have vast populations and mammoth amounts of money under their control? Could crack babies be rehabilitated in days? Could these brain enhancing devices even beat genetic predisposition and change the course of human evolution? Of immediate concern, could these mind-renewers help reverse America's deteriorating scholastic performance and massive illiteracy? Could they save a graying population from the staggering health costs of a memory—weak old age? Right now there are more questions than answers.

After investigating the vast array of new HEAD technology, Robert Anton Wilson asserts, "What concerns me urgently, is the *direction* and *acceleration* of this research . . . my visions of what's coming startle me." The fourth generation of these mind machines "will mark the most important turning point in the evolution of this planet."

The Memory Electric

"I sing the body electric," wrote Walt Whitman in the 1800s. It's taken more than a century to hear the reprise of his song in *The Body Electric* by Dr. Thelma Moss (the body electric explored through Kirlian photography), and Dr. Robert O. Becker's landmark book, also titled *The Body Electric,* covering major discoveries about bio-electric fields. It seemed not only the body, but the "mind and memory electric" should be "sung."

In the early 60s Becker had the idea that consciousness itself was related to a direct electrical current. Testing out his ideas on animals, he observed that "every alteration in a state of consciousness might be associated with a shift in the amount of current. Depressing the flow of current, for example, would decrease excitability, and increasing direct current would cause arousal."

Some fifty years ago, prior to Becker's work, Dr. Harold Saxton Burr of Yale University, an internationally recognized neuroanatomist, made a dramatically important discovery. All living things, from men to mice, from trees to seeds, are molded and controlled by "electrodynamic fields" which can be measured and mapped with standard modern voltmeters. He considered these "L-fields" or "life-fields" to be the basic blueprints of life. He discovered that illnesses such as cancer could be detected long before the usual symptoms develop by monitoring L-fields. Wound healing, both internal and external, could be monitored by Burr voltmeters. And so could processes such as ovulation, simply by monitoring a woman's finger. Burr mapped a grid structure of these electrically significant points on the surface of living organisms and describes them in his book, *Fields of Life*.

Early researchers in the USSR, such as Dr. Alexander Gurvich and Semyon and Valentina Kirlian, had also monitored these electrodynamic fields. Burr came to the conclusion that this energy matrix shapes the living forms of matter. Studying frog's eggs, he found the area giving the highest voltage always came from the frog's nervous system. There was a distinctive pattern of energies that would later form the blob of protoplasm into each element of the physical body. Moving one part of the egg to a new location did not disrupt the final form. The energy fields seemed to control matter in this dimension. Burr also studied plants, finding the voltage not only varied with sunlight and darkness, but also with cycles of the moon and with magnetic storms and sunspots.

Burr's student, Dr. Leonard Ravitz, discovered that altered states of consciousness, from degrees of hypnosis to rage or serenity, could be detected with the Burr voltmeter. Even recalling an emotion such as grief showed a marked energy change. "Emotions can be equated with energy," says Ravitz, and so can memories of emotions. Researching hypnosis for years with the voltmeter, Ravitz asserts that the depth of a hypnotic trance can be defined electrometrically. The Soviets have long used such an instrumented approach to hypnosis.

Burr believed that just as our bodies and brains are maintained by permanent electromagnetic fields which mold the ever-changing material of the cells, so in turn these fields are influenced by the greater fields of the universe, "a new approach to the nature of man and his place in the universe."

The Soviets have researched these electrodynamic fields for decades. Researchers at the Institute of Clinical Physiology in Kiev found acupuncture points on the skin changed their electrical potential when solar flares occurred on the sun. Graphs of sunspot activity and changes in the electrical rhythms of the skin matched closely, though cosmic particles ejected by the sun take two days to reach earth (see p. 301).

Dr. Becker believed the bioelectric field was not only the key to changes in states of consciousness, but also to healing and regenerating tissues and organs. He searched for the source and structure of the bio-electric network pervading the body—a kind of data-transmission system. Like his colleagues in the USSR and China, he looked at acupuncture, which holds that chi flows through the body on meridians. The map of the body's pathways looks like a subway map with different stops and interchanges. Imbalances and clogs in these pathways can cause illness. Attempting to map the bioelectric system, he tested the electrical conductivity of the acupuncture meridians and points. After extensive studies he too concluded, "Electrical correlates have been established for a portion of the acupuncture system and indicate that it does have an objective basis in reality." Electrical stimulation of the entire body's electrical field appeared to have profound effects on mind, body, emotions, and behavior. Becker went on to a major breakthrough—using the electrical stimulation of the body's fields to actually regenerate organs.

Clarence Cone at the Cell and Molecular Biology Laboratory of the VA Hospital in Hampton, Virginia, confirmed that it was possible to stimulate neuron regeneration in the brain by means of "direct electromagnetic changes across the cell surface." NASA patented Cone's discovery and many other scientists have confirmed it.

Becker was soon swept into a maze of fascinating discoveries. Brain and body were affected dramatically by external stimuli such as sound, light, and electromagnetic fields. His latest compelling findings are revealed in *Cross Currents: The Perils of Electropollution—The Promise of Electromedicine.*

Overdrawn at the Memory Bank?

If you sometimes feel overdrawn at the memory bank, and your memory ATM is malfunctioning, the forgetfulness could be caused by the high tech systems all around you. If certain frequencies of electrical stimulation can release neurotransmitters and make you smart, could beaming other kinds of energy waves at you deplete your neurotransmitters and make you foggy and stupid? Unfortunately the answer is *yes*. And it's pouring in from studies from all over the world.

At the navy's Pensacola laboratory, scientists tested people's short term memory while a 1-gauss magnetic field was beamed at them. At the 60 hertz power frequency and 45 hertz frequency, memory declined on the tests. The Soviets tested ELF (extremely low frequency) magnetic or electric fields on animals and people. ELF waves produced hyperactivity and disturbed sleep patterns. Russian biophysicist R. A. Chizhenkov noted that your brain becomes desynchronized (abruptly shifts its main EEG rhythm) for a few seconds when any electric field is switched on or off. The brain's hypothalamus is a crucial link in the stress response. Any interference with it disrupts logical and associational thought. In 1973, Dr. Z. Gordon and Dr. M. Tolgskaya of the USSR Academy of Medical Sciences found that low doses of microwaves changed the nerve cells in the hypothalamus. The cells secreting neurotransmitters began to atrophy after five months. J. J. Noval's studies showed that the ELF electric fields affected brainstem acetylcholine, a substance extremely important for memory. Other Soviet work showed that two more neurotransmitters vitally important for memory, norepinephrine and dopamine, were reduced to brain levels that indicated exhaustion of the adrenal cortex and autonomic system, as a result of microwave radiation.

This was just the beginning. Dr. Becker and others discovered that a variety of artificial electromagnetic fields in the average big city could have disastrous effects on the human mind, memory, and body. Powerful transmissions from TV and radio towers, high-tension electrical wires that crisscross the country, radiation from household appliances like microwave ovens, TVs, computers—all create a kind of electronic smog that can affect memory, cause learning disabilities, depress the immune system, cause diseases such as cancer and a variety of mental and behavioral disorders such as depression. Becker found that magnetic fields averaged 22% higher at homes of suicide victims than at controls. Areas with the strongest fields contained 40% more fatal locations than randomly selected houses. Studies show exposure to high-level electromagnetic fields depletes the important mind/memory neurotransmitter norepinephrine, which can lead to depression.

Dr. Wendell Winters of the University of Texas in San Antonio reported in 1984 that cancer tumors grew 600 percent faster in one day of direct exposure to a 60 hertz field—the same frequency carried by our electric power lines. Few are aware of what a precise subliminal link we may have to our wiring. People in Europe and America were asked to sing a note, any note. In Europe most came forth with a G sharp, which related to the local power line frequency of 50 hertz. In America, the majority hit B natural, relating to our 60 hertz electricity.

In 1984, the World Health Organization in Geneva stated officially that "Exposure to ELF electric fields can alter cellular, physiological and behavioural events. . . . At present, studies serve as a warning that unnecessary exposure to electric fields should be avoided." Or, as *People* magazine headlined in November 1989, "Feeling Fatigued and Forgetful? The Power Line Next Door May be the Source of Your Burnout."

Electro-Smog/Memory Fog Shields

Scientists are developing shields to protect us from harmful electromagnetic smog and these shields may also help clear memory fog. The earth itself has its own magnetic field which oscillates at approximately eight cycles per second. Says Becker, we humans are oriented to living in this natural earth field and it acts as a biological clock for us. If the body is confronted with confusing electromagnetic fields *and* the natural earth field of eight cycles, it will tend to respond to its natural eight cycle earth field and reject the unhealthy ones.

Dr. Patrick Flanagan and other scientists have developed small devices that generate an eight cycle earth field. In independent tests by Dr. Sheldon Deal of the Swan Clinic in Tucson, Arizona, people were radiated with unhealthy, confusing electromagnetic pollution. The changes in their bodies' bioelectric energies were monitored with laser-acupuncture monitoring devices. Then, unknown to the subjects, the eight cycle earth resonance generators were turned on. Their bio-fields returned to normal.

Dr. Flanagan suggests keeping an eight cycle device three to five feet from you if you live in a city or near power lines or radio stations, or work with electrical appliances or computers. Jet lag can often include memory fog. A TWA stewardess used the earth resonance device on international flights and reported freedom from jet lag.

In Toronto, Danish-born inventor and electrical engineer Niels Primdahl developed "Relaxit," a similar eight cycle pulsed magnetic-field generator. It's the size of a cigarette pack and runs on one nine-volt battery. His files bulge with testimonials from people who once were nail-biting wrecks and are now calm and collected. In addition to protecting from electro-pollution, the device has helped people overcome insomnia, motion sickness, migraines, muscle cramps, and stress. Tests by physicist Dr. Michael Persinger of Laurentian University showed that the Relaxit induced a relaxed state. It functions at about an alpha level. The device is able "to harmonize your rhythms back to their relaxed state so you feel calm again," explains Primdahl. To counteract stressful situations and electro-pollution, he suggestions wearing the Relaxit on the solar plexus.

We have used Relaxits for years and recommend them. So could numerous racehorses! The device calms their nervousness. In the case of the Kentucky Derby hero Sunny's Halo, it also helped heal an injured ankle. When the first astronauts returned to earth with severe health disturbances, NASA discovered that these were due to their isolation from the pulsing magnetic field of the earth. Now NASA builds magnetic pulse generators into all manned spacecraft to maintain a health-giving and natural electromagnetic environment.

Dr. Andrei Puharich has also invented the Teslar, a tiny eight cycle earth resonance generator built into an attractive wristwatch so it's easy to wear anywhere. A magnetic chip inside the watch near the battery generates a 7.83 hertz signal that neutralizes the harmful ELF frequencies of electro-pollution and is claimed to strengthen the body. Testimonials by wearers describe less fatigue, less jet lag, and a general sense of well-being along with less irritability. For eighteen-year-old Wendy Fry of England, the Teslar Shielding Device, was a godsend. Wendy had ultrasensitive hearing. Traffic noise, loud radios, and TVs caused agonizing headaches. Dr. John Lester found that the Teslar watch created a small electrical field around Wendy which protected her from these electrical waves and interferences. She could still hear the sounds, but she had no more headaches. Dr. Glen Rein tested Teslars on all cultures while at Stanford University Medical Center, and reports positive results.

Dr. Eldon Byrd, a former navy scientist whose specialty was investigating bio-effects of ELF fields, tested the Teslar using a spectrum analysis of a subject's EEG recordings. His preliminary findings indicate "the shielding instrument appears to block signals that may be harmful to the body; produces a beneficial frequency, and promotes an amplified energy field in the subject wearer. The Teslar shielding instrument performs as advertised."

We have tested Teslar watches and found them helpful, especially while working at computers. (The watchstraps tend to wear out quickly.)

Because electro-pollution tends to desynchronize the brain, devices and cassette tapes that help resynchronize brain activity can be a major help in counteracting electro-smog. For instance, music such as Superlearning music, that entrains and synchronizes, can be a great help (See p. 144).

In addition, electro-pollution depletes essential neurotransmitters on which memory depends. Research shows exposure to electromagnetic fields also depletes vitamins, minerals, and enzymes, damages adrenals, affects sodium-potassium balance, hormone balance, and blood chemistry. Nutrients that replenish these losses can be helpful shields along with the protective instruments mentioned.

A simple test to check your environment for electro-pollution can be done with a battery operated AM radio. Tune the radio between stations, and turn the volume to maximum. Hold the radio a foot from a TV, computer, or microwave, and switch on the device. Check the noise. Move the radio away from the device till the noise disappears. The area with the noise is electro-polluted.

Mini-Guide to the High Tech of Consciousness and Memory

An avalanche of breakthroughs in the neurosciences has led to an avalanche of new devices to monitor, alter, enhance, or prod the human brain, mind, and memory. Since 1986 when Hutchison's *Megabrain* appeared, the number of devices has skyrocketed. Some soared up from garages and cellars worldwide, others appeared from high-profile researchers, still others from declassified scientific investigations.

Hutchison now has a national consumer newsletter, *Mega Brain Report—The Neurotechnology Newsletter,* a catalog and marketing organization and a nonprofit research center in San Francisco. There are dozens of mind-spas coast to coast, and hordes of ads promising to monitor, stimulate, pulse, or enfield you with theatrical modalities—rhythmic sound waves, stroboscopic lights, intense colors, electroluminescent ganzfelds, vestibular stimulation, sensory deprivation, sensory overload—or pulse you with electricity, or magnetism. . . . They promise rapid learning, improved memory, creativity, intelligence, well-being, extended powers and states of awareness. Intense competition has generated "sound and light wars," false claims, stolen technology, malfunctioning devices. To make your way through the claims, here's a miniguide.

The family trees of these devices may come from biofeedback, sound and light therapy, sensory deprivation (float tanks), or something totally different.

ALPHA-STIM.

Delivers a unique electrical signal said to lead to optimal brain functioning, to spur production of endorphins, boost creativity, concentration, and mental functioning. It also aids in pain control and healing. Widely used and recommended by coaches and athletes to cut rehabilitation time.

BINAURAL SIGNAL GENERATOR.

Based on Robert Monroe's discoveries (pp. 47 and 315). He found that pulses of sound called "binaural beat" frequencies are the most effective means of entraining brain waves and synchronizing right and left brain hemispheres. The BSG delivers pleasant tones and is favored for learning. It helps achieve relaxed body and alert mind.

I.S.I.S.

Designed by mind/body expert Jack Schwarz. Uses light delivered through goggles to entrain different brain-wave frequencies: beta (for questioning, thinking), alpha (body/regulation/pain control), theta (working with transpersonal, memory/learning enhancement), delta (body-mind harmony). The I.S.I.S. photodrives and synchronizes both hemispheres of the brain in the alpha frequency. It induces a pleasant state of relaxation and aids in learning mind-body regulation. A new model adds sound. Together with special training exercises developed by Schwarz, the I.S.I.S.can also enable users to extend visual perceptions to subtle energy fields (auras). We have worked with the I.S.I.S. and highly recommend it. Robert Anton Wilson travels with I.S.I.S. "I have found it remarkably efficient when I'm feeling stressed by too much public speaking. . . . The alpha-theta range always seems to take out the muscular kinks of tiredness as efficiently as any neo-Reichian body worker . . . and can be carried airport to airport."

ENDOMAX.

Portable and versatile. It functions via two electrodes attached at the mastoids. It provides sound tapes containing eight frequencies known to stimulate neuropeptides and claims to retrain the brain to operate more efficiently. Robert Anton Wilson recommends the jet-lag tape.

TENS (TRANSCUTANEOUS ELECTRICAL NERVE STIMULATOR) MACHINES.

Widely used in hospitals and clinics for chronic pain control. Electrical stimulation of the nerve fibers blocks pain for hours or days.

MINDGENIC.

Turns a computer into a mind-machine. This Japanese instrument allows self-regulation of brain-wave frequencies and displays them on your PC computer screen.

20. Memory Weapons: Secret Memory Discoveries

The phone rang in the executive office of a New York modeling agency. The director, a famous blond glamour girl, listened intently to her call. It was just a series of rhythmic, electronic bleeps. The strange sounds triggered her into instant action. She was soon aboard a plane bound for San Francisco. From there she sped to a doctor's office in Oakland. Several hours later, a dark-haired, aggressive woman emerged and got into a car. Her voice was deep, strident, and tough as she answered the doctor's questions while he drove her to the airport.

"Here's your passport," he said. The name on it was Arlene Grant. The photo matched her appearance. He handed her a large envelope which she tucked into her handbag. "You will take the plane to Taiwan tonight. A Chinese businessman will meet you at the airport. He'll watch over you while you're there."

When Arlene landed, a conservatively dressed Chinese man approached her. He politely escorted her to his car and whisked her to his beautiful but somewhat institutional home twenty miles outside Taipei on a wooded estate. Arlene spent several days at this deluxe estate. She went sightseeing, enjoyed gourmet meals, and felt fit and relaxed on her return flight to San Francisco. The doctor met her and once again drove her to his Oakland office. She handed him the "Arlene" passport, rolls of film, air ticket stubs, and the black wig. He gave her a "vitamin shot." The next day, she caught the flight to New York.

The staff of the modeling agency was relieved when their boss settled behind her desk. They'd wondered about her week long absence. She didn't tell them about the sights in Taiwan. She couldn't. She had absolutely no memory of her trip to the island; she thought she'd only been in San Francisco.

The glamorous blonde was the famous Candy Jones, America's leading model in the 40s and 50s, featured on countless magazine covers, and the star of a smash Broadway play, Mike Todd's *Mexican Hayride*. For nearly two years, she toured the Pacific war zone, star-

ring in *Cover Girls Abroad*. In the 60s, she headed the well-known
Conover Model Agency. As a part-time broadcaster for NBC, she
interviewed such notables as Teamster boss Jimmy Hoffa. Candy Jones
was on the celebrity circuit, often seen at galas and openings. She was
a frequent guest at columnist Dorothy Kilgallen's parties. In Washington, she socialized with the Nixons.

All the while, for twelve years, as Arlene Grant she also made
scores of trips to Taiwan and other Far Eastern countries delivering
intelligence information. She experienced total amnesia for these trips.
Though she had both beauty and brains, Candy Jones had no conscious clue that she was leading a wild double life, no faint recollection
of her adventures as a female James Bond, no idea she led a bizarre
Jekyll/Hyde existence. Her memory of her life as "Arlene Grant, spy"
had been completely annihilated. Far more stunning was the origin of
Arlene Grant.

Arlene was an artificially seeded multiple personality. The Arlene
alter ego had its own individual memory bank. Like most "original"
personalities, Jones had no access to her alter's memory. Arlene was
loud, tough, and sarcastic. She knew about Candy and called her a
"namby-pamby." She was physically strong and athletic. Arlene, but
not Candy, had received a special education in Virginia. She had gone
to spy school. She had been fully trained in guerrilla warfare, fire
setting, search tactics, and more. It was needed. On some of her secret
trips, Arlene ran into rough times and was tortured.

The Oakland doctor, who used the pseudonym Gil Jensen, was a
covert CIA operative. He used memory-altering drugs and hypnosis
on Candy Jones to elicit and train a multiple personality, Arlene
Grant. This Pygmalion of multiple personality believed he'd created
the ultimate in the intelligence field, the perfect super spy. He paraded
Candy before the CIA's top brass to show off his accomplishment.

"Hypnotism in Warfare: The Super Spy," from *Hypnotism* by world
authority Dr. George Estabrooks describes the "how to": first, induce
a multiple personality with its separate memory. Then give the multiple secret intelligence information. The regular personality is sent to
various places. She carries no secret documents. Only the special hypnotic signal can access the multiple personality who carries the secret
data. Even if tortured, personality A will not, cannot, access personality B's memory. Based on his own experiments, Estabrooks of Colgate
University claimed that the alter ego can withstand far greater torture
than is usual, with little ill effect. In addition, Estabrooks found the

alter could have an expanded memory. Volumes could be memorized and recalled by the seeded personality.

For twelve long years in the 50s and 60s, Candy Jones led her startling double life. Frequently, Candy attended celebrity functions, where she chatted with the famous from politics, military, theater, and media. Afterward, Arlene was summoned by the strange electronic sounds on the phone. Arlene then delivered information at a designated drop. Should Candy be intercepted, she wouldn't divulge anything as she didn't have the data. At the height of the cold war, Candy had been approached by old friends in the government who asked if she'd help out her country by simply receiving and dropping "special" mail. That's all the conscious Candy knew she was doing. Dr. Jensen was an old friend she'd met while touring the Pacific war zone with her show.

Over a decade later, as often happens with multiples, the Arlene personality grew stronger and began to seize control at inappropriate moments—even on her wedding night to new husband Long John Nebel. Nebel, a well-known New York broadcaster, would be out dining with Candy at a sponsor's restaurant, when Arlene would suddenly appear and reenact bizarre, violent scenes from her spy past. On occasion, during these recalls, even torture marks would reappear on her skin. Jensen hadn't created the perfect super spy after all. Nebel, stunned to discover his beautiful new wife was not only a multiple, but also a spy—and a tough, nasty one—called in hypnotherapists, psychiatrists, espionage experts. The unbelievable scenario of Arlene Grant gradually spilled out and began to be validated.

It was shades of *The Manchurian Candidate*, Richard Condon's story of an American sergeant captured in Korea and hypno-programmed to kill on seeing the queen of diamonds in a deck of cards. Not surprisingly, Candy Jones was shattered to discover she'd been sharing her body and mind. Worse, the program called for Arlene, when no longer useful, to commit suicide. With awareness and therapy Jones sidestepped the plan (she died of natural causes in 1989). Long before, in 1976, she turned to the mike and revealed her story on numerous radio shows. A full account appears in Donald Bain's compelling *The Control of Candy Jones*.

In 1963, Linda Macdonald checked in at McGill University's famous Allen Memorial Institute in Montreal. She'd borne five children, including twins, in four years, and felt exhausted. She suffered postpartum depression and low blood sugar. A grotesque therapy began without consent of any kind. Macdonald was given over 100 electroshock treatments and three months of heavy drugs, probably including LSD. Strange tapes played over and over in her room giving her odd instructions, a treatment called psychic driving.

Result? She no longer could recall her name. Her husband and children were strangers. She could not remember how to use a knife and fork. She could no longer read or write. Macdonald's whole memory, her entire life, had been totally erased.

In 1987, Linda Macdonald brought a massive suit against the Canadian government for the loss of twenty-five years of memory. She and at least fifty-three other patients, including the wife of David Orlikow, a member of the Canadian Parliament, had been unwitting guinea pigs in abhorrent memory modification experiments led by Dr. Ewan Cameron at the Allen Memorial Institute. Carried out in the late 50s and early 60s, these experiments were CIA ordered and funded through a "front," the Society for the Investigation of Human Ecology. Nine other Canadians sued the CIA for one million dollars each for the loss of their memories. All, chosen at random and told nothing about experimentation, had undergone similar treatment to wipe out memory and re-pattern personality. "Our lives were destroyed," they claimed. The CIA did not admit guilt—but paid nearly a million dollars in settlement.

Memory control and amnesia were big goals of the CIA, says John Marks, former CIA agent and coauthor of *The CIA and the Cult of Intelligence.* Under a project code named MK-ULTRA, the CIA conducted bizarre memory experiments on thousands of unknowing dupes across the country in 180 hospitals, research centers, and prisons. Spurred by the cold war, fearing the communists had the lead in the "mind wars," the CIA used LSD and other drugs, sensory deprivation, de-patterning, brainwashing, hypnosis, and hordes of other mind control methods. In 1976, the Senate investigated these horrendous practices and ended the program.

What memory weapons did this war-crime style research uncover? Two, according to journalist James L. Moore, who was given documents by ex-CIA men. One was Radio-Hypnotic Intra-Cerebral Control. The other, the Electronic Dissolution of Memory. Here was documentation that artifically seeded multiple personality was indeed a counterintelligence tactic. Moore reports the prospective spy/assassin is hypnotically conditioned and split into a multiple. This alter is controlled by the "sound of a specific tone," and "a person may be placed under this control . . . without his knowledge, programmed to perform certain actions . . ." whenever he hears the tone. "Effective for a lifetime," Moore reports, "control may be triggered weeks, months, or even years after the first hypnosis and programming." Specific frequency sounds, beamed by radio or telephone, activate certain parts of the brain, eliciting the multiple's memory.

The second memory weapon—Electronic Dissolution of Memory, which like most things governmental went by an acronym, EDOM—involves the brain chemical acetylcholine that carries electrical impulses from the senses to the brain. Memory requires the recording of these electrical impulses. Acetylcholine is the "wiring." "By electronically jamming the brain, acetylcholine creates static which blocks out sights and sound. You would then have no memory of what you saw or heard; your mind would be a blank." According to Moore, CIA documents report EDOM can either block access to memory completely or scramble memory so events are out of sequence.

Right from the beginning of the spy business, memory—its expansion, contraction, deletion—has been a major focus. Many spies have been ranking memory stars. The Israeli master spy, Elie Cohen, had a natural, photographic supermemory and in 1967 it was credited with being the key to Israeli success in the Six Day War. Spy Cohen had only a few short minutes to precisely memorize every detail of a massive installation containing most of the enemy's weapons. He did. Mega memory is a necessity when an agent prepares for a foreign mission. He must know the target language, memorize the new persona's family tree, background, culture, and profession, and all details of his assignment. Once there, he often needs almost photographic memory when he glances at a paper upside down on a companion's desk. A memory slip can mean death.

Soviet Multiple Personality Superspies?

Vladimir Raikov conjured rooms full of Rembrandts and Raphaels to unlock talent. The college students with artificially seeded personalities, like Candy Jones, had no memory of their time spent as Renaissance masters. Following Soviet writers, we called this Artificial Reincarnation (see Chapter 15). Raikov's technique resembles Dr. Estabrooks's protocol for seeding multiple personalities. With the techniques trickling into public use, it's very hard to believe other scientists weren't "incarnating" more devious talents—Soviet versions of Candy Jones, super spies, assassins—in ordinary people going about their ordinary business until "biological radio communication" triggered a mission. If the Soviets didn't have multiples, the British apparently did. Sir William Stephenson, the man called "Intrepid," told Jones that in British intelligence he used agents programmed just like she was. W. H. Bowart, author of *Operation Mind Control,* contacted some American Vietnam vets who appeared to have undergone multiple personality programming.

Author Donald Bain, along with many others, reports that Lee Harvey Oswald, accused assassin of President John F. Kennedy, spent time at a behavior modification institute in Minsk during his years in the Soviet Union. Which opens up a can of worms—conspiracy theories. We don't have any answers. Once you understand the mind manipulation pursued by all sides in the 60s, it's easier to understand how one might take a leap of imagination and end up with conspiracy. Imaginations were primed further when Sirhan Sirhan, Robert Kennedy's assassin, was linked to hypnotic programming. One curious death is worth mentioning. Right after the powerful journalist Dorothy Kilgallen interviewed Jack Ruby, after he'd killed Oswald, and claimed she had evidence to "blow the JFK case sky high," she was found dead. Accidental, ruled the coroner. But he forgot to rule what accident made her files go missing. Kilgallen was one of Candy Jones's well-connected, insider friends, a friend that alter ego Arlene probably reported on.

The Electro-Current of Consciousness

In Moscow we noted that the Soviets had gone high tech with hypnosis, seeing it as an energetic phenomenon influencing the body's many energies: bioelectric, biomagnetic, and bioplasmic energy, the chi energy of acupuncture. They devised detectors to monitor these signals to determine the depth and kind of trance. Controlling the body's energies by either hypnosis or electronic machines they could affect consciousness, memory, and behavior.

For thirty years, Soviet researchers have used an effective, undetectable aid to induce hypnosis, a pulsed ELF field instead of the flashing strobe used in the United States. In 1983, Dr. Ross Adey of the Loma Linda VA Hospital revealed a captured Soviet Lida machine and demonstrated its effect. Electronic Lida was used by interrogators on unknowing POWs to induce trance and capture information from their memories. Inducing trance greatly facilitated access to their memories, sped up memory recall, and elicited compliance.

Mapping the body's bioelectric fields, Soviets found that *waking consciousness itself is a function of direct currents that run from nega-*

tive to positive poles in the brain—a central front-to-back flow in the head. By passing a low-voltage current through the front of the brain to the back, you can cancel the normal current of waking consciousness and knock a person out. He will have no memory of what's happening. This electro-zap can also totally anesthetize a person. The speculative possibilities are enough to warm the cockles of the coldest covert heart.

The Soviets had discovered what Dr. Robert Becker of the Syracuse VA Hospital was only to confirm decades later. Chemical anesthesia, acupuncture anesthesia, and hypnotic anesthesia all work the same way. They reverse the polarities of the brain's "electro-current of consciousness."

Publicly, Soviets released their "electro-sleep machine," often dubbed the "sleep gun," to be used for surgical anesthesia, therapeutic relaxation, and sleep therapy. Obviously, undercover use of this consciousness zapper wasn't publicized, but it certainly would be a handy "gun."

In addition to the electro-zap, Soviets found that strong magnetic fields also can interrupt the brain's "consciousness current" and knock out people and animals. Becker made the same discovery. The EEG recordings for magnetic and chemical anesthesia were identical, he saw.

Soon Becker too was on the track of the electromagnetic nature of hypnosis. He too developed instruments to monitor hypnosis and suggestion. As the client sank into deep trance there was an electrical change. (Negative potential at the front of the head dropped to zero.) With hypnosis and suggestion he could change the body's direct current potentials. That caused pain to be upped or decreased. You can do the same with electric or magnetic fields. Hypnosis and EM fields work the same way. Self-suggestion for healing also functions this way, Becker says. It alters the body's electro-potentials. The reverse could also work—alter the fields and produce aberrant behavior and memory loss. One has to wonder how often fields were summoned in the effort to seed multiples, to blank and jumble memory.

One reason the electro-zap didn't sound strange to us is that we were familiar with *the* showcase experiment of Soviet psi. Led by a world famous physiologist, bolstered by mountains of published reports, repeated endlessly for fifty years, "telepathic hypnosis" was well established in the USSR decades ago. Usually this telepathic knockout happened room-to-room but sometimes it stretched over hundreds of miles. Experimenters tried to implant subliminal suggestion in subjects' memories and eventually these researchers also worked with supposedly classified EM fields.

Memory Weapons and Mind Control

U.S. Ambassador Walter Stoessel returned home from Moscow not feeling well. He had constant headaches, bleeding eyes, and poor concentration. Tests confirmed a rare blood disease, similar to leukemia. His two predecessors had also come home sick and subsequently died of cancer. The U.S. Embassy staff didn't feel well either. They suffered headaches and blurred vision. They couldn't concentrate or remember well. Doctors found white blood cell problems.

Stanley Gottlieb, the CIA's MK-ULTRA program director, testified before Congress that when Richard Nixon and his party were in the USSR in 1971, they exhibited aberrant behavior—including depression and crying. From the early 60s to the early 80s, Soviets bombarded our Moscow embassy with microwave radiation including frequencies known to affect mind, memory, and health. Bowart reports that the Soviet's own studies show microwaves can alter brain waves, cause hallucinations and drastic perceptual changes, including a loss of the sense of time.

In 1975, a powerful signal began pulsing at us all from seven colossal radio transmitters in the USSR. These became known as the woodpecker transmissions, pulsing ELF waves. The transmission, between 3.26 and 17.54 megahertz, is pulsed at several key brain-wave rhythms, especially 6 hertz and 11 hertz. These specific ELF waves can affect people negatively. Woodpecker was apparently set up to communicate with submarines or spy satellites, but many believe its major side effects may have been intentional.

Woodpecker periodically caused severe radio blackouts worldwide. Its ELF waves mingled with electromagnetic pollution in the earth's upper atmosphere and was suspected of bringing major weather disturbances. As the ELF waves traveled and fluctuated over certain parts of North America, particularly Eugene, Oregon, they sometimes caused mind, memory, and health problems. They affected concentration, decision-making ability, coordination. They caused mental confusion, irritation, and anxiety. People complained of pressure and pain in the head. They heard high-pitched ringing in their ears.

Raymond Damadian of Brooklyn's Downstate Medical Center, patenter of the nuclear magnetic resonance scanner, says the Soviet broadcasts are designed to induce nuclear magnetic resonance in human tissue. Such broadcasts may also magnify the invisible smog of electro-pollution already with us, increasing damage to mind, memory, and health. Like some malevolent subliminal, it seems fields we are unaware of cloud our memories and mental abilities and wear down our immune systems.

A simple test at the navy's Pensacola laboratory showed the mind's vulnerability to electromagnetic interference. People were asked to add sets of five two-digit numbers. A 1-gauss magnetic field was beamed at them, the same field strength found near high-voltage power lines and household electric heaters. Tests scores declined while people sat in the magnetic field. Scores returned to normal when the field was removed. Electromagnetic fields near radar installations (i.e. airports or military installations) are stronger and presumably have an even more deleterious affect on mental ability.

The Sun, Your Mind, and Memory

When solar flares erupt, vast magnetic storms rage, changing the earth's magnetic fields. These changes produce abnormal behavior in humans and animals. It seems to push some people over the edge. Becker charted the admission of 28,000 patients to eight psychiatric hospitals over four years. He matched the chart with the records of sixty-seven magnetic storms during the same period. Significantly more people needed hospitalization after magnetic storms. Becker believes the storms influence the electrical current of consciousness in the body.

Cosmobiology is the Soviet name for this science. By the 60s, researchers at the Institute of Clinical Physiology in Kiev discovered that when solar flares occur, the resulting magnetic storms affect mind, memory, and reaction time—and can even cause apoplexy. Reflexes slow and traffic accidents soar four times above normal.

Can the sun affect your memory? Can solar flares stimulate memories of old wrongs, grudges, enmities? When the sun rages, and magnetic fields surge on earth, does this stir raging memories of injustice and repression? Yes, says Dr. Alexander Chijevski, and his "yes" came from a vast canvas of research covering millennia. Revolutions, wars, political unrest, vast migrations, outbreaks of disease all appeared to correlate with the eleven-and-a-half-year sunspot cycle. Chijevski, the father of Soviet cosmobiology, said political upheaval is facilitated when the sun rages. The spectacular disturbances on the sun in 1917 coincided with the Russian Revolution. "If unjust conditions exist, they are aggravated by a torrent of radiations that help activate events," declared Chijevski. Becker's findings help confirm how these magnetic field shifts affect the electro-currents of consciousness.

Chijevski's investigations, published as *The Sun and Us,* and *In the Rhythm of the Sun,* revealing how the sun can affect your mind/ memory and thus alter political history, were rewarded with over twenty years in a Siberian prison camp. He did live till 1964 to see cosmobiology scientifically established. He would have predicted a whirl of tumultuous political events for 1989 through 1991. As sunspots soared to the highest activity in 150 years, citizens of Eastern Europe and various Soviet regions were flooded with remembrance of horrors past, injustice, and repression. Vast populations rose up in country after country to throw off oppression, and changed the face of history overnight. The whole of Eastern Europe was altered. The Soviet Union threatened to crumble with ethnic unrest. In Central America and Haiti, dictators were overthrown. Even quiet Canada responded to the powerful solar maximums. "I remember" is the slogan on the Quebec car license plate. And in 1990 remember they did— old injustices, wrongs, and wounds. Quebec threatened to split up Canada. In the Middle East, many Muslims recalled the religious command to unite as a nation and heeded the call to a holy war in the Persian Gulf.

Artificial Magnetic Storms and Your Memory

The KGB and military were fully aware of how electromagnetic storms affect human behavior and affect mind/memory and health. What would happen to your memory if *artificially* created electromagnetic storms were beamed at you? And what about ultra-ultra high-frequency electromagnetic waves—microwaves—that extend from 500 million cycles per second (500 megahertz) up to the frequency of visible light? Could they be memory scramblers and destabilizers? Could they be invisible amnesia producers—the preferred memory weapon of covert operators? Could terrorists beam these waves at selected ethnic groups to produce memory changes, confusion, irritation, hallucinations, perception changes, sickness, depression, criminal behavior, loss of time sense?

In 1984, Warsaw's Radiobiology center found that microwaves beamed at people caused memory loss, brain damage, and health problems. In America, Duke University reported that beaming 10,000 microwatt microwaves slowed the brain's electrons and lowered its energy. Similarly, Dr. Ross Adey recorded chemical changes in the brain caused by microwaves that affected total brain function. Microwaves are linked to the ultimate memory loss—Alzheimer's disease. Monkeys chronically exposed to microwaves developed brain symptoms characteristic of Alzheimer's, according to Dr. Sam Koslov of Johns Hopkins University. Other animals subjected to low-dose microwave radiation showed a big drop in neurotransmitters essential for memory. Rats in the care of Dr. Richard Lovely at the University of Washington spent seven hours a day for three months being irradiated by microwaves and turned into slow learners. Dr. Allen Frey found that pulsed microwave beams increase the permeability of the blood-brain barrier, allowing drugs, bacteria, and poison through. All of these recent microwave findings help explain why the KGB was busily beaming microwaves at the United States Embassy in Moscow. They'd discovered it all decades before.

Frey also found a much more intriguing kind of permeability. If you pulse microwaves of 330 to 3,000 megahertz at a specific rate, people can hear them. They come over as buzzing, hissing, clicking. They are sensed, even by the deaf, in the temporal region of the brain near the ears. If you take a word's sound vibrations and create a pulsed microwave audiogram, then words, codes, or instructions could be beamed directly into someone's brain at a distance. Dr. J.C. Sharp of the Walter Reed Army Institute of Research became a test subject himself. He heard and understood words delivered by microwave. Spies like James Bond could have driven a target crazy with "voices" or delivered secrets or instructions to agents by beam-to-brain.

At Loma Linda VA Hospital, Ross Adey showed that modulated microwaves can enforce specific electrical patterns on parts of the brain, and by sculpting these waves you could even evoke conditioned responses in people and animals. Dr. Jose Delgado, director for fifteen years of Centro Ramon y Cajal, the foremost Spanish neurophysiological laboratory, studied the impact of specific frequencies of magnetic fields on the behavior and emotions of monkeys, without using any implanted electrodes or radio receivers. Using very low strength ELF magnetic fields, Delgado could make the monkeys fall asleep on command, or induce bizarre, manic behavior. *Omni* editor Kathleen McAuliffe, who saw some of these secret experiments, reports that the monkeys resembled battery operated electronic toys, endlessly repeating the same action.

Recent declassified experiments reveal that the Soviets tried to induce hypnotic trances in people through microwaves alone. They had microwave "programmers" like computer programmers. People were unaware they were being irradiated or entranced. They tried "information beams" to blank out and falsify subjects' memories.

Certain toxins generated by bacteria and viruses can greatly damage mind/memory. Bacteria and viruses multiply faster and grow stronger in specific magnetic fields. As Soviet cosmobiologist Chijevski had shown, the naturally occurring cycles of high sunspot activity coincide with outbreaks of disease among plants, animals, and humans. Cholera, diphtheria, and typhoid grew more virulent as the sun stormed. The great influenza pandemic of 1918 occurred during high solar activity. Bacteria and viruses reproduced intensely during high solar activity and electromagnetic storms. Famous British astronomer Sir Fred Hoyle confirmed that viral pandemics and solar maximums have coincided for hundreds of years. The concept was a natural for yet another memory weapon. Soviet Yuri Udintsev discovered that a magnetic field of 200 gauss 50 hertz could make bacteria one fifth stronger. In a memory weapon system, magnetic fields might be used to potentize viruses and bacteria destined for germ warfare, or victims might be beamed with fields to make them more vulnerable to viruses, or both. Conversely, a defense system would involve fields that make you less vulnerable.

In 1968, Moscow scientists told us that their vast research in electromagnetic fields had pinpointed which frequencies are beneficial, which damaging. Certain pulsed magnetic fields speed healing, others greatly heighten human perception—ESP, telepathy, and clairvoyance, they claimed. Psychic spying was taken seriously in Moscow at the time. It was the major reason their government funded psi research. By beaming confusion and anxiety waves at certain key individuals, Soviets believed it could give them great advantages over their competitors in a vast range of areas from commodity trading to sports to political deals. Champions of the cerebral cutthroat sport of chess were said to be targets for secret radiation beams. Defector Boris Spassky claimed he'd lost the world chess championship to Bobby Fischer because he was being bombarded with confusion rays that affected mind and memory. Gary Kasparov and Anatoly Karpov have both complained repeatedly about subtle energies being directed at them to disrupt concentration and memory.

American researchers Dr. Andrei Puharich and Dr. Bob Beck were later to confirm that there are exact electromagnetic field frequencies that can cause depression or riotous behavior as well as positive frequencies that can relieve stress, aid concentration, and make you feel good.

Like the startling high tech missiles and "smart bombs" used in the Middle East War, the military has simultaneously been working on equally sophisticated high tech Memory weapons.

After his years of electromagnetic research, Becker warns, "The ultimate weapon is manipulation of our electromagnetic environment. We're dealing here with the most important scientific discovery ever— the nature of life." His recent book *Cross Currents* reveals some of the Western electromagnetic defense weapons developed by the military. These range from the EMP (Electromagnetic Pulse) to the GWEN (Ground-Wave Emergency Network). There's also the High-Power Pulse Microwave system. All electromagnetic field mind/memory weapons are silent and imperceptible. A 1982 air force review of bio-technology states that the systems would be used for dealing with terrorist groups, crowd control, security control, and antipersonnel techniques in tactical warfare. They would be used to produce mild to severe physiological disruption, perceptual distortion, or disorientation.

What can we do about these disturbing new mind/memory weapons? Says Becker, "An informed public is the only defense."

PART FOUR

21. The Near-Death Experience—A Window on Memory?

With a certain degree of wry amusement, Dr. "Smith," a pediatric surgeon, watched some of his medical colleagues stampede out of the operating room—probably going to check their malpractice insurance, he thought. Then he turned back to his patient on the operating table and saw that the little girl was beginning to come out of the anesthesia. Then he noticed his own body. He lay crumpled on the floor beside the operating table, scalpel in hand. Dr. Smith was clinically dead. Just as he had bent over the patient to make the first incision, he had suffered a massive heart attack. The rest of his colleagues were trying to resuscitate him.

Now they were carrying his body to the emergency room. He began to realize he was out-of-body and floating up near the ceiling. Peering over his colleague's shoulder, he read his blood pressure—40 over 20. Then he lost interest in the resuscitation team. His total focus was directed toward a tunnel. Soon he was spiraling through the tunnel at great speed, traveling toward a brilliant, welcoming light in the distance. He wanted desperately to reach that beneficent light. Suddenly he was back in his body. And back in this dimension again.

"My life's never been the same," he says of his near-death experience. "Nothing in this world seems important anymore in comparison to what I experienced." It was important enough for this surgeon to give a public report, anonymously but in person at the 1989 International Association for Near-Death Studies Conference in Philadelphia.

In the last two decades, resuscitation advances have sparked something genuinely new under the sun, an experience having transformative, life-changing effects on more than eight million Americans. Suspended between life and death for a few minutes, they return with bright memories of remarkable and remarkably similar experiences. Just as 20th century astronauts look out on the sparkle of the universe from an entirely new perspective, so do the near-death experiencers enjoy a new, enlarged perspective on the dimensions of life and most particularly on the scope of memory. The following accounts collected by Raymond Moody, M.D., and psychologist Dr. Kenneth Ring, two of the field's leading researchers, are typical of both the near-death experience (NDE) and of the unfolding understanding of memory it brings.

Tom Sawyer of Rochester, New York, was under a truck, doing repairs, when the supports gave way and he was crushed. He was seemingly dead as a team of paramedics tried to resuscitate him. Suddenly Sawyer found himself out-of-body, shooting through a tunnel to emerge in "this most magnificent, just gorgeous, beautiful, bright, white or blue-white light. . . ." It was an extraordinary brilliance, he added, that didn't hurt the eyes. "The next sensation is this wonderful, wonderful feeling of this light. . . . It's almost like a person. It is *not* a person, but it is a being of some kind. It is a mass of energy. . . . Then the light immediately communicates to you . . . it is a feeling of true, pure love. . . . The second most magnificent experience . . . is you realize that you are suddenly in communication with absolute, total knowledge."

When Sawyer merged with this light being, it seemed as if an enormous amount of knowledge was imparted to him. The experience transformed his life. He returned from the clinically dead with a ravenous desire to study—science, ancient history, parapsychology, cosmology. A lifetime laborer who'd never finished a book, Sawyer shocked his family by enrolling in college to study physics and mathematics. He began asking people about Max Planck's quantum theory, saying he felt a great urge to read about the theory. When he finally got to Planck's concepts, Sawyer immediately related them to the understanding he had so mysteriously picked up during his NDE. After his NDE interdimensional trip, Sawyer also began to feel latent psi abilities kick in.

Across the continent in California, Janis was nearly killed in a car accident. After swirling through a tunnel, she encountered a light, a brilliant, golden, powerful, bright light. A sense of peace, homecoming, warmth, love, and acceptance from this luminous being engulfed her. The luminous entity asked telepathically, "Are you ready to stay?" Before making her decision, Janis experienced panoramic memory. "This review of my life passed by—pssst—just like that. . . . I saw my whole life pass right by me. All chronological. All precise. I was a spectator." It was like an accelerated video replay. "And after my whole life went by—in black and white—zoom . . . and it got into color."

Hank was almost killed in a car accident in Virginia in 1975. He suddenly found himself in a large room with intensely luminous entities so brilliant they engulfed the room with light, warmth, and love. When asked whether he'd stay, panoramic memory was ignited in Hank too. "It was like I knew everything that was stored by my brain. Everything I'd ever known from the beginning of my life . . . I had a total complete clear knowledge of everything that had ever happened in my life—even little minute things . . . just everything, which gave me a better understanding of everything at that moment." The entities also perceived his total life record. Hank felt he now knew the purpose of life in the earth dimension—to realize, learn, and love. "And to realize that every single thing that you do in your life is recorded and that even though you pass it by not thinking at the time, it always comes up later."

Jayne Smith of Philadelphia almost died in childbirth in 1952. She felt she was standing in a mist and knew that she had died but was alive. A light came into the mist and got brighter and brighter. The light seemed to cradle her; the feeling became more and more ecstatically joyful. "If you took 1000 best things that ever happened in your life and multiplied by a million, maybe you could get close to this feeling." She telepathically reviewed everything in her life. Then she asked the luminous entity, "How does the whole thing work?" She was told the secrets of life and death and the universe and of events to come which made perfect sense, she says, at the moment. "I knew it was something I had always known and managed to forget."

Darryl was electrocuted in 1971 when lightning struck his house. For nine minutes he was without pulse or respiration. Life suspended, he says he encountered a radiant being of light filled with an "awesome and pure love" and then his life passed before him. "What occurred was every emotion I have ever felt in my life, I felt." He was shown how those emotions affected his own and others' lives. "I had done a terrible job," he admits. Years later, he was still trying to work out relationships from his new perspective.

Adult NDEers may see this total record of their lives from birth to death or in reverse. Some see the memory record in segments. Instead of dispassionately viewing the memories, some may relive them. "Everything in my life was recorded," they constantly report. Still others saw a replay of a global memory—the records of the earth from its very beginnings.

Children are unlikely to have read psychological literature or to have heard about people in extremis shooting out of the body. Yet, on the edge of death, even small children report that they too leave the physical body, travel through a tunnel, encounter a being of light, meet deceased friends or relatives, choose to return and reenter the body. Dr. Glenn Gabbard of the Menninger Foundation reports the case of a two-year-old boy who bit an electrical cord. Medical records show he had no heartbeat or respiration for twenty-five minutes. The boy pulled through, and later told his mother, "I went into a room. . . . It had a very bright light. . . . There was a very nice man who asked me if I wanted to stay there or come back to you. . . . I wanted to be with you and come home." One significant element is missing in children's experience—panoramic memory, which makes sense. They haven't lived long enough to flesh out much of a record.

Eastern Illinois University researcher Dr. Barbara Walker reports the case of a seven-year-old boy who fell from a stone bridge and hit his head on a rock in the water. He was underwater ten minutes before being rescued. He remained in a coma four days. When he came to, he said he'd been hovering over the bridge, watching rescuers diving to search for him. He spoke of events on the bridge that he couldn't have seen while underwater. He entered a dark tunnel with white clouds in it, he said, and he saw a light. His dog, Andy, who'd died when he was three, rushed down the tunnel and licked his hands and face in a joyful greeting. The family cat, Abby, who'd been run over, greeted him too, the child reported. The next thing he knew, he was in the hospital.

Though it sounds as soupy as a Hollywood formula movie, being greeted by dead relatives, friends, and pets during an NDE is considered by researchers to be part of the universal prototype of the near-death scenario. Recently it's been discovered that even infants who brush death can have a near-death experience with the same basic pattern as adults. The baby NDEers apparently can remember it clearly and describe the event when they are old enough to talk.

A Kaleidoscope of Memory

After panoramic memory, some NDEers travel on to another striking and again remarkably similar experience. They arrive at a "city of light." Electrocution victim Darryl found himself standing beside a soaring cathedral made of light. The building blocks "appeared to be made of Plexiglas. They were square, they had dimension." They were transparent, and in the center of each was gold and silver light. This radiant cathedral "was literally built of knowledge. This was a place of learning . . . I began to be bombarded with data . . . literally all information . . . was coming at me from every direction." It was like a stream with every drop of water a piece of information. The information flowed past him as if his head were in the stream.

Darryl is far from the only person to arrive at this "city." Stella, a North Carolinian, "died" of massive hemorrhaging after surgery in June 1977. Seeming to travel on a laser beam of light, she came to an immense floating city of light. The buildings were of crystalline blocks with a golden radiance. "There was knowledge that was beyond anything that I could possibly try to describe to you . . . and I could hear languages . . . languages that I had never heard before and I could understand them. . . . There was so much more there. . . ." She wanted desperately to stay and experience it.

After twenty years of researching NDEs, Raymond Moody, psychiatrist and author of the landmark books, *Life After Life, Reflections on Life After Life,* and *The Light Beyond,* sums up the basic NDE sequence of events: 1. A sense of being dead. 2. Out-of-body experience, 3. The tunnel experience. 4. Encounter with a brilliant light. 5. Meeting powerful, loving "Beings of light" and luminescent dead friends, relatives, and pets. 6. "The life review" or panoramic memory. 7. Reluctance to return. 8. A sense of entering a different time and space and knowledge base. 9. Transformation and loss of fear of death.

This basic NDE pattern has been reported by hundreds of thousands of people in dozens of countries, by people of all ages, in all walks of life and belief systems. A 1982 Gallup Poll showed that 8 million Americans had experienced an NDE. More recently, George Gallup, Jr., put the figure at over 23 million. Better resuscitation methods worldwide are turning millions more into NDEers. Latest estimates figure 40% of resuscitated patients will have an NDE. Dr. Elisabeth Kübler-Ross was the first M.D. to publicly discuss "near-death" and document the phenomenon in her books. The pioneering research of Kübler-Ross, Moody, and Ring has now been followed by years of investigations by scores of professionals. The International Association for Near-Death Studies (IANDS) has been established, publishes a journal, and holds an annual, well-attended conference. The worldwide chorus of NDE reports has been documented in a profusion of books, scientific papers, articles, TV shows. All the arguments labeling the NDE as hallucination, wish-fulfillment, dreams, chemical patterning, brain damage, insanity, lies—even satanic interference or a messianic complex—have been thoroughly examined. Now researchers are focusing on the significance of the experience. How does it affect people at the time or years later? What can it tell us about our memories?

In *Heading Toward Omega: In Search of the Meaning of the Near-Death Experience,* Dr. Kenneth Ring says that individuals who have the "core transcendental experience" undergo deep value changes. Self-esteem increases. So does love, compassion, and a heightened spiritual awareness. There's a tendency to pay less attention to materialistic pursuits, and to devote more attention to alleviating human suffering. "The NDE is essentially a spiritual experience that serves as a catalyst for awakening and development," Ring maintains. "Afterward, people tend to manifest a variety of psychic abilities that are an inherent part of their transformation." As well as total recall of their past life, many have visions of the future during their NDEs. Interestingly, these too tend to be similar; they foresee global upheaval, war, and then an era of cultural renewal and worldwide cooperation.

The near-death experience has vibrant personal significance to those who have gone down that tunnel of light and directly experienced a transcendental, supersensible realm that almost all agree enlarged their view of life and appreciation of memory. Does the phenomenon have broader significance, are these growing millions yeasting our society? Have they become, as some think, a powerful evolutionary force pressing to break old, stultifying beliefs and open new perspectives on the multidimensional nature of life? Is the cosmic perspective brought back by NDEers necessary, as others think, to help prepare us for radical cultural and physical changes? Dr. Ring believes the thousands of newly awakened people are a "species avant-garde." As they become more loving and compassionate, they become "prototypes of a new humanity, fit custodians of our future."

Phyllis Atwater of Boise, Idaho, underwent three near-death experiences in 1977. Driven to understand the gnawing memory of her experiences, she interviewed hundreds of other NDEers. Her pioneering classic, *Coming Back to Life,* has a unique perspective. Death is a step-up of energy frequencies for the NDEer, she believes. They've been exposed to strong doses of high energies—"The Force." Virtually all report this sense of acceleration of frequency as they spiral through the dark tunnel to the light. Aftereffects should be looked at in energy terms, she feels. They may include: a shifted view of the body and physical reality (the body is worn like a jacket); a sense of timelessness (new memory functions—remembering the future); disorientation in time and space; expanded perceptions (Atwater saw inside body cells and heard people's thoughts; others perceived a weblike substance connecting everything, both living and nonliving, in a glistening network); increased psychic abilities (high-power energy fields, able to heal); spiritual transformation; difficulties with communication and relationships. It may take years to integrate the aftereffects, but as more millions resonate to this different paradigm of what humans are, a global revolution is coming, says Atwater.

She also reveals another constant aftereffect for NDEers. "Almost every single person returns knowing time does not exist. They come back knowing time is a matter of consciousness; past and future are really qualities of perception." NDEers experience timelessness. As a result, many have another strange *aftereffect.* They "remember" the future. Atwater came to regard "future memory" as a process in which time and space merge. These prehappenings were far stronger than déjà vu. They ran from snatches to long scenarios of future events. For instance, many "remembered" seeing American troops and tanks arrayed in the Middle East. Others "remembered" weather changes and earth upheavals.

Memory and Mind—Outside the Body?

The NDE reveals new things about memory and says them loud and clear. The most obvious is that NDEers *remember* their experience even though the body is shut down. This is no puny, hazy, weakling recollection. It is a coherent, lucid, detailed, consistent, superpotent memory. It is a memory that becomes a demarcation line in the lives of some NDEers, as if their identity had been split into two different people—"before" and "after" *the* memory. It is a memory so forceful it demands telling, despite ridicule and disbelief. Persistent recounting of *the* memory even landed some NDEers in mental wards. "I could not forget it," they report. "It haunted me." "It came back—replaying over and over." Recounting their transformative memory and its message, some feel, would help revolutionize society.

During the out-of-body sequence of the NDE, people report they feel like a mobile center of consciousness. Says Atwater about the moment of dying, "The biggest surprise of all is to realize you are still you. You can still think, you can still remember. . . ." NDEers encode memory not just of the kindly light at the end of the tunnel. More evidentially, they remember factual details and events going on back home in this world, both near and far from the body they've left behind. Dr. Smith returned with accurate, detailed memories of what was happening in the operating room, including his own fading blood pressure as he lay unconscious and dying. Dr. Walker found that the drowning seven-year-old had a bird's-eye view of the desperate rescue activities on the bridge above him as his body lay underwater. There are countless, meticulously documented cases of the newly revived startling doctors and rescuers with clear accounts of what people were doing and saying during the emergency, including activities that couldn't be seen from the perspective of the dying body. Memory, it seems, can go about its business quite well without the workhorse brain. Actually, some NDEers report, it seems to resonate more powerfully on its own. Moody reports on a seventy-year-old blind woman who had an NDE during her heart attack and resuscitation. Afterward, she described everything as if with full sight, including the doctor's blue suit. Similarly, cardiologist Dr. Michael Sabom cites the case of a soldier with severe injuries from a boobytrap explosion that perforated his eardrums and burned his eyes. He was unable to see for weeks. Nevertheless, after his NDE, he described what he'd seen in detail while hovering over the battlefield and over the operating table. Later, he identified the surgeon's voice, having heard it during surgery.

NDEers not only remember on-the-spot events, but most also undergo the almost universal experience of panoramic memory, an extraordinary kaleidoscopic rush of memories of one's entire life, a full-color, 3-D profusion of engulfing memories—though brain and body are closed down. This is photographic memory and more, total recall of a kind that even memory superstar Veniamin, the man who remembered everything, couldn't equal. It sounds like the ultimate audit and brings new depth to the meaning of memory. Is this where the idea of Judgment Day comes from? If so, something got twisted in translation, according to millions of NDEers. Your memory doesn't turn state's evidence before a hanging judge; instead memory seems to open for one's own judgment and reflection.

"All of my body is in my mind, but not all of my mind is in my body." It's a statement mindbody expert Jack Schwarz likes to repeat often. Schwarz explains that the body is like an egg yolk, floating in the cosmic egg white that contains our individual minds. The mind operates as much outside as inside the body, he explains. Body/brain is like a computer; mind/memory like the software.

"The mind can function without the help of the nervous system." That's the basic precept of Hindu yoga psychology, says yogi author Swami Akhilananda. Mind controls the brain, the physical instrument through which it expresses. Electricity travels through wires, but electricity and wires are not identical. "Similarly, the mind in its functionings, conscious or otherwise, cannot be identified with the instruments through which it works or has expression."

Swami Rama, founder of the Himalayan Institute, has confounded doctors, particularly at the Menninger Foundation, by demonstrating how mind can control and reorder the matter and systems of the body. He too maintains that consciousness and the nervous system are fully separable entities, and with his colleague, Rudolph Ballentine, M. D., explains in *Yoga and Psychotherapy* that this separation is the basis of Eastern psychotherapy.

Western thinkers have also seen brain and mind/memory as separate entities. French philosopher Henri Bergson summed it up brilliantly in *Matter and Memory:* ". . . any attempt to derive pure memory from an operation of the brain should reveal . . . a radical illusion. . . . Itself an image, the body cannot store up images, since it forms a part of the images; and this is why it is a chimerical enterprise to seek to localize past or even present perception in the brain; they are not in it; it is the brain that is in them."

An ongoing breakthrough has made it possible for anyone to try to see for himself whether mind and memory can cavort outside the body during this life. Several years ago, engineer and broadcast executive Robert Monroe, while sleeping, suddenly realized he was floating above his body. He was up near the ceiling, in a state of panic. Soon he discovered he could go out-of-body at will, and took off on high adventures described in *Journeys Out of the Body* and *Far Journeys.* Getting small help from scientists he petitioned, yet driven to understand the phenomenon, he founded the Monroe Institute of Applied Sciences in Virginia. There, Monroe and researchers discovered that using Hemi-Sync, a system of specific sound patterns on audio tapes, it was possible to train others to have an out-of-body experience. Graduates include many prominent professionals, like Dr. Kübler-Ross. By now, as mentioned in Chapter 11, Hemi-Sync has been developed to help people attain a "best state" for going about the business of this world. Still, at the heart of Monroe's investigations and the Institute workshops is the effort to help "voyagers" develop the capability to explore nonphysical realities, to "unhook from local traffic and travel the interstate," says Monroe.

In words that echo the NDE, Monroe describes how the conscious self with fully functioning mind and memory lifts out of the resting physical form and with another "body" of its own, travels by the power of thought to places far and near. At first most people perceive nothing but a "dimensional blackness." Then they learn to see, eventually moving into a brightly lighted area, the natural home, Monroe says, of the second body. As people grow comfortable in these altered states, they can travel in space without boundary, they can travel in time, observe themselves as youngsters, or travel into the future. Like the NDEers, out-of-body explorers change their relationship to time— and to death, says Monroe. They too return believing physical death is a natural transition. An old burden falls, they claim, letting them live life to the max for they no longer fear losing it. Similarly, NDEers lose all fear of death. According to Moody, everyone who goes through this experience becomes aware that life, love, and knowledge continue on in another dimension.

During the kaleidoscopic memory review, the "being of light" helps the individual see every single act and its rippling effects, both immediate and long term. The review puts events and consequences of one's life into a larger perspective, like seeing one's life from an observation deck. As in Thornton Wilder's play *Our Town,* where the dead heroine participates in the replay of key events in her life, and the town's life too, the past is viewed through different, sometimes more compassionate eyes.

Phyllis Atwater reports she *relived* her life review—every thought, every word, every deed—plus their effects on everyone and anyone within her sphere of influence, even unknown passersby, plus the effect of each thought, word, and deed on weather, plants, animals, soil, trees, water, air. "It was a reliving of the total gestalt of me as Phyllis." No detail was left out, it seemed to her. No slip of the tongue, mistake, or accident went unaccounted. She was stunned and overwhelmed. Everything recorded, remembered, accounted! Every thought, word, and deed seemed to go out and have a life of its own. "It's as if we must live in some kind of vast sea or soup of each other's energy residue and thought waves, and we are each held responsible for our contributions and the quality of 'ingredients' we add. It wasn't St. Peter—it was me judging me."

Some NDEers were told by the being of light that learning doesn't stop when you die. Everything in your memory you can take with you, they were told. One woman told Dr. Moody that the place she found herself in was a big university where they passionately pursued knowledge. She saw people in intense discussions about that realm around them. One man discovered that if he merely thought of something he wanted to learn about, it instantly appeared as though information were available in "bundles of thought."

Many NDEers bring back a compelling urge to learn as though the experience triggered a need to catch hold of that sense of understanding that came with the light, to grasp again, "What I've always known but managed to forget." They seem to glimpse the connectedness and wholeness of the universe. It's given many an intense appetite to understand physics and metaphysics.

George Lucas, creator of *Star Wars,* is the survivor of a brush with death. Although not conscious of the near-death experience at the time, he displayed the memory imprint and classic aftereffects of one, says Atwater. As a youngster, his family considered him a punk. He was a nonachiever, nonathletic and nonstudious. He cruised around and hung out. While in high school he was in a spectacular car crash. He teetered between life and death for three days, and was hospitalized for two more weeks. He returned home dramatically changed. It was almost as if he had become another person, according to his family. He became very philosophical. He believed he was saved for some special mission he had yet to fulfill. It seemed as if he were imbued with a mysterious "force," according to his father. He threw himself into learning. He was intensely goal-oriented. He enrolled in college and later the University of Southern California's Film School. "May *The Force* be with you" and a new view of spirituality became the focus of his films.

To celebrities like Elizabeth Taylor, an NDE brought a deep source of spiritual strength. Taylor, who almost died of pneumonia in London in 1961, finally talked about it in 1990. "I had a near-death, out-of-body experience, but nobody talked about that thirty years ago, because you felt crazier than a bedbug if you did." Taylor saw the tunnel and the light and a deceased person who made her go back. "It's extraordinary. So vivid."

Multidimensional Memory and an Energy Body

Monroe's voyagers remember what happens to them as they supposedly go tooting about an interdimensional universe. Their testimony and that of millions of NDEers is that memory is multidimensional; it can detach from the body. Besides the brain and physical stuff of the body, something else about us must be imbued with memory. It seems we are multidimensional creatures, that life and memory have more dimensions than current philosophies allow for. If a full-bodied memory can live happily beyond solid physicality, what carries it? What lifts out as that mobile center of consciousness? The soul or spirit are traditional Western terms for that something. In more precise Eastern terms, Dr. Shafica Karagulla, the neurosurgeon who used clairvoyants as her instruments, would have said memory lives in the subtle bodies.

Some NDEers echo an ancient description of the vehicle that carries them beyond the body. Many say they feel as if they are inside a finer body, an elliptical field, or cloud of colored light. One man told Moody he studied his hands in this state. He saw they were composed of light with tiny structures in them. He could see whorls of finger-prints and tubes of light up his arms. Moody resuscitated a woman after cardiac arrest who reported she'd been in a diaphanous body. She hadn't wanted to return, she said, and when Moody began to insert a needle in her body, she'd grabbed out to stop him, but her hand went right through his arm. Many NDEers report the frustration of reaching out to relatives only to pass right through them. One woman saw herself encased in a blue bubble. Some traveled in a duplicate energy body during the NDE and were physically seen and recognized when they "visited" friends or relatives. Some felt they were in an energy field of light sparkles. Almost all noted that this mobile energy center was larger than their physical body and when being revived felt the need to shrink or squeeze down to fit back into the body.

Memory—Where and What Is It?

European esoteric theory holds that each of us has a subtle body called the etheric body which underlies and interpenetrates every atom, molecule, and cell of the physical body, and is directly related to the nervous system which it controls and activates. Supposedly, memory makes its home in this body. It's a common idea; from Europe to Africa to Asia, ancient teachings speak of a luminous body, often described as a cobwebby field of light strands like a network of millions of bright fiber optics. Various subtle energies circulate through this body, and all one's experiences, thoughts, and emotions are registered in its substance. The subconscious taps into this network to recall memories in this life, and it is this body of memory that accompanies one to the next life.

But exactly *how* does memory work? What is the precise mechanism of coding and accessing memory imprints? Recovering this secret might help us all recover from a kind of mass memory loss. Out of all the esoteric data, the ancient root wisdom tradition of the Pacific, preserved in isolation for centuries in the Hawaiian Huna system, reveals one of the clearest, most specific, least garbled, precise accounts of subtle energies and a possible esoteric paradigm for the workings of our memories. According to Huna, there is a universal memory field made of a substance called *aka,* which interpenetrates the entire universe as well as every atom and cell of all living things. All living things have an *aka* body made of this universal substance. Kahunas, practitioners of Huna, describe it as a glowing body made of a fine network of light strands.

In Huna, this aka body records memories, stores them, and also transmits energy. Exactly how do memories get stored? Huna explains that there's a powerful subtle energy which circulates through the aka body, called *mana* (equated with chi). Mana, which they specify can be of three kinds, carries thoughts, emotions, actions, and images as pulse patterns, and imprints them in the aka recording substance as memories. To recall them, mana must access aka. The amount of mana energy a thought or emotion receives determines how readily it can be recalled. Traumatic events are recorded with a lot of mana and thus may keep replaying. Mana like chi can be boosted and balanced by oxygen, food, sound, light, magnetism, etc. Thought forms, images, emotions are imprinted on aka in bundles or clusters of energy, says Huna. Many NDEers report having seen information in "bundles." Atwater observed her thoughts floating out like pastel bubbles during her NDE, and focused them into shapes and forms.

The aka body, a glowing web of light with mana circulating through it, can receive, assimilate, and transmit data from a universe of sources, says Huna. It is also the medium of psi communication. Through universal aka we are all linked—plants, animals, people, the universe. NDEers too saw themselves linked through a cobwebby substance to all living things. Telepathy and clairvoyance function through the field of memory, says Huna.

During sleep, and at other times, either by accident or training, this aka body can disengage from the physical body and travel as a mobile center of consciousness, they say. At death, the aka body, imprinted with the individual's lifetime of memories, is said to lift out and shift to another frequency dimension. To summarize, the aka body is sort of like a compact disc on which memories are recorded, and the mana energy is like the CD player's laser beam that plays back the memories.

A shimmering, freewheeling body, the domain of memory, and life-giving subtle energies loaded with data—are they more than metaphor? Millennia of world tradition attests to them, the most gifted psychics claim to see them and use them, and they would seem to be implied in people's experience of prebirth memories and in NDEer's experience of total memory fields and light-encoded data banks. Edgar Cayce maintained that these energies would shortly be discovered and instruments to monitor them developed. The mysterious energy fields of memory might become accessible.

If Huna's paradigm of memory is correct and mana/chi energy is the means by which we store, access, and manipulate our memories stored in aka substance, then we would expect to find leading-edge memory breakthroughs involving boosting, balancing, or manipulating mana/chi. This appears to be the case with many of the memory discoveries in this book. Modalities that stimulate chi have been yielding unexpected memory enhancement. Devices like the BT-5+ stimulate acupuncture points to boost memory; nutrients like germanium, said to be rich in chi, boost memory; high-frequency sound and music that stimulates chi like sonic acupuncture, boosts memory; the Cayce bio-battery replenishes and balances chi to boost memory; "far memories" of past lives are recalled by a new acupuncture method; breathing exercises, like those of Superlearning, boost memory; full sensed visualization that infuses images with energy boosts memory. Conversely, disrupting chi circulation and depleting chi energy through magnetic fields and certain kinds of radiations can disrupt memory and even cause amnesia. Is the Huna idea of memory right? Is there any scientific evidence for it?

Our Bioenergy Fields and Memory

While American NDEers were undergoing a transformation through an exposure to subtle energies, something strange was happening in science in the USSR. "The discovery of the energy behind psychic events will be more important than the discovery of atomic energy!" These were the words of one of the Soviet Union's most respected scientists, physiologist Dr. Leonid Vasiliev. The USSR's top biophysicists, biologists, physicists, and physiologists plunged into an exploration of energies. The energies of acupuncture, the force-fields of Qi Gong masters, the energies behind telepathy, psychokinesis, and eyeless sight—they all became top-priority research projects. Reports about energy fields packed with data that interpenetrate living systems —chi, prana, bioplasma—all made their appearance regularly in top scientific journals.

"We all generate light!" The famous Russian scientist Alexander Gurvich began the hunt in the 1930s, when, after years of experimentation, he announced that all living things radiate an energy more powerful than the ultraviolet light beaming at us from the sun. It took decades and the invention of luminescence detectors, sensitive light amplifiers (photoelectronic multipliers) before biologists worldwide could see the light. Dr. Boris Tarusov, Chairman of Biophysics at Moscow State University, discovered that plants, animals, and humans all radiate ultrafaint luminescence. Why do we glimmer? By the 70s, Tarusov and colleagues showed that plants and people recorded and stored memory data in these energy fields. We flash light signals of *information*. Plants, at least, could "talk" with these light signals. What did they have to say? Recently, the Byelorussian Institute of Physics decoded this glimmering plant light: it contained the *stored memory* of the plant's complete genetic codes. Is this luminous field what the Kahunas see as the aka body, the bright storehouse of memory? Have any scientists found a circulating energy that might correspond to mana?

The German chemist-physicist Dr. Fritz-Albert Popp, of the Biophysics Lab in Worms, reported in *Cell Biophysics* his discovery that living DNA cells emit coherent light, laserlike light, made of biophotons. In Dayton, Ohio, nuclear physicist-engineer Dr. Gianni Dotto found that DNA's coil is a miniature sender and antenna that transmits in the two-megacycle range. Cells bounce these signals out like radar, detect the echo, and rebalance to maintain cell health, he says. False signals can lead to mutated cells. Dr. Dotto patented tuners to help keep the cells in balance, which seems like an instrumented approach to Dr. Deepak Chopra's efforts to re-correct the memory patterns of cells with sound frequency (p. 215). Dr. Herbert Pohl of Stillwater, Oklahoma, also confirmed these minuscule radio signals streaming out of cells. In Moscow, Dr. Alexander Dubrov closed in on similar phenomena: luminescence, high-frequency sound, and possibly other energies emitted by cells. Jack Schwarz says that Dubrov's work sounds like a scientific description of the data-carrying energies he sees clairvoyantly, circulating through patients such as those he accurately diagnosed at the Menninger Clinic.

In Novosibersk Science City, Dr. Vlail Kaznachaev carried out award-winning experiments that showed one sort of information carried by the radiation shooting through the body. He put diseased cells in one stoppered quartz bottle, healthy cultures in another, and placed them end to end. The healthy cells soon showed symptoms of the disease afflicting their cousins beyond the quartz wall. They too sickened and died. It wasn't like catching a virus in the ordinary sense. Lengthy experiments showed *information,* carried on light, transmitted the viral disease from one cell colony to another. Can some disease actually spring from memory codes carried on a beam? *Disease can be transmitted at a distance by light,* Kaznachaev's team reported. They won one of the USSR's highest science awards for this work. The implications, nefarious and otherwise, are stunning.

Meanwhile, Dr. H. Von Rohracher discovered at the University of Vienna that our *skin* radiates sound which bounces out like radar. He recorded sonic microvibrations from human skin that even revealed thought changes. In England, Hugo Zucarelli, discovered that our ears radiate sound beams like radar. As mentioned, this holographic ear radar became the basis of an entire new recording process called "holophonics." At the same time, scientists in Japan, investigating a well-tested psychic, Matsuaki Kiyota, discovered he radiated microacoustic sound waves encoded with data.

Scientists have uncovered unsuspected workings of known energies, light, and sound flashing to and from the body. Did they find any other energies? At the Beijing Institute of High Energy Physics, Dr. Hsu Hung-chang set up photoquantum and other detectors around an esteemed Qi Gong master. He asked him to focus and emit chi. Dr. Hsu's detector's reacted, picking up clear pulses. In Japan, Dr. Hiroshi Motoyama devoted years to developing elaborate computerized detectors for monitoring and decoding chi. These machines are now widely used there. At the Bio-Quantum Lab in Palo Alto, California, Dr. Glen Rein, in controlled experiments, is exploring an "other," nonhertzian energy that has a striking affect on living systems.

As scientists probe further, it seems there is far-flung evidence that living things are shot through with energy radiations, broadcasts packed with information, memory data being received, stored, transmitted. More and more proof turns up of whole "sound and light shows" radiating from us, broadcasts of encoded data. Research seems to confirm that the "information soup" seen by NDEers really exists.

In Moscow some years ago, Dr. Viktor Adamenko, a friend of ours, handed us one of the strangest photos we'd ever seen. It appeared to be a leaf all aglow in a luminous, aurora borealis of colors. "Look closer," he urged. "Part of the leaf has been cut away." In the photo, the entire leaf was still there, but the part that had been cut away looked fainter, like a cobwebby substance. We were looking at the *ghost* of part of a leaf! Were we seeing the etheric body of the leaf? It was a Kirlian photo of a leaf, revealing the same luminous field of data as that picked up by luminescence detectors. Except that here the field was amplified and magnified. Here was a photo of bioplasma, the fourth state of matter, as it was called by physicists at the University of Kazakhstan, who uncovered the mechanism of its workings. All living things have a bioplasma body interpenetrating the physical one, they found. All have bioplasma energy circulating within them. In humans, cascades of colored lights—bioplasma—are seen pouring from the body, light-coded data that can reveal the state of one's health, one's shifting emotions and reactions to music and even sunspots. If your fingerprint were sandpapered away, the Kirlian photo still would show the energy pattern of the fingerprint stored in its fields. The energy matrix would help your finger heal back in the same unique pattern. The bioplasmic body revealed in both photos and moving pictures seemed to be a blueprint for matter.

Kirlian photos of the body clearly showed the acupuncture points, supposed centers of chi, against this luminous energy matrix. They showed as flaring, radiating points of energy. Stimulating these points with lasers, biophysicists could track this energy circulating through the meridians. They could detect the blockages so long insisted on by acupuncturists. Kirlian photos of the death of plants and animals showed bioplasma leaving physical matter. Kirlian photos of documented healings revealed something new. As the healer's radiating hands passed over the patient's body, it was coded *information* that was being transferred to the patient, a corrected *memory* pattern, one might say, for the patient's cells. As postulated by all ancient traditions, subtle energy like chi is strengthened by breathing, food, sound, music, or mental suggestion. Kirlian photos of this bioplasma energy showed major shifts when people did deep breathing exercises, ate different foods, heard different sounds and music, or were hypnotized or anesthetized. Were we seeing in the Kirlian photos the energy fields that are the actual storehouse of human memory—the aka body, the etheric body?

Today, scientists worldwide have replicated the Soviet work and carried it further. They too have photographed the "ghosts" of leaves and circulation of bioplasma energy. Would NDEers find that it matched what they saw on their interdimensional journey? Scientists too have had NDEs, giving them a new research perspective. Are we closer to a technology that can authenticate the testimony of millions of NDEers that memory is stored in an energy field that is part of a mobile field of consciousness? It seems there is beginning to be evidence of a field of memories. Huna maintains that the shimmering aka body that codes our memory is embedded in a larger "body" of memory, planetary memory, an all-pervading field. In physics, the idea of an all-pervasive, all-unifying, all-registering energy field has returned. What used to be called the ether is now called a "neutrino sea." The distinguished French physicist/philosopher Dr. Jean Charon has another name for it. He calls such a universal field the mneumonic field, which he says pervades all things and is a permanent memory register.

Divine Memory

The total, constant recording of every nanosecond of all life, even the earth's, referred to by NDEers, is described in ancient texts from Tibet, Egypt, and India. Again it's that ancient idea of "Divine Memory," "Nousphere," or "Akashic Record." *Akasha* is a Sanskrit word referring to primordial substance, meaning the "unshining light" or Black Light of radiation. *Nou* in Egyptian also meant prephysical matter. This cosmic data bank of the totality of universal happenings was conceptualized as being recorded on a "subtle ether," a kind of invisible, all-pervading, unmanifested medium through which "kasha," or the visible light, passes throughout space as a manifestation of vibration. Not only every individual's memory forms part of the Akashic Record, but seeming more like a camcorder than a record, the Akashic supposedly catches the whole scene, every planetary instant.

It is this Akashic record that many gifted psychics claim they access to obtain detailed data about a person's past. Edgar Cayce once explained how he used world memory to gather demonstrably accurate information about people he didn't know and never met. To do a reading, Cayce first put himself into an unconscious or hypnotic trance state. He then felt himself to be traveling out-of-body. He was a small mobile center of awareness. There was a dark tunnel filled with fog and smoke. "There was just a direct, straight, and narrow line in front of me, like a shaft of white light. . . . As I followed along the shaft of light, the way began to clear. . . ." He perceived shadowy figures in the dark tunnel too. "Yet with the narrow way in front of me, I kept going straight ahead. . . ." There was more and more light. He saw colors, heard music, and saw buildings. "Finally, I came to a hill, where there was a mount and a temple. I entered this temple and found in it a very large room, very much like a library. Here were the books of people's lives, for each person's activities were a matter of actual record, it seemed. And I merely had to pull down the record of the individual for whom I was seeking information."

There are obvious similarities to an NDE, and Cayce himself felt his experiences were close to what happens at death. Consciousness and memory survive, said Cayce, not being dependent on earth coordinates. An entity retains after death "total recall of its worldly experiences, now safely stored in its 'memory bank,' " he said.

"The conscious mind receives the impression from without and transfers all thought to the subconscious where it remains. . . ." said Cayce. "The sub-conscious mind is in direct communication with all other sub-conscious minds," he explained. It can interpret information received and transmit data through this all-embracing memory field. By attuning to other subconscious minds, Cayce said he could also gather data stored in other people's memories.

Other psychics have also claimed to access this cosmic data bank and often note that such a wide body of data—beginning with the birth of time—can be difficult to translate into terms understandable to us at present. In his book *Cosmic Memory,* the German philosopher and teacher Rudolf Steiner describes his reading of the Akashic Record. He claimed to have tapped into humanity from prehistory on. From this overview, sighting long trends and currents, Steiner in the twenties predicted that evolutionary changes were about to occur in humans: a transformed view of themselves, vastly increased psychic and mental powers, a diminishing role for gender. Today, NDEers and many others are beginning to experience such transformative change.

Instead of accessing an all-embracing world memory, some sensitives claim to zero in on the memory of events embedded in objects—a ring, watch, or photo—which is called psychometry. At the University of Utrecht, Dr. Willem Tenhaef was doing experiments in psychometry when he handed a psychic a hat found at the scene of a murder. This subject and many others in Tenhaef's lab would "read" the object, attuning supposedly to unique memory imprints carried by it. Bits of data, clues, occasionally a complete record of an event was read off by the psychic from object memory, making Tenhaef's lab world famous for helping police solve crimes.

Time and Memory

"Time itself is a form of energy!" the internationally known Soviet astrophysicist Dr. Nikolai Kozyrev explained to us. We were in Leningrad at the prestigious Pulkovo Observatory. In a scientific paper that rocked the astrophysics community, Kozyrev had said, "It is to time's properties that we should look in order to find the source that maintains the phenomenon of life in the world." The white-haired Kozyrev radiated a serene spirituality despite years spent in a Stalinist prison camp.

"Time appears immediately everywhere," he said. The altered properties of a certain second of time will appear instantly everywhere at once. Time links us all and all things in the universe."

He postulated the idea that time has density. Our thoughts affect this density of time, he told us. This wasn't just speculation. He had performed years of careful testing with devices he'd perfected to monitor the workings of what he called "time." Some experiments involved gyroscopes like the sea green one on his desk.

"What affects this density of time?" we asked. His tests showed time density could change with storms and climatic changes. Gravity also changes the energy of time, he said. When something occurs to alter time's density, Kozyrev explained, the energy of time remained encoded longer in some things than others.

Time also has a "flow pattern," according to Kozyrev. Left-handed rotating systems have a positive time flow—more energy comes in. Right-handed systems have a negative time flow. Time flows in one direction, from past to future. Once a plant grows from a seed, it can't directly return to being a seed again. In a sense, in Kozyrev's view, time might be considered as receptivity.

According to the laws of physics, all processes in the universe should wind down (entropy). However, says Kozyrev, the universe sparkles with inexhaustible variety, not thermal and radioactive death. What is the cause of stellar energy? He believes it's the all-pervasive energy of time. Scientists at the Crimean Astrophysical Observatory and elsewhere are monitoring star systems to prove Kozyrev's theories. Interestingly, Edgar Cayce once explained that the Akashic Record of memory "is *written on the skein of time and space.*"

Since Dr. Kozyrev's death, his research is being continued in observatories from Latvia to Armenia and by the Soviet biophysicist Dr. Viktor Adamenko, who helped pioneer Kirlian photography. Adamenko has left the USSR to head a laboratory at the University of Athens, Greece. Most significantly, Kirlian photos show the same energy that Kozyrev's "time density detectors" reveal, he told us. As noted, Kirlian appears to show energy fields that encode memory. Did Kozyrev, sighting the same energies on a universal scope, actually find the all-pervasive field of memory and call it time?

In December 1989, Japanese scientists reported in *Physical Review Letters,* a leading physics journal, that they too, like Dr. Kozyrev, detected changes in energy from rotating gyroscopes. Counterclock-

wise rotation caused weight loss. They called this energy "anti-gravity" energy.

Can Instruments Tap Cosmic Memory?

When NDEers tell us they experienced a replay of their entire lives
as if these had been recorded, how do we know they were *entire* or
recorded? We don't. The panoramic NDE recall takes only minutes of
regular time. Maybe it only seems as if every detail was recorded and
replayed. But if we could find objective evidence that a continuous
recording process is going on in nature, it would not only corroborate
NDEers, but give us the master key to understanding our memories.
Could instruments pick up these same memory "recordings"?

Can devices be developed that access energy systems where memory
is stored and actually read off the contents of our memories? Could
devices tap past memories? Could we even decode universal memory
tracings—the Akashic record? Until recently, mind/body experts like
Jack Schwarz were needed to read and decode the data stored in human energy fields. Electrical genius Dr. Charles Steinmetz was convinced that a device could be developed to decode memory tracks and
play them back. Supposedly he was working on the project at the time
of his death. Today, a number of devices have surfaced that may be
candidates for capturing the energies of memory. Many of them sound
like science fiction, but then memory may be more like sci fi than we
thought.

According to ancient theories of yoga and acupuncture, prana and
chi nourish consciousness, memory, and body vitality. Chi is said to be
the energy that encodes memory on a subtle matrix. We can get chi
from breathing, food, drink, sound, music, and perhaps Cayce battery
devices. The more chi we have playing over the memory field (like a
laser beam playing a CD), supposedly the better our memory.

Dr. Hiroshi Motoyama, a scientist with doctorates in psychology,
physiology, and philosophy, after decades of research in Japan, invented an electronic computer-assisted device, the AMI, that measures
and decodes chi energy streaming along the acupuncture meridians of
the body. The AMI reads the acupuncture points and meridians via
twenty-eight electrodes attached to points on the fingers and toes.
Compared to nerve impulses, chi (carrying information and control
signals) travels slowly, Motoyama says, from 12 to 47 centimeters per
second. The AMI decodes the chi signals to diagnose the conditions of
internal organs, detect specific disease tendencies, mental and emo-

tional states, hypnotic and meditative states, even ESP activities and more. Motoyama's equipment is now often used in Japan for annual medical checkups and is in use at the A.R.E. Arizona clinic. A genuine breakthrough was announced at a recent international medical conference: CAT scans can image chi circulation. M.D.s J-C Arris and P. de Vernejoul of the University of Paris injected radioactive tracers on meridians to confirm chi's slow, axial travel patterns.

Dr. Motoyama, whom we met in Canada, also developed another monitor that shows changes over the seven chakras of energy centers of yoga. Feelings and emotional attitudes radiate out from these centers, he says, and the machine detects them. He feels his devices "prove conclusively that the human being is more than a body and a limited intellect."

The acupuncture meridians, he believes, are the link between the chakras and our physical nervous system. Chi mediates mental and physical energies, he says. It would seem that it is to chi we should look to understand mental healing or even the placebo effect. He thinks his devices may eventually clarify the "relationship of consciousness to matter." They may show precisely how memories encode on the memory field. Motoyama also finds that a person's chi interacts with the chi of other people and living things. Soviet geologist Dr. V. Neumann insists that his research shows that the body's acupuncture meridians also resonate with a structural energy network in the cosmos, and Soviet scientists believe they have mapped the frequencies of this cosmic network. Can Dr. Motoyama's devices help reveal the interrelatedness of people and cosmos as seen by NDEers? Would they detect anything when Monroe Institute trainees claim they're lifting out of the body in a mobile center of consciousness?

"I believe I'm on the way to capturing a portion of 'the memory of the world'!" It was Dr. Genady Sergeyev speaking, a foremost Soviet physiologist from the Uktomski Institute, a military lab in Leningrad. Sergeyev, whom we met in Moscow, author of highly respected texts on the brain and a longtime researcher of human subtle energy radiations, says all objects in the vicinity of a person absorb the energies he radiates and are changed by them. The objects become natural magnetic recorders, he thinks. Sergeyev has invented a scanner which he maintains picks up these changes in objects touched by people. A computer does the decoding. It works like an instrumented form of psychometry. Locations where violence has taken place can be readily decoded, he says, because he's found that basic emotions like fear and anger are the easiest to decode. If true, recapturing trace memory imprints of the past could prove a powerful crime-solver and a great aid in mineral and archaeological exploration.

Instruments That Track Memory Through Time and Space

"Startling results"—that's what Soviet scientists got when they used dowsing to track traces of the past. At the battleground of Borodino, where Napoleon staged his onslaught on Moscow, Soviet archaeological dowsers uncovered amazing anomalies, secret caverns, and hitherto unknown mass graves of French soldiers. On the old estate of Czar Boris Godunov (1552–1605), they verified data from Polish sources which up until then had been considered incorrect by Russian historians.

Can a dowsing rod be a memory machine? Some energy in the dowser changes when he walks over the ground and specific movements of the dowsing rod or pendulum simply make this unconscious change visible. They are feedback signals that he's reacting to emanations from deep down gold, oil, or archaeological objects. Soviets have explored dowsing for decades and use it widely in geology. Dowsing ability doesn't stop there, however. Some dowsers can also pick up signals just from the map of a location as if they were somehow tapping into the memory field of minerals or objects.

An electromagnetically amplified form of dowsing may carry us further into the realm of cosmic memory retrieval. U.S. Patent No. 2482773, "Detection of Emanations from Materials and Measurement of the Volumes Thereof" was awarded to T. Galen Hieronymous, an American electrical engineer, on Sept. 27, 1949. Using the device to tap into an all-pervasive data field, Hieronymous claimed he could monitor information about people, crops, even insects at any distance. He tracked the physiological condition of American astronauts on Apollos 8 and 11, throughout the lunar voyages, and his test data matched telemetry from NASA. As noted, we and all matter constantly emit radiation. Instrumented dowsing holds that there's a specific radiation frequency for everything and everybody. Each person's radiation is unique, tuned to its own specific frequency in the universal mneumonic energy field. By tuning into this unique frequency through sound resonance, contact is made and data and information can be obtained over vast distances by a biological detector—the human operator of the device. Instrumented dowsing adds electromagnetic energies to amplify the operator/dowser's responses and make them more precise. Hieronymous called the data-carrying energy "eloptic" (*elec-*

tricity plus *optics*). He could focus it with lenses, refract it with prisms, implant its effects on film.

Years ago, in England, we met George De La Warr and his wife Marjorie at their labs in Oxford. They too worked with instrumented dowsing or "radionics." Like scientists Dubrov, Dotto, and others, De La Warr believed we radiate sound energies, a kind of ultrasonic microacoustic radar that bounces out and echoes back in an all-pervasive field of memory. The devices amplify the dowser's responses. It was sort of like being a ham radio operator on the microsound band. To send out your signal, you stroke a panel on the machine with your hand. The device amplifies the microacoustic, radarlike energies that emanate from your skin and cells. When your radar locks on the target, your skin registers a "stick" on the panel. All matter is in a constant state of vibration. After years of experimenting, the De La Warrs uncovered rates of ultrasonic microacoustic vibrations for different substances. (Interestingly, ancient Mayan texts also speak of these frequencies.) By "dialing" or "tuning in" to the frequency of a specific plant on the radionics device, you could be in resonant communication with it through the all-registering memory field. You could chart the plant's health at a distance. The device could also broadcast treatment as well by re-patterning the plant's memory field. The De La Warrs' instruments were controversial, to say the least, and publicly argued in Britain. Yet for years they were used to treat animals and plants and people. Using his distance detectors as a kind of sonar, De La Warr had a spectacular success: he was able to detect the source of a chemical poison that was making cattle sick, a problem that had baffled British experts because the poison, fluoracetamide, is one of the hardest to detect.

Radionics continues to be practised in Europe and the UK, but in North America flourishes in an underground. (see Resources). Documented data from radionics, going back 100 years, may one day provide instrumented proof of the existence of an all-pervasive memory field. De La Warr showed us his controversial "time and space camera." It was high sci fi. With this experimental radionic device, his team claimed to have photographed plants, animals, and people at a distance. De La Warr believed they tuning in to the mneumonic field that interpenetrates all life and were photographing prephysical matter. Were they getting the etheric energies that store memory? Taking a photo at a distance of a woman in Ireland, the lab confirmed that she was pregnant, and monitored the baby's progress with photos. They were asked to photograph a sick cow at a distance. The camera produced a picture of a metal object and a stone inside the cow. When the vet operated, the objects were in the location indicated. Occasionally, the team claimed to intersect past memory traces—blossom time for a dead plant, for example. Like a dowsing camera, they used the device to prospect for water in the Middle East. Reportedly, they accurately located a subterranean water supply and even assessed its quality. They took 12,000 exposures.

Accounts of the De La Warr camera seem unbelievable, and perhaps they are, or perhaps this dedicated husband-wife team somehow learned how to tune to a universal field of data and retrieve information. The De La Warrs didn't live to see the camera perfected for use by more than a few operators. Today, some of De La Warr's instruments are in Kentucky, where they are quietly used to diagnose and treat some of America's prize racehorses. American radionics pioneer Ruth Drown also developed a memory camera. Foremost practitioner Frances Farrelly has the plans. Instead of being exiled from science, a century of experimental data gathered worldwide from dowsing and radionics might be reexamined, as forming a body of proof for the existence and properties of a mneumonic field, the energy field of memory.

Chronovisor

Benedictine monk Padre Pellegrino Ernetti, professor of Archaic Music in Venice at the Benedetto Marcello Conservatory, has developed a device called the Chronovisor, which he claims can recapture the past. Ernetti, now in his seventies, worked with Portuguese Professor de Matos and twelve physicists to develop the device. In Europe Professor Ernetti is regarded as a serious researcher, says French author Robert Charroux. The Chronovisor is based on the principle that sound and light waves, once generated, continue to travel in the universe. Ernetti says it's possible to reconstitute them. His apparatus includes a cathode oscillograph using the deviations of a stream of electrons. Using his extensive knowledge of sound harmonics derived from ancient texts, he was aware that as sound waves subdivide into harmonics, each has unique characteristics which can be tracked.

TV broadcasts, it is known, continue out into space, and occasionally, thanks to some fluke in the ionosphere, people may see an old program spontaneously on their TV sets. Does Ernetti think human "broadcasts" (like the human laser-light and radio wave emissions found by Drs. Popp, Pohl, and Dubrov) continue to travel in the universe? "Every human being," declares Ernetti, "traces from birth to death a double furrow of light and sound. This constitutes his individual identity mark. The same applies to an event, to music, to movement. The antennae used in our laboratory enable us to "tune in" on these furrows: picture and sound." By intercepting transmissions from all living things, he believes he can reconstruct past events. He claims to have reconstituted the exact pronunciation of ancient languages; a play in archaic Latin, "The Thyestes," a tragedy by Quintus Ennius (Rome, 169 BC), and various religious events. (Can certain kinds of ghosts be spontaneously occurring playbacks of these memory broadcasts?)

Because he is a monk, Professor Ernetti's device, and details about it, remain in the hands of the church, which is fine with Ernetti, who is concerned that the device might be misused by spies or even the "Rona Barretts" of the Akashic records. (Would the secret police have to develop "cosmic memory shredders"?)

With so many scientists closing in on the spectrum of subtle bodies and energies, the luminous webs where memory is said to dwell, one day soon someone—if not Professor Ernetti—may make a decisive breakthrough with a cosmic memory camera or cosmic video player. Perhaps the clues in the testimony given by countless NDEers, about how our individual memories are recorded in the universal archive, will eventually lead us to an instrumented opening of the Akashic record, our cosmic memory bank.

22. Far Memories—Can They Change This Life?

At the gate of a turquoise-tiled house in the village of Taktser in Tibet, the parents of a two-year-old boy greeted several men and immediately led them to the servants' quarters where their child was playing. The little boy rushed up to the eldest, who was garbed as a servant, and climbed onto his lap. Touching prayer beads worn by the old man, he said, "I'd like to have those."

"You can have them, if you can guess who I am," replied the old man.

"You're a lama from the Sera Monastery," the boy said.

"Who is the master of the monastery?"

"Losang," said the two year old.

All day, the elderly men questioned and observed the child. When they prepared to leave, he begged to go with them. The men returned several more times to conduct cautious observations and special tests. Finally, the old man revealed that he was indeed a lama in disguise. The child had passed all the tests: he had identified specific belongings, he had revealed secret knowledge. Before Tibet's thirteenth Dalai Lama died, he'd left indications of where and when he would be re-born and to which parents. All the indicators matched. The two year old was the Dalai Lama come again.

A caravan of fifty people and 350 horses and mules transported the child to Lhasa. On the fourteenth day of the first month of the year of the Iron Dragon (1940), the little boy ascended the Lion Throne of Tibet and became the fourteenth Dalai Lama. Six million Tibetan followers believe him to be the latest incarnation of the line of Tibetan spiritual leaders, dating from 1391. Unlike his predecessors, the little boy was to travel a long way from his turquoise house. He is the Dalai Lama who lives in the United States now and recently won the Nobel Peace Prize.

Through far memory, evidently, murder will out—and in Agra, India, it did with a twist even Agatha Christie didn't anticipate. Six-year-old Titu Singh appeared in a court of law in Agra and convinced skeptical authorities that he was the reincarnation of a murder victim. He demanded that the killer be brought to justice. Titu named his murderer and described how he'd been shot while working in his radio shop in Agra. He showed investigators marks on his skull matching where the bullet entered and exited the head of the dead man. He revealed intimate details of his married life with previous wife, Uma. He convinced his past-life father, with recollections they alone shared. When six-year-old Titu was taken to the radio shop eighteen miles from his current village, he knew every detail of the shop and commented on recent changes. He had an emotional reunion with the murdered man's two sons and elderly parents.

"This is the most remarkable case of reincarnation I have ever seen," says Dr. N. K. Chadha, a parapsychologist at Delhi University. Because of the police involvement, it is one of the very best documented cases of seeming reincarnation. The BBC, finding the evidence so compelling, did a documentary on Titu, who had memory with a vengeance.

For the past twenty-five years, Dr. Ian Stevenson, Chair of Psychiatry at the University of Virginia, has been researching children who claim to have past-life memories. His 1987 *Children Who Remember Previous Lives* is a scholarly, methodical study of over 2000 such cases worldwide. He believes reincarnation memories may account for unusual behavior patterns in children, not attributable to genetics or environment.

In England, three-year-old Dorothy Eady was pronounced officially dead. One hour later, she was sitting up and playing as if nothing had happened. But something extraordinary *had* happened. She was now full of memories of the life of an enigmatic woman called Omm Sety, an Egyptian who lived 3000 years ago and was the passionate love of a Pharaoh. Her story unfolds in Jonathan Cott's intriguing biography, *The Search for Omm Sety.*

From Plato to Tolstoy to General George Patton, many famous people have not only believed but also claimed benefits from reincarnational memories. Patton was convinced he'd been a Roman warrior in a past life, and while commanding his troops in Italy and France had detailed recollections of the terrain. What of child prodigies like Mozart, who composed music at four, and Pascal, who outlined geometric principles at eleven? Some think the explanation lies in past memories.

Reincarnation is a major tenet of religions around the earth, with followers in the millions, if not billions. Some say it was part of early

Christian belief. At least it was known, for in 325 A.D. Emperor Constantine officially declared reincarnation a Christian heresy (it was rumored that neither he nor his powerful Empress Theodora could envision returning as a lesser being). Joe Fisher's *The Case for Reincarnation,* and Head and Cranston's *Reincarnation—an East-West Anthology* reveal some of the background. A heresy punishable by death, for centuries the concept of reincarnation was kept alive only by secret hermetic groups in Christian countries. Today far memories are breaking through again.

In 1956, *The Search for Bridey Murphy* by Morey Bernstein, startled America with its account of a Colorado housewife who, under hypnosis, recalled a previous lifetime in Ireland. With the stirrings of a new age, reincarnation began to expand people's idea of themselves and the potential reach of their memories.

One of the prime stirrers was Edgar Cayce, who shocked himself with the idea. In waking life, he adhered to the orthodox Christian tenets he taught in Sunday school. In trance, Cayce revealed "heretical" past-life readings for hundreds of questioners. His *Readings* unveiled a vast web of worldwide reincarnational transfers of entities from one area of time to another (see Chapter 24). He maintained that we are greatly influenced by past-life memories, whether conscious of them or not. His memory-tracking of each client taken from the "planetary Akashic records" appeared to show that past-life actions affect what is happening to us now, and the choices we make. People were likely to return to work out different combinations of relationships with the same people they'd known before, he said. A husband in a previous life might return as a son, a mother as a daughter, and so on. Like most rebirth philosophies, Cayce's included karma—*accountability* from life to life. *"Karma is memory,"* said Cayce. Noel Langley's *Edgar Cayce on Reincarnation* covers dozens of typical cases.

Volumes of channeled information such as the Seth material dictated through writer Jane Roberts boosted further interest. Seth maintained that our concepts of time and space are altogether inaccurate, and taught that the nature of human personality is not linear but multidimensional, and that so-called "past lives" are coexistent in a hyper-space dimension.

Far Memories That Liberate

Why does everything go right or wrong for you? Why are you prone to certain illnesses or addictions? Why do you have spectacular or

seemingly puny talents? What about relationships or financial affairs—
why do they keep running in certain patterns? If you really could
recover memories of "the late great you" (as in *On A Clear Day You
Can See Forever*) with all your karmic strands, you would certainly
have a more fruitful, secure life, understanding why you'd chosen certain "projects" to work through this time around. Recalling your
grand design would be an eminently practical use of memory. But
reincarnation is not proven in our scientific era. It's become another
leading edge in the supermemory revolution. Whether their past lives
are real or imaginary, thousands of people are experiencing all around
benefits from "recalling" them. There is a genuine memory breakthrough going on in the theater of consciousness. Therapists use this
memory technique "because it works." Far memories in hand, clients
report accelerated improvements in careers, relationships, health, and
a sense of purpose, to name a few. How do you catch hold of these far
memories? Routes include hypnosis, drugs, meditation, psychic or
channeled readings, past-life Hindu astrology, and the latest: acupuncture.

Using hypnosis, clinical psychologist Dr. Edith Fiore was among
the first of a growing number of therapists to delve into people's past
lives in depth, by the century. Fantasy or not, after a trip down an
extended memory lane, clients often returned problem-free. Results
were too startling not to share, and Fiore published *You Have Been
Here Before.* Dr. Brian L. Weiss recently published his cases in *Many
Lives, Many Masters.* A Yale-trained M.D., Chairman of Psychiatry at
Mount Sinai Medical Center in Miami, Weiss also unexpectedly found
treatment with far memory techniques exceptionally effective. His colleagues might wonder, but the method held such healing potential that
it seemed unethical not to report his observations. Weiss is training
other clinicians to help patients reach way back to liberating memories.

Long before, in the 40s, Dr. Dennis Kelsey, an English psychoanalyst, discovered the liberating effect of far memories. Kelsey had an in.
His wife, Joan Grant, was a famous British author—and a powerful
psychic. Grant would take a clairvoyant look into patients' supposed
past lives and give Kelsey bits of data that, real or imaginary, proved
surprisingly useful in treatment. Joan Grant said outright that her
seven best-selling historical novels were really autobiographies drawn
from lives she'd lived in Egypt and the Middle East. Curiously, background details in books like *The Eyes of Horus* were only unearthed
and validated by archaeologists *after* Grant's novels were on the book-

shelves. Her explanation? "I remembered them." With the title of her autobiography of this life, *Far Memory,* Grant set a new term rolling.

Richard Gerber, M.D., describes "the cosmic cycle of regeneration and rebirth" in his *Vibrational Medicine.* He sees the overall Self as a cosmic tree, with each soul pattern a flower blossoming on its branches. Every flower is in constant communication with the tree as it feeds through the "sap lifelines of a common trunk and root system." He believes the human entity is a collective multidimensional consciousness of many individual incarnations, a growing, branching being with many subtle veins of intercommunication. Recovery of far memories, Gerber says, opens powerful new choices in the drive to heal our society and ourselves.

Psychologist Dr. Helen Wambach would agree. Using hypnosis she elicited and intensely analyzed more than 1000 past-life recollections. None of her subjects remembered being the Napoleons or Cleopatras the tabloids write up. They recalled the more or less usual lives one would expect in a normal random sampling of people. Reflecting on their new/old memories, about half felt they'd chosen to be reborn as part of a spiritual learning program. Wambach believes earlier incarnations might help account for existing emotional disturbances. The past life, once surfaced, has been very healing, she says. Past-life therapy might be especially helpful for certain situations, such as the process transexuals go through making the transition to a different body.

"Today—unlike times even in the recent past—people are remembering more and more past-life experiences," observes William McGarey, M.D. "In the field of healing, one cannot bring about a true change unless he takes into account the ongoing experience of life that one moves through over the period of many incarnations. . . ."

Jack Schwarz, director of the Aletheia Foundation, during two years of hypnotic regression experienced the recall of a life as a Berber in 550 B.C. Psychologist Ahmed el Senussi, of Ojai, California, was brought in as interpreter for the mountain Berber dialect Schwarz spoke, not heard since 300 B.C. But Schwarz raises a cautionary. We may resonate with occurrences out of the past, he says. They may not necessarily be our own past lives. Rupert Sheldrake ventures a similar idea. Resonance with morphic forms or memory fields is an alternate interpretation to reincarnation.

Recalling Past Lives Through Acupuncture.

Morphic forms, if the theory holds, are one way for memory to be carried through generations. Various traditions have other, though not necessarily incompatible, ideas about where you can find the memories of the Self. Ancient Yoga texts teach that they reside in one of the subtle bodies, the "causal body," which carries the seeds of karma that will fructify in present and future lives. According to Yogi I.K. Taimni, in *The Science of Yoga,* all yogis of a high order can contact their "causal vehicles" and gain knowledge of their own and others' previous lives.

Historically, prana, as the subtle energy is called in Indian tradition, connects with the subtle bodies. Similarly, Chinese wisdom holds that chi energy fields imprint one's physical body with the memory of the multiincarnational events the Self has experienced. Physically this might be seen in the strange phenomenon of "memory tissue," which hypnotists run across. People undergoing age regression, for instance, will actually develop physical signs of a long-ago injury. A burn as a five year old might suddenly resurface as real blisters—which leads hypnosis expert Dr. John London to think that there is a memory store linked to the cells of our bodies. With her "window to the sky" acupuncture, Chris Griscom extends that idea into multilives and multi "bodies" (see page 220).

One of the troubles with us and our world, Griscom says, is that we're laden with the emotional traumas of other times, which adhere to our emotional bodies like a sort of "stickum." We can get stuck in a rut in this life with old memory baggage. Awareness is the first step to release. The same goes for the old baggage of other lives, Griscom says. The adventure begins with accepting one's multidimensionality and the illusion of the linear nature of time. Acupuncture, she found, can prick the illusion and bring an explosion of memories.

Shirley MacLaine, one of Griscom's early clients, describes this creative big bang of memories in *Dancing In the Light.* In "windows to the sky acupuncture," fine gold or silver needles are placed in the third-eye area in the middle of the forehead, or at the galactic points around the ears, or on the classical psychic meridian points on the shoulders. Occasionally, mid-chest points and those under the chin just above the throat (classically called "controling crowd" points) are used. As Griscom's needles moved the energies of her body, for eleven days MacLaine seemed to vividly relive past lives. She seemed to contact a powerful Higher Self dimension.

"How to get rid of evil and criminals in the world? she asked her Higher Self. Power them out with the revelation of the individuals' spiritual links, came the answer. MacLaine felt a lot of "stickum" was being powered out of her as she flew through hours of filmlike experiences, memories that delineated the meaning behind conflicts involving parents, ex-husband, lover, child, brother, memories moving like musical variations on many themes, transformations keying a multitude of times and countries from the Gobi Desert to Russia. Acupuncture seemed to unfold in the mind's eye memory patterns previously locked in the subtle energies and the body's physical cells. MacLaine felt that the gold and silver needles catapulted her to quantum leaps in spiritual understanding and self-transformation.

At this writing, Griscom has turned daily sessions over to an international group of trainers at her Light Institute in Galesteo. Instead of needles they use acupressure and light-energy massage. One of the authors went to the Institute. In retrospect, the most interesting thing about the supposed past lives that unrolled is that they foreshadowed this book. Themes we were not particularly aware of, themes that only emerged months later in the writing, presented themselves in a variety of historical guises and perspectives. For instance, one particularly vivid "life" later appeared to be in the thick of the wild-and-wooly hermetic memory schools of the Renaissance—systems we'd heard of but not yet researched. Whether this was a life lived, or as Schwarz or Sheldrake might say "a resonance" that memory picked up because we were tuning into mother Mnemosyne, is a very open question.

Griscom maintains that awareness of these old memories brings on real molecular change in the body, one that releases energy and a joyful flow of being. Something is afoot in our time, propelling people to seek far memories. Whether they are real or not seems to be beside the point. No matter what method of accessing them is used, this is an adventure of memory that brings on a new lightness of being.

23. Memory After Death

Dr. Julian Burton and his wife were entertaining relatives at home in California. He was in the kitchen cutting up a pineapple for dessert. "Where's the bowl?" he asked his wife. She'd gone out of the kitchen for an instant, and as he turned to ask her again, suddenly he saw his mother standing beside him. She had died six months before.

"She was fully visible, looking quite beautiful and about ten years younger than at the time of her death. She was wearing a diaphanous pale blue gown trimmed in marabou which I had never seen before," says Dr. Burton. " 'Ma!' I exclaimed. She smiled—and then dissolved. She did not disappear, she *dissolved.*"

Burton felt an enormous weight lift. The next day he called his sister and related the incident. She began to cry. Why hadn't Mother come to see her as well as her brother? "Don't you believe me?" he asked her. "I *know* it's true," his sister replied. Shortly before her mother died, they'd gone shopping and the older woman had tried on the exact pale blue gown Burton described. She looked wonderful in the dress, his sister said, but decided she didn't want to spend $200 on it.

The experience had a profound effect on Burton. He decided to return to college at age forty-two and get a Ph.D. in psychology. His dissertation? "Visitations" from the deceased.

In London, in October 1930, Eileen Garrett, a well-regarded writer and businesswoman—and one of the most throughly tested psychics of the century—received an unexpected visit. It was a presence claiming to be Flight Lieutenant H. C. Irwin, captain of the British dirigible R101. The dirigible had crashed near Paris in a severe storm two days earlier. Almost all aboard, forty-six passengers and crew, had died. Irwin was among the dead. Urgently, the supposed Irwin told Garrett the full details of why the airship crashed. "The whole bulk of the dirigible was . . . too much for her engine capacity. Useful lift too small. Gross lift computed badly. . . . Elevator jammed. Oil pipe plugged. . . ." Although Mrs. Garrett knew nothing of the mechanics of dirigibles, there were quantities of technical data, even details of navigation and topography. Experts at the Royal Airship Works in

Bedford called it "an astounding document," replete with confidential information.

On the far edge of the revolution of remembrance, the last unspeakable in intellectual circles—death—is being discussed after a hiatus of 100 years. In the mid 80s, a significant group gathered in Washington, D.C., under the sponsorship of the Institute of Noetic Sciences and the Office of Smithsonian Symposia. Senator Claibourne Pell initiated the idea, Episcopal Bishop John Spong helped, and Georgetown University offered its facilities. Distinguished scientists and scholars addressed, as Dr. Willis Harman put it, the "awkward" question of "Survival and Consciousness." Will you survive? To many, that means will your memory survive? Conferees from a catalogue of disciplines mostly agreed that in one manner or another, some sort of survival is a reasonable bet.

Dr. Candace Pert spoke of psychoneuroimmunology and traced the many new discoveries about the complexity of the body's inner communication system. "It's possible now to conceive of mind and consciousness as an emanation of emotional information processing," she said, "and as such, mind and consciousness would appear to be independent of brain and body." What about survival? "Matter can neither be created nor destroyed, and perhaps biological information flow cannot just disappear at death and must be transformed into another realm." Pert, the scientist, concludes, "Who can rationally say 'impossible'?"

The files of psi research societies around the world bulge with thousands of cases of people reporting they have seen, heard, or dreamed they were in communication with the dead. They describe the dead as being in possession of their memories and often able to communicate complicated data, as in Mrs. Garrett's case. Until recently, perhaps the best indication that memory survives came from the "cross-correspondence" experiments of the British Society for Psychical Research early in this century. The supposed communicator from the beyond was the respected classical scholar F.W.H. Myers, a founder of the society. The experiment worked like a puzzle. Fragments of messages were picked up by different mediums on two continents. Like the odd-shaped pieces of a puzzle, they only made sense when fit together. Even then they didn't ring much of a bell with most people. What finally appeared were extremely obscure passages from Greek and Roman literature—Myers's specialty. These lengthy experiments suggest, as the researchers said, that both Myers and his memory survived.

A similarly ingenious experiment was devised in the 80s by Dr.

Wolfgang Eisenbeiss, a Swiss investment consultant, psi researcher—
and chess lover. Eisenbeiss worked with a medium supposedly in contact with Geza Maroczy, a Hungarian chess champion who departed
this earth in 1951. The deceased master correctly answered the usual
questions about his life, even recounting moves he'd made in long-ago
championship play. Interesting perhaps, but like most such instances
hardly proof of anything. If he really was Maroczy, how about a
match with a peer? Like the famous grandmaster Viktor Korchnoi—
someone neither the medium who didn't know chess nor the amateur
Eisenbeiss could possibly play. Korchnoi and "spirit" agreed, setting
up a genuinely long-distance match. Thirty moves and three years
later, the departed was holding his own.

A 1987 survey by the University of Chicago's National Opinion
Research Council revealed that nearly half of all American adults
(42%) believe they've been in contact with someone who has died,
usually a dead spouse or sibling. A University of North Carolina team
led by Dr. Richard Olson found 64% of widows at two Asheville
nursing homes had at least "once or twice felt as though they were in
touch with someone who had died": 78% saw the dead person, 50%
heard, 21% touched, 32% felt the presence, 46% a combination; 18%
talked with the departed. Helpful, not frightening, was how they described their encounters. Dr. Andrew Greeley, priest-sociologist, remarked in *American Health*, "What has been 'paranormal' is not only
becoming normal in our time—it may also be health-giving." He
points out that millions have undergone profoundly spiritual experiences from NDEs to out-of-body travel to transformative encounters
with the dead. "That many people . . . can have a lasting effect on
the country," says Greeley.

"Gedenke, Ich Bin."—"Just Think, I Am."

Evidence that memory can cross the border of death has been
largely anecdotal until a quiet technological breakthrough occurred. It
was Thomas Edison who first started working on instruments to communicate with the dead. Many quite reasonable people think Edison's
vision began to be realized thirty years ago on a machine the great
inventor didn't create—the tape recorder. If they're right, this is the
breakthrough par excellence, the headline of the century, yet unless
you're part of a small but far-flung, self-selected group, you've probably never heard of people picking up voices of the dead on their tape
recorders. Voices of the dead? It sounds like a tabloid fantasy. Those

not directly involved don't know what to do when they come across the evidence, and generally head for the exit, making this a potentially comic as well as cosmic breakthrough.

In 1959, Friedrich Jurgenson, a prominent Swedish filmmaker whom the Vatican chose to document the life of Pope Paul VI, was listening to tapes of birdcalls he'd recorded in a Swedish forest. To his astonishment, he heard voices discussing birdcalls in Norwegian. A wandering radio broadcast? He listened some more. There were other voices, some that seemed familiar. They addressed him by name. They claimed to be the dead. He even heard what he believed to be his dead mother's voice on the tape with a personal message. He began experimenting. Soon Jurgenson had recordings of hundreds of voices, all claiming to be the deceased. "Electronic voice phenomena" (EVP) was on the air.

In Europe, other researchers joined in on voice phenomena recording, among them Dr. Konstantine Raudive, a well-known psychologist, professor, writer, and student of C. G. Jung; Theodor Rudolph, a high-frequency engineer with Telefunken at Ulm, who had worked with such radar pioneers as Messerschmitt; a Swiss physicist, Dr. Alex Schneider. Another Swiss, the Reverend Father Leo Schmid, a well-known theologian, was given permission by his superiors to record in his church. He obtained 10,000 snatches of strange voices, including, he believed, that of his deceased Monsignor. Jung Institute co-founder, Dr. Gebhard Frei, a cousin of Pope Pius XII, announced that the full scope of the phenomena pointed toward the voices belonging to "transcendental personalities." Soviet writer Valery Tarsis, author of *Ward Seven,* also experimented. He believed he had picked up the voice of the deceased Boris Pasternak, who commented on Tarsis's current work. Even NASA engineers and officials quietly investigated the electronic voices in Germany.

What were they doing? For the bare-bones experiment, you simply switch on a tape recorder along with a source of noise—the hiss between stations on the radio dial, the white noise of a sleep machine. Ask for a communication, then wait silently as the blank tape runs ten minutes or so. On playback, sometimes something is heard that shouldn't be there. Voices.

Dr. Raudive, after an intensive investigation of Jurgenson's tapes, devoted full time to EVP research from 1965 on. He soon had over 100,000 phrases spoken by enigmatic voices on tapes. At first, messages were compressed, rarely longer than ten or twelve words against a background of static. One of the clearest is a female voice exclaiming, "Gedenke, Ich Bin!" Just think, I am! Typically, Raudive was addressed by his full name or his nickname, Kosta. The speech was usually double speed and pulsed in rhythms. One had to strain to hear, as though trying to catch words over a very bad phone connection. When Raudive published his findings in *Breakthrough,* a record of the voices was also released. Thousands more were drawn into the controversial experiments. Peter Bander, Raudive's British publisher, was so struck that he did something unusual for a publisher: he began his own research and eventually published a book on the unaccountable voices he himself had gathered. Where were the voices coming from? Why were they coming? Some British clergy thought they shouldn't be coming. "How can we stop them?" they asked.

Voices were always recorded on factory-fresh tape. Men, women, children, spoke in hurried snatches. Voices would identify themselves, give names and hometown. They addressed people in the room by name. Eventually, they responded to questions and commented on conditions in the room—even the clothes the questioners were wearing—and discussed transmission technicalities. This stumped those critics who had insisted that the voices were simply wandering bits of radio broadcasts picked up by mistake. British and European media played EVP recordings. Interest was so intense that shows ran overtime. Hundreds more began patiently sitting with recorders and trying to improve the equipment.

Austrian electronics engineer Franz Seidl developed instruments that improved the clarity of transmissions. The odd voices began to get helpful. Parents of a missing girl appealed to Seidl. Voices came through on the tape giving information on her whereabouts. Helpful or not, the voices still weren't supposed to be there.

Belling & Lee Ltd., of Enfield, England, conducted experiments inside radio-frequency-screened labs used by the British military. No broadcast signal could possibly penetrate the facility. Again paranormal voices appeared on the tapes. Researchers from every field studied the unbelievable voices—audio engineers, physicists, electrical specialists, parapsychologists, broadcasters, clergy, even the Vatican became involved. EVP was gone over with a fine-tooth comb by some of the best labs and experts in Europe. (There is great deal of documentation and published research, particularly from Germany. See References.) No one has been able to explain the voices away. The voices themselves keep on explaining that they are "the dead."

Voiceprint Technology and After-Death Memory

Would the voice of a person recorded during his lifetime match the paranormal voice purporting to be that same person? Various researchers analyzed the voices in detail on sound spectrographs and oscilloscopes. They used the latest voice print technology to test individual voices recorded by Otto Koenig. Voiceprints are as individual as fingerprints. The supposed after-death voiceprint of an individual was compared with before-death prints of the same person. They matched! "This is very strong proof," says Sarah Estep, founder of the American Association for Electronic Voice Phenomena. Prior to matching voiceprints, identities of after-death communicators had to be established by memory-matching.

Several years after Raudive's own death, Koenig was at a meeting of 500 people in Fulda, Germany. A voice was recorded in distorted German that said, "The dead greeting!" A woman in the audience asked about Raudive. After a few seconds a low-pitched, slow-speaking voice answered "Raudive." Replayed at higher speed, voiceprint technology matched it with Raudive's predeath voice.

Once, Koenig unexpectedly heard on his tape the voice of a close friend, Walter Steinoekel, hospitalized at the time. Fifteen minutes later, Steinoekel's wife called and said her husband had died—fifteen minutes earlier. After that, Koenig succeeded in recording two-minute, two-way conversations with, he believes, the gone but not departed Walter. The voice, in dialect and tone, was a match. In 1983, Radio Luxemburg invited Koenig to hold a supervised recording session on the air. Voices came through, precise, strong, clear and noise-free. Response was so great that EVP became a regular on Radio Luxembourg.

Like some others in the field who are technically sophisticated, Koenig went far beyond using a simple tape recorder. He recorded with ultrasonic electronic equipment and also added a monitor for chi energy which he claimed improved voice reception and quality of recordings. (See Motoyama's work, pg. 328).

Sarah Estep, a retired Maryland schoolteacher, became interested in the voice phenomenon after reading our *Handbook of Psi Discoveries.* She taped for six days and got nary a peep. Finally bored, she asked, "Please tell me what your world is like." On playback, a clear voice replied on tape, "Beauty." Estep was hooked. She heeded later voices instructing, "Don't give up." "Keep it up." Some experimenters have had to wait patiently for months before catching a voice. Slowly Estep's transmission problems remedied. Voices got louder, clearer, more tonal. When her Aunt Jane died, she tried to keep in contact by recorder, and reports that various voices appeared on tape. "She's right here." "Very good now. Go ahead, speak!" Then a voice Estep says was her Aunt Jane's, "I'm good. I'm back here now."

In 1982, Estep founded the American Association for Electronic Voice Phenomena. She has tirelessly encouraged hundreds worldwide to join in the research and she has selflessly tried to assuage the grief-stricken who seem to appeal to her at all hours of day and night. It should be noted that instead of making money from their endeavors, voice experimenters spend much of their own on tapes and equipment. The AAEVP publishes a newsletter and hosts annual conferences. Recently Fawcett published Estep's *Voices of Eternity,* about her rather mind-boggling, cosmic adventures while sitting at home in her office with her tape recorder.

At one of Estep's conferences in Maryland, we met Dr. Ernst Senkowski, a German researcher, an electrical engineer and professor of physics at Bingen Technical College in Mainz, who's taped voices for years. We heard some of his recordings and learned more about the technology behind them, more about the quirky ways of these impossible voices. Often voices are found on the reverse side of tapes, where they doubly shouldn't be, as well as on the recording side. Senkowski played tapes on which children killed in car accidents replied to their parents' questions. There also seemed to be reunions with family pets with a bark here and there.

If only one person or fifty came up with voice tapes, it would make matters easier. One could say, "deluded" or "fraud." But thousands have caught these impossible voices and apparently millions could if willing to sacrifice the time. No one seems to have profited, at least in a worldly sense. Mercedes Shepanek, the wife of a top-ranking naval officer and originally a skeptic, told us that her own EVP experiments, in which she taped dozens of inexplicable voices speaking directly to her, made her reexamine her views of death and life. She didn't turn into a "true believer" or run shouting through the streets. She did expand her sense of her own self, her own memory, and how far it may extend.

Currently, in Luxembourg, Jules and Maggie Harsch-Fishbach of Hesperange have one of the most advanced taping centers in Europe. Jules, a lawyer with the Luxembourg Department of Justice, and Maggie, a schoolteacher, started taping with the basics in our handbook.

After several sessions, a voice appeared, claiming to be a technician. He gave complex data on how to make technical improvements.

"He astounded us with his exceptional knowledge of electronics, physics, math, astronomy, the natural sciences, and about the future and the past," says Maggie. "Technician" instructed them to set up two complex electronic systems, one a two-way system that permits conversation back and forth out loud during taping. The other makes use of intricate European telephone technology.

Dr. Ralf Determeyer, a West German engineer, asked Technician if EVP could help world peace. "It is the most important instrument to awaken human consciousness out of early dawn's sleep. To do this takes bridges and bridge-builders between your world and the world of spirit," came the reply. Sometimes Technician, like an electronic Edgar Cayce, gives helpful medical advice—a special medicinal tea that helped a stroke victim recover, specific medicine for back trouble that proved effective.

How is he talking to them? Technician explained that people on "the other side" have to impress their thoughts through a system that sets up oscillations and then goes through a relay bridge in order to be picked up on our magnetic tape recorders. He said he used something like a computerized translating machine containing the syllables and phonemes of all languages. He has to draw on the vocabulary in the system to express what he wants to say. He suggested they read *The Seth Material* by Jane Roberts to better understand.

When Sarah Estep visited the Harsh-Fishbachs in Luxembourg, a voice purporting to be Konstantine Raudive came through with a seven-minute message. "Beyond the astral world [there exists] yet another range of experience, the mental, and beyond that others of still finer nature respond to still more spiritual aspects of consciousness. All these rates of vibrations interpenetrate each other in the same way that solids, liquids, and gases are all present in a sponge filled with water."

Remembering Raudive's research in this life, the voice continued, "Sometimes the voices I captured were more real than the people around me and then they became phantoms swirling in motion, disappearing like the summer mists. . . . Don't be afraid of death. It is not the end but a transition to a better, a finer world."

Videos from The "Beyonders"

Genial, retired fire-inspector Klaus Schreiber, of Aachen, Germany, gathered with three friends one evening for their regular card game. Why not try to record these voices they'd heard about? They set up the tape recorder, asked, and listened. On playback, they heard clear voices addressing them by name, talking directly to them! The three card-playing friends fled, never to gather again. But Schreiber, fascinated, went on recording. There, clearly on the tape, was the voice, he decided, of his young daughter Karin, who'd died tragically at seventeen. The voice recalled events during her last terrible days of blood poisoning and reassured Schreiber that she was completely well now.

If you'll set up your VCR and camcorder the way we tell you, we can send you video pictures, she supposedly told him. What happened next moved EVP further toward the evidential or toward the unbelievable, depending on your point of view. As various accounts go, Schreiber rigged up an elaborate system for his camcorder and VCR in his basement. When he played the video back, there were pictures of Karin. They were like vibrating, fuzzy, still photos, gradually taking form on the screen. Eventually more of his "beyonders," as Schreiber called them, came through: his mother Katharina, first wife Gertrude, second wife Agnes, and others he did not know appeared on tape and video.

Working with Martin Wenzel, an engineer, Schreiber steadily improved the equipment. Audio came through with the video. One day he heard, "I'm on the video! Call me Kosta!" A picture of Konstantine Raudive took shape and stayed on the TV screen for 137 seconds.

Multidimensional TV Call-In Show

Rainer Holbe, a well-known talk show host on Luxembourg TV, set up a "multidimensional call-in show" to highlight the "beyonders." Schreiber installed his equipment in the studio and demonstrated his work to a fascinated audience on TV network RTL PLUS. Then fellow-guest Ernst Senkowski revealed his experiences with EVP technology. He told of a voice claiming to be a Hamburg steam engineer dead since 1959, who instructed him through the tapes to phone his widow, gave the phone number, and said to tell her the message was for "Little Dwarf." Senkowski did. The wife was stunned, saying it was a very personal pet nickname known only to her and her husband. In another instance a woman's voice remarked on Senkowski's tape, "There's a gold chain around your neck today, not a silver one. I have been observing you." It was true, he said, he usually wore a silver chain. The voices have shown us "wit, personality, memory, and an active mind," says Senkowski. "They are as much 'alive' now as when they had physical bodies."

Broadcaster Holbe, after further investigation in 1987, wrote *Pictures From the Land of the Dead,* covering Schreiber's research and including over two dozen photos. Physicist Senkowski provided an afterward with full details of technical specifications and how-tos. Senkowski's own book was published recently, detailing ongoing research on the phenomenon.

Dr. Walter Uphoff, Professor Emeritus at the University of Colorado, president of New Frontiers Center, and a knowledgeable, bilingual EVP investigator, presented Schreiber's work to the 1988 International Psychotronics Conference in Carrollton, Georgia, attended by scientists from over a dozen countries including the Soviet Union. In Georgia, we watched Schreiber's videos a few times over, saw faces seem to slowly shape themselves together, and heard scientists discuss various technical points they felt argued against the videos being faked.

This is just a small sampling from over three decades of EVP research. What is one to say? The advent of video into the field seems to leave more room for fraud, yet what is so appealing about EVP is that there is no academic establishment; everyone from housewife to priest to physics professor seems to have an equal chance and is self-taught. Anyone with a reasonably open mind, plus a good dose of patience and commitment, can try to prove for himself that memory survives. It's the province of amateurs in the true sense of the word—those who love their chosen field. It is a democratic investigation, and in that sense similar to Rupert Sheldrake's effort to open the doors of research a little, when he invites one and all into competitions to find the best experiments to prove his morphic theory.

As with near-death research, the focus today in EVP is moving to *what* the voices are saying, rather than trying to prove or disprove the phenomena. Transmitted data is surprisingly consistent around the world. The nature of consciousness, memory, and the universe described is similar to channeled material such as that in Jane Roberts's Seth books. The complexity of philosophical and technical data transmitted has steadily increased. Unlike material channeled through human messengers, with "electronic channeling" the message and the medium don't mingle. If the current gaps and nothing comes through, the tape recorder doesn't come up with a message to meet expectations. It's not distorted by ego, philosophical prejudices, or money-making needs. EVP doesn't damage the health of the receiver, as some channeling has done. For more than thirty years, these supposedly impossible voices have been coming through with ever increasing strength, clarity, urgency. Like it or not, it's doubtful the broadcasts could be stopped.

A hundred years ago, Americans strained to hear the first faint voices reaching them over primitive telephones. Do we stand on a similar frontier today, as thousands of people strain to hear through their tape recorders the first transmissions of voices addressing them personally from the "next world"? Has Edison's dream finally been realized? Evidence that at least "something" is happening comes from the intriguing fact that the technical instructions the voices have dictated appear to work—transmissions have steadily improved. Is it to technology—surprise, surprise—that we should look for ultimate proof of the survival of individual memory and consciousness?

Many, like Dylan Thomas, have stormed at death of his father's dying he wrote "Do not go gently into that good night / Rage, rage against the dying of the light." Could we now, with new hi tech EVP, find it more comforting to accompany a loved one through this stage of an ongoing journey?

Otto Koenig did just that in Germany. He took his equipment to the hospital where his friend Anna K. lay dying. She had asked him to record at her deathbed. The doctors and nurses agreed to the experiment. When the oscillograph showed no brain waves, the doctor declared Anna dead. Koenig turned on the recording equipment. Half an hour went by. Then, after another ten minutes, there was a sound. According to published reports, Koenig, the doctor, and nurse clearly heard Anna's voice saying, "I see my body. . . ." To be sure this wasn't a fluke, Koenig tested the voice, just as he had tested all the other voices he received, with ultrasonic voiceprint technology. The before- and after-death prints matched.

Can you really take it with you? Does memory survive without the body? What about people in cryonic suspension or people in comas? Could they too be contacted by EVP? Nothing can stop an idea whose time has come. Nothing can ignite the fireworks of an idea whose time has *not* come in the collective mind. EVP is waiting on the threshhold. The voices aren't going away. They keep on talking out of left field, adding to the possibility that memory survives. Trumpets and drum rolls? Perhaps it is best to stick with the businesslike approach of the theosophical philosopher Alice Bailey, who in 1936 predicted coming electronic contact between "seen and unseen," in *Esoteric Psychology.* "Communication will be eventually set up and reduced to a true science," Bailey predicted. "Death will lose its terrors, and that particular fear will come to an end." Perhaps the day is nearing when we will truly know that memory shall find no end.

24. Remembering Who We Are

"Immemorial memories," authors Louis Pauwels and Jacques Bergier call them. "The persistent memory," author Charles Berlitz calls it. For Rudolf Steiner it was "cosmic memory" and for Richard Heinberg it is murmurings deep in the mind of a lost "golden age." Whatever it's called, hovering just at the rim of human recollection is a haunting, ancient memory of "better days." The murmurings are getting louder, more persistent, as though evoked by hordes of anomalous artifacts that have begun to surface, as though Mnemosyne were stirring up the greatest recollection of them all, memory that could transform the race as surely as memory transforms individual NDEers.

Tracing these elusive wisps in *Memories and Visions of Paradise,* Richard Heinberg uncovered an unusual consistency. In almost every culture on the planet, one encounters myths, legends, and tribal tales of how humankind originated in a world of peace, plenty, and miraculous power. It's the Garden of Eden story, though most accounts speak of a much more sophisticated life than Adam and Eve enjoyed. Eventually, as the stories go, some cataclysmic mistake or failure occurred and humans took a tumble, a big tumble into the struggle and toil of recorded history. Finally, the stories come full circle as one finds—again in nearly every tribe and society on earth—ancient legends or texts detailing a purifying cataclysm to come that will bring the flowering of a new Golden Age. "Much of our civilization's greatest literature and many of its most inspiring social theories and experiments seem to derive their vitality and appeal from these mysterious memories and visions of Paradise," Heinberg says.

Is our collective human remembrance accurate? Was there a Golden Age, was there a Fall, did global catastrophes occur within the range of human memory? "Of all the world's myths, that of a universal deluge must surely be the most persistent and widespread," remarks Francis Hitching. "The idea that a great flood destroyed almost all mankind, or at least a substantial part of it, can be found in virtually every country." For his *The Mysterious World* Hitching scoured old texts, including such venerables as the Indian *Mahabharata* and *Ramayana* and the Mayan Codex to compile a map of eighty-three deluge accounts spanning the globe. Worldwide, accounts conform to the same pattern: a race leader receives warnings of disaster; cosmic disturbances occur, followed by floods; some escape in boats or climb mountains; birds/animals are sent out as "deluge scouts"; eventually groups reach dry land, usually a mountain, and find other survivors; societies slowly rebuild under devastating conditions.

From the memory of myth to the material of science, one finds a record of cataclysmic disaster. For instance, Professor Frank C. Hibben, in *The Lost Americans,* marshals clear evidence that 12 to 14,000 years ago mammals over three-fifths of the earth's land surface were decimated—fast frozen at lightning speed in mid-mouthful. 40 million died in North America. "This death was catastrophic and all-inclusive . . . of such colossal proportions as to be staggering to contemplate," says Hibben. In Alaska "it looks as though the whole world of living animals and plants was suddenly frozen in mid-motion in a grim charade." In the Yukon, "evidence of violence is as obvious as in the horror camps of Germany. Such piles of bodies of animals or men simply do not occur by any ordinary natural means." In Siberia, Soviet scientists found the same devastation, their biggest bit of proof being a huge wooly mammoth iced on the hoof, with a mouthful of violets still clinging to his ancient tusks.

Tangible proof that Gaia has gone through many cataclysmic changes accumulates. To give just a very few examples, as early as 1963 Soviet geologist Dr. M. Klionova reported that rocks 6600 feet under the ocean off the Azores had existed 17,000 years ago in the atmosphere. Beach sand, formed only along shorelines, has been found thousands of feet down in the mid-Atlantic along with the remains of freshwater plants. Off Bimini, explorers continually photograph submerged artifacts, columns, and seeming roads. Shades of Atlantis. On the other side of the earth, George Cronwell states that coal and ancient flora found on Rapa Iti Island in French Polynesia "provide irrefutable testimony that there was a continent on that part of the ocean"—shades of the lost Pacific land of Mu. The Mayan Troano Codex fixes the date of the last cataclysmic breaking up of lands at 9937 B.C. Plato, writing of the final destruction of Atlantis, gives the same date. It's become a safe bet that the old race memory of something godawful happening and of lands being lost is accurate.

Disaster, though, doesn't give the immemorial memories their energy. What persists so are those shadowy, shimmering recollections of a better place and a better way, of a civilized sophistication and ease that we are just beginning to approach. Misplaced concreteness, unconscious longings for the womb or a childhood gone? Perhaps, yet contrary to general belief we are only starting to learn about what life has been up to on this planet of ours. Not very long ago, Westerners, at least, believed the earth was only 4,006 years old; now we mark its age in billions and the appearance of humanoids in millions.

It was only in this century that scholars followed Lord Carnarvon through the door to begin to reclaim the glories that were Egypt. It was only in the last decade that Dr. Stephen Schwartz, in the unprecedented Alexandria Project, combined high tech equipment with highly skilled psychics to finally find the site of the legendary Library of Alexandria, the tomb of Alexander, and remains of the Lighthouse of Pharos, one of the seven wonders of the ancient world. These are the material of known memories. Much stranger relics are showing up, a hodgepodge of cryptic objects that resonate to the immemorial memories of wondrous times lost. "Is modern science catching up with ancient knowledge?" asks respected archeologist Zecharia Sitchin in *Genesis Revisited.*

Remembrance of "Things" Past

The gallery of things that "shouldn't be there" is getting crowded. Anomalies of prehistory and history are popping up at an accelerating clip, perhaps because we now have the technology to find them and understand them. Some of the better known include:

- Two thousand-year-old electric batteries discovered in Baghdad that were used for electroplating and—what else, one wonders. Replicas worked. In Egypt, engravings on tomb walls in Dendera show devices disconcertingly like electrical insulators and electric lights.

- A thousand-year-old gold artifact from a Colombian tomb, thought to be a bird or fish, later found—after extensive calculations by the noted zoologist Ivan Sanderson—to have the attributes of a delta wing jet aircraft like the Swedish SAAB. An ancient model glider was unearthed near the Saqqara pyramid in Egypt. In 1979 in Mysore, India, a prehistoric text was finally translated. It turned out to be on aeronautics (the Vymaanika-Shaastra Aeronautics), which surprised everyone but scholars of ancient Indian texts, which contain hundreds of references to flying machines and their usage.

- A metallic device found by sponge divers off Greece, dating 65 B.C. Derek de Solla Price of the Institute for Advanced Study at Princeton discovered it to be a basic analogue computer designed to short-cut astronomical calculations.

- Fabrics superior to current parachute material found in ancient tombs at Nazca, Peru, along with pottery depicting hot-air balloons in flight, and "burn pits" for the required hot air. Balloon pilots Woodman and Knott successfully flew a replica, Condor I, over Nazca, famous for its mysterious markings—lines and designs of creatures so huge they are only understandable from the air.

- Ancient maps, particularly the famous Piri Reis Map, a 1513 A.D. copy of an older map that accurately charts the coasts of the Americas, mountains of South America, coasts and interior of Antarctica. Some of the topography of Antarctica still under ice was only verified after the maps were discovered.

- Agricultural evidence including the ancient, widespread *seedless*-banana. Today, seedless fruit require genetic engineering.

- Precision building techniques. The forty-square-foot casing stones of the Great Pyramid fit together so neatly that the cracks between them measure less than 1/50 of an inch. The same precision is found in Peruvian ruins; 1/50 of an inch is less than the allowable error in the fitting together of the all important tiles that coat our space shuttle.

- Ground glass lenses dated 8th-century B.C., held in the British Museum.

- Advanced astronomical knowledge found in remote societies. The Dogon tribes of the South Sahara shared their ancient and correct knowledge of the tiny Sirius B star two decades before astronomers finally photographed it in 1970. Ituri pygmies in central Africa know about the moons of Saturn. From ancient Samoa to Japan, from the Navajo nation to pre-Inca Peru, to Berber tribes and Greece, our ancestors seemed fixated on the Pleiades, a speck of a star cluster 500 light years away. All called them the seven sisters, virgins, or goddesses, though only six can be seen with the naked eye. In ancient Britain, Julius Caesar long ago noted Druids who had memorized a 25,000 verse ephemeris giving the planets' placements for hundreds of years.

- Pyramids found worldwide that embody advanced knowledge of geometry, mathematics, astronomy, geography, and perhaps "other" energy spectrums.

- Vast megalithic engineering works like Carnac in Brittany, Newgrange in Ireland, and Stonehenge in England now shown to have had highly sophisticated architects. They share a common sacred geometry, astronomical alignments, and units of measure. Almost all stand near magnetic anomalies or "sacred sites," and are often found to emit forms of radiation and pulsed ultrasound. All are now being studied by serious scientists who postulate a worldwide megalithic grid system, an amplifier, some have reason to think, of cosmic and earth energies.

Like crocuses in the spring, anomalous things are popping up at random across a vast landscape of time to bolster the immemorial memories of a finer heritage than we find in our history books. They witness to an arresting discovery made by Dr. R. A. Schwaller de Lubicz, one of the most interesting Egyptologists of the century. The further back one goes in Egyptian science, medicine, mathematics, and astronomy, he discovered, the more *advanced* they are. Egyptian civilization, de Lubicz concluded, must be the offspring of a prior even more developed culture, one that he associated with legends of Atlantis and the Golden Age. Others see Egypt as the heir to Sumer, a culture on the horizon of history that we have just begun to sight, a culture that seemingly sprang into existence all at once, in full blossom.

Another archaeologist, a veritable new-age Indiana Jones named David Childress, searches all around the earth and under the waters to recapture traces of highly evolved civilizations. One trace, the underwater city of Nan Modal on Pohnpei in the Caroline Islands, covers eleven square miles. Childress is one of the few to explore this vast sunken "City of the Gods." Gifted with the endurance of a triathlete and an encyclopedic mind, he combines local legend, esoteric teaching, and scientific theory to evaluate sites in the round. If you feel any delight in wondering, check his books: *Anti-Gravity and the World Grid,* plus an adventure-filled series, *Lost Cities and Ancient Mysteries of* . . . most known and unknown spots on the planet, for there are dozens and dozens of lost civilizations (see References).

Scuba diving through the watery streets of Nan Modal, Childress discovered petroglyphs (What do they say?) and also came to muse about how the sixty-ton building blocks of the city were put in place when it stood under the sun. Local legend has it that they were "floated" in air from one side of the island to the other. Could they have been "floated," he speculates, by the use of sound frequencies between short radio waves and infrared radiation, causing the crystalized blocks of basalt to lose their weight?

And what of the famous "walking statues" of Easter Island? We often see pictures of a few lonely statues gazing across the empty sea, but Childress emphasizes that there are hundreds of 300 ton statues on Easter Island, some that have been raised vertically to be placed in niches on cliffs. Native memory insists that statues were "walked" to their proper places. Were the walkers an ultratall race that the Soviet Dr. Alexander Kondratev writes of in *Riddles of Three Oceans?* Studying the Rongo-Rongo texts of Easter Island, he found accounts of large people who destroyed their continent in the Pacific and fled to the island, bringing the magic of technology.

Now that we are better able to recognize what is found—the relic is not a religious juju but an analog computer—Gaia's exotic past seems to be surfacing all over. It's coming up inside the psyche too.

Back to the Future

"In Atlantis, when there was the breaking up of the land—came to what was called the Mayan land or what is now Yucatan—the entity was the first to cross the water in the plane or air machine of that period."

With such past-life readings, Edgar Cayce astounded clients in the 30s and 40s. He told hundreds that sealed like a time-release capsule in their memories were recollections of life on a lost continent that once boasted spectacular technological marvels and a supremely harmonious social order. According to Cayce's *Readings,* greed and corruption eventually ate away this mighty civilization. Toward the end, scientists misaligned the megapowerful Atlantean energy generators. Energy run wild plus massive changes in the solar system produced a colossal cataclysm. Foreseeing disaster, Atlanteans sent out colonists in planes, ships, and subs to South America, Egypt, Europe, and America. There, engineers set up installations to help refugees, to re-seed civilization, and store the knowledge and archives of their dying land. Pyramids and megalithic structures were parts of this old planetary system, Cayce said.

Cayce is one of many who have made the story of Atlantis part of our culture; accounts spring from respected texts of old, they gather details in the complex writings of mystics like Rudolf Steiner and Theosophy-founder Helena Blavatsky, and roll right on down through Friday night fright movies. What sort of people does this ubiquitous tale portray? At the very beginning—Atlantis supposedly existed through three long stages—Atlanteans were unisexed, inhabiting more diaphanous bodies than ours. Eventually they settled into male and female, living in sparkling cities of canals and lush gardens, where they enjoyed a golden age of art, science, and education. They had analogs of our technology from lasers to plumbing, phones to TV. Mastery of the life force was theirs, as they perfected genetics, reproduction with cloning, in vitro fertilization, and cosmobiology. In decline, they mingled human and animal cells to hatch horrible hybrids as slaves. They brought agriculture to full promise using sound and telluric energies. Like us, they held ultimate weapons of destruction. (Curiously, the ancient writers of the *Mahabharata* describe what clearly seem to be atomic explosions during great prehistoric wars.)

As the story goes, Atlanteans had much we don't have. Spectacular intelligence and memory was common. Levitation was possible. Psi ability was normal and allowed communication with those in the afterlife and other dimensions. They lived hundreds of years in fine fettle, using sound, color, crystals, electromagnetic fields, and other energies, and treated the subtle matrix body to maintain health. To power their world, they discovered clean energy, free energy which they focused through enormous grids.

Many of these legendary marvels don't sound as far out today as they did when Blavatsky spoke of them in the 1800s and Cayce in the 1930s, before lasers, nuclear power, genetic manipulation. Other "Atlantean" skills beyond the fringe just two decades ago are edging the mainstream: the use of electromagnetics, sound and subtle energies in healing, out-of-body experiences, self-control of states of consciousness, the use of sound in agriculture. We seem to be growing into the legend. In a sense Cayce predicted it. As technological discovery or "recovery" increased, he said, data about Atlantis would start to surface. He cautioned clients that they would encounter situations which resonated with their Atlantean past. Today about 24 million Americans believe in reincarnation and many claim recall of lives in old Atlantis. And we have channelers galore, one of the interesting things about them being how often their teachings agree. Here too there is common talk about triggering of ancient memories, about people encoded long, long ago who will suddenly come into awareness, remem-

ber a divine heritage, and realize the powers of extraordinary ancestors. Interestingly, many channeled voices claim to be from that
faraway star cluster the Pleiades that so captured the ancient world.
(Understandable, according to Navajo legend, for it was from the Pleiades, they said, that humanity descended to earth.) If nothing else
there is a social phenomenon going on.

The memory of myth is rarely literal. The underside of things has
curious ways to catch our attention. Past-life therapists use the technique because it works; similarly, perhaps something is using the Atlantis "technique" on all of us. The truth at the heart of the legend of
Atlantis may be telling us simply that we did not descend only from
troglodytes. Unearthed, it would be an expansive recollection and a
cautionary one. Or is it something else, a memory sleight of hand in
the supposed eternal now. Are these future memories? Is it the story of
an evolutionary seed of Paradise planted at the beginning, growing
into flower? Whatever sort of memory breaks through, all the wonders
won't have been told. As the old legend becomes more commonplace,
the face of a new myth is coming over the horizon—literally, on Mars.

What looks to be a sculptured face, one mile in length, resembling
the Sphinx, was photographed in the Cydonia region of Mars by
NASA's Viking probe. Some of the best minds of the space world have
become involved with the face on Mars. By itself the face would be
striking, what makes it gripping is that it appears to be accompanied
by pyramids and honeycomb buildings. High resolution computer
analysis seems to show that this is an artificial complex, that is, someone built it. The major structures are aligned—just like the megalithic
structures on earth—with the summer and winter solstice sunrise
sightlines. The mathematical ratios are the same as those at earth's
"sacred sights."

It's a face to stir immemorial memories even deeper than those of
lost continents—the persistent idea that the "gods" or man descended
from space. "We were all lost children of the stars," as the poet A. E.
wrote. Space science consultant Richard Hoagland, who's organized
ongoing scientific study of the face, can't resist indulging in a little
speculation too. Eons ago, was Mars a base camp for some star travelers, he wonders, a temporary home while they seeded their race on
earth? Hoagland goes on to marshal enough scholarly clues from ancient Sumerian and Egyptian texts, both from content and etymology,
to fuel anyone's fancy. For instance, *El-Kahir*, the Arabic word for
Cairo, site of earth's most famous pyramid and the Sphinx, means—
Mars. Looking further back to immemorial times, Hoagland writes,

"in these archetypal glimmerings, shadows moving in the mists from a time on earth lost forever to the written word, there is the suggestion . . . of an extraordinary resolution to the ultimate dilemma of finding an image of ourselves . . . on Mars."

All of which has the makings of a myth for our times. "The face is one of the few wild cards in the human deck," anthropologist Richard Grossinger points out. "It has the potential . . . to transform us." Sometime soon, astronauts, or more likely Soviet cosmonauts, will check the face on Mars firsthand. Even if it's just a heap of rocks, perhaps what's important is that an idea has risen on a far horizon. The immemorial memories are unhooking from a geocentric focus and moving outward. If the face is real, earth's human race, like a growing number of individuals, may begin to recover prebirth and birth memories. Either way, as myths go, the face on Mars can help one get off the ground and rise like the ancient hot air balloons over Nazca to a wider perspective. A loftier view might reverse the typical response of those who hear of the face. "Oh, you mean *they* came down and pulled us out of the mud." Instead of identifying with the lesser part of the equation, we might start to think, *"We* came down."

25. Opening the Universal Palace of Memory

"Humanity is about to blow its amnesia circuits!" Of all the milling millennial predictions, that idea borrowed from the ancient Mayans may be closest to the mark. Mayan mathematicians, astrologers, and astronomers were said to possess a high degree of knowledge about the universe. Their buildings, like the Yucatan stepped pyramid El Castillo, still an accurate solar calendar and clock, prove the precision of their calculations. Supposedly, these ancient scientists calculated into the future—and concluded that a memory revolution would erupt right now.

Why now? Because, says Mayan scholar Jose Arguelles, the Mayans figured cycles, and determined that by our era humanity's evolutionary pattern would be out of sync and in need of a memory correction. They foresaw a highly toxic society, he reports, people sickened within and without and the earth in trouble, which sounds familiar. In response, people "will unlock ever deeper levels of memory." We will begin to remember who we are, where we came from, how we got here, and why. Supposedly widespread recall will culminate in 2012—or so Arguelles hopes. Without the correction, no next phase of evolution is predicted. Recall or be recalled? It's a curious prediction that grows more tantalizing. People are re-membering, waking from long cultural amnesia all around the earth.

When memory magus Giulio Camillo stretched awake, a host of characters laden with information came awake too, greeting each other in the long shadows of nuance and corridors of relationship that filled his memory palace. When we started to come awake in our five-year journey through Mnemosyne's domain, as we sifted leading-edge and sometimes underground explorations of hundreds of researchers, the walls blew out of the old memory palace. We found memory sprung from its compartments, memory informing the human body, unbounded by time and space, a unifying and transformative power: memory at the very center of the long-heralded consciousness revolution. Memory at the center isn't a new idea.

"Life is that property of matter whereby it can remember—matter which can remember is living," philosopher Samuel Butler wrote in the 1870s. A few years later, Rupert Sheldrake points out, Butler went further: "I can conceive of no matter which is not able to remember a little. . . ." This 19th-century observation has come into 21st-century focus. What appears is a vision of the universe closer to the heart than the old mechanistic picture. What is revealing itself is a companion closer to us than our breath. Just in time, it seems, for as Arguelles says, "When the Light hits, the Dark gets tough."

Memory—A Companion for Tough Times

Memory has unique powers to help us find our way through tough times. Continuity and self-reliance are the stabilizing gifts of Mnemosyne. At the same time, her creative juices can lead us down avenues of change to shape the new that will rise from the old.

Keys to quicken learning, strengthen memory, turn subliminal memory and the vivid powers of imagination into positive channels, are available in the master memory systems. Gingko, L-glutamine, dozens of substances hold promise of greater lucidity for young and old. We have only begun to plug in mind machines, the tech some believe will "mark the most important turning point in the evolution of the planet." And if Dr. Ernest Rossi is right, understanding how state dependent memory weaves the substance of our lives can begin to spring us from our ills. As we finally draw on our innate brightness, as we re-member, the sense strengthens that we can run our lives from the inside, rather than being run off our feet by the outside.

The memory revolution has brought a deep sense of belonging and connection to some. Contemplating her near-death experience, Patricia Bahr says, "We are headed toward a chance for a quantum leap in consciousness where all beings will remember who they really are and be able to communicate at a level where we'll know the truth of another. . . ." With panoramic memory, NDEers become aware of how closely they are enmeshed with the whole of life, how intricately bound to others. Victimization of others can be seen as victimization of self.

They wake up to something else too. Psychologist Richard Chamberlain, who started from the opposite end of the spectrum with prebirth memory, says it nicely. "The fact that even the most advanced memory activities can take place without benefit of body or brain means that memory is our faithful and constant companion on a long journey." A very long journey. As viewpoints expand and data mounts not just from NDEers but from many experiencing the memory revolution, the numbers grow of those who have gained the greatest sense of stability one can have. Life is a continuum, they think, death is not a dead end.

Yet, we all know that the idea of nonphysical cause—or just the nonphysical—still raises the snicker effect in sections of the intelligentsia and the media. Though more thinkers are lining up with Sheldrake, though seventy years of intensive research has not found the site of memory storage in the brain, orthodoxy can not look at his idea that your brain is analogous to a TV receiving set, a tuning device to pick up memory stored beyond it in a nonphysical dimension.

Chamberlain takes aim at overpreoccupation with the physical parameters of the brain and fragmented research. "This scientific amnesia for birth, womb, and past-life memory—one of the sins of science—has delayed discovery of who we really are," he contends. If he's right, when that discovery is made will we see the "cleansing" predicted by all the old myths? Les miserables, newly awakened, aren't exactly storming through the memory palace tumbling the old and established. That various foundations are shaky, however, is apparent.

To historian Morris Berman "society has reached the limits of its old-paradigm learning, and much of it now is in the midst of the social analogue of either madness or creativity—that is re-creation." The way out of the wasteland, he says in The Reenchantment of the World, lies in recovering what humanity has forgotten or repressed, and in the rediscovery of interconnectedness—in our terms, in the gathering tide of remembering and re-membering.

That we verge on some sort of revolution—call it consciousness or memory—seems likely. The well-known physician-writer Brugh Joy foresees "a revolution of the most astonishing proportions. . . . I sense the approach of a psychological earthquake the magnitude of which has not been experienced in the human awareness for millennia. . . ."

Swiss Sophrologist Dr. Raymond Abrezol says it is not revolution but, literally, "re-evolution" coming. British psychologist Peter Russell, author of The Global Brain, believes that "humanity could be on the threshold of an evolutionary leap, a leap that could occur in a flash of evolutionary time, a leap such as occurs only once in a billion years."

"It is a revolution. Make no mistake about that," NDEer Phyllis Atwater writes. "It is a revolution of consciousness. And it is truly global. . . . It is happening, with or without anyone's permission. Some see this revolution as the reemergence of divinity. . . ."

Teilhard de Chardin, perhaps the first in this century to point to this revolution in the making, noted that "the consciousness of each of us is evolution looking at itself and reflecting upon itself." That would seem to be the leap: from here on, evolution is not automatic but conscious. As Arthur Young, another deep student of evolution contends, choice has entered the equation, our choice. Our "faithful companion" might do a lot to inform that choice.

Revolution is a hot word. In tough times, it may be better to use the cooler terms. We're changing paradigms, worldviews, we're told. That's where all the friction comes from, as the new paradigm emerges, the old resists. It's a resistance with a familiar outline; the body politic seems ridden by "state" bound memories in more ways than one. The microcosm reflects the macrocosm, the memory magi taught, and many of the insights of memory research could be used to ease change and allow new, healthy growth in the group as well as the individual.

What if we looked at our dogmas, from state to education, medicine to conflict resolution, through the widening perspective of state dependent memory? What new solutions, what new avenues of transformation might open? And there is the fine art of creating future memories. Future memories, better memories can be shaped, imagined, energized for just about anything—groups, institutions, the earth herself. These are only two of many possibilities. If we come to see that memory is inherent in nature, Sheldrake believes, new ways of thinking will emerge "better adapted to life in a world that is living in the presence of the past—and is also living in the presence of the future, and open to continuing creation."

Memory at the Center of a New Paradigm

Personal experience, research, bits of data from everywhere are adding new facets to our picture of memory. Those involved would probably agree with most of the following: One's being and consciousness is within a multidimensional, all-embracing, all-unifying mneumonic field. Memory shapes physical forms and is intimately involved with sickness and health. Memory lives outside of our dimensions and there is no death. Death is a change of frequency in the memory field. One's true source and power lies beyond the physical realm. Through the memory field, one is linked with all people, animals, plants, earth, the universe itself. Various repressed human abilities like higher sense perception—telepathy, clairvoyance, precognition—function through the memory field. Finally, everything one does is "remembered," which is why Edgar Cayce insisted, "karma is memory." The new view of memory raises an intriguing question. Could the all-embracing mneumonic field turn out to be the long-sought unifier that brings together again physics and metaphysics, intellect and spirit, self and nature?

We searched around for a myth of Mnemosyne and finally found at least the crosscultural seeds of one in the ancient Mayan story. In one particular, it has a surprisingly contemporary ring. The Mayans saw memory comprised of basic patterns of resonance. In his *The Mayan Factor*, Arguelles reports that they thought these resonant patterns formed a huge memory circuit moving like a great horizontal numeral 8, connecting past, present, and future. To Arguelles, this is an explanation of synchronicity and perhaps an opening to time travel. And an opening to something more splendid, if we come to understand memory as a central unifying pattern of resonance, Arguelles predicts. "Through this knowledge, rung as the sonorous tones of collective synchronization, the palace of universal memory will open."

The Mayans had predicted a jolt of galactic energy would coincide with the opening of universal memory. Interestingly, a Japanese satellite has recently detected a rare quasar burst of energy in our galaxy which scientists say is equal to a million years of sunlight.

The old memory palace has turned into something truly vast, dynamic, ever unfolding—which sounds a lot like life itself. And life should be worth living. Over and over, as we sorted through very disparate memory research, we came upon the same thing, an insistence on the necessary emergence now of what Chris Griscom calls "a new frequency," what many others call bliss, call joy. With a note of joy, we might alter the lyrics of poet Leonard Cohen just a bit, to sing out: Memory is alive. Memory never dies. Magic is alive!

Appendix A—Three Steps to Superlearning

How to Make Your Course

1. If you're working by yourself, put the key material you want to embed in your memory on tape:

Organize your data into four-second fragments.

When recording repeat each fragment three times.

If you wish, follow a cycle of intonations for the three—speak normally, then softly, confidentially, then commandingly! Keep repeating the cycle.

Pace your reading. Speak for four seconds, be silent four seconds, speak four seconds, be silent, and so on.

To keep your timing right, buy a timer tape or make your own. For example, click a pencil against a table every four seconds. You can listen to this with earphones if you don't want the click on your memory tape.

Keep sessions about eighteen to twenty minutes long.

2. The only other thing you need is the special music. A number of commercial tapes have been specifically sequenced for Superlearning. Check Resources (p. 373).

Or, you can make your own. Use the largo movements of baroque compositions, preferably in 4/4 time, played at around sixty beats per minute. You'll have to listen to various renditions because different conductors lead the same pieces in varied tempos.

Put together about twenty minutes of slow baroque music, finish with two to three minutes of upbeat, fast baroque music.

How To Superlearn

3. Before beginning your memory session, relax your body and calm your mind. Warm yourself up with some positive suggestions. Reexperience for a moment a time when you were a grand success. (For how-to help, see page 48.)

The first time through, silently read the material along with the memory tape.

Try to hold your breath when something is said, and breathe out and in during the pauses. If this is distracting, just breathe rhythmically.

Once through the lesson, close your eyes and relax. Play the same lesson again, but this time backed by the special Superlearning music on a second player.

Keep sessions short in the beginning. Remember that the effect snowballs.

This is a very bare-bones description. For a much better discussion of the system, including such tricks of the trade as to how much data will fit in a lesson, or how to learn languages and longer material, self-testing, etc., see the *Superlearning* book or materials in Resources (pages 373-375).

Appendix B—Memory Shortcuts

To Remember Random Lists

To remember long lists of things, "chunk" them, separate them into smaller groups. 1194827691 looks formidable. (119) 482-7691 doesn't. A shopping list of broccoli, butter, toothpicks, cheese, apples, cocktail napkins, milk, lettuce, paper towels, and onions is easier to remember in sets: broccoli, lettuce, onions, apples; milk, butter, cheese; toothpicks, paper towels, cocktail napkins. You can devise a variety of ways to group disparate objects.

Another way to remember random things is to make a vivid cartoon. Say your chores are: fix watch, get birdseed, pick up dress at cleaners, buy hotdogs, go to Post Office, find a window cleaner. A giant hotdog in a postman's cap hunches behind the wheel of a mail truck, speeding, checking his huge pocketwatch over and over, anxious to get the mail through on time. Hotdog takes his eyes from the road once too often, smashes into a cleaning shop and catapults out of the truck into the racks of clothes. Stuffed in your red dress, he runs out of the shop, the cleaner in close pursuit. In desperation, Hotdog hops a passing canary, a giant bright yellow canary, and they zoom up the avenue to disappear into the wide open window of a tall apartment house. . . .

This sort of story list can easily go on and on. The key is to be really "loony tunes," make it bizarre, unexpected, violent, silly. Or if you have a mind to, use the sort of images our most erudite ancestors swore by—they've been called "naughty," actually many standard memory images were downright scatological and pornographic.

To Remember Numbers

It may be worth your time to concoct your own images to go with the numbers one to ten. These can be used to recall things in order or as small cartoon loops to remember numbers. A common approach is to use objects that rhyme—one-ton, two-shoe, three-tree. Choose concrete objects you can easily visualize. Learning expert Tony Buzon suggests using objects that look like the numeral: 1 = a pen, 2 = the curving neck of swan. You'll do best if you seek out your own. Choose your system and stick with it.

Another approach is to assign images of people you know to numbers—perhaps a family hierarchy: grandpa, grandma, mother, father, siblings, cousins. You can also order objects or facts on your own body. Number one is atop your head, two on your forehead, and so on.

Remembering Phone Numbers

If you're nuts for anagrams, try a maneuver that amuses some memory mavens. Write out the three letters that accompany each number on the phone. Choosing one letter from each triad in order, try to spell a word. Digits 1 and 0 have no letters so may be assigned Q and Z. Scanning a fairly long address book, we only found one number, 467-7437, that readily fell into a "word"—horsies.

It's much easier to look at the letters and make up a sentence, preferably one that relates to the owner of the phone. For instance, a friend owns two small dogs. Her number, 532-7982, readily turns into *L*ittle *d*ogs *2, s*he *w*alks *t*hem *b*oth. Most aren't that neat, but bizarre phrases are memorable. Digits 1 and 0 can now also be assigned the words yes or no, or symbols like ?, =, +.

If you're one of the few people who are serious about memorizing many long strings of numbers, use an alphabet code. An easy one is to assign different consonants to numbers zero through nine. Let's say you have a serial number that translates in your system to the consonants: KTSLRMTBKS. Vowels are free. What phrases can you make? *K*ats *l*ure *m*e *t*o *b*oo*k*s. Or, *K*ate's *a*larm *a*t *b*i*k*s. Or lots of other phrases. With a little practice one can become a whiz and astonish friends by rattling off long chains of numbers.

Remembering Names

If you genuinely want to remember everyone's name, pay attention, become interested in the person, take time to shake hands, and repeat the name aloud. If that's boring, make it a game, see how many creative, crazy associations you can make.

If a stranger has the same name as a friend, a favorite celebrity, even a brand name product, use it as a hook, imagine them interacting.

Some names—Rosie, Bill, Peg, Woods, Bush, Red-ford—have obvious images. Others like Candace take a little creative touch to turn into a can full of aces.

You can use foreign words. A woman named Rue might conjure a Parisian street or Dr. Weissberg a white mountain.

Generally one has to make a small cartoon. Take names in this book, for instance—the memory magus Metrodorus brings to mind an image of a friend named Doris swaying on the subway. Biologist Glen Rein can be imagined sitting in a green, leafy glen swigging Rhine wine from a huge goblet decorated with a colorful picture of the Rhine. What about Rupert Sheldrake? If you don't know someone named Rupert or even Rue, how about a glittering Indian rupee sitting in the sand beside a beautiful shell that's just been uncovered by a large drake. Or Deepak Chopra?—a man with very deep pack on his back chopping up a Egyptian sun disc of Ra. Reaching? Yes, but the energy you expend looking for an association helps fix the name. All you really need is a clue or two to later prime the memory pump.

And of course it helps to fit the name to the person. Most memory experts suggest that you adopt the eye of a caricaturist and focus on the person's most prominent features, usually on the face—bushy brows, knifelike nose, rosebud lips. Relate one or more to your cartoon name. Usually, though, by the time you've imaged the name, you have the face pretty well in mind.

Remembering Facts

In 1492, Columbus sailed the ocean blue. Since long before 1492, students have reached to rhyme and doggerel to fix facts in mind. Make up rhymes, set facts to familiar tunes. Following "the foot bone connected to the shin bone" principle, one of the authors hummed her way through college biology with such delights as human hormones set to "How Dry I Am." If you talk with a doctor about mnemotechnics, odds are that this pillar of society will grin and say, "On old Olympus towering top, a fat assed German vaults and hops." As generations of medical students know, the first letter of each word recalls the twelve cranial nerves.

In her *Active Learning: Rappin' and Rhymin',* Rosella Wallace gives you the right answer when someone asks what states border the Great Lakes. Just say, "I'm no wimp!" In other words, Illinois, Michigan/ New York, Ohio/ Wisconsin, Illinois, Minnesota, Pennsylvania. Wallace's book is chock full of mnemotechnic quickies. How about the two smallest countries in the world? Well, they are "very minute": Vatican City and Monaco.

For complex subjects, one has to blossom, at least a little, into classical mnemotechnics as described in Chapter 13. Set story images of what you need to remember in your house—bathrooms, kitchen, and garage are particularly useful as they have a wealth of objects to hang images on. Organize and separate your subjects. Each room at home can hold an aspect of biochemistry. Familiar locations around your neighborhood: trees, parks, houses, shops, bus stops can be sites for the facts of Chinese history. We all have a multitude of organizing sites if we think about it—familiar shops, church, offices, homes of relatives and friends, schools, camps, clubs, playgrounds of childhood.

Automatic Memory

Make the most of habit. For instance, always drop house keys and car keys in the same place. Develop "unthinking" habits: designate a place near the door where you always place what is to go with you in the morning; always return your flashlight, checkbook, current tax papers to the same drawer. Hook reminders to deeply ingrained activity—brushing your teeth reminds you, "Who do I have to talk with or phone today." After-breakfast coffee means take your vitamins.

Check the index for the many memory boosters in this book from imagery streaming to sense cues and special music. When all is said and done, perhaps what can most add sparkle to your memory is to use it. Trust it. Start with small things. Leave your list home and take your images to the supermarket. Ask your memory to remind you to phone Aunt Betty on Saturday—you may have to hook it to a Saturday activity. Or ask your memory to wake you at seven-thirty tomorrow. The more interested you are, the more you wonder and question, the more you delight in the ever changing miracle of life, the stronger your memory will become.

Chapter 1

Resources and References

You can find ongoing information about a great many topics covered in this book from these highly recommended sources:

Association for Research & Enlightenment, Box 595, Virginia Beach, VA 23451. (804) 428-3588. Founded by Edgar Cayce, membership $30, introductory $15 for 9 months, includes magazine, membership projects, borrowing *Readings,* bookstore catalog, plus data on regional groups across the United States and abroad, conferences. Outstanding library in Virginia Beach, VA.

Association for Transpersonal Psychology, Box 3049, Stanford, CA 94309. (415) 327-2066. Membership $65, includes newsletter and biannual journal.

Brain/Mind Bulletin, Box 42211, Los Angeles, CA 90042. Monthly, $35. (800) 533-mind. Founded by writer Marilyn Ferguson, also offers excellent theme packs.

Institute of Noetic Sciences, Box 909, Sausalito, CA 94966. (800) 525-7985. Founded by astronaut Edgar Mitchell, membership $35, includes journal, newsletter, special new-science reports, data on conferences and travel programs.

The Quest: A Quarterly Journal of Philosophy, Science, Religion & the Arts. Box 270, Wheaton, IL 60189. (708) 665-0230. Theosophical publishing, quarterly $14. Also data on borrowing metaphysical books by mail.

Chapters 2 and 3

Resources

Superlearning Inc. 450 Seventh Ave., Suite 500, New York, NY 10123. (212) 279-8450. Free Catalog. Mail order tapes and materials produced under the direction of Ostrander and Schroeder. *Superlearning.*

Hardcover: $14.95. Tape 101: Relaxation/concentration exercises plus 20 minutes special Superlearning baroque music, $14.

Tape 102: How-to guide to producing your own Superlearning course, $10.95.

Tape 103: All-music tape, special slow baroque music to speed learning, boost memory, $14.

Learn How To Learn: Taped "workshop" and booklet by Ostrander and Schroeder, $9.95.

SPECIAL: Order Tapes 101 & 103 for $27.95 and receive *free Superlearning* book. Ship/Hand. $3 first item, $.75 per each additional.

Also available: Superlearning foreign language phrases, math review, children's tapes. Superlearning subliminals and related material. Send for free information.

In Canada: Superlearning tapes and books from Ostrander Associates, 1290 W. 11 Ave., Suite 105, Vancouver, BC, Canada V6H 1K5. (604) 736-5287.

The Society for Accelerative Learning & Teaching (SALT), 3028 Emerson Ave. S., Minneapolis, MN 55408. Professional society, quarterly journal, newsletter, international conferences, directory, networking.

Abtracts for articles in *Journal SALT* beginning 1976 can be accessed via the national ERIC computer database. Printed hard copy can be ordered by ERIC number from Center for Applied Linguistics, 3520 Prospect St. NW, Washington DC 20007.

Dr. Rosella Wallace, Box 57, Anchor Point, AK 99556. Consulting, teacher training, workshops.

Also available: *Active Learning: Rappin' & Rhymin',* book and tape $9.95 each plus $2.50 Ship/Hand. Upbeat Publishing, P.O. Box 70, Anchor Point, AK 99556.

Brian Hamilton, CSW, 460 West 24 St. Suite 1C, New York, NY 10011. (212) 807-8810. Superlearning workshops for students and teacher training, some one-on-one with therapeutic emphasis. Also teaches support network.

Bruce Tickell Taylor, Accelerative Tutoring & Transformations Institute, 45350 Ukiah St., Mendocino, CA 954670. (707) 937-4591. Lectures, accelerative learning plans, international networking.

Dr. Donald Schuster's books: Research into Mind, Box 8987 Welch Station, Ames, IA 50010. Powerlearning Systems, Dr. Don Lofland,

638 Escalona Dr., Santa Cruz, CA 95060. Language, business, student and teacher training.

Lorne Cook, Sound Learning Systems, 32 Hedgewood Dr., Unionville, Ontario, Canada L3R 676. (416) 477-3816. Workshops for teachers and students of all ages, distribution of Superlearning materials.

Mankind Research Unlimited, Inc., Dr. Carl Schleicher, President, 1350 Apple Ave. Silver Spring, MD 20910. (301) 587-8686. Accelerated learning materials including those for the blind and for literacy.

Karen Sands, Futureworks, 63 Greene St. Suite 205, New York, NY 10012. (212) 431-5590. Master trainer for business and educators, consultant in continuous improvement and marketing.

Al Boothby, 1254 Sunland Vista, Sacramento, CA 95631. Education consultant, teaching, some one-on-one counseling.

International Language Services, Inc., 17041 Prairie Lane, Minneapolis, MN 55346. (612) 934-5678. Accelerated language training and language learning trips abroad.

Dr. W. Jane Bancroft, University of Toronto, Scarborough College, West Hill, Ontario, Canada MIC 1A4. International consultant on Superlearning. Lectures.

References

Altorfer, Otto. "Mobilizing 'Reserve Energy' at Work: a Composite of Common Learning Elements." *Journal of the Society for Accelerative Learning and Teaching (SALT)*, Vol. 10, No. 4.

Croucher, Charles and Hope. "Accelerated Learning in Japanese." *Incorporated Linguist*, 1981.

Dineen, Janice. "Superlearning: Relaxation, Baroque music key to new teaching." *The Toronto Star*, Nov. 22, 1988.

Erskine, Ron. "A Suggestopedic Math Project Using Nine Learning Disabled Students." *Journal SALT*, Vol. 11, No. 4.

Hallmark, C.L. "Superlearning Presentation." *OF0704 AT&T*, 1990.

Hand, James, and Stein, Barbara. "The Brain & Accelerative Learning, Part III." *Journal SALT*, Vol. 11, No. 4.

Lozanov, Georgi. *Suggestology and Outlines of Suggestopedy.* New York: Gordon and Breach, 1978.

———. "Problems of Suggestology." *Proceedings of the First International Conference on Suggestology,* Sophia, 1971.

Ostrander, Sheila, and Schroeder, Lynn. *Superlearning.* New York: Delacorte, 1979; Delta, 1981.

———. eds. *The ESP Papers: Scientists Speak Out from Behind the Iron Curtain.* New York, Bantam, 1976.

———. *Learn How To Learn.* Los Angeles: Audio Renaissance, 1990. Tape.

Prichard, Allyn. "College Developmental Mathematics." *Journal SALT,* Vol. 11, No. 3.

———; Schuster, D.; Gensch, J. "Applying SALT to Fifth Grade Reading Instruction." *Journal SALT,* Vol. 5, No. 1.

———, and Taylor, Jean. *Accelerating Learning: The Use of Suggestion in the Classroom.* Novato, CA: Academic Therapy Press, 1980.

———. "Adapting the Lozanov Method for Remedial Reading Instruction. *Journal SALT,* Vol. 1, No. 2.

Render, Gary, and Anderson, Lynn. "Superlearning & Retention." *Journal SALT,* Vol. 11, No. 3.

Schuster, Donald. "Using Accelerative Learning in a Large University Class for Teaching Pascal Computer Language." *Journal SALT,* Vol. 11, No. 4.

Schuster, D.H., and Gritton, C.E. *Suggestive Accelerative Learning Techniques.* New York: Gordon & Breach, 1986.

———, and Schuster, Locky. "Educating the Children of Changing Cultures." *Journal SALT,* Vol. 13, No. 1.

Seki, Hideo. "Alpha Brain Wave Formation by Sine Wave Stereo Sounds." *Journal SALT,* Vol. 13, No. 3.

———. "Japanese Language & SALT." *Journal SALT,* Vol. 12, No. 3/4.

———. "Application of SALT Method to a Large Number of Students." *Journal SALT,* Vol. 6, No. 4.

Taylor, Bruce T. "An Attempt to Transform International Education." *Journal SALT,* Vol. 11, No. 4.

————. "Low Budget Introduction of Elementary Accelerative Mathematics." *Journal SALT,* Vol. 9, No. 2.

Walker, Ann. "Implementing Whole-Brain Methods for Reading Instruction." *Journal SALT,* Vol. 13, No. 3.

Wallace, Rosella. *Active Learning: Rappin' and Rhymin'.* Anchor Point, Alaska: Upbeat Publishing, 1990.

Chapter 4

References

Bower, G.H. "Mood & Memory." *American Psychologist,* Vol. 36, 1981.

————, and Hilgard, E.R. *Theories of Learning.* New York: Prentice-Hall, 1981.

"Emotional Quality of Memory Can Be Altered by Changing Facial Expression." *Brain/Mind Bulletin,* Feb. 14, 1983.

Erickson, Milton, and Rossi, Ernest. *The Collected Papers of Milton H. Erickson on Hypnosis.* New York: Irvington, 1980.

Fisher, R. "Arousal-Statebound Recall of Experience." *Diseases of the Nervous System,* Vol. 32, 1971.

Laird, James; Wagner, John, et al. "Remembering What You Feel: Effect of Emotion in Memory." *Journal of Personality and Social Psychology,* Vol. 42:646, 1982.

"Memory: It Seems a Whiff of Chocolate Helps." *New York Times,* July 10, 1990. See also: *Journal of Experimental Psychology: Learning, Memory and Cognition.* July 1990.

Rossi, Ernest. *The Psychology of Mind-Body Healing.* New York: W.W. Norton, 1986.

Sheldrake, Rupert. *The Presence of the Past.* New York: Times Books, 1988.

————. *A New Science of Life: The Hypothesis of Formative Causation.* London: Blond, 1985.

————, and Bohm, D. "Morphogenetic Fields and the Implicate Order." *ReVision,* No. 5. 1982.

Chapter 5

Resources

Progressive Awareness Research Inc., Box 12419, Las Vegas, NV 89112. Eldon Taylor's firm, diverse research studies in subliminal perception and special experimental programs. Also at the same address: The International Society of Peripheral Learning Specialists. Professional and corporate membership. Newsletter, research review.

References

Antel, M. "The effect of subliminal activation of sexual and aggressive drive derivatives on literary creativity." *Dissertation Abstracts International,* (Univ. microfilms No. 70-03033). Vol. 30, 1969.

Ariam, Sima and Siller, Jerome. "Effects of subliminal oneness stimuli in Hebrew on academic performance of Israeli high-school students: Further evidence on the adaptation-enhancing effects of symbiotic fantasies in another culture using another language." *Journal of Abnormal Psychology,* Vol. 91 (5), 1982.

Barratt, P.E.H., and Herd, J.M. "Subliminal conditioning of the alpha rhythm." *Australia Journal of Psychology,* Vol. 16, 1964.

Becker, H.C., and Charbonnet, K.D. "Applications of subliminal video and audio stimuli in therapeutic, educational, industrial and commercial settings." Eighth Annual Northeast Bioengineering Conference, M.I.T., 1980.

————, and Glanzer, N.H. "Subliminal communication: Advances in audiovisual engineering applications for behavior therapy and education." *Proceedings of the 1978 Institute of Electrical and Electronics Engineering, Region 3 Conference,* 1978.

Black, R.W., and Bevan, W. "The Effect of subliminal shock upon the judged intensity of weak shock." *American Journal of Psychology*, Vol. 73, 1960.

Bryant-Tuckett, Rose, and Silverman, Lloyd. "Effects of the Subliminal Stimulation of Symbiotic Fantasies on the Academic Performance of Emotionally Handicapped Students." *Journal of Counseling Psychology*, Vol. 31, 1984.

Cheek, David. "Unconscious Perception of Meaningful Sounds during Surgical Anesthesia as Revealed under Hypnosis." *Journal of Clinical Hypnosis*, Vol. 1:101, 1959.

Cook, H. "Effects of subliminal symbiotic gratification and the magic of believing on achievement." *Psychoanalytic Psychology*, Vol. 2(4), 1985.

Cuperfail, R. and Clarke, T. Keith. "A New Perspective of Subliminal Perception." *Journal of Advertising*, Vol. 14, No. 1.

Dixon, Norman, F. "The conscious-unconscious interface: Contributions to an understanding." *Archiv Fur Psychologies*, Vol. 135 (1), 1983.

———. *Preconscious Processing*. New York: Wiley, 1981.

———. "Subliminal perception and parapsychology: Points of contact." *Parapsychology Review*, Vol. 10 (3), 1979.

———. *Subliminal Perception: The Nature of a Controversy*. London: McGraw-Hill, 1971.

Flanagan, Patrick. "The Neurophone, Principles of Operation." Novato, CA: *Flanagan Research*, 1984.

Goldstein, M.J., and Davis, D. "The impact of stimuli registering outside of awareness upon personal preferences." *Journal of Personality*, Vol. 29, 1961.

Goleman, Daniel. "Research Probes What the Mind Senses Unaware." *New York Times*, Aug. 14, 1990.

Hayden, Brian, and Silverstein, Robert. "The effects of tachistoscopic oedipal stimulation on competitive dart throwing." *Psychological Research Bulletin*, Lund University, Vol. 23 (1), 1983.

Kazhinsky, B.B., *Biological Radio Communication.* Springfield, VA: Clearinghouse for Federal Scientific and Technological Information, AD 415-676, April 1963.

Key, Wilson. *The Clam Plate Orgy.* New York: Signet, 1981.

––––––. *Media Sexploitation.* New York: Signet, 1978.

––––––. *Subliminal Seduction.* New York: Signet, 1974.

McGinley, L. "Uncle Sam believes message about mom helps calm nerves." *Wall Street Journal,* Jan. 1, 1986.

Morrison, Andrew P. "Reflections on 'Unconscious oneness fantasies.'" *International Forum for Psychoanalysis,* Vol. 1 (2), 1984.

Packard, V. *The Hidden Persuaders.* New York: Affiliated Publishers, 1957.

Palmatier, J.F., and Bornstein, P.H. "Effects of subliminal stimulation of symbiotic merging fantasies on behavioral treatment of smokers." *Journal of Nervous and Mental Disease,* Vol. 168, 1980.

Parker, Kenneth A. "Effects of subliminal symbiotic stimulation on academic performance: Further evidence on the adaptation-enhancing effect of oneness fantasies." *Journal of Counseling Psychology,* Vol. 29 (1), 1982.

"Recent Studies Show Strong Role For Unconscious In Everyday Life." *Brain/Mind Bulletin,* March 5, 1984.

Romberg, L. *Workings of Your Mind.* Burlington: Audio Cybernetics, 1973.

Shevrin, H. "Evoked potential evidence for unconscious mental processes: a review of the literature." *International Symposium on the Unconscious,* Tbilisi, USSR, 1979.

Shurtman, Robert, et al. "On the activation of symbiotic gratification fantasies as an aid in the treatment of alcoholics." *International Journal of the Addictions,* Vol. 17 (7), 1982.

Silverman, L.H. "A comprehensive report of studies using the subliminal psychodynamic activation method." *Psychological Research Bulletin,* Lund University, Vol. 20 (3), 1980.

Silverman, L.H., and Candell, P. "On the relationship between aggressive activation, symbiotic merging, intactness of body boundaries and manifest pathology in schizophrenics." *Journal of Nervous Mental Disease,* Vol. 150, 1970.

Silverman, L.H.; Klinger, H.; Lustbader, L.; Farrel, J.; Martin, A. "The effects of subliminal drive stimulation on the speech of stutterers." *Journal of Nervous Mental Disease,* Vol. 155, 1972.

Silverman, L.H.; Lachmann, Frank M.; Milich, Robert H. "Unconscious oneness fantasies: Experimental findings and implications for treatment." *International Forum for Psychoanalysis,* Vol. 1 (2), 1984.

Silverman, L.H., et al. "Effect of subliminal stimulation of symbiotic fantasies on behavior modification treatment of obesity." *Journal of Consulting Clinical Psychology,* Vol. 46 (3), 1978.

"Subliminal messages: Subtle Crime Stoppers." *Chain Store Age,* July 1986.

Taylor, Eldon. *Subliminal Learning, An Eclectic Approach.* Salt Lake City: Just Another Reality Publishing, 1988.

———. *Subliminal Technology.* Salt Lake City: Just Another Reality Publishing, 1987.

———. *Subliminal Communication.* Salt Lake City: Just Another Reality Publishing, 1986.

Tharp, Paul. "Shopping Will Get Homier Feel." *New York Post,* Feb. 27, 1990.

Tyrer, P., et al. "Treatment of agoraphobia by subliminal and supraliminal exposure to phobic cine film." *The Lancet,* Feb. 18, 1978.

"Unconscious Interpretation Precedes Seeing." *Brain/Mind Bulletin,* March 15, 1976.

Westerlundh, Bert. "The motives of defence: Percept-genetic studies: I. Shame." *Psychological Research Bulletin,* Lund University, Vol. 23 (7), 1983.

Zuckerman, S.G. "An experimental study of underachievement: The effects of subliminal merging and success-related stimuli on the academic performance of bright underachieving high school students." *Dissertation Abstracts International,* Vol. 41 (12-B), 1981.

Chapter 6

Resources

Doe Lang, Charismedia, 610 West End Ave. New York, NY 10024. (212) 362-6808. Consultant public speaking, speech training, charismatic presentation. Tapes and book; also available from Superlearning Inc. see p. 373.

Foundation for Mind Research, and The Mystery School, Box 3300, Pomona, NY 10970. Directed by Dr. Jean Houston, training in human development and spiritual studies.

Mead Institute, 325 W. 101 St., New York, NY 10025. (212) 666-5036. Founded by Dr. Elaine de Beauport. Workshops, training in triune brain and multiple intelligence.

References

Abrezol, Raymond. *Adventuring With The Brain.* New York: Superlearning Inc. 1987. Tape.

"Breath technique selectively activates hemispheres." *Brain/Mind Bulletin,* Vol. 13, No. 4, Jan. 1988; also see: *Brain/Mind Bulletin,* Vol. 4, No. 17 and *Science,* 204:1326.

Dotto, Lydia. "REM Sleep: 40 Winks Are Worth Remembering." *The Globe & Mail,* March 24, 1990.

de Beauport, Elaine. *Your Multiple Intelligences, New Access Routes into the Three Brains.* New York: book in progress.

Durden-Smith, Jo, and deSimone, Diane. "Interview, Jerre Levy." *Omni,* Jan. 1985.

Gazzaniga, M. *The Social Brain: Discovering the Networks of the Mind.* New York: Basic Books, 1985.

Gray, William, ed. *Theory and the Psychological Sciences.* Seaside, CA: Intersystems, 1980.

Goleman, Daniel. "Studies Offer Fresh Clues To Memory." *New York Times,* March 27, 1990.

Hand, James, and Stein, Barbara. "The Brain & Accelerative Learning, Part III." *Journal SALT,* Vol. 11, No. 4.

Hooper, Judith. "Want to keep your brain from aging? Lead a more exciting infancy." *Wholemind,* July 1988.

Lorber, John. "The Disposable Cortex." *Psychology Today,* April 1981.

Lang, Doe. *The Charisma Book.* New York: Wyden Books, 1980.

MacLean, Paul. "A Mind of Three Minds: Educating the Triune Brain." *Education And The Brain,* Chicago: University of Chicago Press, 1978.

————. "The Imitative-Creative Interplay of Our Three Mentalities." *Astride the Two Cultures: Arthur Koestler at 70.* H. Harris, ed. London: Hutchinson, 1976.

"New Theory: Feelings Code, Organize Thinking." Special Issue, *Brain/Mind Bulletin,* March 18–29, 1982.

Schwarz, Joel. "Training Memory." *Omni,* March 1988.

Shannahoff-Khalsa, David. "Rhythms and Reality: the Dynamics of the Mind." *Psychology Today,* Sept. 1984.

"Thought, Concentration, and Memory, A New Look at the Edgar Cayce Readings." *Commentary,* Dec. 1986.

"Thought, Concentration, and Memory." Virginia Beach, VA.: *Association for Research and Enlightenment,* Circulating File.

Chapter 7

Resources

Dr. W. Jane Bancroft, international consultant, see page 375.

Eli Bay, Director, Relaxation Response Ltd. 858 Eglinton Ave. West, Toronto, Ontario, Canada M6G 2B9. (416) 789-7261. Consulting, stress management for corporations, government, individuals. Books and tapes. In the United States, Bay's relaxation tapes are available from Superlearning Inc.

Lisa Curtis, President International Sophrology Institute, 381 Park Ave. South, Suite 1519, New York, NY 10016. (718) 849-9335. Lectures on "turning stress into energy," optimal health, goal achievement. Tape available from Superlearning Inc.

Elizabeth Reudy, M.A., Consulting and one-on-one coaching for memory and learning problems generally, but especially for math and acting. Contact: Ivy Stone at the Fifi Oscard Agency, 19 West 44 Street, New York, NY. (212) 764-1100.

References

Bancroft, W. Jane. "Yoga Factors in Accelerative Learning." *Journal SALT,* Vol. 8, No. 3.

————. "The Tomatis Method & Suggestopedia, A Comparative Study." *Journal SALT,* Vol. 7, No. 1.

————. "The Lozanov Method and its American Adaptations." *The Modern Language Journal,* 1978.

————. "Sophrology & Suggestology." *Journal SALT,* Vol. 4, No. 2.

Begley, Sharon. "The Search for the Fountain of Youth." *Newsweek,* March 5, 1990.

Felix, Uschi. "Student Attitudes Towards the Use of Music & Mind-Calming." *Journal SALT,* Vol. 12, No. 3/4.

Goleman, Daniel. *The Meditative Mind.* Los Angeles: Tarcher, 1988.

————. "Concentration Is Likened To Euphoric States Of Mind." *New York Times,* March 4, 1986.

"How-to Instructions Inhibit Optimal Performance?" *Brain/Mind Bulletin,* Vol. 7, No. 13, Aug. 2, 1982.

Huxley, Laura. *The Timeless Moment.* Millbrae, CA: Celestial Arts, 1968.

Jacobson, Edmund. *Progressive Relaxation.* Chicago: University of Chicago Press, 1933.

Reudy, Elizabeth. *Where Do I Put The Decimal Point?* New York: Holt, 1990; Avon, 1991.

Sacks, Oliver. "Neurology and the Soul." *New York Review of Books,* Nov. 22, 1990.

Schultz, J., and Luthe, W. *Autogenic Training: A Psychophysiological Approach in Psychotherapy.* New York: Grune & Stratton, 1959.

Selye, Hans. *The Stress of Life.* New York: McGraw-Hill, 1976.

Chapter 8

Resources

The Institute in Culture and Creation Theology, Holy Names College, 3500 Mountain Blvd. Oakland, CA 94619. (415) 436-1046. Directed by Matthew Fox. Also his magazine *Creation,* 160 Virginia St. #290, San Jose, CA 95112. (408) 286-8505. Bimonthly, $20.

Dr. Teri Mahaney, Supertraining Press, 133 E. de la Guerra, Suite 409, Santa Barbara, CA 93101. (800) 762-9937. Lectures, workshops, book includes scripts for self-taping, also music tapes for suggestive background.

NeuroLinguistic Programming. Information on centers, workshops, training in various localities: (317) 636-6059.

References

Bandler, Richard. *Using Your Brain—For A Change.* Moab, Utah: Real People Press, 1985.

———, and Grinder, John. *ReFraming.* Moab, Utah: Real People Press, 1982.

Borysenko, Joan. *Guilt Is the Teacher, Love Is the Lesson.* New York: Warner, 1990.

Caycedo, Alphonso. *Le Professeur Caycedo, Pere de la Sophrologie Reconte sa Grande Aventure.* Paris: Retz, 1978.

———. *La India de Los Yoguis.* Barcelona: Editorial Andes Internacional, 1977.

Fox, Matthew. *Original Blessing.* Santa Fe: Bear & Co., 1983.

Mahaney, Teri. *Change Your Mind.* Santa Barbara: Supertraining Press, 1989.

"Proverbs That Go With Heart Trouble." *Science Digest,* April 1982.

"Unhappy Anniversary." *Psychology Today,* Oct. 1985.

Chapter 9

Resources

Rebirthing International (800-641-4645, ext. 232); International LRT, Box 1465, Washington, CT 06793. Rebirthing Centers (available most U.S. cities, see new age directories): programs that help you recall and explore birth and prebirth memories.

California Institute of Transpersonal Psychology, and (Stan Grof's) Spiritual Emergency Network (40 centers worldwide). 250 Oak Grove Ave., Menlo Park, CA 94025. Assist with deep memory exploration and integration.

Hawaiian Prenatal Cultural Center. P.O. Box 727, Molokai, HI 96748.

References

Abrezol, Raymond. *Sophrologie et Evolution—Demain L'Homme.* Lausanne: Editions du Signal; Paris: Chiron, 1986.

"Born Under Water." *Northern Neighbors,* April 1987.

Chamberlain, David. *Babies Remember Their Births.* Los Angeles; Tarcher, 1988.

———. "The Outer Limits of Memory." *Noetic Sciences Review,* Autumn 1990.

Clark, Seward and Bailey. "Giving Birth Underwater." *Newsweek,* Jan. 16, 1984.

Dansby, B. "Underwater Birth." *Life Times,* Winter 1986/87.

Grof, Stanislav. *Realms of the Human Unconscious.* New York: Dutton, 1976.

Haber, D. "What Is Water Birth?" *Life Times* No. 4.

"Hypnotized Children Recall Birth Experiences." *Brain/Mind Bulletin,* Jan. 26, 1981.

Odent, Michel. "Birth Under Water." *The Lancet,* Dec. 24/31, 1983.

Poole, W. "The First 9 Months of School." *Hippocrates,* Jul./Aug. 1987.

Rauhala, A. "Suicide by Teen-agers Linked to Difficulties During Birth Process." *The Globe & Mail,* Oct. 31, 1987.

Sidenbladh, Erik. *Water Babies.* New York: St. Martin's Press, 1986.

"Social Character May Be Set By Birth Practices." *Brain/Mind Bulletin,* Jan. 25, 1982.

Tomatis, Alfred. *L'oreille et le langage.* Paris: Editions du Seuil, 1978.

————. *L'Oreille et la Vie.* Paris: Editions Robert Laffont, 1977.

Verny, Thomas, and Kelly, J. *The Secret Life of the Unborn Child.* New York: Dell, 1982.

"Water for Life and Health." *Northern Neighbors,* August 1989.

Weintraub, P. "Preschool?" *Omni,* August 1989.

Wyllie, Timothy. "Waterbirthing: Where the New Masters Come In." *Metapsychology,* Winter 1987.

Chapters 10 and 11

Resources

Sound Therapy, St. Peter's Press, Box 190, Muenster, Saskatchewan, Canada S0K 2Y0. For high-frequency Sound Therapy cassettes. The basic set of four 90-minute metallic cassettes in ascending frequencies that constitute the program are available for $200 plus $10 shipping. *Sound Therapy for the Walkman,* the book by Pat Joudry, is $10. A catalog outlines other tapes.

Centre Tomatis, 68 Blvd. de Courcelles, 75017 Paris, France. Treatment for hearing problems and dyslexia.

Scientific Enterprises, Inc. 708 119 Lane, Blaine, MN 55435. Cassette tapes of Carlson's high-frequency sounds for accelerated plant growth. There's also a plant kit and a video available.

References

Bancroft, W. Jane. "The Tomatis Method and Suggestopedia: A Comparative Study." *Journal SALT,* 1982.

Bloom, Pamela. "Soul Music." *New Age Journal,* Mar./April 1987.

"French Research Links Hearing to Body Dynamics." *Brain/Mind Bulletin,* Theme Pack, Vol. 8.

Chang, S. T. *The Complete Book of Acupuncture.* Berkeley, CA: Celestial Arts, 1976.

Halpern, Steven, and Savary, L. "Tools for Transformation." *New Realities,* Summer 1985.

———. *Sound Health: The Music and Sounds That Make Us Whole.* San Francisco: Harper and Row, 1985.

"Hearing Deficits May Be Source of Confusion That Causes Dyslexia." *Brain/Mind Bulletin,* Theme Pack, Vol. 8.

"High Frequency Sound and Hormone Sprays: A Solution to World Hunger?" *New Frontiers Center Newsletter,* Spring/Summer 1984.

" 'Holophonic' Sound Broadcasts Directly to Brain." *Brain/Mind Bulletin,* Theme Pack, Vol. 8.

Joudry, P. *Sound Therapy for the Walkman.* St. Denis, Sask: Steele and Steele, 1984.

———. "Sound Therapy Documentary." Tape. Muenster, Sask: St. Peter's Press.

Martin, S., and Isaacson, C. "Are You Wired for Sound?" *Here's Health,* Nov. 1985.

McGarey, W. *The Edgar Cayce Remedies.* New York: Bantam, 1983.

"MEG's Localize Vision, Epilepsy." *Brain/Mind Bulletin,* Vol. 9, No. 16. Oct. 1, 1984.

Pillai, Patrick A. *Sonapuncture—Acupuncture Using Intrasound.* Toronto: Electro-Medica, 1990.

"Sound and Nutrients in Agriculture." *Acres, USA,* Nov. 1984.

Tomatis, Alfred. *Vers l'ecoute humaine.* Paris: Les Editions ESF, 1974, Vols. 1 and 2.

————. *L'Oreille et le langage.* Paris: Editions du Seuil, 1978.

————. *L'Oreille et la vie.* Paris: Editions Robert Laffont, 1977.

————. *Education et dyslexie.* Paris: Les Editions ESF, 1978.

Revue Internationale d'Audiopsychophonologie.

"The Noise/Disease Effect." *Frontiers of Science,* Vol. IV, #2, May/June 1982.

MacIvor, V., and LaForest, S. *Vibrations.* New York: Weiser, 1979.

Superlearning Music

Resources

Superlearning Inc., 450 Seventh Ave., Suite #500, New York, NY 10123. Ostrander Associates, 4325 Steeles Ave. West, Suite 410, Downsview, Ontario, Canada M3N 1V7. Superlearning Music tapes available prepared by the authors; freshly minted 60-beats-a-minute music by contemporary composers to use with the Superlearning system; courses and learning materials backed with Superlearning music.

References

Maleskey, G. "Music That Strikes A Healing Chord." *Prevention,* Oct. 1983.

Ostrander, S., and Schroeder, L. *Superlearning.* New York: Delacorte, Delta, Dell, 1979.

Sophrology Musical Memory Method

Resources

Superlearning Inc. (See page 389.) Sophrology programs by Dr. Raymond Abrezol and Sophrology music tapes (Turning Sound) available for North America.

Collège International de Sophrologie Médicale, 50 avenue de la Gare, CH-1003, Lausanne, Switzerland, and International Sophrology Institute, 419 Park Ave. South, New York, NY 10016. Additional Sophrology materials.

References

Abrezol, Raymond. *Sophrologie Dans Notre Civilization.* Neuchatel, Switzerland: InterMarketing Group, 1973.

———. *Vaincre par la Sophrologie (Become A Winner With Sophrology).* Chêne Bourg, Geneva, Switzerland: Diffusion Soleil, 1983.

Boredom-Beating Beats

Resources

Edrington, Devon. "A Palliative for Wandering Attention." Tacoma, WA: 1985.

———. "Hemi-Sync: Treatment for Wandering Attention." Conference presented by the Monroe Institute for Applied Sciences, Faber, VA., Aug. 11, 1984.

———. "Neomorphosis: The Art of Radical Change." Tacoma, WA: 1984.

———. "Binaurally Phased Sound in the Classroom." Tacoma, WA: 1985.

———. and Allen, C. "1984–1985 EEG Experiments with Binaurally Phased Audio Stimuli." Tacoma, WA: 1985.

Morris, S.E. "The Facilitation of Learning." Madison, Wis.: 1985.

Oster, Gerald. "Auditory Beats in the Brain." *Scientific American,* Sept. 1973.

Pawelek, Y., and Larson, J. "Hemispheric Synchronization and Second Language Acquisition." *Education Services Division,* Fort Lewis, WA

Chapter 12

Resources

Dr. Raymond Abrezol, Sophrology Institute, Avenue de la Gare 50, 1003 Lausanne, Switzerland. Sophrology for sports, health, creative living. English tapes by Abrezol available from Superlearning Inc., page 373. For information on Sophrology in English contact: International Sophrology Institute, page 384.

International Imagery Association, P.O. Box 1046, Bronx, NY 10471. Conferences, workshops, *Journal of Mental Imagery,* edited Dr. Akhter Ahsen. Also available: Ahsen's books and tapes on introductory and advanced imagery.

Vera Fryling, M.D. Tapes on imagery and autogenics available from Superlearning Inc., page 373.

Dr. Win Wenger. Books and workshop data available from Psychegenics Press, P.O. Box 332, Gaithersburg, MD 20877. Same address: information on CELT, a planned encyclopedia of Enhanced Learning Techniques. Also Wenger's *How To Increase Your Intelligence,* from United Educational Services (800) 458-7900.

References

Abrezol, Raymond. *Win With Sophrology.* Chêne Bourg, Switzerland: Diffusion Soleil, 1983. French.

————. *Sophrologie dans Notre Civilization.* Neuchatel: Inter Marketing Group, 1973.

————. *Winning Stance.* New York: Superlearning Inc., 1988. Tape.

Frankel, Victor. *Man's Search For Meaning.* New York: Touchstone, 1984.

Fryling, Vera. *"Survival, Creativity and Transcendence."* New York: Superlearning Inc., 1986. Tape.

"Image Memory Pegs Aid Language Recall." *Brain/Mind Bulletin,* 1979.

Luria, Alexander. *The Mind of a Mnemonist.* New York: Basic Books, 1968.

McNeill, Barbara. "Beyond Sports: Imaging in Daily Life." *Newsletter IONS,* Summer 1985.

Sparrow, Scott. "Mental Practice Improves Performance." *Perspective,* May 1984.

Wenger, Win. *Beyond Teaching & Learning.* East Aurora, NY: United Educational Services, 1987.

————. "Dual-Plane Awareness Techniques Other Than Lozanov's, for Accelerating & Enriching Training & Learning." *Journal SALT,* No. 3/4, 1987.

Chapters 13 and 14

References

Ad Herrenium. Tr. Harry Caplan. New York: Loeb Classical Library, 1968.

Dictionary of Mnemonics. London: Eyre Metheun, 1972.

Hersey, G.L. *Pythagorean Palaces: Magic and Architecture in the Italian Renaissance.* Ithaca: Cornell University Press, 1976.

Mead, G.R.S. *Thrice Great Hermes.* London: John Watkins, 1906.

Plato. *The Encyclopaedia of Platonic Philosophy.* New York: American Classical College Press, 1989.

Powell, James N. *The Tao Of Symbols.* New York: Quill, 1982.

Shear, Jonathan. "Maharishi, Plato and the TM-Sidhi Program on Innate Structures of Consciousness." *Metaphilosophy* 12:1, 1981.

Smalley, Beryl. *English Friars and Antiquity in the Early Fourteenth Century.* Oxford: Oxford University Press, 1960.

Sorabji, Richard. *Aristotle On Memory.* Hanover, NH: University Press of New England, 1972.

Spence, Jonathan, D. *The Memory Palace Of Matteo Ricci.* New York: Penguin Books, 1985.

Yates, Frances, A. *The Rosicrucian Enlightenment.* New York: Ark, 1986.

————. *The Art Of Memory.* Chicago: University of Chicago Press, 1966.

————. *Giordano Bruno and the Hermetic Tradition.* Chicago: University of Chicago Press, 1964.

Chapter 15

Resources

Society for the Study of Multiple Personality & Dissociation, c/o Dissociative disorders program, Rush Presbyterian-St. Luke's Medical Center, 600 South Pauline, Chicago, IL 60612.

References

Allison, Ralph. *Minds in Many Pieces.* New York: Rawson Wade, 1980.

Bearhs, John. *Unity and Multiplicity.* New York: Brunner Mazel, 1983.

Cochran, Tracy. "Multiple Personality Twins." *Omni,* Dec. 1986.

Damgaard, Jacqueline. "The Inner Self Helper." *Noetic Sciences Review,* Winter 1987.

Gilman, Robert. "Memory and Morphogenetic Fields." *In Context,* Summer 1984.

Hartley, Robert. "Imagine You're Clever." *Journal of Child Psychology,* Vol. 27, No. 3, 1986.

Keyes, Daniel. *The Minds of Billy Milligan.* New York: Bantam, 1981.

Mahlberg, A. "Evidence of Collective Memory." *Journal of Analytical Psychology,* Vol. 32, 1987.

"Multiple Personality No Longer Considered Rare." *Brain/Mind Bulletin,* Nov. 1988.

"Multiple Personalities Proof of Brain's Versatility." *Brain/Mind Bulletin,* Oct. 3, 1983.

Myers, F.W.H. *Human Personality and Its Survival of Bodily Death.* London: Longmans Green, 1907.

O'Regan, Brendan, and Hurley, Thomas. "Multiple Personality." *Investigations, Institute of Noetic Sciences,* Vol. 1, No. 3/4, 1985.

Raikov, Vladimir. "Reincarnation by Hypnosis." *The ESP Papers: Scientists Speak Out,* New York: Bantam, 1976.

————. "Reincarnation by Hypnosis." *Science and Religion,* Moscow, No. 9, 1966.

————, and Adamenko, V. "Questions of Objective Research of Deep Hypnotic States." *Therapy of Mental Disease,* Moscow: Society of Neuropsychiatrists, Sechenov Medical Institute, 1968.

Ross, Colin. *Multiple Personality Disorder: Diagnosis, Clinical Features and Treatment.* New York: Wiley & Sons, 1989.

Schreiber, Flora. *Sybil.* New York: Warner, 1974.

Sperling, J., and Wolensky, W. "Superlearning: Can it be Effectively Adapted to Technical Education?" IBM *Technical Report,* 00.3014.

Taylor, Eugene. *William James on Exceptional Mental States.* New York: Scribners, 1983.

Tennaeff, Willem. "Psychoscopy." *Pursuit,* Vol. 21, No. 4, 1988.

Virato, Sw., "An Interview with Rupert Sheldrake." *New Frontier,* April 1988.

Chapters 16 and 17

Resources

There are M.D.s practicing holistic medicine and alternative clinics across the United States; check local directories. Listed here are those mentioned in the text.

Aletheia Psycho-Physical Foundation, Jack Schwarz director, 1809 North Highway 99, Ashland, OR 97520. (503) 488-0709. Personal health training, internships re human energy systems and self-regulation, workshops, publications.

American Holistic Medical Association, 4101 Lake Boone Trail, Suite 201, Raleigh NC 27607. (919) 787-5146.

Ayurvedic Medicine. Maharishi Ayurveda Association of America, Box 282, Fairfield, IA 52556. (515) 472-8477, for data on centers and treatment.

Creighton Health Institute, 275 Elliot, Menlo Park, CA 94025. (415) 327-6166. Help for those with cancer.

Ahmed Elkadi M.D., director Akbar Clinic and Resource Institute, Panama City Clinic, 236 South Tyndell Parkway, Panama City, FL 32404. (904) 763-7689. 24 hrs. Holistic treatment.

Foundation for the Advancement of Innovative Medicine, Box 338, Kinderhook, NY 12106. (800) 462-FAIM. Professional and lay group working to spread data and protect complimentary, alternative, and nutritional medicine from the attacks of orthodoxy. Symposiums, journal, membership: indiv. $25, prof. $125.

International Society for the Study of Subtle Energies and Energy Medicine. Newsletter, workshops, conference. Professional dues $35. Contact Penny Hiernu, executive director, ISSSEEM, 356 Goldco Circle, Golden, CO 80401.

Subtle Energies: An Interdisciplinary Journal of Informational and Energetic Interactions. Quarterly, $35, from the address above.

The Light Institute of Galisteo, Rt. 3, Box 50, Galisteo, NM 87540. (505) 983-1975. Chris Griscom, director, one-on-one intensives, books and tapes available.

Science of Mind Magazine, Box 75127, Los Angeles, CA 90075. Monthly, $18.

Bernie Siegel M.D., ECaP (Exceptional Cancer Patients), 1302 Chapel St. New Haven, CT 06511. (203) 865-8392. Support groups, comprehensive directory of support and healing programs nationwide, tapes and books.

STEPS, 263A Cumberland, San Francisco, CA (415) 864-6518. Offshoot of the Creighton Institute, empowerment for people living with HIV, AIDS.

Third Opinion: An International Directory to Alternative Therapy Centers for the Treatment and Prevention of Cancer by John Fink, Avery Publishing Group, 1988. Not a discussion of merits, but a guide to alternative treatment and data banks here and abroad.

United Church of Religious Science, Office of Ecclesiastical Affairs, 3251 W. Sixth St., Los Angeles, CA 90020. (213) 388-2181. Data on churches, national and international study groups.

World Research Foundation, 15300 Ventura Blvd., Suite 405, Sherman Oaks, CA 94103. (818) 907-5483. Computer data bank of latest medical developments worldwide. Search for nominal fee, library open to public.

References

Achterberg, Jeanne. *Imagery Healing.* Boston: New Science Library, 1985.

Bronson, Matthew. "Healing With Mind and Heart." *Magical Blend,* No. 23, 1989.

Caycedo, Alphonso. *Progress in Sophrology.* Barcelona: Emerge, 1969. Spanish.

Chopra, Deepak, *Quantum Healing.* New York: Bantam, 1990.

Davrou, J., and LeClerq, F. *The Astonishing Possibilities Of Your Memory Through Sophrology.* Paris: Retz, 1982. French.

————. *Sophrotherapy: Psychotherapeutic Application of Sophrology.* Paris: Retz, 1982. French.

Evans, F. "Expectancy, Therapeutic Instructions and the Placebo Response." L. White et al., eds. *Placebo: Theory, Research and Mechanism.* New York: Guilford Press, 1985.

Gagnon, T. and Rein, G. "The Biological Significance of Water Structured with Non-Hertzian Time Reversed Waves." *Journal of the U.S. Psychotronics Association* 1991.

Graves, Florence. "The High Priest of Healing." *New Age Journal,* May/June 1989.

Griscom, Chris. *Time Is An Illusion.* New York: Fireside, 1988.

————. *Ecstacy Is A New Frequency.* Santa Fe: Bear & Co., 1989.

————. *Desert Trilogy: Chris Griscom Interviewed by Biannca Pace on Sexuality, Healing, Radiation.* Cosmic Renaissance Foundation, 1988. Tape Set.

"Harvard Tests Mother Theresa Effect." *Brain/Mind Bulletin,* July 29, 1985.

Holmes, Ernest. *The Science of Mind.* New York: Dodd Mead, 1938.

Karagulla, Shafica. *Breakthrough to Creativity.* Los Angeles: De Vorss, 1967.

————, and Kunz, Dora. *The Chakras and The Human Energy Field.* Wheaton, IL: Quest Books, 1989.

Langer, Ellen J. *Mindfulness.* New York: Addison-Wesley, 1989.

Murphy, Michael. "Dimensions of Healing." *Noetic Sciences Review,* Autumn 1987.

O'Regan, Brendan. "Barriers to Novelty: Can Energy Medicine Come of Age?" *Noetic Sciences Review,* Fall 1989.

————. "Spontaneous Remission: Studies of Self-Healing." *Noetic Sciences Review.* Spring 1988.

————. "Positive Emotion: The Emerging Science of Feelings." *IONS Newletter,* Fall 1984.

Parsons-Fein, Jane. "Interview with Ernest Rossi, Ph.D." *NYSEPH Newsletter,* Sept. 1988 and Nov. 1989.

Pert, Candace. "Neuropeptides: The Emotions and Bodymind." *Noetic Sciences Review,* Spring 1987.

————; Ruff, M.; Weber, R.; Herkenham, M. "Neuropeptides and their Receptors: A Psychosomatic Network." *Journal of Immunology,* Vol. 135, No. 2.

Rein, Glen. "Psychoenergetic Mechanism for Healing with Subtle Energies." *Mechanisms of Psychic Perception.* J. Millay, S-P. Sirag, Eds. Forthcoming.

Rossi, Ernest. *Psychobiology Of Mind-Body Healing.* New York: Norton, 1988.

Siegal, Bernie, *Peace, Love and Healing.* New York: Harper & Row, 1989.

Simonton, C.; Simonton, S.; Creighton, J. *Getting Well Again.* Los Angeles: Tarcher, 1978.

Chapter 18

Resources

International Academy of Nutrition and Preventive Medicine, P.O. Box 5832, Lincoln, NE 68505.

Linus Pauling Institute of Science and Medicine, 440 Page Mill Road, Palo Alto, CA 94306.

The Academy of Orthomolecular Psychiatry—Huxley Institute for Biosocial Research, 900 N. Federal Hwy., Suite 330, Boca Raton, FL 33432.

Canadian Schizophrenia Foundation, 7375 Kingsway, Burnaby, B.C., Canada V3N 3B5.

People's Medical Society, 462 Walnut St., Allentown, PA 18102. (Grassroots organization for information on freedom of choice in health care.)

Price-Pottenger Nutrition Foundation, P.O. Box 2614, La Mesa, CA 92041. (Registry of nutritionally oriented health care professionals.)

See additional health resources, following.

Brain Foods and Choline and Lecithin

References

Bland, Jeffrey. *Choline, Lecithin, Inositol and Other "Accessory" Nutrients—The Exciting New Uses of Powerful Nutrients for People With Special Needs.* New Canaan, Conn.: Keats Publishing, Inc., 1982.

Bell, Stuart. "Phosphatidyl Choline—Aids in the Fight Against Neurological Disorders and Aging." *Let's Live Magazine,* Los Angeles: April 1982.

Huerner, Richard. "Brain Food—Neurotransmitters Make You Think." *Let's Live,* Dec. 1981.

Pearson, Durk, and Shaw, Sandy. *Mental Alertness.* International Institute of Natural Health Sciences, Inc., Huntington Beach, CA: 1981.

"Phosphatidyl Choline—The Power Base of Lecithin." Del Mar, CA: Biosource.

Pines, Maya. "Food *Does* Affect Your Brain." *Reader's Digest,* Nov. 1983.

Yepsen, Roger, Jr. *How To Boost Your Brain Power, Achieving Peak Intelligence, Memory and Creativity.* Emmaus, Pa.: Rodale Press, 1987.

Ginkgo

References

Chatterjee, S.S., and Gabard, B. "Protective effect on extract of Ginkgo Biloba and other hydroxyl radical scavengers against hypoxia." Eighth International Congress of Pharmacology, Tokyo, Abstract 866, 1961.

Chatterjee, S.S., and Gabard, B. "Studies on the mechanism of action of an extract of Ginkgo Biloba." Symposium, 1982.

Gebner, B.; Voelp, A.; Klasser, M. "Study of the long-term action of a Ginkgo Biloba Extract on vigilance and mental performance as determined by means of quantitative pharmaco-EEG and psychometric measurements." *Arzneim Forsch* 35: 1459–65, 1985.

Hindmarch, I., and Subhan, Z. "The psychopharmacological effects of Ginkgo Biloba extract in normal healthy volunteers." *International Journal of Clinical Pharmacology,* Res. 4: 89–93, 1984.

Hoffmann D. "A New Paradigm of Western Herbal Medicine." 1987.

Huber, W., and Kidd, P.M. "Ginkgo Biloba Extract, a critical assessment." Berkeley, CA: HK Biomedical, 1988.

McQuade, A. "What is Ginkgo Biloba?" *Health World,* Burlingame, CA: July/Aug. 1988.

Murray, Michael. "Ginkgo Biloba: 'The living fossil.'" *Phyto-Pharmica Review,* Vol. 3, No. 6, Nov. 1990.

———. "Ginkgo Biloba Extract: Is Europe's most popular medicine a miracle drug?" *Phyto-Pharmica Review,* Vol. 3, No. 6, Nov. 1990.

Schaffler V.K., and Reeh, P.W. "Double-blind study of the hypoxia-protective effect of a standardized Ginkgo Biloba preparation after repeated administration of healthy volunteers." *Arzneim-Forsch*, 35:1283–6, 1985.

Vorberg, G. "Ginkgo Biloba Extract (GBE): A long-term study of chronic cerebral insufficiency in geriatric patients." *Clinical Trials Journal*, 22: 149–57, 1985.

L-Glutamine

References

Elwood, C. *Feel Like A Million!*. New York: Pocket Books, 1965.

Fredericks, C. *Psycho-Nutrition*. New York: Berkley Books, 1988.

Hoffer, A. *Orthomolecular Psychiatry*. D. Hawkins and L. Pauling, eds. San Francisco: Freeman and Co. 1973.

Rogers, L.L., and Pelton, R.B. "Effect of Glutamine on IQ Scores of Mentally Deficient Children." *Texas Reports on Biology and Medicine*, Vol. 15, No. 1, 1957.

"Sweet Remembrances." *Science News*, Sept. 22, 1990.

Williams, R., *Nutrition Against Disease*. New York: Bantam Books, 1971.

L-Phenylalanine and DLPA

References

Garrison, R. *Lysine, Tryptophan and Other Amino Acids—Food For Our Brains . . . Maintenance for our Bodies*. New Canaan, Conn.: Keats 1982.

DLPA in the Nutritional Control of Arthritis and Chronic Pain. Pomona, CA: Nutrition News, 1983.

"Lack of Endorphins in Alcoholics Can Be Corrected." *Brain/Mind Bulletin*, Vol. 9, No. 8. April 16, 1984.

Mark, V., and Mark, J. *Brain Power*. New York: Houghton Mifflin, 1989.

Pearson, D., and Shaw, S. *Life Extension—A Scientific Approach*. New York: Warner Books, 1982.

L-Tyrosine, Vasopressin, RNA-DNA

References

Banderet, L.E., et al. "A Preliminary Report on the Effects of Tyrosine Upon Altitude and Cold-Induced Stress Responses." Natick, MA.: U.S. Army Research Institute of Environmental Medicine, 1988.

"Brain Peptide Vasopressin Offers Clue to Depression." *Brain/Mind Bulletin*, Theme Pack No. 9, Vol. IV.

Eisenberg, Jacques, et al. "A Controlled Trial of Vasopressin Treatment of Childhood Learning Disorder." *Biological Psychiatry*, Vol. 19, No. 7, 1984.

Gelenberg, A. "Tyrosine for the Treatment of Depression." *American Journal of Psychiatry*, 147:622, May 1980.

Goldberg, I. "Tyrosine in Depression." *Lancet*, 364, Aug. 1980.

Purser, J. "Treatment of Hayfever in General Practice." *Current Medical Research Opinion*, 556, 1976.

Growdon, J.H., and Wurtman, R.J. "Dietary Influences on the Synthesis of Neurotransmitters in the Brain." *Nutrition Review*, 37:129, 1979.

Miller, A. "A Comparative Trial in the Treatment of Hayfever." *Clinical Allergy*, 556, 1976.

Goleman, D. "Food and Brain: Psychiatrists Explore Use of Nutrients in Treating Disorders." *New York Times*, Mar. 1, 1988.

Pearson, D., and Shaw, S. *Life Extension*. New York: Warner Books, 1982.

Pearson, D., and Shaw, S. "How To Prevent Jet Lag." *Anti-Aging News*, 13, Feb. 1981.

Pines, Maya. "Food *Does* Affect Your Brain." *Reader's Digest*, Nov. 1983.

Stein, et al. "Memory Enhancement by Central Administration of Norepinephrine." *Brain Research*, 84:329–335, 1975.

Weingartner, H., et al. "Effect of Vasopressin on Human Memory Functions." *Science,* 211: 601–603.

Octacosanol

Resources

Naseer, Ahmad, c/o Ontario's Common Ground Magazine, 320 Danforth Ave., Suite 204, Toronto, Ontario, Canada M4K 1P3. 416-964-0072. Information re octacosanol and autistic children.

References

Ahmad, Naseer. "Autism—One Man's Story About Overcoming an 'Incurable' Illness." *Ontario's Common Ground Magazine,* Fall 1990.

Fredericks, Carlton. *Nutrition, Your Key to Good Health.* Hollywood, CA: London Press, 1964.

————. "Nutrition For the Damaged Brain." *Let's Live,* May 1984.

Fieldman, Anita. "Octacosanol—The Big Word That Causes Controversy." *Whole Foods,* Hester Communications, Feb. 1982.

Germanium

Resources

Dr. Parris Kidd, Former Director, Germanium Institute of North America, c/o HK Biomedical Inc., 1200 Tevlin St., Berkeley, CA 94706.

(CAUTION: *Never ingest inorganic germanium—the metallic kind used in transistors. This form is poisonous.* It took Dr. Asai years to develop an organic, safe form of germanium.)

References

Asai, Kazuhiko. *Miracle Cure, Organic Germanium.* Tokyo and New York: Japan Publications, 1980.

Kamen, B. *Germanium, A New Approach to Immunity.* Larkspur, CA: Nutrition Encounter, 1987.

Hyper-Oxygenation

Resources

Hyper-oxygenation therapy is available and inexpensive. Food-grade hydrogen peroxide (diluted to therapeutic levels, 1/2 of 1 percent) is available in some health food stores. (Nonfood grades have extra ingredients.) Use only a few drops in at least 6 oz. of pure spring water or juice. It can be drunk or rubbed on the skin. (CAUTION: *If not diluted, it can burn and when drunk can cause nausea.*) Dr. Donsbach's H2O2 formula, Superoxy, is available in five flavors and contains aloe to prevent nausea. Oxy Toddy contains diluted food grade H2O2 along with aloe, vitamins, minerals, and twenty-two amino acids. Dr. Farr strongly suggests taking antioxidant vitamins A, C, and E and antioxidant enzymes with H2O2 to counteract the hydroxyl radical given off in the process. Gingko is also an excellent antioxidant scavenger to take with H2O2. For bathing, 6 fluid oz. of food-grade H2O2 to a full bathtub. H2O2 is also ideal for swimming pool and hot tub purification. Peroxy Gel is available for the skin. Baking soda and hydrogen peroxide have long been recommended by dentists for cleaning teeth. A new formula, Peroxyl, is available as a mouthwash. We personally prefer the safer oxygen electrolyte supplements and have had superior results with them. EQ O2, a safe, nontoxic oxygen supplement is available from Pure Action, Lynnwood, WA 98046; AEROX, Box 3052, Iowa City, IA 52244.

Information Resources Hyper-Oxygenation: Ed McCabe, 99-RD1, Morrisville, NY 13408.

International Bio-Oxidation Medicine Foundation, P.O. Box 61767, Dallas/Fort Worth, TX 75261.

Hospital Santa Monica, Rosarito Beach, Mexico.

International Ozone Association, 83 Oakwood Ave., Norwalk, CT. 06850.

Artzlich Gesellschaft fur Ozontherapie, Stuttgart, Germany.

Clinica Medica de Ozone Therapie, Baja California, Mexico.

Waves Forest, Newsletter—NOW WHAT, P.O. Box 768-OT, Monterey, CA 93942.

ECHO Newsletter, Box 126, Delano, MN 55328.

"Search for Health." APW, Box 3052, Iowa City, IA 52244.

Rex Research, Box 1258, Berkeley, CA 94701.

Izone International, 470 Granville St., #1027, Vancouver, B.C., Canada V6C 1W3.

Medizone International, 123 East 54 St., 2B, New York, NY 10022.

References:

Berkowsky, B. "Bio-Available Oxygen." *HealthStore News,* Feb./Mar. 1989.

Bradford, R., and Culbert, M. "Perils of H2O2 Overuse." Townsend Newsletter for Doctors, No. 49-8707.

Clifford, D., and Repine, J. "Hydrogen Peroxide Mediated Killing of Bacteria." *Molecular and Cellular Biochemistry,* No. 49, 143–149, 1982.

Crook, W. "Yeast Can Affect Behavior and Learning." *Academic Therapy,* Vol. 19, No. 5, May 1984.

———. *The Yeast Connection.* Jackson, Tenn.: Professional Books, 1986.

Donsbach, K. *Hydrogen Peroxide—H2O2.* Rosarito Beach, Mexico: Hospital Santa Monica, 1989.

Farr, D. "The Therapeutic Use of Intravenous Hydrogen Peroxide." Dallas, Tex.: International Bio-Oxidative Medicine Foundation.

Forest, W. "Cancer, AIDS Cured by Hyperoxygenation?" *Life Times,* No. 4.

———. "Hyperoxygenation—AIDS, Cancer Cured By." *Health Freedom News,* June 1988.

Khoudary, Kevin. "The Power of Ozone." *Water Technology,* May 1986.

McCabe, E. *Oxygen Therapies.* Morrisville, NY: Energy Publications, 1988.

"Medical Applications of Ozone." Norwalk, Conn.: International Ozone Association.

Naj, A.K. "Water Standards of U.S. Questioned: Microbe Is Cited." *Wall Street Journal,* May 2, 1989.

Philpott, W., and Kalita, D. *Brain Allergies: The Psycho-Nutrient Connection.* New Canaan, CT: Keats, 1980.

Silversides, A. "Acid Rain-Alzheimer's Link Suspected." *Toronto Globe & Mail,* May 20, 1987.

Thomson, Bill. "Do Oxygen Therapies Work? The AIDS-Ozone Connection." *East-West,* Sept. 1989.

ABCs of Memory—Minerals and Vitamins

References

Adams, R., and Murray, F. *Improving Your Health With Niacin.* New York: Larchmont Books, 1978.

Cheraskin, E.; Ringsdorf, W.M.; Brecher, A. *Psychodietetics.* New York: Stein & Day, 1974.

Davis, A. *Let's Have Healthy Children.* New York: Signet, 1972.

Fredericks, C. *Psycho-Nutrition.* New York: Berkley Books, 1988.

Malevsky, Gale. "Boost Your Brainpower." *Prevention,* Jan. 1985.

Mark, V. and J. *Brain Power: A Neurosurgeon's Complete Program to Maintain and Enhance Brain Fitness Throughout Your Life.* New York: Houghton Mifflin, 1989.

Martin, P. "Mentally Ill Children Respond to Nutrition." *Prevention,* Feb. 1974.

Mindell, E. *Vitamin Bible.* New York: Warner Books, 1981.

Murray, F. "Niacin Therapy: Physicians Report Results." *Better Nutrition,* Oct. 1985.

Sheinkin, D.; Schachter, M.; Hutton, R. *Food, Mind and Mood.* New York: Warner Books, 1980.

Mann, J. *Secrets of Life Extension.* New York: Bantam Books, 1982.

Williams, R. *Nutrition Against Disease.* New York: Bantam, 1973.

Wilson, Eugene. "How To Improve Your Memory." *Health Freedom News,* Mar/April 1990.

Wolf, R. "Brains Work Better With Vitamin C." *Prevention,* Sept. 1973.

Chapter 19

Resources

ELF Cocoon International, Route 1, Box 21, St. Francisville, IL 62460.

Essentia, 100 Bronson Ave., Suite 103, Ottawa, Ontario, Canada K1R 6G8. BT-5+s and other devices and information.

American Association of Acupuncture and Oriental Medicine, 50 Maple Place, Manhasset, NY 11030.

　Acupuncture Foundation for Canada, 10 St. Mary Street, Toronto, Ontario, Canada M4Y 1P9. Information.

References

Beck, Robert. "BT+5 Plus . . . The Alternative." Tape and pamphlet. St. Francisville, IL: ELF Cocoon, 1985.

Beck, Robert. "Bibliography of Cranial Electro-Stimulation." St. Francisville, IL: ELF Cocoon, 1985.

Chang, S. *The Complete Book of Acupuncture.* Berkeley, CA: Celestial Arts, 1976.

"Cranial-Electrical Stimulation: reduces anxiety and depression." *Focus on Alcohol and Drug Issues,* Hollywood, Fla., Vol. 6, No. 1, Jan./Feb. 1983.

Lerner, Fred. "The Quiet Revolution: Pain Control and Electromedicine." *California Health Review,* Apr./May 1983.

Maleskey, Gale. "Electricity's Healing Potential." *Prevention,* Nov. 1985.

McAuliffe, Kathleen. "Brain Tuner: The Black Box—Secret Drug Treatment of Rock Superstars." *Omni,* January 1983.

Patterson, Margaret. *Addictions Can Be Cured.* Berkhamstead, England: Lion Publishing, 1975.

———. *Getting Off The Hook.* Wheaton, IL: Harold Shaw Publishers, 1983.

———. "Electro-Acupuncture in Alcohol and Drug Addictions." *Clinical Medicine,* Vol. 81, Oct. 1974.

———. "Effects of Neuro-Electric Therapy (NET) in Drug Addiction: an Interim Report." U.N. Bulletin on Narcotics, Oct.–Dec. 1976.

———. "Neuro-Electric Therapy: Are Endorphins Involved?" *Mims Magazine,* Sept. 1981.

Schmitt, R., et al. "Cranial Electrotherapy Stimulation Treatment of Cognitive Brain Dysfunction in Chemical Dependence." *Journal of Clinical Psychiatry,* 45:60–63, 1984.

Smith, R.B., and Day, E. "The effects of cerebral electrotherapy on short term memory impairment in alcoholic patients." *International Journal of Addiction,* 12:575–582, 1977.

Taub, Harald. "Addicts Are Cured With Acupuncture." *Prevention,* Sept. 1973.

Wen, H.L., and Cheung, S.Y. "Treatment of drug addiction by acupuncture and electrical stimulation." *Asian Journal of Medicine,* 9:138–41, 1973.

The Graham Potentializer

Resources

David Graham, 2823 E. Malapai, Phoenix, AZ 85028. Information on Graham Potentializer. STARR (Stress Technology and Relaxation Research) Labs, P.O. Box 22165, Phoenix, AZ 85028. Machines feature rotation with soothing sound.

Mega Brain Report, Neurotechnology Newsletter, Box 2744, Sausalito, CA 94965.

References

Clark, D.L., et al. "Vestibular Stimulation Influence on Motor Development in Infants." *Science,* Vol. 196, June 10, 1977.

Ertl, J.P., "Louisiana Study of Learning Potential by Brain Wave Analysis." Louisiana State Dept. of Education, June 1976.

―――. "Electromechanical Therapeutic Apparatus." Neuro Models Limited, March 7, 1978.

Graham, D. J. "The Effects of the E.T.A. on the Electrical Activity of the Brain." Toronto: David John Institute, 1979.

―――. "Summary of Findings: The Effects of the ETA on Brain Dysfunctioning." Toronto: David John Institute, 1979.

―――. "A New Model for Medicine—The Electro-Magnetic Man." Toronto: David John Institute, 1979.

―――. "Electromechanical Therapeutic Apparatus." Toronto: David John Institute, 1979.

Hutchison, Michael. *Megabrain.* New York: William Morrow, 1986.

―――. "Mind Expanding Machines: Can the Graham Potentializer Do For The Brain What Nautilus Does For the Body?" *New Age Journal,* July/Aug. 1987.

Kantner, R.M., et al. "Effects of Vestibular Stimulation on Nystagmus Response and Motor Performance in the Developmentally Delayed Infant." *Physical Therapy,* Vol. 56, No. 4, April 1976.

Llaurado, J.G., et al. "Biologic and Clinical Effects of Low-Frequency Magnetic and Electric Fields." Springfield, IL: Charles C. Thomas, 1974.

Wilson, Robert Anton. "Adventures With Head Hardware." *Magical Blend,* July 1989.

Memory Batteries and Rejuvenation

Resources

Bruce D. Baar, 1645 Farnham Lane, Downington, PA 19335; The Heritage Store, Box 444, Virginia Beach, VA 23458-0444. Joseph Myers, Route 5, Box 257, Lexington, NC 27292. Cayce devices, plans and supplies.

A.R.E. Clinic, 4018 N. 40th St., Phoenix, AZ 85018.

A.R.E., Box 595, Virginia Beach, VA 23451. Information on the Cayce device and its use.

Superlearning Inc., 450 Seventh Ave., Suite 500, New York, NY 10123. Information on the memory battery.

References

Carter, M.E., and McGarey, W. *Edgar Cayce on Healing.* New York: Paperback Library, 1972.

Grady, Harvey. "The Cayce Impedance Device—A Gift On The Doorstep." *Venture Inward,* May/June 1989.

Karp, Reba Ann. "Edgar Cayce Cures Still Baffle Science." *Fate,* Feb. 1976.

Layne, Meade. *Vitic: Vitality From Carbon and Magnets.* Garberville, CA: BSRF, 1989.

McGarey, W. *The Cayce Remedies.* New York: Bantam, 1983.

Myers, Joseph. *The Radio-Active Appliance for Physical, Mental, Spiritual Regeneration.* Lexington, N.C.: 1969.

Taubes, Gary. "An Electrifying Possibility—A Swedish Radiologist Posits An Astounding Theory: The Human Body Has The Equivalent of Electric Circuits." *Discover,* April 1986.

Thomas, P. "Why The Wet Cell"; Proceedings, U.S. Psychotronics Assn., Dec. 1988.

———. "Edgar Cayce and the Wet Cell"; Proceedings, U.S. Psychotronics Assn., Dec. 1988.

Turner, G.D., and St. Clair, M.G. Virgina Beach, VA.: "Individual Reference Files of Extracts from the Edgar Cayce Records." 1970.

Mind/Memory High Tech

Resources

Aletheia, 1809 N. Highway 99, Ashland, OR 97520 I.S.I.S. devices and info.

ELF Cocoon and Essentia (listed above) have Teslar Watches and other devices.

Electro Medica, 32 Goodmark Place, Rexdale, Ontario, Canada M9W 6J4. For Relaxits, TENS machines, Sonafons, (sonic acupuncture) and other equipment and information.

Western Educational Systems, 3734 71st Avenue West, Tacoma WA 98466. Binaural Phasers.

Inner Technologies, 51 Berry Trail, Fairfax, CA 94930. Catalog of mind machines.

Management Work Co., Eternal Nishiya, 46 Banchi, Nishi 21 Chome, Odori, Chuo-ku, Sapporo, Japan. "Mindgenic."

References

Becker, Robert O. "Electromagnetic Fields—What You Can Do." *EastWest,* May 1990.

"Feeling Fatigued and Forgetful? The Power Line Next Door May be the Source of Your Burnout." *People Magazine,* Nov. 27, 1989.

Hooper, Judith and Teresi, Wick. *Would The Buddha Wear A Walkman?* New York: Simon & Schuster, 1990.

Huebner, Albert. "Healing Cancer with Electricity." *EastWest,* May 1990.

Leviton, Richard. "Current Affairs: Electro-Magnetism." *EastWest,* May 1990.

Paros, Lawrence, "The Technology of Consciousness." *Common Ground of Puget Sound,* Spring 1990.

"Power Play." *Discover Magazine,* Dec. 1989.

Puharich, Henry K. "Method and Means For Shielding A Person From The Polluting Effects of Extremely Low Frequency (ELF) Magnetic Waves and Other Environmental Electro-Magnetic Emissions and Pollution." U.S. Patent No. 616-183, June 1, 1984.

Rein, Glen. "Biological Interactions With Scalar Energy-Cellular Mechanisms of Action." Intl. Psychotronics Assoc., Dec. 1988.

Johns, B. "Sunny Takes a Rest." *Toronto Sun,* June 16, 1983.

Chapter 20

References

Alpert, Ya., and Figel, D. *Propagation of ELF and VLF Waves Near the Earth.* Institute of the Earth's Magnetism, Ionosphere and Radio Wave Propagation, USSR Academy of Sciences, Moscow, 1970; New York: Plenum Press, 1971.

Bain, D. *The Control of Candy Jones.* Chicago: Playboy Press, 1976.

Beck, R.C. "Extreme Low Frequency Magnetic Fields Entrainment: A Psychotronic Warfare Possibility?" *Association for Humanistic Psychology Newsletter,* April 1978.

Becker, Robert. *The Body Electric.* New York: William Morrow, 1984.

———. *Cross Currents: The Perils of Electropollution—The Promise of Electromedicine.* Los Angeles: Tarcher, 1990.

Blumenthal, S. "Mind Wars—The CIA's Secret Acid Test." *New Age,* Jan. 1978.

Bowart, W.H. *Operation Mind Control: Our Secret Government's War Against Its Own People.* New York: Dell, 1978.

Brodeur, P. *The Zapping of America.* New York: Norton & Co., 1977.

———. "Annals of Radiation—The Hazards of Electromagnetic Fields." *New Yorker,* June 19, 1989.

Chijevski, A. L. "L'action de l'activité périodique solaire sur les phénomenes sociaux." Traité de Climatologie Biologique et Médicale. Paris: Masson, 1934.

————. *The Sun and Us.* Moscow: 1969.

————, and Shishina, Y. *In The Rhythm of the Sun.* Moscow: Nauka, 1969.

Cruickshank, J. "Brainwashing—Ottawa Sued Over Its Role in Psychiatric Experiments." *Toronto Globe & Mail,* Dec. 23, 1987.

Ebon, M. *Psychic Warfare: Threat or Illusion?* New York: McGraw-Hill, 1983.

"Electrifying Effect: Overview of EM Research." *Brain/Mind Bulletin,* October 1988.

Hilts, P. "Study Says Electrical Fields Could Be Linked To Cancer." *New York Times,* Dec. 15, 1990.

McAuliffe, Kathleen. "The Mind Fields." *Omni,* February 1985.

Ostrander, S., and Schroeder, L. *Psychic Discoveries Behind the Iron Curtain.* Englewood Cliffs, N.J.: Prentice-Hall, 1970; Bantam, 1971.

————. *Astrological Birth Control.* Englewood Cliffs, N.J.: Prentice-Hall, 1972.

Paul, B. "Men Exposed to Electromagnetic Fields In Study Have Slower Motor Responses." *Wall Street Journal,* Dec. 6, 1989.

Peick, E. "A Way to Peace, Through ELF Waves." *Journal of Borderland Research,* Mar./April 1983.

Stevens, W. "Scientists Debate Health Hazards of Electromagnetic Fields." *New York Times,* July 11, 1989.

Strauss, S. "Research Finds Sunspots Are Nothing to Sneeze At." *Toronto Globe & Mail,* Jan. 25, 1990.

Vienneau, D. "Ottawa Paid For '50's Brainwashing Experiments, Files Show." *Toronto Star,* April 14, 1986.

Chapter 21

Resources

International Association for Near-Death Studies (IANDS), c/o University of Connecticut Health Center, Department of Psychiatry,

Farmington, CT 06032. Also P.O. Box 7767, Philadelphia, PA 19101. Publication: *Vital Signs.*

International Foundation for Survival Research, Inc., P.O. Box 291551, Los Angeles, CA 90029. The Monroe Institute, Route 1, Box 175, Faber, VA 22938. Training in mobile consciousness.

A.R.E., 215 67th St., Virginia Beach, VA. Cayce material.

The Radiance Technique Assn. Intnl., Box 40570, St. Petersburg, FL 33743-0570. Subtle energy health applications. Publishes a journal.

United States Psychotronics Association (USPA), 2141 Agatite, Chicago, IL 60625. Information on subtle energy research.

The Planetary Association for Clean Energy, Inc., 191 Promenade du Portage, Suite 600, HULL, Quebec, Canada J8X 2K6. (Founded by Canadian Senator Chesley Carter, Chairperson, Canadian Senate Committee on Health, Welfare and Science.) Information on emerging subtle energy science.

Radionic Association, Witney St., Burford, Oxon, England. Information and quarterly. See also ISSEEM pg. 395.

References

Adamenko, Viktor. "The Problem of Time and Psi." International Psychotronics Assn., 1988.

Atwater, P.M.H., *Coming Back To Life: The After-Effects of the Near-Death Experience.* New York: Ballantine Books, 1988.

Bassior, J.N. "Astral Travel." *New Age Journal,* Nov./Dec. 1988.

Berendt, Joachim-Ernst. *Nada Brahma—The World Is Sound.* Rochester, Vt.: Destiny Books, 1987.

Blavatsky, H.P. *The Secret Doctrine.* Wheaton, IL: Theosophical Publishing, 1966.

Byrd, Eldon. "The De La Warr Camera: Theory of Operation, History and Implications." Tape. Pleasant Grove, UT: USPA, 1990.

Charroux, Robert. *The Mysterious Past.* London: Futura Publications, 1974.

Chijevsky, A. *Terrestrial Echoes of Solar Storms.* Moscow: Edit. Myal, 1976.

Cayce, Hugh-Lynn. *Venture Inward: The Incredible Story of Edgar Cayce.* New York: Harper & Row, 1964.

Davis, A.R., and Rawls, W. *Magnetism and Its Effects on the Living System.* Hicksville, NY: Exposition Press, 1974.

Davidson, John. *Subtle Energy.* Saffron Walden, England: C. W. Daniel, 1990.

Delawarr, George, and Day, L. *Matter In The Making.* London: Vincent Stuart, 1966.

Dubrov, A. "Geomagnetic Fields and Life." *Geomagnetobiology.* New York: Plenum Press, 1978.

"Electronic Device Reads Acupuncture Meridians." *Brain/Mind Bulletin,* Dec. 14, 1981.

Ford, A. *The Life Beyond Death.* New York: Berkley, 1971.

Fortune, D. *Through The Gates of Death.* Wellingborough, Northamptonshire, England: Aquarian Press, 1968.

Goodavage, J. "The Incredible Hieronymus Machine." *Saga,* Sept. 1972.

Goncharov, N., et al. "Is The Earth A Huge Crystal?" *Khimia y Zhizya Journal,* No. 3, Moscow, 1974.

Greeley, A. "Mysticism Goes Mainstream." *American Health,* Jan./Feb. 1987.

Greyson, B., and Flynn, C. *The Near-Death Experience: Problems, Prospects, Perspectives.* Springfield, IL: C.C. Thomas, 1984.

Gris, H., and Dick, W. *The New Soviet Psychic Discoveries.* Englewood Cliffs, N.J.: Prentice-Hall, 1978.

Hieronymus, Sarah, and True, Jack. "Eloptic Instruments." Tape. Pleasant Grove, UT: USPA, 1990.

Hills, C. *Supersensonics.* Boulder Creek, CA: University of the Trees, 1975.

Jones, L. "Elizabeth Triumphant." *People,* Dec. 10, 1990.

Kaznacheyev, V., et al. "The Role of Superweak Light Flows in Biological Systems." *Bioenergetika i Biologischeskaya Spektrofotometriya.* Moscow: Nauka, 1967.

Kenyon, J. *Acupuncture Techniques.* Rochester, VT.: Healing Arts Press, 1988.

King, Serge, *Mastering Your Hidden Self.* Wheaton, IL: Theosophical Publishing House, 1985.

Kozyrev, N. "Possibility of Experimental Study of the Properties of Time." Springfield, VA: Joint Publications Research Service, NTIS, 1968.

————. "Time As Physical Phenomenon." in "Modeling and Forecasting in Bioecology." Riga: Latvian State University, 1982.

"Living Cells Emit Light, German Scientist Reports." *Brain/Mind Bulletin,* Aug. 19, 1985.

Long, Max F. *The Secret Science Behind Miracles.* Santa Monica: DeVorss & Co., 1948.

"Luminescence Spectrum To Guide Plant Breeders." *Soviet Science and Technology Almanac,* Moscow: Novosti, 1985.

"Machines Hint At Existence of Subtle Energies." *Brain/Mind Bulletin,* Dec. 14, 1981.

MacIvor, V., and LaForest, S. *Vibrations—Healing Through Color, Homeopathy and Radionics.* New York: Weiser, 1979.

McEwen, E. "Citizens of the Cosmos: Life Between Death and Rebirth." *Venture Inward,* July/Aug. 1989.

Mishlove, J. *Roots of Consciousness.* New York: Random House, 1975.

Monroe, Robert. *Journeys Out Of The Body.* New York: Doubleday, 1971.

————. *Far Journeys.* Garden City, New York: Doubleday, 1985.

"Robert Monroe: Update on Journeys Out of Body." *Brain/Mind Bulletin,* Mar. 26, 1984.

Moody, R. *Life After Life.* Atlanta: Mockingbird Books, 1975.

————, and Perry, P. "The Light Beyond." *New Age Journal,* May/June 1988.

Motoyama, Hiroshi. "The Motoyama Device: Measuring Psychic Energy." The Unesco Press: *Impact of Science on Society,* Vol. 24, No. 4, 1974.

────. *Science and the Evolution of Consciousness.* Brookline, MA: Autumn Press, 1978.

────. *Theories of the Chakras.* Wheaton, IL: Theosophical Publishing, 1981.

"Near-Death Experiences Defy Single Explanation." *Brain/Mind Bulletin,* Sept. 14, 1981.

Neal, V., and Karagulla, S. *Through the Curtain.* Marina del Rey, CA: DeVorss & Co., 1983.

Neumann, V. "Framework of the Universe." *Tekhnika-Molodiezhi,* No. 9, Moscow, 1973.

Ostrander, S., and Schroeder, L. *Psychic Discoveries Behind The Iron Curtain.* Englewood Cliffs, N.J.: Prentice-Hall, 1970.

────. *Handbook of Psychic Discoveries.* New York: Berkley, 1974.

────. *Psychic Discoveries Behind the Iron Curtain—Audio Update.* Los Angeles: Audio Renaissance Tapes, 1989.

Ostrovsky, B. "Why Does A Cell Emit Light?" *Znanyiye Sila,* No. 9, 1967.

Powell, A.E. *The Astral Body.* Wheaton, IL: Theosophical Publishing, 1927.

────. *The Etheric Double.* Wheaton, IL: Theosophical Publishing, 1925.

Rama, S.; Ballentine, R; Ajaya, S. *Yoga and Psychotherapy—The Evolution of Consciousness.* Honesdale, Pa.: Himalayan International Institute, 1976.

Ray, B. *The Reiki Factor.* St. Petersburg, Fla.: Radiance Associates, 1983.

Rein, Glen. "Psychoenergetic Mechanism for Healing with Subtle Energies." *Mechanisms of Psychic Perception,* J. Millay and Sirag, S-P. Forthcoming.

Ring, K. *Life at Death.* New York: Coward, McCann & Geoghegan, 1980.

———. *Heading Toward Omega: In Search of the Meaning of the Near-Death Experience.* New York: Morrow, 1984.

Roberts, J. *The Nature of Personal Reality: A Seth Book.* Englewood Cliffs, N.J.: Prentice-Hall, 1974.

———. *Seth Speaks: The Eternal Validity of the Soul.* Englewood Cliffs, NJ.: Prentice-Hall, 1972.

Rogo, Scott. "The Near-Death Experience." *Fate,* Oct. 1989.

Sabom, M. *Recollections of Death.* New York: Harper & Row, 1982.

Sampson, Catherine. "Chinese Revive Ancient Taoist Healing Rituals." *Toronto Globe & Mail,* May 18, 1990.

Schwarz, Jack. *Human Energy Systems.* New York: Dutton, 1980.

Sergeyev, G. "Magical Crystal." *Niodiolia Journal,* No. 36, Moscow, 1978.

Steiner, Rudolf, *Cosmic Memory.* New York: Harpers, 1959.

Swami Akhilananda, *Hindu Psychology.* Boston: Branden Press, 1946.

Taimni, I.K. *The Science of Yoga.* Wheaton, IL: Theosophical Publishing, 1975.

Tenhaef, W. "Proscopy." *Pursuit,* 4th Qrtr., 1988.

Tansley, David. *Subtle Body.* London: Thames and Hudson, 1977.

Tocquet, R. *Votre Memoire.* St. Jean-de-Braye, France: Editions Dangles, 1981.

Uphoff, Walter. *Mind Over Matter.* Oregon, Wis.: New Frontiers Center, 1980.

White, John, and Krippner, S. *Future Science.* New York: Doubleday, 1977.

White, Stewart E. *The Unobstructed Universe.* New York: Dutton, 1940.

Chapter 22

Resources

Light Institute, Route 3, Box 50, Galisteo, NM 87540. Griscom programs for recovering past-life memories through acupuncture. See also Resources, Chapters 17 and 19.

References

Armstrong, P. "Reincarnation: Contemplating the Wheel of Life." *The New Age Connection,* Winnipeg, Canada, Winter 1989/90.

Chang, Stephen. *The Complete Book of Acupuncture.* Berkeley, CA: Celestial Arts, 1976.

Cott, Jonathan. *The Search for Omm Sety.* New York: Doubleday, 1987.

Grant, Joan. *Eyes of Horus.* New York: Avon, 1942.

————. *Far Memory.* New York: Avon, 1969.

Griscom, Chris. *Ecstasy is a New Frequency.* Santa Fe, NM: Bear & Co., 1987.

————. *Time Is An Illusion.* New York: Simon and Schuster, 1989.

Into The Unknown. Pleasantville, NY: Reader's Digest Association., 1989.

Langley, Noel. *Edgar Cayce on Reincarnation.* New York: Paperback Library, 1967.

MacLaine, Shirley. *Dancing in the Light.* New York: Bantam, 1985.

Roberts, Jane. *The Seth Material.* Englewood Cliffs, N.J.: Prentice-Hall, 1970.

Rogo, Scott. "Other Lives Than This." *Fate,* June 1988.

Chapter 23

Resources

American Association for Electronic Voice Phenomena, 726 Dill Road, Severna Park, MD 21146. (301) 647-8742. Newsletter covering worldwide research, information, sample EVP tapes and how-to.

New Frontiers Newsletter, Fellowship Farm, Route 1, Oregon, WI 53575. Reports on current research worldwide.

Bill Weisensale, P.O. Box B-Q, Barstow, CA 92312. How-To Instructions for EVP Research.

METAscience Foundation, P.O. Box 737, Franklin, NC 28734. Info on survival and communication.

MTFD Group for Transcommunication, Herderstrasse 19, D-6000, Frankfurt / M. 1, Germany. Research and information. Newsletter (in German).

References

Bander, Peter. *Carry On Talking.* Gerrards Cross, England: Colin Smythe, 1979.

Bender, Hans. "The Phenomena of Friedrich Jurgenson—An Analysis." *Journal of Paraphysics,* Vol. 6, No. 2, 1972.

Burton, J. "Contact with the Dead: A Common Experience?" *Fate,* April 1982.

Estep, Sarah. *Voices of Eternity.* New York: Fawcett, 1988.

Fuller, John. *The Ghost of 29 Megacycles.* New York: New American Library, 1986.

Gardner, Alex. "Chess With A 'Dead' Partner." *Pursuit,* 4th Qtr. 1988.

Holbe, Rainer, *Bilder aus dem Reich der Toten: Die paranormalen Experimente des Klaus Schreiber.* Munich: Verlag Knaur, 1987.

Jurgenson, Friedrich. *Sprechfunk Mit Verstorbenen* (Radio-Link With the Beyond). Freiburg, Germany: Verlag Hermann Bauer, KG, 1967.

Ostrander, S., and Schroeder, L. *Handbook of Psychic Discoveries.* New York: Berkley, 1974.

Raudive, Konstantine. *Breakthrough, An Amazing Experiment in Electronic Communication with the Dead.* New York: Taplinger, 1971.

Schaffranke, Rolf. "Spirit Voices Tape-Recorded." *Fate,* July 1970.

Senkowski, Ernst. *Instrumentelle Trans-Koummunikatin: Dialog met dem Unbekannten* (Instrumental Transcommunication). Mainz, Germany, 1989.

Smith, L. "The Raudive Voices—Objective or Subjective? A Discussion." *Journal of the American Society for Psychical Research,* Jan. 1974.

Spirit Summonings. New York: Time-Life Books, 1988.

Welch, William. *Talks With The Dead.* New York: Pinnacle Books, 1975.

Chapter 24

Resources

Adventures Unlimited, Box 22, Stelle, IL 60919. (800) 345-7979. Archaeological expeditions to ancient civilizations.

A.R.E., Box 595, Virginia Beach, VA 23451. Cayce data on ancient civilizations.

References

Arguelles, Jose. *The Mayan Factor: Path Beyond Technology.* Santa Fe, NM: Bear & Co., 1987.

———. *Surfers of the Zuvuya.* Santa Fe, NM: Bear & Co., 1988.

Berlitz, Charles. *Mysteries from Forgotten Worlds.* New York: Dell, 1972.

———. *The Mystery of Atlantis.* New York: Avon, 1976.

Blavatsky, H.P. *The Secret Doctrine.* Wheaton, IL: Theosophical Publishing, 1966.

Cayce, Edgar Evans. *Edgar Cayce on Atlantis.* New York: Paperback Library, 1968.

Childress, D. H. *The Anti-Gravity Handbook.* Stelle, IL: Publisher's Network/Adventures Unlimited Press, 1985.

———. *Lost Cities of Ancient Lemuria and the Pacific.* Stelle, IL: Adventures Unlimited Press, 1985.

———. *Lost Cities and Ancient Mysteries of South America.* Stelle, IL: Adventures Unlimited Press, 1986.

———. *Lost Cities of China, Central Asia and India.* Stelle, IL: Adventures Unlimited Press, 1987.

———. *Lost Cities of Africa and Arabia.* Stelle, IL: Adventures Unlimited Press, 1987.

———. *Lost Cities of North and Central America.* Stelle, IL: Adventures Unlimited Press, 1987.

———. *Anti-Gravity and the World Grid.* Stelle, IL: Adventures Unlimited Press, 1987.

Churchward, J. *The Lost Continent of MU.* New York: Paperback Library, 1931.

Devereux, Paul. *Earth Memory.* St. Paul: Llewellyn Press, 1991.

Heinberg, R. *Memories and Visions of Paradise.* Los Angeles: Tarcher, 1989.

Hitching, Francis. *The Mysterious World; At Atlas of the Unexplained.* New York: Holt, Rinehart, Winston, 1978.

Hoagland, R. *The Monuments of Mars: A City On the Edge of Forever.* Berkeley, CA: North Atlantic Books, 1987.

Into the Unknown. Pleasantville, NY: Reader's Digest, 1981.

Josyer, G.R. *Vymaanida-Shaastra Aeronautics* by Maharishi Bharadwaaja. International Academy of Sanskrit Investigation, Mysore, India, 1979.

Kondratov, A. *The Riddles of Three Oceans.* Moscow: Progress, 1974.

Landsberg, A. and S. *In Search of Ancient Mysteries.* New York: Bantam, 1974.

"Mystery Megaliths of North America." *Frontiers of Science,* Vol. IV, No. 2. May–June, 1982.

Mystic Places. Alexandria, VA.: Time-Life Books, 1987.

Pauwels, L., and Bergier, J. *Morning of the Magicians.* New York: Stein & Day, 1964.

Rho Sigma. *Ether-Technology: A Rational Approach To Gravity-Control.* Lakemont, Ga.: Rho Sigma, 1977.

Schwaller de Lubicz, R.A. *Sacred Science: The King of Pharaonic Theocracy.* New York: Inner Traditions International, 1982.

Schwartz, S. *The Alexandria Project.* New York: Delacorte, 1983.

Scurtton, R. *Secrets of Lost Atland.* London: Sphere, 1979.

Sitchin, Zecharia. *Genesis Revisited: Is Modern Science Catching Up With Ancient Knowledge?* New York: Avon, 1990.

———. *The Earth Chronicles* (4 Volumes). New York: Avon, 1976.

Steiner, R. *Cosmic Memory.* New York: Harpers, 1959.

Tomas, Andrew. *We Are Not The First.* New York: Bantam Books, 1971.

———. *Atlantis From Legend To Discovery.* London: Sphere, 1973.

Index